"In *Queer Imaginings*, David Gerstner offers a provocative meditation on the relationship between cinema, queerness, and the radical promise located at their intersection. Sweeping in his objects of study, Gerstner's collected essays span time, place, and scholarly categorization to create a rich and multilayered vision of the possibilities for cinema and cinema studies. With an approach to both classic discourses and emerging queries in the arts that demonstrates a profound and moving level of care, *Queer Imaginings* is a stunning reminder of the love for their work that both artists and scholars share."

—Racquel Gates, author of *Double Negative: The Black Image and Popular Culture*

"In *Queer Imaginings*, David Gerstner delves into relations of relations—queer self and other, critic and artist, critic and self, reader and writer, friendship, queer auteurist and queer auteur, and more—pushing and pulling and blurring boundaries in an almost erotic way. The result is a rich collection of metacritical essays that are politically insightful, aesthetically sensitive, and frequently very moving."

—Kyle Stevens, editor of *The Oxford Handbook of Film Theory*

"*Queer Imaginings* takes up the question of the auteur and sheds new light on the overlapping processes of filmmaking and film writing. Gerstner expands our understanding of where the labor of cinema happens by foregrounding the economy of queer friendships—intimate exchanges built through conflict, 'burgling,' remembering, and generosity."

—Tara Mateik, associate professor of media studies, College of Staten Island/CUNY

"In this essential collection of writings by one of our foremost contemporary film theorists, the category of authorship finds itself both defended and queered: as écriture, as biography, and as a concept that connects the queerness of lived experience to the aesthetic deterritorializations of cinema. Tantalizing readings of Epstein, Eisenstein, Riggs, Minnelli, Honoré, and others are supplemented by a series of profound reflections on politics, aesthetics, and friendship, demonstrating that the project of queer film criticism and theory is one of film studies' most crucial and enduring legacies."

—Damon Ross Young, associate professor of French and film
and media, University of California, Berkeley

QUEER
IMAGININGS

QUEER
IMAGININGS

On Writing and Cinematic Friendship

David A. Gerstner

Wayne State University Press
Detroit

Library of Congress Control Number: 2022946412

ISBN 9780814350218 (paperback)
ISBN 9780814350201 (hardcover)
ISBN 9780814350225 (e-book)

On cover: *17 fois Cécile Cassard* (Christophe Honoré, 2001). Used by permission of Christophe Honoré.

David A. Gerstner, "Introduction," from *Queer Pollen: White Seduction, Black Male Homosexuality, and the Cinematic*. Copyright © 2011 by the Board of Trustees of the University of Illinois. Used with permission from the University of Illinois Press.

David A. Gerstner, "An Interview with Peter Wells." *Interdisciplinary Literary Studies* 2, no. 2 (2001): 105–16. http://www.jstor.org/stable/41209076. Copyright © 2001 by The Pennsylvania State University Press. This article is used by permission of The Pennsylvania State University Press.

Wayne State University Press
Leonard N. Simons Building
4809 Woodward Avenue
Detroit, Michigan 48201-1309

Visit us online at wsupress.wayne.edu.

CONTENTS

III: ON WRITING AND CINEMATIC FRIENDSHIP

INTRODUCTION

Without the critical faculty, there is no artistic creation at all, worthy of the name, . . . and no one who does not possess this critical faculty can create anything at all in art.

—Oscar Wilde, "The Critic as Artist"

The images are for myself . . . and a few others.

—Jonas Mekas, *Walden*

On Writing

This book is about writing. It is, at the same time, a book about friendship. Specifically, this book is about writing on the subject of cinema whose very aesthetic form necessitates an exchange—a friendship—with the other arts. The volume is not, therefore, a "how to write about film" book; rather, it is a book about "how *to think about* writing" on cinematic art and the intertwined relationships it generates, aesthetically and otherwise. *Queer Imaginings: On Writing and Cinematic Friendship* is a collection of writings dedicated to sensuous encounters with time and space. It is a selection of published and unpublished works that gathers nearly thirty years of work, investigating questions focused on auteur theory as a generative cross-disciplinary discourse. It brings together previously published essays as well as writings that were held from view for various reasons. The collection principally concerns itself with *écriture*, the act of writing by both the film critic *and* the filmmaker; pointedly, it centers itself on the oft-times-at-once *queer* film critic and filmmaker. The collection thus brings together critical essays, book and film reviews, interviews, and other jottings related to cinematic practice in which queerly formed dimensions appear. *Queer Imaginings* is thus a *graphology*. It seeks to discover the "author's" presence—*a queer touch*—as it permeates the dynamic in which the work, artist, and spectator find themselves entangled with one another.[1]

Overall, the volume brings into relief the contours of a history and the ongoing discussions, debates, and queries I have followed during my career in which queer and auteur theories in film studies are situated. These two key areas of concentration—queer and auteur theories—remain highly relevant (certainly, deeply contested) not only in film studies. Film studies, however, introduces discrete, if, to be sure, formal, elements not available to the other arts. As such, the theoretical tensions around matters of the artist from within the discipline take on a unique perspective. Recently, attention to the auteur debate succinctly took place in the pages of *Cinéaste* and *Film Quarterly*.[2] Against the backdrop of intense critical engagement with cultural identity and aesthetic practices, critics and filmmakers have again raised the ante on the terms for the auteur and precisely the queer auteur. *Queer Imaginings* participates—directly and indirectly—with these conversations in that the essays included here trace a history of ideas that spotlight an ever-shifting terrain associated with auteur theory—*indeed, queer-auteur theory.*

Published or unpublished, my thoughts about writing on the cinema are not easily separated from the art of filmmaking. I studied filmmaking as an undergraduate, where I quickly realized that my interest in and talents with the cinema were best served by pen and paper and not hands-on production (a life immersed in, as I saw it then, bagels and cables). Throughout, Oscar Wilde stood as my guardian angel while I rethought my relationship to film, my relationship to *la caméra-stylo*, as it were. Yet the more I write *about* film, the more I desire to return to write *for* film, to make film.[3] What I have come to realize—perhaps always already knowing—is that to write *about* film is no different in fact than to write *for* film. With all due respect to Wilde, while there is no art without the critic, there is, in turn, no critic without art. No stronger does this intermingled and generative exchange reveal itself than in the history of the cinema (think Sergei Eisenstein, Jean Epstein, Germaine Dulac, the *Cahiers du cinéma*'s "Young Turks," Maya Deren, and so on). Artist and critic—*often one and the same*—provide each other with what Christophe Honoré calls "good company."[4] The work of art makes available an exchange, a gift tendered, for and among comrades. And because a gift is never free of self-interest, it is not insignificantly an offering that serves the pleasure of oneself. "The images are for myself . . . and a few others," Jonas Mekas insists in his film-diary *Walden* (1970).

These are, to be sure, not dissimilar terms for queer auteurs. They are the *écrivains extraordinaires* insofar as they are a singular voice enduringly dependent on the Other. To write about and for the cinema, therefore, is to act in concert with history in which theory and practice remain indissoluble. In this way, the *queer auteur* thinks and acts cinematically; this is to say, to act cinematically queer is to embody—*to be indistinguishable from*—the multimediated world in which they live. As such, the queer auteur recognizes that there is no cinematic Self without the forcing presence of the Other. Is "not the function of the Other's look," Jean-Paul Sartre queries in his study of Charles Baudelaire, "to transform him[self] into a *thing*?"[5] Baudelaire's "aim" in cutting the queer figure of the dandy, Sartre argues, "was to exist for himself as an object, to dress up in all his finery and paint himself in order to be able to take possession of the object, to remain long in contemplation of it, and finally to melt into it" (135). In doing so, the "melting" together of Self and Other reveals the queer auteur's delightfully mischievous self-centered role as matchmaker. Forged together, subject and object "melt into" each other. Enfolded and inseparable, the queer auteur's Self-*as*-Object sets the stage for unexpected and deliciously surprising works of cinematic art.

The queer auteur is a multidimensional actor whose hands grab aesthetic and critical debris from a wide assortment of what Walter Benjamin refers to as "les pochettes-surprise."[6] "One should either be a work of art," Wilde reminds us, "or wear a work of art."[7] The queer auteur, however, manages both and more as they rummage through others' dusty concepts and creative imaginings. Thus, when Andy Warhol and his Superstars paraded through New York clubs, they presented Andy's axiom that their very presence confirmed that no distinction existed between the everyday and the movies. *They were the movie!* Others such as Barbara Hammer insisted that her queer body was not inseparable from her camera *and* her subject. Susan Sontag reencountered her signature tropes of seduction, desire, and metaphor through aesthetic registers that gave life to her own-branded *nouvelle-vague* cinematic form in *Duet for Cannibals* (1969). James Baldwin noted, during his failed adventure making biopics in Hollywood, that filming the complexity of Black lives could only be rendered as an experimental film. Hollywood narrative-style biopics effectively "assassinated" Black bodies (Baldwin had Malcolm X on his mind). In a different register, Kenneth Anger embraced gossipy and debris-ridden Hollywood culture that littered the pages of movie magazines and other paraphernalia. He jammed his home, movies, and books with all the cinematic excess he could find. Across the globe, Sergei Eisenstein intensively worked at his writing table *and* flatbed-editing table to stitch together imagistic pleasures in which the rubble of bourgeois culture collided with muscular proletarian enthusiasm. The queer auteur, in other words, envisages cinematic aesthetics in the way Peter Wollen describes Jean-Luc Godard's formal designs on cinema: "a process of writing in images, rather than a representation of the world."[8] Queer ducks all, queer auteurs resist representation as such and, instead, wrestle with aesthetic form and its debris to reach for the malleability of queer identity and desire by "writing in images."

The queer auteur I consider here tantalizes the viewer, redirects their expectations, and unsettles queerness itself. The queer auteur makes way for an imbricated and decidedly intimate *writerly* relationship between themselves as film critic *and* filmmaker *across media*. Indeed, the queer auteur thus gestures toward Jacques Derrida's generous concept of *écriture*, since, for him, the act "to write" is not reserved for pen and paper.[9] Two Derridean examples—not irrelevant for my purposes here—include choreography and cinematography.[10] Cinema is therefore something more. It is intertextual writing. As one invested in cinema's capacious aesthetics—*its possibilities*—the queer auteur positions themselves uniquely, because "to write" *about and for* the cinema requires nimble legerdemain, a deft pickpocketing of the other arts. Queer cinematic practice is the art of aesthetic thievery.

Not dissimilar to Jean Genet's eroticized thievery, cinematic *écriture* demands skills about which he teaches us in *The Thief's Journal*. Theft, we learn, "requires a host of movements," ideally "performed in the heart of darkness," "walking on tiptoe," in which "groping hands organizing in the darkness gestures of an unwonted complexity and wariness."[11] In one way or another, for Genet, thievery bundles Self and Other into an intimate, seductive, and unanticipated dance.

With one hand, then, the queer auteur traces Genet's elegant techniques for pilfering, a precise act so magisterially described in his spirited guidebook. With the other hand, the queer auteur embraces what Georges Bataille refers to as "potlatch"—*a compulsive exchange*, an act in which Self and Other set out to *outdo* each other: while potlatch "excludes all bargaining and, in general, of humiliating, defying, and *obligating* a rival," it, at the same time, raises the stakes for the recipient.[12] In accepting the gift, the recipient "must satisfy the obligation" by giving in turn a "more valuable gift" (121). Queer Self and Other simply cannot do without each other because they cannot relieve themselves from exponential giving and taking.

Queer auteurist potlatch is an existential realization of desire; it operates "*at the mercy of a need for limitless loss*" (Bataille, "Notion of Expenditure," 123; emphasis in original). The queer auteur *performs* games of desire because, for them, cinema is a driving force, a conduit for exchange. To write about and for cinema draws the queer auteur into endless flows of giving and taking. Because of this, to write for and about cinema demands what Peter Wollen calls "an orgy of *dépense*."[13] Wollen argues that the auteur engages cinema as a way to discover and *to revel* in cinematic expenditure, its excesses, its histories. And because cinema mixes itself as a multidisciplinary media, it is a "jewel, like excrement"; it is "brilliant waste."[14] Auteurs, such as Wollen, are thus drawn into a "deliriously formed ritual poker" between friends from across the arts (Bataille, "Notion of Expenditure," 122). Always a perverse rivalry in which one-upmanship commands its raison d'être, the queer auteur's multimediated interactions with the other arts involve (over)generous aesthetic giving *and* taking in which destructive transformation is generated.

In effect, the queer auteurist exists at once as artist and critic—"the artist-as-critic" *and* "critic-as-artist." Because of this, the queer auteur dances with themselves *as* Other.

Together, they maneuver the twin poles of theory and practice—*praxis*. Hand in hand (indeed, "groping"), they juggle a broad and complex aesthetic terrain in which the histories of art relentlessly borrow, beg, and steal from one another. With perceptive fingering, they write *about and for* the cinema, folding in the other arts, passing from one to the other ("performed in the heart of darkness"), invariably surprising, delighting, and bewildering both robbed and robber.[15] The queer auteur is one and the same.

Sergei Eisenstein is, of course, an excellent case study in this regard (as my essay "In Excess of the Cut," chapter 7 in this volume, shows). Eisenstein's cinematic largesse would reward us less today if his theories of montage were narrowly defined as "film editing." Eisenstein—a superlative queer auteur—enthusiastically asserted that cinema is nothing if not the interrelationship among the arts. Indeed, as Genet is quick to remind us (and Eisenstein fully brings to life in his films), the supple handing off of the pilfered objet d'art requires a "host of movements" ("brilliant as a facet of a jewel"; *Thief's Journal*, 29) that involves the "invisible, nervous presence of the accomplice" (30). At turns willing and unwilling accomplices, the other arts' artists *and* their critics keep wary eyes on the cinema's movements. Eisenstein formidably wrestled with his Soviet colleagues who looked askance at his magnanimous (homoerotic?) theories of montage. Eisenstein's admiration for bourgeois and aristocratic French culture along with other forms of perverse decadence contradicted Marxist-Leninist dreams that circulated in Soviet filmmakers' circles. With his queer eye, Eisenstein offered a muscular proletariat that appears in ways not much different from the homoerotic figures who people Anne-Louis Girodet-Trioson's luminous male-to-male erotics (consider *The Sleep of Endymion*, 1791) and his teacher's Jacques-Louis David revolutionary esprit de corps (consider *Léonidas aux Thermopyles*, 1799–1814).[16] Eisenstein placed high value on aesthetic thievery in which the revolution involved a unique form of homoerotic impulses.

Theft, Genet tells us, "makes of us a very ball of presence." It is, for him, a religious rite, an act of friendship:

> But within myself, this total presence, which is transformed into a bomb of what seems to me terrific power imparts to the act a gravity, a terminal oneness—the burglary, while being performed, is always the last, not that you think you are not going to perform another after that one—you don't think—but because such a gathering of self cannot take place (not in life, for to push it further would be to pass out of life); and this oneness of an act which develops (as the rose puts forth its corolla) into conscious gestures, sure of their efficacy, of their fragility, and yet of the violence which they

give to the act, here too confers upon it the value of a religious right. (*Thief's Journal*, 30)

Burglar and burgled fold together—fragilely, violently; they move together in consecrated frisson with "the value of a religious right." Pitched this way, to burgle—*to write as ritual*—is to violate the willing, the "accomplice." Film and its relationship to the other arts aptly render the enriching dynamic between robber and robbed, artist and critic. Together, they raise the stakes on cinematic praxis because their subtle, often outrageous, and deliciously penetrative intermingling of media "makes of us a very ball of presence."

Such an exchange, for Genet, is a sacred deal (the "oneness of an act"). It is one meant to be sealed with a dedication to a friend, an "homage" to "beauty." Genet's first sensual burglings were memorialized with a dedication to his amputated friend—a young, thieving, and corporeally mutilated companion who "initiated" him into the terpsichorean precision that thievery entails. "To his beauty [the "splendid cripple"], to his tranquil immodesty," Genet writes, "I dedicated my first thefts." Genet's "obsession with his body" is the hinge on which so much depends, since his concentrated "obsession" with disfigured "beauty," performed through the ritual of a dedication, sustains the care Genet brings to the act since it "kept [him] from flinching" (*Thief's Journal*, 30). Not "flinching," however, does not suggest a lack of movement; Genet simply does not hesitate during the act. The "very ball of presence"—the holy trinity: robber, robbed, and deformed beauty—is at once rigorously sculpted yet ever malleable. Thievery is a trembling between Self and Other. It is the gift of friendship.

But something comes of all that giving and taking. In the cinema, a unique exchange economy (an "orgy of *dépense*") is made crystal clear. The queer auteur's work on the screen brings into relief what amounts to a penetration between film and the other arts, between critic and filmmaker. As it turns out, then, the cinema is an exchange of Self *as* Other. Cinema is the queer work of art.

On Cinema

The friendship economy therefore actively gives and takes. The queer auteur shamelessly ravages the other arts that are beholden to other critical disciplines. They crumble the rigid disciplinary boundaries traditionally aligned with the history of the arts. By plundering the historical arts, the queer auteur reveals cinema's adulterous aesthetic enterprise. They seduce their accomplices into an impure cinematic hermeneutic, a ritual of heretical interpretation.

Queer auteurs are migratory gleaners. They assiduously scavenge art history's land-scape, then carry off the remains from rich multiaesthetic fields. They mix the found leftovers and incorporate the aesthetic debris into their creative and intellectual ener-gies. To think cinematically is therefore to reimagine the other arts. In their role as the queer auteur's accomplice, the other arts at once wittingly and unwittingly participate in the cinema's ritual that seduces while it violates. To glean (a form of thievery) is thus an aesthetic ritual involving a complicit, deliberate, and allegedly naturalized chore-ography in which cinematic beauty is nothing less than the violation of the other arts.

In this way, the queer auteur desires to surmount time and space, to overcome its limitations, to dismantle aesthetic constraints. Hence, the cinema's view toward these limitations is one that can see its possibilities precisely because of the friendly exchange it inaugurates with the other arts. In attending to a composition of fleeting images and sounds, the queer auteur necessarily rehearses fresh vocabulary and rede-signs grammatical phrasing in order to evoke the cinema's rich *transformative move-ments*. Specifically, the queer auteur discovers the aesthetic tensions—the giving and taking—that effectively define cinematic movement.

The queer auteur thus revels in *écriture* and takes pleasure in conceptualizing move-ment's transmogrification on multiple fronts (whether we are speaking of cinematic *movement* as an aesthetic property or as a school of filmmakers galvanized around a particular impulse: *an art movement*). In the introduction to the anthology *Meta-Morphing: Transformation and the Culture of Quick Change*, Vivian Sobchack tells us that to morph depends on not only "dexterity" but "also articulated 'traces' of transfor-mation and movement that point to the gaps, fissures, spaces, and ruins that constitute the 'blur' left by all this shape-shifting."[17] If movement manifests itself through com-plexity, intricacy, and dexterity, then to write for and about transforming (a) move-ment involves wrestling with and, in some instances, *reinventing* terminology to *get at* its malleability.

In Sobchack's edited collection, Matthew Solomon draws our attention to the his-torical challenge in which early film critics and filmmakers found themselves when hoping to describe the cinema-machine's most astonishing achievement: visualizing movement. From the start (ca. 1895), Solomon writes, "excursus[es] on nomencla-ture" were a common occurrence as critics and filmmakers alike sought "poly-syllabic words" to grab onto cinematic movement. Neologisms such as "shadowgraphy" ("writ-ing in shadows") emerged alongside "cinematography" because, in the mind of the modern cinéaste, "the moving-picture" experience could not be nailed down as a sin-gular event, as an aesthetic discipline *as such*. Precisely because the cinema moves still images, which are wrapped in multiple artistic and cultural practices, the cinéaste must reckon with "an extensive performance culture [that emphasized] transformation." In trouble with language, Solomon rightfully refers to the cinéastes (performers all!) as "conjurers."[18]

Cinéaste-conjurers—filmmakers and film critics—are, in short, illusionists.[19] A queer occupation to be sure. They are schemers. Indeed, they are thieves. They are skilled in delivering an impression of one thing at the expense of another, "the real" for "the real." With their *caméra-stylo* they cunningly offer a perception of "the real," while, with their other hand, they mischievously steal it away. Before our very eyes, the queer conjurers resurrect the dead (a memory of what has past, a peculiarity of "the real," as André Bazin reminds us). Through ekphrastic precision, the cinéaste gives life to *nature morte*, always keeping their behind-the-scenes hand in the picture. The function of the cinéaste-conjurer is thus to engage cinema's unique capacity to invoke life and death simultaneously. They recognize that the cinema-machine, in all its various iterations, merely materializes the aesthetic dream held by a long lineage of cinéaste-conjurers, stretching back well before the arrival of the cinema-machine itself (Plato, Da Vinci, Kircher, Mallarmé, and other cinéastic magicians).[20] To be sure, savvy critics-as-artists from the traditional arts cannot be ignored for their cinematic desire to represent movement and reimagine time and space. Some of the most satisfying cinéaste conjurers derive from peripheral critics, some who dabbled at times in the art of filmmaking: Erwin Panofsky, Rudolf Arnheim, E. H. Gombrich, Lotte Eisner, Pablo Picasso, Gloria Anzaldúa, Marcel Duchamp, Gustave Flaubert, John Dos Passos, William Faulkner, James Baldwin, Gertrude Stein, and, of course, Jean Genet.

Hence, if the cinema is an art form that derives its formal and aesthetic dimensions from the pilfering of the other arts, writing about the cinema requires a critical approach that is equal to the medium's interaesthetic burgling. Historically, the film critic and filmmaker have an indissoluble partnership in crime because, unlike other critic-artist relationships, they take pleasure in the cinema's violable capacity to choreograph across several media at once. There were those early modernists whose theoretical tomes on the cinema's relationship to the other arts fed directly into their film practices. And there were those whose critical appetite for the cinema drew them away from the well-defined aesthetic properties in which they trained. Whether through the theatrical imaginations of the directors Sergei Eisenstein and Detlef Sierck, or Panofsky's and Arnheim's delightfully blasphemous art-historical likening of cinema with that of the architectural dimensions of cathedrals and whores, or the prolific critical writing and filmmaking of Maya Deren and Laura Mulvey, in which the terms for cinematic form took shape precisely because the stakes for the critic-as-filmmaker/filmmaker-as-critic's body were high, queer auteurs, in particular (but not always), discover flexibilities *across the formal dimensions of the arts*. For many, the thrill to write *about* the cinema coincides with the intimately connected impulse to write *for* the cinema, and back again.

Taken together, then, writing film criticism and making film are at their strongest when intertwined. This indissoluble relationship yields the cinematic dream in too many ways to count. The symbiotic dynamic just traced reveals what is assuredly the most salient definition of the cinéaste, *the auteur*. In the dazzling (if sometimes dizzying) discipline we call "cinema studies," the auteur is not merely the author who makes work related to the cinema (as critic, as filmmaker); the auteur is the artist-conjurer who imagines the world in cinematic terms and acts on it as such. The auteur is an abiding, if vexing, friend to film studies.

On Friendship

A thing that has unquestionably influenced my development as a creator of films is water. I cannot conceive of cinema without water. There is an inescapable quality in the movement of a film which relates it to the ripple of streams and the flow of rivers. The truth is that the affinity between the film and the river is the more strong because it cannot be explained. Lying on the bottom of the skiff with [schoolboy chum] Godefer, with the branches brushing our faces, I had a thrill very near to what I feel when watching a film which moves me deeply. I know I cannot go back upstream, but I am free to relive in my own fashion the sensation of leaves stroking the end of my nose. For me that is what a good film is, the caress of foliage in a boat with a friend.

—Jean Renoir, *My Life and My Films*

For to love friendship, it is not enough to know how to bear the other in mourning; one must love the future.

—Jacques Derrida, *The Politics of Friendship*

HUBERT FICHTE: Does living without an address, without an apartment, make it difficult to maintain friendships? You can't invite anyone over, you can't cook. . . .
JEAN GENET: I don't like to cook.

—Hubert Fichte interview with Jean Genet

It is difficult not to smile when watching Jean Renoir and actor Michel Simon recollect their rewarding comradery established during a long career making films together. The director Renoir's avuncular disposition coyly prompts actor Simon's subtle devilishness when past innuendos are recalled and "in-the-know" secrets from the past sneak into their conversation. Their casual yet obviously staged get-together at a bistro, arranged in advance by the producers for the French television program *Cinéastes de notre temps* (1967), hints at a partnership realized cinematically. Their fond recollections and jovial exchanges from the vantage point of old age, and not unimportantly presented publicly for the camera, give life to a friendship enabled precisely because of the cinema. To watch Renoir and Simon chuckle about shared experiences underscores cinema's uncanny ability to time and again forge—and reignite—intimate friendships. And yet (curiously ignored in their jovial recollection of the past), Simon had once wished to kill Renoir after filming *La Chienne* (1931).[21] Friendships are complicated affairs, enlivened by their "defects."[22]

Renoir developed many—indeed, many lovingly fraught—friendships during his career in the cinema. Besides actors such as Simon, Renoir latched onto the *Cahiers du cinéma*'s enthusiastic group of young cinéastes. The critics-soon-to-be-filmmakers held Renoir as representative of *the* French auteur. Jacques Rivette and François Truffaut, along with their mentor, André Bazin, were confirmed acolytes. Truffaut, especially, maintained a long-standing friendship with the director, serving as the editor for a comprehensively annotated Renoir filmography (completing a project begun with Bazin). For Rivette's part, he and Renoir spent well over an hour in a 1961 television interview, *Jean Renoir parle de son art*, exploring in detail the director's approach to filmmaking. Set in a restaurant, critic and filmmaker (*who is who?*) chatted effortlessly about their love for film, concepts about making film, and philosophical possibilities for the cinema.

For me, to watch Renoir's exchange with others about cinema reminds me of the crucial role friendship plays for cinematic practice. It is an experience with friends that lends itself to the "sensation of leaves stroking the end of my nose," while I sometimes recognize that I, like Genet, have no desire to cook for them. Film collaboration—in its making, its viewing—is as intense as it is brief (even the change in exhibition platforms such as mobile phones does not eliminate cinematic friendship; friends continue to engage one another about their likes and dislikes, what to see and what not to see).

It is certain, as Derrida reminds us, that "it is not enough to know how to bear the other in mourning; one must love the future."[23] Looking back at the fortunate cinematic exchanges I have shared with friends—some no longer with us, some encountered only in books and archival materials—I see a career built on writing about cinema that only came to be because of friendship. I also see that I am well placed in a history of cinematic friendships that led to a wide body of creative and intellectual writing. Consider the *amité* between kindred thieves, Jean Genet and François Truffaut; Marlon Riggs and his crush on the white boy, Phillip, that took on complex feelings because of the movies; André Breton and his youthful friend Jacques Vaché, who darted in and out of movie theaters, never staying for an entire film; Derrida's intense relationship with Robert Abirached as they practiced "applied filmology" at the movies; Andy Warhol's parade of Superstars and "celebrity" screen tests, in which the movies and "real life" blurred; Gloria Anzaldúa's prosaic recollections, rendered cinematically, of intimate connections with friends and their political commitments; Rainer Werner Fassbinder's long-standing ensemble of political misfits and sex radicals who people his theater and film; and on and on.[24]

Queer Imaginings mourns the passing of these and other past creative and intellectual relationships, while, at the same time, it recalls their shared intimacies that allow us to "love the future."

Putting It Together

Taken together, the essays in *Queer Imaginings* envisage an immersive entanglement at once sensual, political, and creative. In short, the essays invite the reader to imagine modes of *cinematic doing*. As I reviewed and selected essays for this book, it became clear that the texts dialogue with one another. While I assembled the book's bibliography, something more was clarified: the parade of works included in *Queer Imaginings* give off something of an echoic memory. What I mean by this is that, to my ear, the meeting ground on which the bibliography is assembled recalls the lively timbre of a queer bar, or the chatter of colleagues as they circumvent the halls at a Society for Cinema and Media Studies conference, or the buzz of excitement as spectators wait for the movie to begin.

The volume is organized around three parts. Part 1, "Politics, Love, and the Queer Auteur," considers theoretical inquiries that reflect on the place in which the queer auteur finds themselves pushing against white-heterocentric crosscurrents, a pushback that makes way for a politics of cinematic imaginings. Part 1 opens with the introduction to my second book, *Queer Pollen: White Seduction, Black Male Homosexuality, and the Cinematic*. This project came about when it struck me that James Baldwin's unmatched literary brilliance was deeply indebted to cinematic tropes. To this day, I can think of no other English-language writer who can match Baldwin's magisterial *cine-literariness*. I read his work voraciously. Given his movements between Paris and New York, Baldwin facilitated a bridge for me from my first book, *Manly Arts*, to *Queer Pollen*. It was clear to me that much more was to be said about New York's queer-modernist impulses during the 1930s, as well as the international connections it drew on, particularly from France. For instance, the last chapter in *Manly Arts* ("The Queer Frontier: Vincente Minnelli's *Cabin in the Sky*") had touched on the back-and-forth movements between "downtown" and "uptown" queer culture, where interracial mixing was crucial to the queer aesthetics that brought to life Katherine Dunham's and George Balanchine's all-Black-cast productions of *Cabin in the Sky* (New York, 1940) and, later, Vincente Minnelli's Hollywood version (1943). In effect, the queer Harlem Renaissance artists and their cinematic imagination remained undertheorized, and a study of the interracial cultural milieus was critical to grasping the contours of queer-cinematic aesthetics. And though Baldwin flirted well at the margins of the "Niggeratti" (the deliciously queer ensemble that included the likes of Zora Neale Hurston, Langston Hughes, and, provocatively, Richard Bruce Nugent), it was clear to me that queer-modernist Black artists were indeed modern because they envisioned their artwork through a multidisciplinary and cinematic vernacular to tackle racism, homophobia, and sexual desire.

Richard Bruce Nugent's poetry is particularly acute when identifying the central role that queer, Black, American artists occupied during this period. His prose poem "Smoke, Lilies, and Jade," as well as his drawings, marshaled cinematic concepts and (as I hope to have proved in *Queer Pollen*) put into relief a cine-aesthetic drive to complicate queer Black men's sexual desire. His participation in the Harlem Renaissance allowed me to explore auteur theory as a concept based on an exchange—nay, a cross-pollination—of bodies. Together with Baldwin and Marlon Riggs, a triptych developed around queer cinematic desire in which sexual desire and race moved front and center. The introduction to *Queer Pollen* importantly opens this volume because, to my mind, it lays out what gets closest to my methodological turn on auteur theory more generally and, specifically, queer auteur theory in relation to race. More broadly, the work in *Queer Pollen* registers my concerns around auteur theory as it brings into focus—precisely because the auteur is committed *to act* on its subject—the ideological systems and institutions that come to bear on questions of race, class, gender, and sexuality. US "queer modernism" comes to be queer precisely because the queer-modernist impulse brings to life the dissemination of bodies across race and across aesthetics. Queer moderns resisted systemic racism and homophobia.

My colleague once informed me that the term "penetration" recurs with some frequency in my writing and in conversation with friends. Looking back, I see that my colleague is not mistaken. Part 2 of the book, "Archival Penetration," presents writings in which the lure of penetration prompts my desire, my pleasure, to enter fields of knowledge that give way to a writerly discharge. In other words, engagement with established parameters of knowledge (the book, the archive) generates epistemological transformations precisely because of those institutional containments. In this way, "to penetrate" is a seductive way to conceptualize my embodied relationship to *écriture*, since it promises sentient insight through disciplined and thoughtful action. The filmmakers and writers to whom I am drawn in this part indeed kindle penetrative energies to the extent that their cinematic doing drives my desire to write, to enter into an economy of exchange. What strikes me about this cinematic energy is the gestures discovered between critic and filmmaker. The relationship reveals an interactive performance (at times under historical constraints) in which a scholarly and creative commingling occurs.

Part 3 of the book is titled "On Writing and Cinematic Friendship." Since beginning my work dedicated to Christophe Honoré's cinema (and French cinema more broadly), colleagues have asked on numerous occasions, "Why Honoré?" A similar question was posed to me earlier in my career: "Why Vincente Minnelli?" As I considered how to respond to these queries, it occurred to me that a biographical intimacy was somehow involved in what drew me to these two queer filmmakers.[25] The short response: (1) small-town boys moving to and embracing an unconditional love for big cities (from Carhaix in Brittany to Paris for Christophe and from Delaware, Ohio, to [ultimately] New York City for Vincente; I myself departed Buffalo, New York, for New York City); (2) an insatiable appetite for cinema *as it relates to the other arts*; and (3) a desire to explore the complexity of relations between men (ideologically, creatively, aesthetically, sexually).[26]

When I began writing my dissertation in 1995, Minnelli was no longer alive. As a young scholar, I was eager to identify Minnelli—not necessarily to "out" him—in relationship to queer-modernist aesthetics in cinema (a queer auteur to be sure). At the time, the methodological approach to my thesis was fortuitously, if complexly, riddled by the rich and prolific stream of queer theory by the likes of Eve Kosofsky Sedgwick and Judith Butler that then filled bookstores and libraries. The early to mid-'90s were heady days for queer theory, with new and exciting concepts appearing, it seemed, without pause. I took it as a challenge to embrace the rush of new ideas and filter them through new realizations of the auteur. The start was bumpy. At the very least, the connection was tenuous given queer theory's commitment to poststructuralism, in which (sometimes hasty readings of) Roland Barthes's "The Death of the Author" reigned supreme. Fortunately, Peter Wollen gently queried me at my doctoral oral exams about whether I was treating Minnelli as a "ghost." In my graduate-student intellectual stupor, I was unclear about what he meant (or I cavalierly chose to think I knew better). Upon reflection, it became clear that what Wollen had cautioned against was vaporizing my subject (Vincente Minnelli) into a mist of somebody else's poststructuralist theory. Where did I exist in relation to Vincente Minnelli's body of work?

What ultimately clarified Wollen's remarks and my thinking on auteur theory was my visit to Minnelli's home in Beverly Hills. Minnelli's wife at the time of his death, Lee, kindly invited me to discover Vincente's personal creative world. His office was filled with art books as well as copies of André Bazin's *What Is Cinema? Volumes 1 and 2*. His private bedroom was adorned in deep "Minnelli" red; velvet-textured wallpaper and curtains framed the room, while crêpe de chine lined chairs and bed coverings. From the French doors of his bedroom, one could see the rose garden gifted to him by Elizabeth Taylor. Vincente was no longer a "ghost." My encounter with the director's films and the remains of his lived world materialized the queer auteur. I thank Peter Wollen for a lesson well learned.

Later, and fortunately, Vivian Kleiman granted me access as the first person to explore the Marlon Riggs archive (then housed at University of California, Berkeley). Like time spent within Minnelli's haunt, I discovered the artist's work put into sharp relief. Auteur theory's sensual impact was further escalated. Immersed in the confined space of a storage room in Berkeley, in which the artist's personal remains embraced me, the queer auteur and his critic could no longer exist as a ghostly figure, a figure set in the distance. Surrounded by Riggs's film scripts, props, scribbled notes, diary entries, graduate-student papers on topics such as George Platt-Lynes and *A Clockwork Orange*, Christmas cards from family and friends, and letters of encouragement from friends as AIDS slowly and painfully destroyed his body, I entered Marlon's world and in doing so anticipated his death that had already arrived.[27] The introduction to *Queer Pollen* that is placed up front in this volume makes the case for why Riggs's cinematic imagination lent itself to my critical rethinking of auteur theory. In my 2007 review of the then newly released remastered DVD of *Tongues Untied* neatly summarizes Riggs's milestone contribution, while it hopes the remastering of the film sets the stage for fresh critical writing about Riggs and queer-Black filmmaking.

To realize that the dead live on (*and how art never lets us forget that they do!*) resonates deeply in my attraction to Christophe Honoré's work, a director who is alive and well. It is a far different privilege to have the opportunity to move near a director as his career develops. As the author of films, theater works, operas, novels, and children's books, Honoré is the contemporary queer auteur extraordinaire. The opportunity to attend a working film set or to break bread with a director brings home a very different experience for the auteur critic. Yet death—and the tradition of French thought that explores it in such profound and unsettling ways—circulates vividly in each of Honoré's works, as it does in my relationship to the director. But it is precisely his persistence *to make art as a process in order to engage death as a living force* that draws me to his projects. In making art through his journey with and toward death, the possibilities to open existential iniquities into gender, sexual desire, race, and relationships are endlessly rewarding and vividly complex.

The intellectual crux—and that which keeps me magnetized to Honoré's work—is his exploration of these questions through an experiment with aesthetic form, across the arts. Honoré is positioned within a history of the French arts in which an intense interdisciplinary aesthetic informs his cinematic vision. (Minnelli was not dissimilar in his approach to a multimediated filmmaking; he painted, directed, and produced theater—art forms that were critical for his cinematic eye). To my mind, film criticism is no different. To measure up to the art form it engages, scholarly writing must experiment with form and style. I am indebted to Christophe Honoré (as I am to Vincente Minnelli and others) for their cinematic friendship. In "getting to know them," a sentient bond is shared as the intense international parade of images and sounds disseminate into our contemporary cinematic worlds.

Hence, "Speculations on the Origin of the World: Notes toward Queer Feminism, Gustave Courbet's *L'Origine du monde*, and Christophe Honoré's *17 fois Cécile Cassard*" is included here for several reasons. First, *17 fois Cécile Cassard* is a film I had longed to write about but until now had not found a home for. Thanks to colleagues such as Matthew Solomon at the University of Michigan, who invited me to speak on the film, as well as Cindy Lucia and William Luhr, who host the Columbia University Seminar on Cinema and Interdisciplinary Interpretation, "Origin of the World" has had public airing with rewarding critical input. I am especially grateful to Lucia and Luhr because their salon sets the stage for a fast-disappearing forum where artists and critics gather to fully immerse themselves in vigorous discussion about film (and food and wine). "Origin of the World" discovered reception among a group of friends and students that confirmed, for me, the *aliveness* that scholarly practice yields. To engage my writing in this way is at the heart of *Queer Imaginings*. It is a pleasure I hope to share.

Second, *17 fois Cécile Cassard* challenges the critic to approach questions about feminist queer theory without allowing for sweeping generalizations and oversimplifications. This is to say, queer-feminist film criticism (and, to be sure, cultural criticism more broadly) is often stymied when adhering to reactive admonishments (good/bad; positive/negative) or neglecting rigorous close analysis of the text.[28] For me—and in many ways this is true of French auteur cinema—Honoré's films address the body (and all its possibilities) in complex and paradoxical ways. The strength of his filmmaking rests in his aesthetic management—and it is not incorrect to call this *choreography*—of cinematic practice. In short, to dismiss filmmakers such as Honoré as not queer *or* feminist enough is to assume a reactionary position that seeks to authorize meaning once and for all.

Finally, since writing my dissertation and completing my first monograph (*Manly Arts*), I have been preoccupied with the bodies of men. Manliness, masculinity, patriarchy, and homosocial/homosexual relations are indefatigable topics. To be sure, to discuss "masculinity" is to discuss its purported opposite, "femininity." In effect, the powerful dialectic that enforces the demands for gender *to be* as such cannot be ignored by the critic, who must necessarily grapple with this ideological policing. To disembody abstract terms (male/female), it is the job of the critic to dismantle by engaging those very terms. This is no easy task since claims to liberation in toto already carry the burden of totalitarianism.

Thus, *17 fois Cécile Cassard* affords me the opportunity to address the struggle of the body, the resistance to the dialectics of masculinist ideology, especially taken in hand by a woman (Beatrice Dalle as the film's protagonist, Cécile, cannot be overlooked as a quintessentially queer and resistant body). In Honoré's film, Cécile is a navigator; she is a discoverer of Self through, against, and with the masculinist Other. She makes way for the body of Woman; as she discovers herself, hermetically sealed into a world peopled only by men, Cécile must not only resist the demands made by men for women; moreover, she must assert herself *by choosing* the terms for Self to engage the broadest possible desire.

The materials collated in *Queer Imaginings* are thus notes and queries about queer-auteur practices as much they are about my relationship to a queerly lived world. They make way for the peculiar intimate distance that auteur theory makes available for the living and the dead. My encounters with Marlon Riggs's collected papers, my immeasurably pleasant meetings in Auckland with the soft-spoken and now-departed New Zealand filmmaker-author Peter Wells ("Interview with the New Zealand Filmmaker Peter Wells"), my delightful weekend spent in Orléans with an international group of Duchampians ("Queer Turns: The Cinematic Friendship of Marcel Duchamp and Charles Demuth"), and my tireless warmth for Christophe have made way for auteur theory *as* a theory of queer friendship. Auteur theory, more generally, is thus an invitation to critically engage the Self-Other relation in the throes of Eros and Thanatos. It allows the queer auteur to invoke friendships past (Duchamp and Demuth, for instance) in such a way so as to participate in their historical camaraderie and shared pleasures. Auteur theory longs for those who have passed—some known intimately, others known from a distance. Yet the dead give life to the very work the queer auteur takes on. It is also a theory in flux. This is especially realized when filtered through the work of an artist who continues to make film; the conceptual possibilities remain incomplete since the body of work is on the move. Whether engaging the living or the dead, auteur theory is very much an *alive* theory. What is crucial to bear in mind, therefore, and as Pascale-Anne Brault and Michael Naas remind us in their introduction to Derrida's collection of eulogies to friends and colleagues, even "while the bodies of these friends and thinkers have been spirited away, their bodies of work remain; they remain with us, though it is not certain that we understand or can ever completely understand them, that is, interiorize them."[29] Indeed, our debt to friends, Derrida realizes, "is in some sense incalculable."[30]

As I reread the essays contained in this volume, it occurs to me that even in its entirety, it constitutes an impossible gratitude to so many people for years of friend-ship and "good company." In writing, then, I am moved. I am moved to write precisely because I am moved by others. I am moved by their kindness, their competitiveness, their deceptions, their thievery, their defects (*perhaps, above all, their defects!*), their generosity, and their disappearances.

Wollen is right. As queer artists and critics, our encounters with one another give way to something more than merely dancing with ghosts. Queer-auteur theory haunts—*here and there*—causing us to shudder, invariably prompting us to write.

A Note on My Better (Queer) Angels

The privilege to introduce new works alongside already-published material is at once deeply rewarding and humbling. In returning to one's work, the opportunity to revise material that has passed the muster of editors and colleagues is a tremendous gift for an author. With this said, one is confronted with an ethical challenge: To what extent does one revise work that has been cited, applauded, challenged, and reviewed? I find the question vexing. On the one hand, preparing a collection that includes past and familiar publications serves as a useful handbook for researchers, scholars, and stu-dents; on the other hand, it opens the door to a return where revisions may deliver what is tantamount to a new essay. In most instances, *Queer Imaginings* preserves previously published work with little or no changes, aside from cleaning up typos and minor tidying of sentence structure for clarity. "Queer Angels of History Take It and Leave It from Behind" is the exception. When I revisited this essay—an essay cobbled together from material not included in my dissertation—I was taken aback by the lack of clarity in a publication of which I had been so fond. My delight in seeing the essay come to light in the pages of the *Stanford Humanities Review* derived from enthusiasm in discovering Walter Benjamin's foray into Parisian gay bathhouses with acquaintances of Proust. Ideas of camp and aesthetic debris (*les pochettes-surprises*) danced in my head, and, in many ways, that very swirl of ideas landed in a pile of detritus that would assuredly make Benjamin smile. Thus, something more than simple tidying was necessary. Indeed, I am grateful for the anonymous readers of this volume, who engaged my work with critical and decisive rigor. My revision of "Queer Angels," hence, responds in kind to a reader's disagreement about my positioning of Benjamin as queer. The reader's comments prompted me to clarify—expand on—my situating of Benjamin as queer in relationship to, specifically, the question of *aura*. In any case, the version included here is a significant revision. And keeping with the spirit of delightful spinning, friendly exchanges, and ideological *frisson*, the remains that linger from the former essay for all intent and purposes may be considered profanely "new."[31] Its title is now, "Queer Angels . . ."

And it is to the many queer angels in my life that I must give gratitude: Mal Ahern, Elizabeth Alsop, Luisa Alvary, Bráulio Amado, Joey Arias, Zari Asgary, Beste Atvur-Özdemir, Jillian Báez, Matt Bell, Caitlin Benson-Allot, Billy Berman, Gilberto Blasini, Matt Brim, Rebecca Brown, Tara Burk, Cathy Burke, V. J. Carbone, Michael Carroll, Darrell Carter, Lucio Castro, Silvia J. Cho, Cynthia Chris, Rhea L. Combs, Michael DeAngelis, "The Doll," Camille Domaine, Victoria Duckett, Erik Endsley, Jeff Engel, Mert Erdem, Vicki Evans, Kerry Falloon, Jarim Farciert-Vivar, Stephen Ferst, Matthew J. Fick, Mathieu Fournet, Seth Friedman, Amélie Garin-Davet, Racquel Gates, Dave and Geneviève Gerstner, Emmanuel Grant, Sean Griffin, Roy Grundmann, Omar Hammad, Bang Geul Han, Jeff Harris, Kristin Hatch, Wayne Hoffman, Monica Holowacz, Christophe Honoré, Marcus Hu, Jim Hubbard, Jason Hughes, Dan Humphrey, Victoria Ifastusin, Daniel Ioffreda, Nick Jastrzebski, E. Patrick Johnson, Josh Johnston, Wilma Jones, Peter Jurado, James Kaser, Andrew Katz, Cáel M. Keegan, Sarah Keller, James Kenny, Vivian Kleiman, Karolina Koziel, Sarah Kuntoh, Mark and Claire Long, Mitchell Lovell, Cindy Lucia, Richard Mailman, Edward Malta, Stephen Mamber, Carla Marcantonio, Annie Martin, Paula Massood, Jonathan Mastro, Tara Mateik, Dwight McBride, Joe McElhaney, Lauren McKenna, Edward D. Miller, Sally Milner, Anna Miranda, Adeline Monzier, Pierre-Alexandre Moreau, Valérie Mouroux, Sue Murray, Amber Jamilla Musser, Julien Nahmias, Daniel Nasset, João Nemi-Neto, Sandrine Neveux, Suzanne and Carl Nixon, Ken Norz, Edward O'Neill, J. Todd Ormsbee, James Park, Reece Peck, Ludivine Petit, Patrice Petro, Gary Pizzolo, Michelle Plochere, Joe Radoccia, Asher Remy-Toledo, John David Rhodes, Bill Ritter, John Rizzo, Jasmine Rogers, Justin Rogers-Cooper, Sarah Schulman, Margaret Schultz, M. M. Serra, Usman Shaukat, Marc Siegel, Frank and Joanne Signorile, Laura Silverman, Jason Simon, J. Reynolds Smith, Paul Julian Smith, Beretta E. Smith-Shomade, Vivian Sobchack, Matthew Solomon, Janet Staiger, Amy Stempler, Kyle Stevens, Garret Stewart, Marie Sweetman, Sarolta Takács, Valerie Tevere, Polly

Thistlethwaite, Matthew Tinkcom, Laura Truffaut, Daniel Trujillo, Michael Trus- novec, Edward Baron Turk, Camille Vidal-Naquet, Robert Wallace, Stephanie Ward, Samuel Weber, Judith Weisenfeld, Fritz Westenberger, Patricia White, Siona Wilson, Bilge Yesil, and Damon Young. Throughout my career, Michelangelo Signorile has been my stalwart and loving companion. I am forever grateful.

Finally, to those whom I mourn yet have provided me the love for the future: Brian Henderson, Andrew Hewitt, Charles Silver, Thomas Wirth, and Peter Wollen. And to the shining queer, David Pendleton, I dedicate *Queer Imaginings*.

Notes

1   Cáel Keegan introduces a form of queer imaginings, a "trans* *imaginary of the senses*." Similar to my interests, Keegan seeks a "cross-pollinating discus- sion" in his auteur study of Lana and Lily Wachowski in order "to turn trans* studies toward the sensorial field as activated by film theory" (*Lana and Lily Wachowski*, 5).

2   See, for instance, Girish Shambu's "Time's Up for the Male Canon," in *Film Quarterly*; and my own response to the debate, "With 'Gay Abandon,'" chap- ter 13 in this volume.

3   As this collection came together, I completed a short film, *Between Men, Act 2: A Historical Fantasy*. It reimagines an encounter between Jean Genet and François Truffaut in 1951.

4   See Gerstner, "NYFF Interview."

5   Sartre, *Baudelaire*, 119. Further references to this work are cited parentheti- cally in the text.

6   Benjamin to Gershom Scholem, January 25, 1930, in *Correspondence of Walter Benjamin, 1910–1940*, 362. We will return to this and other Benjaminian delights in my essay "Queer Angels . . . ," chapter 4 in this volume.

7   Wilde, "Phrases and Philosophies for the Use of the Young," 1206.

8   Wollen, "Godard and Counter-Cinema," 123. On Warhol, see Warhol, *War- hol Diaries*, 180; on Hammer, see Sarah Keller's forthcoming *Barbara Ham- mer: Pushing out of the Frame*; on Sontag, see Moser's *Sontag*, 328; on Baldwin, see my introduction to *Queer Pollen*, chapter 1 in this volume; on Anger, see Landis, *Anger*; and on Eisenstein, see my "In Excess of the Cut," chapter 7 in this volume.

9   Derrida loved cinema, as we discover in this volume. But he did so because cinema housed his most intimate friendships.

10   See Derrida, *Of Grammatology*, 9.

11   Genet, *Thief's Journal*, 29. Further references to this work are cited parenthetically in the text.

12   Bataille, "Notion of Expenditure," 121 (emphasis in original). Further references to this work are cited parenthetically in the text.

13   Wollen, "Out of the Past," 27.

14   Wollen, 28. Wollen quotes Bataille here: "Jewels, like excrement, are cursed matter that flows from a wound."

15   It is difficult to target one word to describe the unconscious-consciousness that the robbed experiences during the theft. Genet: "The perfect act: inadvertently putting my hand into the pocket of a handsome sleeping negro, feeling his prick stiffen beneath my fingers and withdrawing my hand closed over a gold coin discovered in and stolen from his pocket" (*Thief's Journal*, 30).

16   Still the most convincing on these painterly homoerotics is James Smalls's "Making Trouble for Art History."

17   Sobchack, introduction to *Meta-Morphing*, xvii.

18   M. Solomon, "Twenty-Five Heads under One Hat," 5, 14.

19   Gerald Mast's essay "Projection," is worth noting:

> To emphasize projection is also to reiterate that an essential condition of the cinema experience is viewing flickering light in an enveloping darkness. This piercing of darkness by projected light is the source of cinema's hypnotic power, paralleling the way that the professional hypnotist entrances a subject by focusing attention on a bright and rhythmically flickering source of light. This light-in-darkness also generates several paradoxes that infuse and influence our experiencing of cinema: we both sit in darkness and are bathed in light; the experience is both private and public at the same time; the projected images both speak to our personal dreams and fantasies and seem to depict the most public and familiar realities. Projection gives us both the concreteness of visual images and the abstract play of light itself. (304–5)

20   "For cinema persists," Garret Stewart persuasively and elegantly tells us, "as institution and as narrative form, regardless of what subsists in the film stock's former place" (*Cinemachines*, 10).

21   Simon's anger with Renoir, whom he blamed for the accidental death of *La Chienne*'s young star, Janie Marèse, is recounted in Mérigeau, *Jean Renoir*, 155–56; see, further, Boston, *Boudu Saved from Drowning*, 37–38.

22 On Renoir's views regarding his friendship with Simon and, among other things, Simon's ("rumoured") "unorthodox sexual practices," see Renoir, *My Life and My Films*, 110–11. On friendship and defects, Marcel Proust writes, "Each of our friends has his defects to such an extent that to continue to love him we are obliged to console ourselves for them—by thinking of his talent, his kindness, his affection—or rather by ignoring them, for which we need to deploy all our good will" (*Remembrance of Things Past*, 797).

23 Derrida, "Loving in Friendship," 29.

24 On Truffaut and Renoir, see de Baecque and Toubiana, *Truffaut*; along with François Truffaut's correspondence with Renoir, in *Truffaut: Correspondences*; on Riggs and his cinematic infatuation with Phillip, see Gerstner, *Queer Pollen*, 145–46; on Breton and Vaché's "flitting" from "cinema to cinema," see Polizzotti, *Revolution of the Mind*, 39; on Derrida and friends' "applied filmology," see Peeters, *Derrida*, 61; on Anzaldúa's queer-cinematic metaphors, see her *Borderlands/La Frontera*, as well as my discussion of this work in this volume; on Fassbinder's cinematic milieu, see Crimp, "Fassbinder, Franz, Fox, Elvira, Erwin, Armin, and All the Others."

25 As I look back at the interview with Peter Wells (chapter 16 in this volume), it is clear that Peter held appeal for me, similar to that of Minnelli and Honoré, in relationship to my scholarly interests.

26 To include my writings on masculinity and cinema would require another volume. If masculinity is queer—which to my mind it is—space is needed to explore the peculiar intimacies in which the likes of Gene Kelly or Theodore Roosevelt explored the cinematic framework for manhood. For those who are interested, see my book *Manly Arts*.

27 And for this I am forever grateful to Marlon's friend Vivian Kleiman for her generosity, giving me unfettered access to the artist's world. Along with my own work on Riggs, Rhea Combs's dissertation intervened in important ways to elevate Riggs's stature for Black-queer auteur studies. I am grateful to Rhea's friendship for sharing Riggs's intimate cinematic world.

28 On this, see Racquel Gates's elegant *Double Negative*; see, further, Cáel Keegan's considered and persuasive essay "On the Necessity of Bad Trans Objects."

29 Brault and Naas, *Work of Mourning*, 28.

30 Quoted in Brault and Naas, 28.

31 In revising this way, I am reminded of Christian Metz's and Gayatri Chakravorty Spivak's endless revision of their publications for new editions, reprints, and anthologies (*Film Language* and *A Critique of Postcolonial Reason: Toward a*

History of the Vanishing Present, respectfully). For them, the *re*-marking of their work with cascading footnotes reveals what Spivak posits as her struggle to reach the present with "the printed word." In effect, she recognizes the "futility" to "update" that which is already printed. In fact, since the "printed word . . . can't be updated," the reader, Jane Gallop tells us, is "moved by 'the challenge' of reading the footnotes, compelled by the drama of 'seeking to catch the vanishing point'" (*Deaths of the Author*, 128). Rather than a relentless plotting of footnotes, I wish to share the concept for "Queer Angels Take and Leave It from Behind" yet in an airing that is more precise.

I

POLITICS, LOVE, AND THE QUEER AUTEUR

INTRODUCTION TO *QUEER POLLEN*

White Seduction, Black Male Homosexuality, and the Cinematic

This, then, is writers' work—to concern themselves with the letter, the concrete, the visibility of language, that is, its material form.
—Monique Wittig, "The Point of View"

Performing Black and Queer

In Wallace Thurman's *Infants of the Spring* (1932), Paul Arbian (that is, RBN, a pseudonym Thurman assigned to his Harlem Renaissance gay compatriot Richard Bruce Nugent) commits an aestheticized suicide at the novel's conclusion. The suicide is performed as a nineteenth-century decadent ritual (the act took place wearing "a crimson mandarin robe . . . [and] a batik scarf of his own designing"); Arbian "slashed his wrists with a highly ornamented Chinese dirk."[1] Appropriately, his Orientalist dramatic exit was further theatricalized with the dedication he inscribed—a suicide note of sorts—for his final book (appositely titled *Wu Sing: The Geisha Man*). In his dedication, Arbian pays homage to queer-decadent, fin de siècle white aesthetics: "To Huysmans' Des Esseintes and Oscar Wilde's Oscar Wilde / Ecstatic Spirits with whom I Cohabit / And whose golden spores of decadent pollen / I shall broadcast and fertilize / It is written."[2]

Thurman's portrayal of Nugent, the first Black queer considered in *Queer Pollen*, is most apt. The queer and very "out" Harlem Renaissance artist, Nugent, was indeed taken, if not emboldened, by white nineteenth-century queer aesthetics. Not unlike the white historical decadents to whom he paid homage, he delighted in expressing his homosexuality through art forms that traversed a wide range of artistic practice. From poetry to prose, from painting to drawing, from dance to theater, he intermingled media to elicit the eroticized pleasures of homosexual desire. But Nugent takes things further than his white queer predecessors; his homoerotic intermingling occurs interracially. This is forthrightly announced by Nugent in his novel *Gentleman Jigger*, where he recounts not only the 1920s heyday of "Niggeratti Manor" (as Thurman had); moreover, he follows through on the transitions and departures from that scene into the early 1930s. Nugent's movements from Washington, DC, to Harlem to Greenwich Village to Chicago find him both seducing and being seduced by Italian American gangsters who are strikingly reminiscent of the Hollywood gangsters who populated the screen at this time.

Significantly, Nugent concludes *Jigger* with his alter ego (Stuartt) performing in a Hollywood musical, an imagined experience where he describes himself as "the perfect medium" for Hollywood's pleasure-production machine because he was "amenable to their every sensational suggestion."[3] To be sure, Nugent's friendship with Langston Hughes, his working relationship with the filmmaker and theater director Rouben Mamoulian, and his socializing with the influential filmmaker Dudley Murphy brought him into close proximity with a range of cinematic production and spectatorship. Through these encounters, his homoerotically and, de facto, interracially charged aesthetic experiences—echoing at once Joris Karl Huysmans, James Cagney, and Busby Berkeley—slid between high nineteenth-century Aestheticism and Warner Bros. spectacles.

The second Black queer discussed in *Queer Pollen* is James Baldwin. In *If Beale Street Could Talk* (1974), Baldwin corporeally channels—as he will do on many occasions in his novels—the different races, genders, and sexual desires that compose his characters. In *Beale Street* he embodies a young Black woman named Tish. When a racist cop mockingly offers to carry her parcels, a revelation of historical anger and frustration surfaces:

> I looked into his eyes again. This may have been the very first time I ever really looked into a white man's eyes. It stopped me, I stood still. It was not like looking into a man's eyes. It was like nothing I knew, and—therefore—it was very powerful. It was seduction which contained the promise of rape. It was rape which promised debasement and revenge: on both sides. I wanted to get close to him, to enter him, to open up that face and change it and destroy it, descend into the slime with him. Then, we would both be free: I could almost hear the singing.[4]

Throughout his career, Baldwin tangled with and anticipated the seductive lie within the "[white] man's eyes" and its "promise of rape"—*on both sides.* He introduced a style—a lived writerliness—that is both elegant and caustic. His often horrifyingly beautiful language explores while testing the aesthetic ground under which the complexities of race, gender, sexuality, and nation collide. Hence, his aesthetic embodiment of white and Black, male and female, homosexual and heterosexual characters provides a richly textured rendering that plays across bodies and desire. Baldwin melds the elusive identities shaped and reinforced by white heteromasculinist ideology; he is unrivaled for the way he simultaneously eroticizes while excoriating the seductive powers of whiteness. Whereas Nugent's queer Black body moved through an array of artistic practices for his creative enterprises, Baldwin's journey through his queer world turned on the properties of multiple media—most pronouncedly the cinema and theater—through which he filtered a singular art form: the novel. *Queer Pollen* demonstrates the cinema in Baldwin's novels as an industrial art form and a conceptual device for the development of his narratives.

Finally, Marlon Riggs is the third Black queer discussed in *Queer Pollen*. In *Tongues Untied* (1989), Riggs evokes the dramatic effect of white seduction where, in a controversial passage, he fondly recalls the "immaculate seduction" of a white boy's kindness. His encounter with the white boy left an "imprint" permanently etched in his memory, ultimately permeating his adulthood sexual desire. The scene of seduction, a penetrative and sentient kindness, is cinematically presented in *Tongues Untied* through an overlap dissolve of the boy's gray/green eyes with Riggs's own deep brown eyes. In the video, the image of the blond, gray/green-eyed white boy who seduced him is superimposed on the image of a Black man, victim to what appears to be a Black-on-Black gay bashing. Through the uneasy juxtaposition of these sequences—sequences that are not unimportantly viewed through a dissolve heightened by the voices of Roberta Flack singing "The First Time Ever I Saw His Face" and Riggs's recounting the touch of the white boy—Riggs cinematically positions himself and his experience of being a gay Black man between two overlapping, yet paradoxical, images: the threat of Black-on-Black violence against his queer body and the affectionate warmth evoked by the look of the gray/green-eyed white boy. For Riggs, seduced by the white boy, is left *caught between*: the white boy's seduction, he tells us, is a "blessing" and a "curse."

What is this "powerful" white "seduction" that, as Baldwin describes it, is at once so alluring and perfidious that the only way to "change it and destroy it," and to set each other "free," is through a mutual "rape" where Black and white together "descend into the slime"? Is it possible to submerge oneself into the "slime" of this deceitful pleasure, this white seduction, and rewrite the corporeal inscription that Paul Arbian determinedly confirms with the blood from his slashed wrists? "It is," his dedication unabashedly tells us, "written." *Queer Pollen* thus argues that Nugent, Baldwin, and

Riggs embrace, yet rewrite, the experience of white seduction as it filters through their work and personal lives (consider their intimate and often controversial relationships with white men: Riggs's white lover, Jack Vincent, who is acknowledged for his "loving support" in *Tongues Untied*; Baldwin's white lover, Lucien Happersberger, to whom *Giovanni's Room* is dedicated; and Nugent's affair with the white French poet Edouard Roditi, as well as his lifelong sexual encounters with Italian and Italian American men who appear in his paintings, poetry, and novel).

Engaging white seduction as a "decadent pollen" to be "fertilized" through Black men's bodies demands some tricky footwork, footwork choreographed, I suggest, through cinematic means. The cross-fertilization of Black and white culture—the "rape . . . on both sides" about which Baldwin speaks—is most prescient and troubling, however, when queer Black men confront homophobia from within Black culture.[5] White homophobia, for these queer artists, was practically a given since it was already a composite of the racist agenda. "A black gay person," Baldwin tells Richard Goldstein, "who is a sexual conundrum to society is already, long before the question of sexuality comes into it, menaced and marked because he's black or she's black. The sexual question comes after the question of color; it's simply one more aspect of the danger in which all black people live."[6] What is most disturbing for many Black queers, therefore, is when Black masculinist culture turns against them.[7]

If white America's "negrophobia" was considered less a concern than hetero- and homo-Black relations, it is not to suggest that white America did not react violently to Black queers. Indeed, history tells us otherwise. Political and cultural difficulties arise—especially for the Black-male queer artists—when white-male queer aesthetics are imitated and perceived as the creative imperative for Black queers. Hence, the potency that queer whiteness carries weighs heavily on the ways Black males' queer identity is envisaged for themselves or by Black culture in general. Thus, while the aesthetics of white queer culture (Oscar Wilde, Aubrey Beardsley, Joris Karl Huysmans, Walt Whitman, Henry James, George Platt-Lynes, Hollywood) played a critical role as a creative tool for Nugent, Baldwin, and Riggs, they also marked these Black artists as quintessentially queer. Or worse, they were considered queer Uncle Toms.

Queer Pollen considers what is at stake, what are the material outcomes, when Black queers turn to a tradition of homoerotic whiteness that invites, and therefore seduces, them to "cohabit" with these "ecstatic spirits." The risks of such cohabitation are many. And though the promises of a sensual bodiliness and aesthetic pleasure appear through queer white aesthetics, the cohabitation nonetheless presses the question: Is it possible—*is it necessary*—to make available a queer Black identity through the filters of white culture? Is it possible, in other words, to articulate queer Blackness by sidestepping the charge that this identity is nothing more than a perverse manufactured body of whiteness?

This is an important query and served as a crucial point of entry for these Black queers' artistic goals. They recognized that the aesthetic encounter between (queer) Black and (queer) white was unavoidable; it was, however, an encounter not foreclosed *as* white.[8] From Nugent's, Baldwin's, and Riggs's perspectives, neither is whiteness dismissed as the pervasive force that it is understood to be, nor is it viewed as the final word on queer Black desire. Whiteness is, as Baldwin puts it, a "seduction which contained the promise of [sodomitic] rape." But, and instead, the decadent spores that this rape disseminates drags both Black and white "into the slime." It is, indeed, at these moments when we "almost hear the singing."

What, then, is "written"? What is inscribed, "slashed," with a "highly ornamented Chinese dirk," into the skin of Black queers? Why is it desirable for, even incumbent upon, Black queers to return to an aesthetic of whiteness, albeit queer, to assert their identity? In what way might the slashed skin of the Black queer, written by the "golden spores of decadent pollen," conjure a history of scarring and slashing that Black bodies underwent time and time again? For Nugent, Baldwin, and Riggs, it appears they saw no choice but to take on this powerful seduction, this forceful penetration that paradoxically evokes a hyper-charged sense of the erotic that simultaneously collides with the violent. The results of their labor in contending with this troubled history that tears into their black skin invariably made manifest an ambiguously realized identity.

In this book, then, I discuss what I identify as a decadent cross-pollination between Black and white, queer Black-male artists who manufacture a *method of cultural production* that rewrites, cinematically I contend, that which is "written." For Black queers, not only is the spirit of queer whiteness rewritten; more crucially, the experience of white seduction, which "contained the promise of rape," is sodomitically fertilized, "on both sides." That is, the white aesthetics that purportedly infuse the terms for Black-queer cultural identity are saliently explored in the hands of Nugent, Baldwin, and Riggs as sentient experiments around forbidden sexual and erotic experiences. What is notable about this erotic commingling is that the cinematic—as a concept and an industrial apparatus—leads these artists down the road toward sexual and racial desire that has little do to with the ontology of race and sexuality. In other words, queer-pollination of artificial boundaries assigned to "Black" and "white," "heterosexual" and "homosexual" are thus dispelled and dispersed by resisting a fixation on concrete identities and desires.

Queer Pollen, then, does not eke out a "gay-Black aesthetic" or a "queer-Black aesthetic" by "gay"-identified "Black" artists divorced from or wedded to "whiteness";

instead, it looks specifically at artists who, through various historical and cultural purviews, queried reductive characterizations of themselves and their work as "gay" and "Black."[9] Hence, testing and challenging the aesthetic terrain of the twentieth century, one anointed by white culture (queer and otherwise), proved for Black queers to be a key occupation in the exploration of their identity. What we come across in the sodomitic cross-pollination between Black and white is an aesthetic *process*, the work that gives fresh life to the relations between Black men. Baldwin, for one, encourages these relations between Black brothers as the necessary "sensual . . . force of life."[10] Riggs later, following Baldwin and the author Joseph Beame, develops "brother-to-brother" relations as a revolutionary act through a revelatory aesthetic where white and Black relations are directly confronted.

Nugent's, Baldwin's, and Riggs's movement across the arts takes on this complex act of entangling—and, indeed, *not disentangling*—the cultural-political matrices that stimulate the force of life between Black brothers. With exacting and disarming erotic precision, the artists here delve into and bathe in the messiness, "the slime," that white heteronormative culture historically delivers and claims for itself as superior, natural, and obvious. In this way, these artists restage the very logic that determines whiteness as such. To be sure, Nugent, Baldwin, and Riggs do not treat their seduction by whiteness as a matter to be simply adopted, assimilated, or reasoned as an ontological phenomenon. Yet, as noted, these artists are quick to acknowledge that they do not seek to secure, by negating whiteness, a "Black" or "Black-homosexual" identity. Additionally, these artists—especially Baldwin and Riggs—were highly attuned to urgent political matters affecting Black culture. During the twentieth century, the demands for political action were often immediate and elicited a direct response. The aesthetic and the personal were thus inseparable from the political formations that shaped Black queers' raced lived world. But to assert a claim for identity as such during a political crisis (the civil rights movement, AIDS) does not preclude the malleability of identity production that, for Black queers, consistently involved navigating wide swaths of Black and white cultures. The work of art reviewed in these pages—its labor, its material presence—is dynamic; it is an active agent (to be sure, an act of agency) instrumental to a queer-Black sensual world.

Queer Pollen is a perverse triptych that tells the tales about cultural agency and the work of art. That is, I place three Black queers side by side in order to enlist the historical repetitions, interaesthetic relationships, and political variations they come to represent and through which they are conjoined. Placed side by side, Nugent, Baldwin, and Riggs deliver a fascinating story about living queer and Black. All told, the attention they give to envisaging queer Black culture, and the multiple threads on which Black culture hinges, makes for an ideal triptych in the art-historical sense. The resonance of the altarpiece as a religious artifact with three distinct but interconnected panels, in fact, should not go unnoticed, especially since the drama and theatrics of religion played a role in these artists' rendering of queer Blackness.[11]

In order to proceed, I wish to briefly address the concepts (conveniently divided by three) assigned to the subtitle of my book: "white seduction," "Black-male homosexuality," and "cinematics." Each term bears on the other, perversely fertilizing one another.

White Seduction

In December 1989, Riggs submitted *Tongues Untied* to be considered for entry into the Black Filmmakers Hall of Fame in San Francisco. The report Riggs received from the Hall of Fame is archived at Signifyin' Works (Riggs's cofounded production company in Berkeley, California). In the report, three judges are listed (numbers 24, 42, and 45) along with their comments about the work. While Judge 42 found the piece an "exceptional poetic work," Judge 45 declared that it was "too much like radio" (albeit "compelling"). According to Judge 24, however, although *Tongues Untied* did have "creative scenes" and "imaginative presentation with humor," it was quite simply a "homosexual promotion film" that did not have "any merit" and, therefore, "not very relevant to the Black community." As Judge 24 saw it, the video was "fine until the intrusion of White admiration and seduction."[12] But what is this "intrusion of White admiration and seduction" that ultimately stripped the work of its creative possibility and made it, according to this judge, not suitable for inclusion in the Black Filmmakers Hall of Fame? Why did whiteness not only ruin the artistic merits of the film but also confirm Judge 24's anxiety about Black homosexuality? Is it, then, that the judge realized that the issue of Black homosexuality was "not very relevant to the Black community" only when "White admiration and seduction" entered the scene? Is it that, in this assessment, white seduction troubled the relevance of Black homosexuality in the Black community to the extent that Riggs's representation displays the possibility that both are inextricably linked? Although the film was a "homosexual promotional film" in which the Black community would purportedly find no purpose, would Judge 24 have tolerated the issue of Black homosexuality if white seduction had not been raised in the film? After all, the video was "fine until [this] intrusion."

From the notes left behind, it is not exactly clear what Judge 24 found most disturbing: white seduction or Black homosexuality. Yet, the judges' comments echo the earlier anxieties that white seduction elicited and that the activist-writer Eldridge Cleaver leveled against James Baldwin's homosexuality during the 1960s. Judge 24's dismissal of Riggs's video raised again the ante on just what the significant effects of white "seduction" are on Black homosexuality and, by extension, the Black community. For Riggs, these connections were extremely "relevant." Cleaver, as Sterling Brown before him, had already made it clear that Baldwin's seduction by white culture was the reason for his homosexuality. In effect, whiteness is equated with homosexuality.[13] Black men, according to Cleaver, who fall prey to the seduction of whiteness are poisoned by its "succulent fruit" and "malignant root."[14] "Negro homosexuals" who wish to "have a baby by a white man" are sodomized ("bending over and touching their toes for the white man") not only into homosexuality. More insidiously, Cleaver posits that the Black man, because of this penetration, "becomes a white man in a black body." By "redefin[ing] himself in the image of his white idols," the Black man has homosexualized himself and, therefore, is no longer Black (we will return to Cleaver's remarks about Baldwin's sexuality).[15]

Indeed, Nugent, Baldwin, and Riggs *were* seduced by white culture, especially (but not always) by queer "white idols." But seduction is no simple matter. To be seduced by the very system of cultural practice and ideology that, historically, shames, humiliates, and injures their queer Black bodies (a shame that Didier Eribon describes in a different context as an *insult* "so deeply interiorized")[16] demands that we redress the questions we pose. Why did a certain group of Black queers envisage their Blackness and their sexuality as pollinated through queer white culture? Why, moreover, would they turn to an aesthetic that, although queer, historically excluded their existence? (What, after all, could Oscar Wilde's Eurocentric-Orientalist Aestheticism, Hollywood's gangster genre, Bette Davis, and George Platt-Lynes possibly have to do with queer African Americans?) It is no wonder that the interracial "baby" (the work of art) that these Black queers reproduced put hetero Black *and* white men on edge.

Mae Henderson's reading of Baldwin's David in *Giovanni's Room*, through Julia Kristeva's concept of the abject, offers one way to get at this peculiar seduction that conjoins race, sexuality, and aesthetics. Henderson stresses that abjection "refers to the feelings of revulsion and seduction experienced by the subject in encountering 'an-other'; it is a reaction triggered by certain images, literal or fanciful." The theory of abjection provides Henderson with an ideal canvas on which to map the novel's queer spatial terrain, since it is in these spaces where she situates Baldwin's complex and ambiguous characterization of David's identification with his whiteness and homosexuality that "both defines and empties agency"; David, therefore, "remains 'betwixt and between' homosexual desire and [white] heterosexual imperative." Thus, Henderson's argument successfully draws out the "symbolic framework of the novel" to the extent that *Giovanni's Room* "is both specular and spatial."[17] Read this way, the abject foregrounds character interiorization that, in turn, displays itself through spatial mise-en-scène (organization of rooms, dirt, filth, and so on).

But Henderson's approach takes us only so far, since it interprets the relationship between character and narrative structure by studying Baldwin's textual thematic that portrays a white boy's homosexuality. How might we, instead, approach Baldwin's novels (and, for that matter, Nugent's drawings and writings and Riggs's videos) as a materialization of historical production inscribed by a "revulsion and seduction" that works through the (queer) by-products of white culture in order to exhibit queer Black desire? Without dismissing the remains of the text Henderson aptly explores, is it possible to get at the "seduction" of "certain images, literal or fanciful," without relying strictly on an analysis of narrative, place, and character—that is, of representation?[18] How might we signal queer Black cultural production and the marks left behind on the page, on the canvas, and on the screen—the *presence* of authorship—as a dynamic power relation at work across the ideological realms of race, gender, and sexuality? In what way do the authorial gestures of Black queers make present what Marx once called the "invisible threads of production" in white Western-industrialized culture? What aesthetic shape does the debris of white culture take, in other words, when it is consumed, then reappropriated, by Black queers as a work of art? To what extent do Black queers disable the homophobic "white" authority that often arrives packaged in white or black skin? To these ends, in what ways do Nugent, Baldwin, and Riggs defuse the rigid, yet combustible, boundaries marked precisely by "Black and white"?

"Shame" is a useful and provocative place to take up these inquiries in that, as Eve Kosofsky Sedgwick. In her essay "Queer Performativity: Warhol's Shyness/Warhol's Whiteness," Sedgwick argues that shame "functions as a nexus of production: production, that is, of meaning, of personal presence, of politics, of performative and critical efficacy."[19] In her later work on the concept, she invites Silvan Tomkins's thoughts on affect into her discussions around shame and Black queers. Here, Sedgwick points to a "history of radical denial." Queer Black bodies, she writes, find themselves hindered at the "intersection" of a "tacitly racist white gay community for whom a black queer body, however, eroticized, might stand as a representation of blackness but could never seem to embody queerness itself, and a more or less openly homophobic African American community by whom the queerness of any black figure must be denied, suppressed, or overridden for that figure to be allowed to function as an embodiment of black identity or struggle." And yet, this shame foist upon Black queers "floods into being as a moment, a disruptive moment, in a circuit of identity-constituting identificatory communication."[20]

With Nugent, Baldwin, and Riggs, historically racist and homophobic shame is redirected, made aesthetically mobile, in order to reproduce art that displays its work in identity formation. Their aesthetic movements across Black and white cultures exercised a sharp and bittersweet queer cross-pollination that (re)writes—*inscribes*, *scars*, *awakens*—their artist-bodies and their art. It is this stimulating and aestheticized act of sodomitic pollination that so distressed Cleaver as well as white liberal critics such as Irving Howe, albeit in quite different ways.[21] The thought that Black liberation might find its richest possibilities through an eroticized brother-to-brother love went strictly against the masculinist and deeroticized homosocial playbook held by both Black activists and white critics. Shame, when it rewrites the "written," I argue, "floods" the processes of creativity with a range of incongruous, but thrilling, possibilities: "Shame," Sedgwick suggests, "points and projects; shame turns itself skin side out; shame and pride, shame and dignity, shame and self-display, shame and exhibitionism are different interlinings of the same glove."[22]

Sedgwick's thoughts guide us toward an investigation where the dissemination of queer Black aesthetics and identity thus flowers with rancid, poisoned beauty—*les fleurs du mal* to be sure. If the abject, as Henderson posits it, is the "expulsion, of that part of the self, which is, in effect, discharged from the self, and thereby rendered *ab-ject* or 'Other,'" shame, from Sedgwick's perspective, is, instead, a mode of writing (*écriture*) that *bridges and intermingles* the production of "personal presence" with the work itself.[23] If there is a "discharge" of the self as Other, the discharge takes place through the work of art as an act of queer insemination, queer reproducibility, allowing for a back-and-forth penetration of self and Other. At work here is a *re/disfiguration* of agency through aesthetic production that is manipulated in the hands of queer Black cultural producers. Re/disfiguration is, therefore, an inter- (between Black and white heterosexual culture) and intra- (among Black queers) penetrative inscription. It is a gesture that tears at the flesh, which is met at once with pleasure and pain. Re/disfiguration is the simultaneous engagement with, yet dismantling of, the very thing that white and Black heterocentric critics aligned with (white) homosexuality and, de facto, accused Black queers of embracing: white seduction. Nugent, Baldwin, and Riggs re/disfigured the "powerful" contours of the detested white seduction with which they were so uniformly accused. The act to re/disfigure the complexities of shame thus creates a materialized presence for the artists' body *and* their work of art so as to signify an active and mobile inquiry into queer Black identity.[24]

What do we see in these rematerialized presences where subject and work of art commingle? What do we hear? What sensual experiences are aroused for spectator/reader when Nugent, Baldwin, and Riggs investigate a sodomitic intermingling of Black and white aesthetics? What do their choices in selecting aesthetic form tell us about queer Black experiences? *Queer Pollen* takes up the racist and homophobic insults ("on both sides") that are "so deeply interiorized." It suggests that the thrusts, the cuts, the "rape," and the penetrative inscriptions that flow between Black and white are precisely where Black queers permeate, sodomize, and make erotic the ambiguity that gives queer life to race, gender, and sexuality.

Indeed, "it is written."

Black Male Homosexuality

In 1984, James Baldwin and Audre Lorde sat down for a conversation that was subsequently published in *Essence* magazine. To have this dialogue in 1984 was significant because it was situated at a critically historical and intellectually vibrant moment when the transition between "second-" and "third-wave" feminists fomented, led in part by lesbians of color.[25] This major segue in feminist thought announced a new political task that was couched in a critique of white patriarchal privilege and its mimicking by white feminists, who during the 1970s had theorized middle-class liberation for themselves, often at the expense of women of color's lived-world experiences.[26] At the same time, Black feminists who were instrumental for this transitional moment also challenged the heteromasculinist assumptions underlining the Black Power and Black Arts movements.[27] At the forefront of this shift in feminist discourse were the writings by lesbians of color such as Lorde and, later, Angela Davis, as well as the Chicanas Cherríe L. Moraga and Gloria Anzaldúa.[28]

In this historical context, then, the discussion between Lorde and Baldwin is revealing insofar as it brought to the table the misogyny and the representational disregard that Black women experienced in relation to the Black cultural and political movements. Their conversation further revealed that even the queer Black man of a certain public stature and letters (i.e., Baldwin) lacked an awareness of and sensitivity to the issues that Black women faced. Moreover, the interview indicates the theoretical conundrum on which both authors sometimes found themselves perched. On the one hand, it is clear that Baldwin sympathizes with Black hetero-androcentric culture, while Lorde, on the other hand, appeals to traditional family structures (motherhood, fatherhood) to suggest a framework where the older generation of Black men should take "responsibility" for teaching the new generation of Black men that the violence they perpetrate against Black women must stop.[29]

Curiously, neither Lorde nor Baldwin announces their queer sexuality in the article or directly relates it to their concerns to harness Black-masculinist violence.[30] Indeed, their dance around and embrace of the traditional trappings associated with heterocentric male and female gender roles is disappointing. It should be noted that the direction their conversation takes may be due, in part, to the forum in which Baldwin and Lorde find themselves: a five-hour interview whittled down to a few pages in a commercial magazine. Nevertheless, the omission of in-depth discussion about Black homosexuality—or Black sexuality in general—for which these writers are recognized is unfortunate since their larger body of work is more nuanced when dealing with these areas.

It is not my intention to take up the well-rehearsed debate about essentialism or hetero-conservatism identifiable in Lorde's and Baldwin's work.[31] I am more interested in the method of writing, of inscription and translation, that these author-producers (to borrow Walter Benjamin's terms) assume. Both writers are quite often messy, contradictory, yet elucidating, about the aesthetic concepts they adopt. At the same time, their work gives life to the uneasy formations that generate queer Black identity. I am interested, therefore, in the modes of (messy) aesthetic production that Black queers choose when they assert their lived experiences through the work of art. Hence, it is worth reading beyond the limits of the overedited text for *Essence*, which promises much in the way of its queer Black star power yet delivers very little in terms of the stars' elegant and controversial thoughts on America's repressed sexuality in relationship to race.

What the Lorde/Baldwin interview highlights is, on the one hand, the ideological shortcomings on queer Black men's part when matters regarding Black women's issues and identity are discussed. On the other hand, the interview begs that we redirect our reading of the text in order to parse the historically different aesthetic concepts to which queer Black men and women turned. And though, for example, Nugent and Baldwin were sensitive to the intersections of race, class, gender, and sexuality, they channeled women's experiences through masculinist assumptions. Riggs, however, arrives on the scene as the Lorde and Baldwin conversation occurs. For Riggs, the feminist voices of the 1980s lent a new perspective for the way he approached questions surrounding queer Black-male identity. Unlike his predecessors, he integrates the emerging voices of queer Black women and multiculturalists to render his own queer Black masculinity. Queer Black feminists' decentering of heteromasculinity and its solidifying hold on Black identity brought to bear a new set of theoretical and aesthetic possibilities that opened Riggs's critical perspective toward a consciousness not readily available in Baldwin's and Nugent's work.

But what did Lorde, Moraga, and Anzaldúa exact in their rethinking of gender, sexuality, and race? In *Essence*, Lorde contends, for example, that "Black women are the blank" in the "American Dream" and only made visible as a body when they are assaulted, especially by Black men. With this position, it is incumbent upon Black feminists to develop a new language in order to situate their subjectivity as something more than a tableau vivant to be filled in by Black and white male culture. Lesbians of color urgently called for a rewriting of language and the ideological structures that informed it under the rubric of white patriarchy (a structure of language, they argued, assimilated by white feminists). For queer women, the expression of oneself artistically and intellectually meant that one's personal life was intimately intertwined with the political world.

Importantly, to give form to a woman-grounded language, it was necessary to resist the use of what Lorde now famously referred to as the "master's tools" ("For the master's tools will never dismantle the master's house").[32] Language as political strategy was, instead, to be varied in style *and* form. "Third World women and/or women of color," as Moraga and Anzaldúa refer to the writers included in their groundbreaking anthology *This Bridge Called My Back: Writings by Radical Women of Color*, contributed work that ranged "from extemporaneous stream of consciousness journal entries to well thought-out theoretical statements; from intimate letters to friends to full-scale public addresses. In addition, the book includes poems and transcripts, personal conversations and interviews. The works combined reflect a diversity of perspective, linguistic style, and cultural tongues."[33] By the 1980s, an unequivocal link had been made between the experiential and the structure of language. For lesbians of color, this "bridging" gave fresh translation to queer corporeal materialization.

For queer Black men of the twentieth century, a new sensual language was also in order. *Queer Pollen* demonstrates that while lesbians of color challenged and remodeled words' grammatical and structural use ("better words," as Moraga phrased it), Nugent, Baldwin, and Riggs also searched for a new "language" that emphasized the visual and aural, or what I identify as the cinematic. All three artists grasped the urgency to envisage radically new terms for communicating queer Black-cultural experience. What stood out for me while researching this book, however, was their emphasis on new language through cinematic concepts.[34]

Although Black women played central parts in the lives of these Black-male queers (Nugent with Georgia Douglas Johnson and Zora Neale Hurston; Baldwin with Maya Angelou, Toni Morrison, and from afar, Angela Davis), it is Riggs, between 1986 and 1994, when he died from AIDS, who incorporates the critical, political, creative, and *"generically* polyphonic" energies that lesbians of color and the new generation of "multicultural feminists" evoked in their writing and artwork.[35] It is precisely these multimediated possibilities that (multi)cultural feminists stoked and galvanized and in which Riggs participated.[36] The queer cross-fertilization of multicultural feminism with Riggs's own conceptualization of his own queer Black-male body left an indelible presence on the queer cinematic that emerged in his work.

The Cinematic

In my book *Manly Arts: Masculinity and Nation in Early American Cinema*, I studied the discourses of nineteenth- and twentieth-century masculinity and nation in relationship to the emergence of the cinematic as both an aesthetic concept—one that allowed for an envisioning of dynamic modern space and time—and an industrial apparatus that formalized these conceptualizations through the discrete properties that the camera-machine offered. As the book demonstrates, the cinema, in both its aesthetic concept and industrial form, proved powerful in its ability to secure Anglo-Saxon masculinist ideals for an aspiring young nation. Under the auspices of an ideology of realism that the cinema so alluringly promised, the New World discovered the artistic means for its break from Old World aesthetic and cultural traditions. But those androcentric and nationalist ideals that many American cultural producers hoped to achieve with the cinema often came up short or revealed themselves as more ambiguous and contested when in the hands of, for example, African American and/ or queer cultural producers. Nonetheless, Americans clung to the cinematic as integral to their creative imagination when rendering masculinist ideals.

In *Queer Pollen*, I seek to extend the discursive and aesthetic practices I took up in *Manly Arts* to investigate what is at stake, specifically, in the production of queer Black identity when the cinematic is put to use—aesthetically *and/or* industrially—in this quest for cultural expression. I say "and/or" because it is important to stress the way that the cinematic occurs through different aesthetic and industrial registers for Nugent, Baldwin, and Riggs. Nugent, for example, relies less on the cinematic as an industrial tool and more as a modernist sensibility, although film production is not entirely jettisoned as an imagined possibility in his writings. Baldwin and Riggs, however, put into service a cinematic aesthetic *as well as* the apparatus in their work. Yet, here again, the emphasis and extent to which Baldwin and Riggs make the link between cinematic concept and medium are not necessarily focused in the same way. Regardless, what is apparent in the use of the cinematic, whether as apparatus or sensibility, is the cultural producer's investigation of *the look*: to look, to be looked at, to be looked down on, to look back at, and to look outward. *Queer Pollen* traces a cinematic methodology that enables the look as it unfolds through painting, poetry, dance, novels, film, and video. Specifically, Nugent, Baldwin, and Riggs turn to the cinematic to mark the queer Black look in relation to the ideological possibilities that inform the contours of race, gender, sexuality, nation, and, death.[37]

In *Queer Pollen*, the cinematic takes place in two ways. First, the cinema is revealed for Nugent, Baldwin, and Riggs as site specific. That is, we encounter the cinema in these artists' works as places, especially movie theaters, sound stages, or other film-set locations. As a place, the cinema plays an important role insofar as it facilitates experiences that illuminate the tensions with which queer Black identity is fraught. Second, the cinematic here suggests an aesthetic and conceptual act. Nugent, Baldwin, and Riggs, in other words, think and produce cinematically. *Queer Pollen* makes clear, I believe, that the coupled relationship between cinema-as-place and cinema-as-concept intricately overlaps in the works discussed here and is instrumental to their exploration of race and sexuality.

For some time, I have been seduced by ideas held by several writers who introduced to me ways of broadly—yet with great precision—conceiving a theory of what I am calling the cinematic. Their writings offered me a conceptualization of aesthetics that opened the formal dimensions of the cinema as a truly multimediated apparatus (technically, ideologically). For example, Peter Wollen's rich body of work on the intersections between film and the other arts; Samuel Weber's writing on "theatricality as medium, . . . *not* as medium of representation, but as a medium that redefines activity as reactivity"; Andrew Hewitt's study of "social choreography," where he proposes "ideology as performance" to signal a "materiality redefined through aestheticism"; Gloria Anzaldúa's cinematic imagery in forging a radical vision of queer-feminist culture and politics; and Eve Sedgwick's and Judith Butler's preoccupation with the corporeal sensuousness of the performative in relationship to gender have, together, bundled the discrete properties of cinematic production so as to envisage a conceptualization of the cinematic.[38] Finally, I follow Laura Marks's methodological suggestion in *The Skin of the Film*, where the works she examines "are themselves works of theory, many explicitly so. They are not waiting to have theory 'done' to them; they are not illustrations of theory but theoretical essays in their own right."[39]

These theorists amply provide the means by which a theory of the cinematic—especially when these theories are stitched together—relays a concept that configures multimedia properties with historical material affect. It is these theoretical impulses and expansive concepts that inform *Queer Pollen*. In intimate proximity, for me, with these aforementioned theoretical models are Derrida's particular turn on writing—*écriture*—and Deleuze's theory of the cinema that is "*not* 'about' cinema." As Deleuze puts it, his theory of cinema is "about *the concepts that cinema gives rise to and which are themselves related to other concepts corresponding to other practices.*"[40]

In short, Derrida's concept of writing is not merely inscribed with the mark made by the pen; rather, his concept of writing includes such modes of production as "cinematography" and "choreography."[41] The "pen," instead, has expanded how and what it writes.[42] Though Derrida does not fully develop cinematography-as-*écriture* in his later writings, several scholars have discussed the philosopher's writing and concepts of deconstruction in relationship to film theory.[43] To be sure, the cinematographic, in Derrida's hands, conjures cinematic properties (conceptually, materially). As Tom Conley aptly puts it, Derrida is the "cinéaste of écriture."[44]

For Deleuze, the cinematic image, the shot, is a "plastic mass." To write or speak about the dynamic cinematic image, however, is not easily executed given the limitations that written and oral language offer. Therefore, the shot for Deleuze is "a *signaletic material* which includes all kinds of modulation, features, sensory (visual and sound), kinetic, intensive, affective, rhythmic, tonal, and even verbal (oral and written)."[45] This tactility, this kinetic experience, is critical for many feminists' and queer theorists' conceptualizing (as it is for my work here) of a "cinema of bodies," or a cinematic corporeality.[46]

In directing us toward these "modulations," Deleuze makes clear that this "plastic mass is not an enunciation": "It is an *utterable*. We mean that, when language gets hold of this material (and it necessarily does so), then it gives rise to utterances which come to dominate or even replace the images and signs, and which refer in turn to pertinent features of the language system, syntagms and paradigms, completely different from those we started with." Because language "dominates" our encounter with images, Deleuze suggests that we turn to "'semiotics' . . . as the system of images and signs independent of language in general." By doing so, we recognize that a "language system only exists in reaction to a *non-language-material* that it transforms."[47]

How, then, do we take account of the "non-language material" if words are positioned as the hegemonic system through which "plastic mass" is articulated? How do we get at that which is expressed, including cultural identity, through "non-language material" and which reveals more than words can possibly explain? How might a theory of the cinema be "not 'about' cinema, but about the concepts that cinema gives rise to and which are themselves related to other concepts corresponding to other practices"? *Queer Pollen* is, therefore, invested in work that, at times, is "not [always] 'about' cinema" yet consistently displays the queer cinematics that Nugent, Baldwin, and Riggs put into play and "gives rise to."

Finally, I want to note that Deleuze stresses the radical qualities of what he calls the "time-image" in *Cinema 2*. In this work, he suggests a form of the cinematic that lends itself to the ambiguity of subjectivity. For Deleuze, the "time-image" disrupts the repetition of what he terms the "cliché-image," or the "movement-image" or "action-image" most often associated with the Hollywood film. The cliché-image, however, is not a failure because of "cinematographic unity" (an "excess of theatricality" invariably involved in the well-hidden manufacturing of the industrial image); rather, it is attached to "truthful narration" or a "form of the true" that is "unifying and tends to the identification of a character (his discovery or simply his coherence)."[48] Here, Deleuze provocatively introduces what he calls the "power of the false" as a critical negation of the "form of the true." Importantly, and key to our journey toward envisaging queer Black cinematics and the ambiguity of queer Black subjectivity, the power of the false "cannot be separated from an irreducible multiplicity. 'I is another' [*J'est un autre*, as Deleuze puts it in his invocation of the queer poet Rimbaud] has replaced Ego=Ego."[49]

Hence, the cliché-image's reliance on cinematographic unity that leads toward an imaginary fulfillment of a unified Self (nationally, sexually, racially) is, as Deleuze puts it, "developed organically, according to legal connections in space and chronological relations in time." Through the work of experimental-narrative filmmakers, such as Resnais and Godard, Deleuze finds a cinematic "power of the false" wherein "falsifying narration . . . frees itself from this system of judgment."[50] How might the cinema's conceptual *and* industrial means offer freedom from a "system of judgment"? How might a cinematic conceptualization of "falsifying narration" furnish power? *Queer Pollen* attends to this "power of the false"—*J'est un autre*—that seeks freedom from systems of judgment. It does so by tracing a cinematographic *écriture* that gives shape to queer Black identity not as a form of the true but as a mobile process that comes to terms with the power of the false.

Notes

1   Thurman, *Infants of the Spring*, 282–83.
2   Thurman, 284.
3   Nugent, *Gentleman Jigger*, 318.
4   Baldwin, *If Beale Street Could Talk*, 284.
5   On this, see Barbara Smith's "Blacks and Gays," 649–52; and, further, see her "Homophobia: Why Bring it Up?"
6   Goldstein, "Go the Way Your Blood Beats," 180.
7   Cheryl Clarke points out, for example, in her discussion about black homophobia against lesbians, "While most political black lesbians do not give a damn if white America is negrophobic, it becomes deeply problematic when the contemporary black political community (another male-dominated and male-identified institution) rejects us because of our commitment to women and women's liberation" ("Lesbianism," 130).

8   Toni Morrison, in *Playing in the Dark*, reminds us of the way "American literature," consciously and unconsciously, came to presume its canonical framework as white. She rightly queries why a black author is "at some level *always* conscious of representing one's race" while white authors' works are understood to be "race-free" (xii; emphasis in original). Decidedly missing from Morrison's account, however, are those queer black and white Americans who turned *toward* (or back[side] toward, if one prefers) Old World aesthetics, translated through fin de siècle decadence. The implications are significant for the new canon of queer literature.

9   Critiques about the rigidity of a "black nationalist aesthetic" include Josef Jařab's "Black Aesthetic." Lisa Gail Collins and Margo Natalie Crawford's anthology *New Thoughts on the Black Arts Movement* provides both an excellent overview of the movement as well as a wide range of thoughtful essays by a number of writers who address the breadth of cultural practice during this period (see, especially, the individual essays by the editors). Riché Richardson's *Black Masculinity and the U.S. South* dedicates a chapter to Malcolm X's misogynist and homophobic rhetoric (see chapter 4), while Ron Simmons and Marlon Riggs, in "Sexuality, Television, and Death," discuss this iconic black-masculinist figure in relationship to his rumored homosexual affairs as well as, in Riggs's terms, an "unfinished text" that is mobile (141).

Additionally, Simmons ties Amiri Baraka's homophobia to repressed homosexual desire while taking Frantz Fanon and Eldridge Cleaver to task for their homophobia ("Some Thoughts on the Challenges Facing Black Gay Intellectuals"). In Hemphill's own introduction to *Brother to Brother*, he further glosses homophobia within the black creative and political movements of the twentieth century (see, especially, xlv–xlviii), while Charles I. Nero, in the same volume, describes a detailed history of homophobia and homosexuality in black culture that extends back through slavery ("Toward a Black Gay Aesthetic"). Darieck Scott's essay "Jungle Fever?" works through the essentialist quagmire that "brother-to-brother" polemics yield in black gay men's everyday life.

The direct links between homophobia, misogyny, and black nationalism may be found in Cheryl Clarke's cornerstone article "The Failure to Transform"; Dwight A. McBride's transitional article "Can the Queen Speak?"; Phillip Brian Harper's *Are We Not Men?* (39–53); Jane Rhodes's *Framing the Black Panthers* (107–11 and 164–66); Joy James's introduction to *The Angela Y. Davis Reader* (7–8); and Davis's article "Black Nationalism." It is important to note, as Davis does, the call of the "Supreme Commander" of the Black

Panthers, Huey P. Newton, for gays and women as part of the revolutionary coalition (Newton, "Women's and Gay Liberation Movements"). In specific relationship to Baldwin, see McBride's "Straight Black Studies"; Emmanuel Nelson's informative "Critical Deviance"; Lee Edelman's "The Part for the (W)hole," in *Homographesis* (42–75); Douglas Field's "Looking for Jimmy Baldwin"; and Andrew Shin and Barbara Judson's "Beneath the Black Aesthetic."

10   Baldwin, *Fire Next Time*, 57.

11   Here, Baldwin's work most fully displays the complex interactions that occur where religion, sexuality, and art meet. Although Baldwin's relationship to religion is emphasized in this book, Nugent's tantalizingly erotic "Bible Stories," written during the 1920s and 1930s, reveal the artist's aesthetic interests in religion, while Riggs, who once considered occupation as a preacher, directly deals with the figure of the preacher in *Tongues Untied* and *Black Is . . . Black Ain't*.

12   Memo dated December 19, 1989, from the Black Filmmakers Hall of Fame, Inc. *Tongues Untied* is entered as work number 22. Signifyin' Works collected papers, Folder 98242243, Box 4. I'd like to thank Vivian Kleiman, the other cofounder of Signifyin' Works and Riggs's creative partner, for her generous assistance in my review of Riggs's collected papers.

13   See, especially, Cleaver's essay "On Becoming."

14   Cleaver, 130. In chapter 2 [of *Queer Pollen*], I will more fully address Cleaver's assault on Baldwin and those queer theorists who critique his attack.

15   Cleaver, 128.

16   Eribon, *Insult and the Making of the Gay Self*, 19.

17   Henderson, "James Baldwin," 318, 319, 320, 323.

18   I, by no means, wish to disregard analyses such as Henderson's. I seek to shift the study into an alternative direction that, clearly, draws on the sort of textual analysis we see in her work while ascertaining the bodily histories and gestures—aesthetic methodologies—that mark the text.

19   Sedgwick, "Queer Performativity: Warhol's Shyness/Warhol's Whiteness," 135.

20   Sedgwick, *Touching Feeling*, 31, 36.

21   As Robert Corber points out in relation to Baldwin, "Writers such as Irving Howe and Eldridge Cleaver did not regard him a legitimate spokesman for the black community because he was gay, and they compared his work unfavorably to that of Wright, who they thought more accurately represented 'the black experience.'" (*Homosexuality in Cold War America*, 188–89). We will return to Howe's argument in chapter 2 [of *Queer Pollen*].

22 Sedgwick, *Touching Feeling*, 38.

23 Henderson, "James Baldwin," 318 (emphasis in original).

24 My concept of re/disfiguration is beholden, in part, to Sedgwick's reminder that, in the spirit of deconstruction, "shame and identity remain in very dynamic relation to one another, at once deconstituting and foundational, because shame is both peculiarly contagious and peculiarly individuating" (*Touching Feeling*, 36). Sara Ahmed's critique in *Queer Phenomenology* of Sedgwick's concept of shame is important to note and instructive to briefly sketch, insofar as Ahmed calls attention to what she sees as the dialectical failings intrinsic to Sedgwick's logic about shame. Whereas Sedgwick, as Ahmed sees it, flags shame as "the primary queer affect because it embraces the 'not,'" it does so to the extent that it "embraces its own negation from the sphere of ordinary culture": "To say 'yes' to the 'no' is still a 'yes.'" In other words, to negate one position (say the "ordinary") is simply a reaffirmation of the negation into the positive (the not-ordinary). Is the "yes," therefore, "to be inaugurated as the proper signifier of queer politics?" (175). I find, however, that Sedgwick's comments regarding "contagious" and "individuating" expand "shame" as a "dynamic relation" rather than simply an experience of negation. In this way, my work is most interested in tracing the particular (the cultural producer's "individuating" signature-mark and their reshaping of white historical inscription) as it puts into play a broader palette of the general ("contagious") theory (here, shame).

To a certain extent, my neologism "re/disfiguration" also nods toward José Esteban Muñoz's concept "disidentification." Muñoz's book is significant for drawing attention to the vacuum that queer studies perpetuated around race at the time of his writing (and perhaps to this day). It is not clear to me in this work, however, if Muñoz, on the one hand, considers "disidentification" as a concept critical of, specifically, Freudian psychoanalysis (*Disidentification*, 12, 26, 29, 30) or, on the other hand, he designates "disidentification" as a concept reliant on Freudian psychoanalytic-theoretical discourses. Because of this slippery articulation of identity positions, his book runs the risk of essentializing desire and reducing it to "wanting" (15). Additionally, and through a different theoretical register (more in line with Althusser and Foucault perhaps), Muñoz posits disidentification as a double articulation through which creative practice is enacted within and against the ideological sphere (19, 23, 25, 31, 79). And though Muñoz states that this concept may be thought of as "a way of shuffling back and forth between reception and production" (25), the analytical legs on which he makes his proposition leave the following declaration evacuated of any sort of theoretical precision: "The power of this painting [referring to Basquiat's *Untitled (Sugar Ray Robinson)*, 1982] has to do with the masterful way lack and desire are negotiated. The painting stands in for another lost object, childhood" (52). As I see it, Muñoz does not successfully draw out the psychoanalytic or discursive practices that lead to such conclusions.

25 I remain cautious when I use these terms. As Ella Shohat reminds us, "U.S. women of color and Third World women's struggle over the past decades cannot conform to the orthodox sequence of 'first waves' and 'second waves'" (introduction to *Talking Visions*, 19).

26 For a critique of this transitional moment in feminist thought, see Susan Gubar's "What Ails Feminist Criticism?" and Robyn Wiegman's response, "What Ails Feminist Criticism? A Second Opinion." Ann duCille's essay "The Occult of True Black Womanhood" examines the effects of black women's entry into academia, where, from her perspective, white feminist scholars and (black and white) men reassert their marginalized identification with black women's oppression. For duCille, post-1970s feminist scholarship fetishizes black women through what is ultimately a privileged position (white and/or male) in the academy (see, especially, 622).

27 Lisa Gail Collins's essay "The Art of Transformation" profitably draws the parallel interests shared between Black Nationalists and arts organizations and women's liberation political and arts movements during the 1960s and early 1970s (292).

28 In a 1979 essay, "The Black Lesbian in American Literature," Ann Allen Shockley explains the dearth of black lesbian writings during the twentieth century yet points to their re-emergence during the 1970s. By 2005, however, Jewelle Gomez, in "But Some of Us Are Brave Lesbians," takes stock of the thinning availability of lesbian-of-color writings as the twenty-first century gets under way.

29 In this light, Lorde tells Baldwin, "Your responsibility [is] not just to me but to my son and to our boys. Your responsibility to him is to get across to him [her son] in a way that I never will be able to because he did come out of my body and has another relationship to me. Your relationship to him as his father is to tell him I'm not a fit target for his fury" (Lorde and Baldwin, "Revolutionary Hope," 130).

30 There is a slight exception to this when Lorde discusses violence against black lesbians, but she does so in the third person. When Baldwin seeks to defend

the circumstances with which black men must contend in American culture and asks Lorde to sympathize, Lorde turns the tables and asks Baldwin to think about black women who are abused by the very black men Baldwin defends. As Lorde reminds Baldwin, black women are "so full of frustration and anger" with their living conditions or find themselves in a situation where, for example, a lesbian "sees her woman and her children beaten on the street while six other guys are holding her" (Lorde and Baldwin, 133).

31 When Baldwin tells Lorde that he still believes in the American Dream, with all the misgivings it affords African Americans, she counters his steadfastness with, "I don't honey, I'm sorry. . . . Deep, deep, deep down I know that dream was never mine. . . . I was Black. I was female. And I was out—*out*—by any construct wherever the power lay" (Lorde and Baldwin, 74; emphasis in original). It is never clear in this published version of the dialogue if Lorde refers to "out" with regard to her lesbian identity or being black and female.

As Dwight A. McBride points out, Baldwin often positioned himself as the "race man," in which his "performance includes the masking of his specificity, his sexuality, his difference. . . . The image of the black man as protector, progenitor and defender of the race . . . is what Baldwin assumes here [McBride is discussing Baldwin's comments on *The Dick Cavett Show*]" ("Can the Queen Speak?," 376). Baldwin's interview with Goldstein ("Go the Way Your Blood Beats") further demonstrates Baldwin's less-than-enthusiastic response to the emergence of a "gay"-identified culture. Gail Lewis also queries Lorde on her much-used trope of mothering: "But what of those amongst us for whom the label or identity of 'mother,' actual or symbolic, not only doesn't fit but excludes from the orbit of political dialogue?" ("Audre Lorde," 105). Lewis strongly praises Lorde's work while recognizing its limitations, especially her "tendencies to essentialism" (113), where Lorde delimits identity by categories and/or representations such as "woman," "lesbian," and "black" (111–12).

32 Lorde, "The Master's Tools," in *Sister Outsider*, 112. In Moraga's essay "La Güera," written in 1979 and included in the 1983 *Loving in the War Years* (42–51), she also explained the need for a new language: "We need a new language, better words that can more closely describe women's fear of, and resistance to, one another, words that will not always come out sounding like dogma" (46). See G. Lewis, "Audre Lorde," for critique of this strategy as opening the door to essentialism. Deborah E. McDowell also raises concerns over "many feminist critics' stubborn resistance to the critical methodology handed down by white men" (193). McDowell, while maintaining that

such "resistance is certainly politically consistent and logical," follows Annette Kolodny's argument, published elsewhere, "that feminist criticism would be 'shortsighted if it summarily rejected all the inherited tools of critical analysis simply because they are male and western'" (193). On black women's writings during the 1970s and 1980s that challenged black androcentric writers, see Kaplan, *Sea Changes*, 180–82.

33 Moraga and Anzaldúa, introduction to *This Bridge Called My Back*, xxiv. Pointedly, and Moraga stresses this in the preface to the collection, "The materialism in this book lives in the flesh of these women's lives: the exhaustion we feel in our bones at the end of the day, the fire we feel in our hearts when we are insulted, the knife we feel in our backs when we are betrayed, the nausea we feel in our bellies when we are afraid, even the hunger we feel between our hips when we long to be touched" (xviii). In a contribution by Anzaldúa in the same anthology, writing is not only positioned as a corporealized experience but also posited as a *multimediated* corporealized experience: *"Write with your eyes like painters, with your ears like musicians, with your feet like dancers. You are the truthsayer with quill and torch. Write your tongues of fire. Don't let the pen banish you from yourself. Don't let the ink coagulate in your pens. Don't let the censor snuff out the spark, nor the gags that muffle your voice. Put your shit on the paper"* ("Speaking in Tongues," 173; emphasis in original). See, further, Yvonne Yarbro-Bejarano's "De-constructing the Lesbian Body," in which she discusses Moraga's poetry in relation to the body.

34 Gloria Anzaldúa stood out from other feminists' emphasis on language by drawing connections between language's materiality and the cinematic for her political methodology. With the publication of *Borderlands/La Frontera: The New Mestiza*, Anzaldúa lays stress on imagery and, indeed, the cinematic (in its multimediated sense) as vital to her conception of Chicana-lesbian aesthetics and politics. Though she does not forgo her determination to change the terms of the dominant language, she recognizes that "working with images and writing became connected" (87). Chapter 6 of *Borderlands* is elegiac in its emphasis on the cinema (images, sound, light and dark) as instrumental to Anzaldúa's project. Her work is described as a process of "montage" (88); her stories are "performances" (89); the creative process involves gathering "voices and scenes to be projected in the inner screen of [her] mind" (91), some of which are "film-like narratives" or "'movies' with soundtracks" (92). I quote in full here the way Anzaldúa describes her aesthetic method because, of all her colleagues, she unequivocally uses the cinematic as a conceptual model to explore

questions of identity: "Gradually I become so engrossed with the drama. I have to struggle to 'disengage' or escape from my 'animated story,' I have to get some sleep so I can write tomorrow. I am film director, screenwriter, camera operator. Inside the frame, I am the actors—male and female—I am desert sand, mountain, I am dog, mosquito. I can sustain a four- to six-hour 'movie.' Once I am up, I can sustain several 'shorts' of anywhere between five and thirty minutes. Usually these 'narratives' are the offspring of stories acted out in my head during periods of sensory deprivation" (92). Hence, while "in *Borderlands*, this new consciousness is created through writing; Anzaldúa's project is one of discursive self-formation. Through writing she constructs a consciousness of difference," Yvonne Yarbro-Bejarano tells us ("Gloria Anzaldúa's *Borderlands/ La Frontera*," 13). This is true to the extent that "writing" itself is opened up, cinematically, by Anzaldúa in such a way as to be a multimediated experience that extracts the possibilities of difference. By 1993, the Chicana feminist and film scholar Rosa Linda Fregoso explicitly acknowledges Anzaldúa, in an epigraph, for these very possibilities (*Bronze Screen*, xiii).

35   Following a series of panels titled *Cross Talk: A Multicultural Feminist Symposium*, at the New Museum in 1993, Shohat defines "multicultural feminism" as a critical and theoretical approach that "[yokes] multiculturalism and feminism not as distinct realms of politics imposed on each other, but rather as coming into political existence in and through relation to each other" (introduction to *Talking Visions*, 2). Expanding the mediated possibilities that "Third World feminists" espoused for their political and creative goals, "multicultural feminists" were, as Shohat states, "part of a visual culture project" that was "*generically* polyphonic, in that [their] texts partake of many genres: reflective essay, testimonial dialogue, digital collage, prose poem, photo montage, [and] performance piece" (3; emphasis in original). The queer filmmakers Cheryl Dunye and Yvonne Welbon subsequently directed their work around this creative and intellectual exchange.

36   In 1998, Judith Halberstam's book *Female Masculinity* led the discussions around "multicultural feminism" toward the complexity and, again, "polyphonic" practices of transgender cultures. See, especially, Halberstam's chapters "Lesbian Masculinity: Even Stone Butches Get the Blues" and "Transgender Butch: Butch/FTM Border Wars and the Masculine Continuum" for an overview of the feminist and queer debates emerging during this period.

37   My work expands on Sara Blair's contention, "Without these writers [that is, Ellison, Baldwin], the canon of American literature at midcentury is

unthinkable. Without their engagements with photography, . . . their work as we know it would have been impossible" (*Harlem Crossroads*, 11). Blair, I suggest, finds her argument trapped within the Barthesian gilded cage of photography. As I will point out in chapter 3 [of *Queer Pollen*], Barthes's dismissal of the cinema ignores the medium's radical interventions.

38   See, for example, Peter Wollen's *Raiding the Icebox* and his essay, "Viking Eggeling"; Samuel Weber's *Theatricality as Medium*, 28–29 (emphasis added); Andrew Hewitt's *Social Choreography*, 42; Anzaldúa's *Borderlands*; Judith Butler's *Gender Trouble*; Eve Kosofsky Sedgwick's "Queer Performativity: Henry James's *The Art of the Novel*" and *Touching Feeling*; and Sedgwick and Andrew Parker's *Performativity and Performance*.

39   Marks, *Skin of the Film*, xiv.

40   Deleuze, *Cinema 2*, 280 (emphasis added).

41   Derrida, *Of Grammatology*, 9.

42   Lighting, camera movement, mise-en-scène, editing, sound, sound mixing, fades, and dissolves, as well as Derrida's invitation to read the text in this way, conjure a spectator's cinematic experience. Consider, for example, Derrida's "The Double Session," where Mallarmé's "cine-poetics," as well as Derrida's own densely packed footnotes, run side by side with Derrida's "primary" text. Derrida's cinematic "operation" highlights Mallarmé's thoughts on the cinematic: "I am for—no illustration; everything a book evokes should happen in the reader's mind: but, if you replace photography, why not go straight to cinematography, whose successive unrolling will replace, in both pictures and text, many a volume, advantageously" (quoted in *Dissemination*, 208n26; see, further, Brunette and Wills, *Screen/Play*, 83–84). Or consider Derrida's turn on "tympanum" in his essay "Tympan" (a performative *écriture*, "framed" by side-by-side texts, that serves as the introduction to *Margins of Philosophy*). Here, Derrida evokes the tympanum in relation to the aural life of the text; the Derridean "tympan"—the fine membrane that permeates the text—makes way to posit, as Mallarmé does, the book as cinematic "unrolling" (xiv–xx). As Brunette and Wills show, "the tympan is obviously important in any discussion of the cinema," particularly because of its "reliance on orality/aurality," but it is also significant because the "tympan performs contradictory functions, both separating and transmitting, functions that destroy any self-evident sense of the inside and outside" (79). There is something Warholian or Paul Sharits–like with the split-screen cinematic at work in Derrida's writing; similarly in this Derridean-Mallarméan light, Viking Eggeling's "attempts to create

a universal alphabet" through cinematic scrolls confirm the cinematic impulses that artists considered through various art forms (see Wollen, "Viking Eggeling," 49).

43   Brunette and Wills in *Screen/Play*, for example, query whether or not Derrida "has already written 'about' cinema" without doing so specifically. In fact, "the image becomes a central part of Derrida's reasoning, from the question of what takes place (the matter of positions and posting that depends on and opens the function of *technē*) to his ideogrammatization of language—the hieroglyph and anagram—a field including the play of the signature" (99). Tom Conley additionally shows in "Site and Sound" how Derrida invites us to "see" *as well as* hear cinematics at work in his texts without an articulation of a film theory as such (852).

44   Conley, "Site and Sound," 852.

45   Deleuze, *Cinema 2*, 29 (emphasis in original).

46   See chapter 8 in Deleuze's *Cinema 2*. Many scholars find Deleuze useful for their projects on corporeal materiality and cinema. See, for example, Theresa L. Geller's "The Cinematic Relations of Corporeal Feminism"; Elizabeth Grosz's *Volatile Bodies*; D. N. Rodowick's "Unthinkable Sex"; and Steven Shaviro's *The Cinematic Body*.

47   Deleuze, *Cinema 2*, 29 (emphasis in original). Deleuze makes this point all the more clear in the preface to *Cinema 1*: "The cinema seems to us to be a composition of images and signs, that is, pre-verbal intelligible content (*pure semiotics*), whilst the semiology of a linguistic inspiration abolishes the image and tends to dispense with the sign" (ix; emphasis in original).

48   Deleuze, *Cinema 2*, 133.

49   Deleuze, 133 (emphasis in original). It is useful to note in this regard and, in particular, in relation to the project undertaken in *Queer Pollen*, Louis Chude-Sokei's study of the West Indian–born performer Bert Williams and the critique the artist leveled through "black-on-black minstrelsy" against the staunch masculinist African-centrism taking hold during the early twentieth century in the United States. Chude-Sokei argues that Williams's minstrelsy of mimicry "should be read as a corrective to the growing nationalistic chauvinism of an African American cultural politics that, despite its resistance and marginalization, veered too often toward an exceptionalism that severely limited the transnational borders of race and culture" (*Last "Darky,"* 6). Chude-Sokei further explores the black queer author Claude McKay in this vein.

50   Deleuze, *Cinema 2*, 133.

PAST THE POST?

Screening Progress and Reappearing Fascism

The 2016 presidential election triggers many unanticipated responses. Emotions run high. Political activists discover newfound energy. One's place in the world has been unfixed, troubled, and unsettled. Philosophers and artists, stunned, rethink the terms for their critical positions and the formal aesthetics that shape their work. The moment is thus rife with anxiety in search of a response. As a film scholar, I find myself driven to script a response. As I write, I feel paused in time and space. My unfixedness in the shadow of the election put in motion what can best be described as quivering *stasis*. From my troubled place, an intellectual processing unfolded. I conjured ideas and images that invariably failed to yield a satisfactory response to what had come to pass. What had I seen? Felt? My psychical and physical response to current events might be likened to what Adorno refers to as "the capacity to shudder, as if goose bumps were the first aesthetic image."[1]

It's not a pretty picture. But we've known this all along.

1.

It was commonplace during the presidential election to describe Donald Trump's candidacy as a moment mirroring a return to historical fascism. New Hitler biographies were trotted out and reviewed in prestigious newspapers, where uncanny resemblances were made between the figure of fascism past and fascism present. Elsewhere, "Germany 1933" stood in as the historical benchmark, a tale of caution. By invoking "Germany 1933," we were encouraged to recall how easily large national populations blindly rode the wave of populism directly into the arms of totalitarianism. Such comparisons are not unwarranted given the "alt-right's" "Heil Victory"

"Past the Post? Screening Progress and Fascism's Return." In *Triple C: Critical Theory Interventions on Authoritarianism and Right-Wing Extremist Ideology in Contemporary Capitalism.* 15, no. 1 (2017). DOI: https://doi.org/10.31269/triplec.v15i1.838.

salutes at their postelection conference in Washington, DC. Breitbart News, "reality TV," and "fake news" resounded as if to mimic Goebbels's news-making machinery.

Nevertheless, the weight given to "fascism" during the 2016 election in the United States and its reauthorization for sustained use in popular discourse remained remarkable. Not too long ago, those who publicly uttered "fascism," with intent to disparage political movements and high-profile figures, were called into question. In charging others with behavior or articulating ideas that aped Nazi-like tactics, "neutral" pundits and politicians lamented the overuse of the term. By pointing to "fascism" at every ideological turn, they argued, the horror of historical fascism was cheapened. "As with 'Nazi' or 'Hitler,'" Michael Kinsley writes in the *Washington Post*, "it is often said that in any discussion, the first person reduced to using such a word has lost the argument." It is, Kinsley reminds us, "an all-purpose epithet."[2]

Indeed, as early as 1944, George Orwell in his essay "What Is Fascism?" illustrated the way redundant and random claims to fascism quickly became meaningless. For Orwell, "fascism" was *le mot du jour*, applied to just about anything and anyone, from "farmers" to "fox-hunting." For twenty-first-century American media pundits, Orwell is the go-to thinker who shores up their criticism when they perceive fascism reduced to empty rhetoric and political gain. During the run-up to the 2016 election campaign, the term and the debate returned. Geoffrey Wheatcroft, in the *New York Times*, found it necessary to remind readers of Orwell's warning: "we should take care not to wear the word 'fascism' out with overuse, lest we fail to recognize the *real thing, if it does reappear*."[3] But, and if we are to pay heed to Wheatcroft's argument, how do we know the "real thing," when and "*if* it does reappear"? How will we know when it is appropriate to reintroduce "fascism" into political and everyday discourse? What if Wheatcroft's cautionary "if" neglects fascism's complex schedule for arrival *and* departure? Indeed, is there such a thing as "historical" fascism that one may decidedly mark with a beginning and an end?

Because this is no easy set of questions to answer, more pressing questions might be posed: If fascism has returned in the body of Donald Trump, when did fascism officially "end"? Is Trump the worrisome "if" about which Wheatcroft warned? If we abide Kinsley's and Wheatcroft's historical markings of fascism, it would seem that fascism took a break at the end of World War II. In doing so, postwar (1945) yielded a "postfascist" period. But did fascism just arrive, once again, with Trump in the seat of the presidency? Or have we seen it all before in more complex divinations? To consider how we might "see" fascism "if" and when it takes the stage (or, if one prefers, how we see it *here and now*), it is helpful to return to the writings of those who lived through the severe thrust of historical fascism and its mediation in the twentieth century. It is useful, therefore, to pause and return to the work of intellectuals and artists whose reflections on fascism emerged at a moment when a particular stream of ideology and practice came to power carrying the very name, "Fascism." By making a return to those (as is often done) who lived through the terror of the period and to those who then reckoned with fascism's declared end, we discover an immediacy of a moment in their writing. We encounter writing, in other words, that queries the time and place of fascism and whether or not the final curtain has, "if" ever, fallen on it.

At the risk of repeating well-worn theoretical enterprises, I nonetheless find myself drawn to the Frankfurt School's reflections on fascism and culture, particularly their ruminations on whether or not the "post-" may be assigned to fascism. It seems to me that their work is worth revisiting (repeating *and* revising) since new generations are now actively engaging in discussions about the return of "Fascism" in our day and age. A revisit to Walter Benjamin's essays "The Work of Art in the Age of Its Technical Reproducibility" and "Theses on the Philosophy of History," as well as Max Horkheimer and Theodor Adorno's essay "The Culture Industry: Enlightenment as Mass Deception," is once again timely.[4] On the one hand, Frankfurt School writings provide clear fascist signposts, especially those manufactured through the media industries (movies, radio, advertising); on the other hand, Frankfurt School critical theory requires that we invest in fascism something more than its material realization. These writings also reappear, over time, strengthened during opportune moments when ideological awakenings occur in the midst of political unrest and strident authoritarianism. Hence, under different historical circumstances during the 1960s, French thinkers and artists returned to the tricky mechanisms of fascism to untangle the difficult relationship between abstract thought and material practice. By posing Frankfurt School concepts side by side with French "poststructuralist" thought, we can at once take account of fascism as it is witnessed in the thick of world war and as it is reconsidered in the late 1960s and early 1970s far from the war zone. My sense is that, following the election in the United States (if not recent elections around the world), the Frankfurt School and the French poststructuralists who followed in their wake are perfectly placed for their encore in 2017.

1.1.

So many questions, so few answers.

—Samuel Weber, *Mass Mediauras*

What is striking about these writers who form the Frankfurt School (and there are, of course, others) is that they challenge what we so readily accept as *post*fascism. The logic is simple: by marking fascism as "post-," we create a narrative to protect ourselves from a fascism-yet-to-come. As the Frankfurt School saw it, however, there is more to fascism than meets the eye and ear. The German philosophers made clear in no uncertain terms that there is no "if" and when regarding fascism's reappearance. Fascism is *always already* present. It is an impulse, an ideological and psychological drive; it is not easily cordoned off by past, present, and future. While fascism reaches its modernist heights through twentieth-century technical reproducibility so as to press forward models of capitalist efficiency and functionalism, fascism is not dateable as such. This is not to say that authoritarian regimes that identified as "Fascists" cannot be historically documented. Historical Fascists are recognized—*made visible*—for their actions against humanity. "Fascists" exist. Indeed, we are witness to their historical atrocities as recorded in history books, films, photographs, diaries, and so on. As such, it is worth considering a distinction between "fascist" and "fascism."

The three essays taken up here are prescient not only because they offer insight from *within* fascism and point clearly to its visible signposts; these essays also put on notice those who oversimplify fascism as a singular historical event, marked by a beginning, a middle, and an end. To hastily conflate the historical Fascist period with fascism's ideological currents is to confuse a significant theoretical and affective point.

Setting aside the view that fascism may be discretely framed in time and place, the Frankfurt School (and their outlier, Benjamin) offered a less-than-cheerful version of "post"-fascism. In short, they leave us with "bad news" and, arguably, somewhat "better news." The "bad news" is that we will never see fascism "appear" as such. Why is this "bad news"? Because it is impossible to recognize fascism's *reappearance* since it is always already on the scene. Each and every day, media-culture apparatuses inculcate ideology, disciplining mind and body. Most chillingly, Horkheimer and Adorno argue in "The Culture Industry," mediated inculcation does not instill Pavlovian response; instead, it deceives the masses that their individuality is unique and that their "opinions" matter. The culture industry generates a ruse of difference. Bifurcating "left/right," or "liberal/conservative," the media industry narrativizes politics through the lens of "good guy" and "bad guy." To "choose" a side, in other words, is to make no choice at all. Mediated battles between Republican and Democrat, Fascist and Social Democrat, give the appearance of ideological difference when they are, in effect, "constant sameness" (134). Why? Because the perception of political difference as presented through the media is part and parcel of consumer culture. Entertainment masquerades as the political, and, in turn, the political—in assuring media coverage—must masquerade as entertainment. One coin, two sides, with very little distinction when tossed.

One need only attend a White House Correspondence Dinner (where opposing forces break bread with folks in the media industry) to witness the "bipartisan" celebration of difference-as-unity. The "culture industry" is the sweetened poison that masks the horrifying existence in which the modern world finds itself: "The ruthless unity in the culture industry is evidence of what will happen in politics. Marked differentiations such as those of A and B films, or of stories in magazines in different price ranges, depend not so much on subject matter as on classifying, organizing, and labeling consumers. . . . Consumers appear as statistics on research organization charts, and are divided by income groups into red, green, and blue areas; the technique is that used for any type of propaganda" (Horkheimer and Adorno, "Culture Industry," 123). It is not inaccurate to draw parallels between Horkheimer and Adorno's remarks on the culture industry's color-coding of consumers in 1944 ("into red, green and blue") and the 2016 news-media industry's categorization of consumer-voters (into "red and blue states").

The "better news"? Because we cannot mark fascism's intrusion by strict calendar dates, we may, nonetheless, disrupt its always-already-*ness*. For Benjamin (and later French poststructuralists), the culture-industry's "propaganda" makes way for unexpected turns of events when authoritarianism strikes. Unlike his colleagues, Benjamin was less willing to disavow the effect of variation, the unexpected. Hence, while Horkheimer and Adorno contend that "whenever Orson Welles offends against the tricks of the trade, he is forgiven because his departures from the norm are regarded as calculated mutations which serve all the more strongly to confirm the validity of the system" ("Culture Industry," 129), Benjamin pushed a bit harder on the point. He, instead, turned a critical eye on the dynamic between the mass-produced movie image and the mass-produced audience. More collectively sensual than Adorno's individualized "shudder," the cinematic experience and the "calculated rudeness" it allowed for, on- and off-screen, made way for what Benjamin conceptualized as en masse *frisson*.

If it is true that Welles's departures from the norm were mere deviations from aesthetic consistency in order to sell something "new" and different, Benjamin argued for a clear distinction between the films of, say, Charlie Chaplin and Leni Riefenstahl. Both drew the masses to the mass-produced work of art but reached differing ends. It is important to recall, however, that Benjamin's vision for political possibility by the masses turns on spectators' experience while assembled before a large movie screen. The giant screen is a crucial element for Benjamin's assertion since he envisaged the politicization of the masses precisely through the emergence of mass-media reproducibility. The point is significant for the political moment in which we find ourselves. How do we consider "mass politicization" when the mediated landscape turns on very different screens? For "the work of art in the age of its technical reproducibility" to mobilize political movement on the part of the masses, it necessarily involves mass participation. The cinema in the early twentieth century functioned as a kinetic force in a social field. The dynamic launched within the time-and-space specificity of the cinema is precisely "aura" in the age of mechanical reproducibility. Writing under the intensifying cloud of fascism, Benjamin argued that the cinematic experience "shocked" the spectator; it prompted bodily movement and involvement *within a movement*. Today's screen redirects the spectator to the field of individualism. The jury is out on how we come to identify "aura" in the twenty-first century, or if the "new" technology unexpectedly returns us to nineteenth-century "contemplation" before the singular work of art.

A caveat must be inserted before one celebrates the "masses" and their political engagement. Benjamin underscored that the cinematic experience may generate politicized mass movements, but the politicized masses may move, ideologically, in unanticipated ways. If the work of art's "aura" gives life to a politicized spectator—a commingling of aesthetic properties, content, and spectator—Benjamin's task was to understand how twentieth-century "technical reproducibility" revises the contours of the aura it generates. What is it that transforms within the shift from the individual encounter with a "unique" work of art (nineteenth-century painting) to that of a mass encounter with a mass-produced copy of the work of art (cinema)? During the nineteenth century, on the one hand, the viewer's experience with a painting secured "aura" as a reaffirmation of bourgeois individualism: *l'art pour l'art*. The privileged one-on-one experience between viewer and work allowed for "contemplation," or a transcendence of self through art. Hence, the unique work brought into conveyance an ideal commingling of the "in-itself" and the "for-itself." Although the experience with the work of art radically changes with twentieth-century technology, the concept of aura does not evaporate. It is, quite simply, revised. Because aura alters through the technology of reproducibility, the aura it manufactures raises the stakes on the politicized individual. The work of art's auratic transformation from the nineteenth to the twentieth century thus metamorphosed the relationship to art. The reaffirmation of the individual was now the reaffirmation of the masses. Mass aura is fascism's seedbed. The political implications are significant. As such, every work of mechanically reproduced art lends itself to fascism's reappearance.

To different degrees, then, Horkheimer, Adorno, and Benjamin "recognized" fascism's appearance under the Nazis. They witnessed fascism's enhancement and expansion through technology. As the tools for modernity heightened fascism's dissemination, its ideology saturated media culture and politics, yielding material effects. On the one hand, fascism comes at us with violent mediated force (Nazis, Goebbels's Ministry of Propaganda); on the other hand, fascism naturalizes its own violence through the media channels that reproduce its ideology (Hollywood, the culture industry). Media is the critical tool that not only sustains fascist ideology in recognizable forms but also holds together "not aura as such but the aura of art as a *work* of representation, a work that would have its fixed place, that would take its place in and as a world-picture."[5] This is "progress." And this is fascism.

1.1.1.

"When I recognize all these merits of the Frankfurt School," Foucault reflects, "I do so with the bad conscience of one who should have known them and studied them much earlier than was the case. Perhaps if I had read those works earlier, I would have saved useful time, surely. . . . If I had encountered the Frankfurt School while young, I would have been seduced to the point of doing nothing else in life but the job of commenting on them."[6] Foucault's remarks are stunningly worrisome for the cultural critic who grapples with the ever-returning concern that is fascism. Indeed, Foucault laments the late arrival of Frankfurt School thought in France, especially since the wartime "experiences" shared between the earlier generation of Germans and Foucault's own generation in France were, if not "identical," then "in some ways very similar" (Foucault, *Remarks on Marx*, 117). If the Frankfurt School tightened terms for theoretical rigor in advance of the unaware Foucault, they have indeed raised the ante for those of us who now must navigate rather pressing circumstances in the United States—circumstances that are certainly not "identical [but] in some ways very similar." To put ourselves in the game where the stakes are so high, a detour through French thought and its intersection with Frankfurt School philosophy (purportedly unread by the likes of Foucault) sheds useful light on the anxiety that surrounds fascism's imminent reappearance.

Since, as Foucault noted in 1978, the Frankfurt School "set problems that are still being worked on" (*Remarks on Marx*, 117), the "problem" for French thinkers came about with what soon became the left's metonymic calling card, "May 1968." Like Benjamin et al. before them, Foucault's contemporaries remained unconvinced that "progress" was sailing along through political activism. They remained wary of doctrinaire claims made by both "left" and "right." Like their German postwar colleagues, French philosophers were concerned that fascistic impulses circulated on all political fronts. Specifically, they sensed fascism hovering over culture and politics in the name of progress (De Gaulle to the right, student activists to the left). The seduction of progress, the modernist ideal in the public imaginary, rests on a promise that modern life is a life that advances. It is the endless procession of the new. With progress, "it only gets better."

Indeed, "progress" was a key concern for Benjamin. "Progress," as he viewed it, requires equal critical attention as that to "fascism." It is not incorrect, in fact, to suggest that the terms are coupled for Benjamin. Together, they envelop ideological principles invested in final outcomes, strengthened by glittering waves of technology. Whether from the left or from the right, to champion "progress" as a cultural ideal is to pin false hopes on the political. If movement "forward" suggests ideological and/or material gains, then "progressive" politics is a ruse. To take a political side demonstrates consumer culture at its finest: "Social Democratic theory, and even more its practice," Benjamin contended, "have been formed by a conception of progress which did not adhere to reality but made dogmatic claims" ("Theses," 260). Like the poststructuralists who followed in his wake, Benjamin remained suspect of those who envisaged a utopic future that awaited them while they clung to a strictly defined movement. "The concept of the historical progress of mankind cannot be sundered from the concept of its progression through a homogenous, empty time. A critique of the concept of such a progression must be the basis of any criticism of the concept of progress itself" (261).

Progress is thus the crux of the "problem" set by the Frankfurt School, similarly understood by postwar French critics. For most, however, the challenge to the problems ("still being worked on") involved eking out modes—albeit limited—of resistance. If Adorno never came around to what were later marked by poststructuralists as "fissures" and "slippages" in culture-industry ideology (although it has been said that vaudeville and the circus were promising for Adorno), his friend Benjamin delighted in identifying—nay participating in—a perversion of progress (consider his notes on "les pochettes-surprise" that he discovered at a Parisian gay bathhouse).[7] Although mediauras (to borrow from Weber) permeated culture and art in such a way that it could tilt toward fascist rule, he nonetheless believed that it is precisely through aura that the spectator is nevertheless politicized. The risk, of course, is that politicizing the spectator can slip toward communism or fascism.

For post–May 1968 thinkers, locating breaks in fascist ideology was no less nuanced and complex. Since aura emanated from the material world, the French, like Benjamin (who embraced Parisian decadence), argued that resistance took place within it. Althusser, for example, wrangled with the distinction between Ideology and ideology and their intermixing within state and cultural institutions. He provocatively drew on Freud and Lacan to grab onto historical practice as it materialized abstract ideology. Foucault's intricate and highly creative archival tracing of discursive practice as repetition illustrated the epistemological formation of "Discourse" (madness, sexuality, meaning itself). If he claimed the "death of man" in *The Order of Things* he later introduced in *The History of Sexuality, Volume 1* "points of resistance" and "reverse discourse" to signal an ounce of wiggle room within ideological containment.

Mirroring Horkheimer and Adorno's thinking in the "culture industry," the French Situationist Guy Debord restated under different circumstances the Frankfurt School's ideological premise. His 1967 book *The Society of the Spectacle* described, as Peter Wollen puts it, "how capitalist societies East and West (state and market) complemented the increasing fragmentation of everyday life, including labor, with a nightmarish false unity of the 'spectacle,' passively consumed by the alienated workers (a term understood in the broadest possible sense of non-capitalists and non-bureaucrats)."[8] For Debord, then, students deceived themselves that liberation awaited them once they manned the barricades (they further deluded themselves that their political concerns were equal to those of the workers). As the Situationists saw it, student activists merely paraded their privileged bourgeois individualism and called it revolt. In their tract "On the Poverty of Student Life," the Situationists spotlighted the students' sham-Bohemian protest as "phantastic compensation in the opium of cultural commodities."[9] Again, the French response to fascist impulses inherent to progress may not have been "identical" to the Germans, but they were indeed "very similar."

1.1.1.1.

Does modern technology, ironically, return the work-of-art experience into one similar to nineteenth-century contemplation? Does the individual screen that absorbs and endlessly fascinates merely give the appearance of collective participation and political engagement? In short, there is no "if" in, or calendar marking of, fascism's return. But if fascism permeates dimension of time and space ("History"), as the aforementioned theorists claim, it follows that political movement(s) do occur. Bodies intermingle, and they resist the pull toward authoritarianism. Yet, there is more. Until we come to terms with the ideological and bodily limitations launched by the techno-aesthetic mechanisms currently at play in the twenty-first century work of art, we will remain unable to disrupt—indeed, *act within and against*—the "storm we call progress."

Notes

1   Adorno, *Aesthetic Theory*, 437.
2   Kinsley, "Donald Trump Is Actually a Fascist."
3   Wheatcroft, "Whose Fascism Is This, Anyway?"
4   Benjamin, "Work of Art in the Age of Mechanical Reproduction," 217–52 (although many people follow Zohn's translation of this title—"The Work

of Art in the Age of Mechanical Reproduction"—I follow Samuel Weber's translation from the German, "The Work of Art in the Age of Its Technical Reproducibility" [*Benjamin's -abilities*, 58–67]); Benjamin, "Theses on the Philosophy of History," 253–64; Horkheimer and Adorno, "Culture Industry." Further references to these works are cited parenthetically in the text.

5   S. Weber, "Mass Mediauras," 107.

6   Foucault, *Remarks on Marx*, 119. Further references to this work are cited parenthetically in the text.

7   See my "Queer Angels . . . ," chapter 4 in this volume.

8   Wollen, "Situationist International," 123.

9   Internationale Situationiste Students, "On the Poverty of Student Life."

AUTHORSHIP, A QUEER DEATH

Review of Jane Gallop's *The Deaths of the Author: Reading and Writing in Time*

The moment one reads Jane Gallop's book *The Deaths of the Author* is the moment one becomes an author. Such banal description, engagement, and creative exchange between work and reader have become something of a truism since Roland Barthes penned what Peter Wollen once described as his "squib-like" essay, "The Death of the Author."[1] Although Barthes took up similar theoretical terrain in his article "From Work to Text," it is "The Death of the Author" that resonates—if not for its critical concept, then certainly for its "militant, elegant slogan" (Gallop also refers to the "slogan" as "world-renowned," a "poststructuralist catchphrase," both "theoretical" and "familiar"). Indeed, the renown of Barthes's memorable title has been such that it has come to obscure the complexity of the problem it originally named, reducing his description of a rich relationship to a dull defense of personal interpretation. Gallop wants to remind us that matters are not, and never were, so simple.

Nevertheless, Gallop must necessarily return to and raise the specter of Barthes and the sloganism that attends his "renowned essay." Revisiting this by-now-familiar trope reengages the authorial-reader experience, an experience that is resonant with a sensualness precisely because of the author's death. Her return, then, depends on the obligatory (yet thankfully brief) historical detour around the oft-paired essays Barthes's "The Death of the Author" and Michel Foucault's "What Is an Author?" Gallop thus begins her book by rightly pointing out that these two writings are *the* "go-to" texts where critical authorship discourse is concerned. If one essay ostensibly kills off the author, the other is more properly read as a discursive recounting of authorial practices in Western commodity culture. Gallop is also right to note that neither of

"Authorship: A Queer Death." Review of Jane Gallop's *The Deaths of the Author: Reading and Writing in Time* (Durham, NC: Duke University Press, 2011). *Reviews in Cultural Theory* 3, no. 1 (2012): 51–55.

these well-rehearsed (arguably, *over*rehearsed) articles do away with the author as such. Foucault is easy to defend on this count because his essay makes clear that he is not declaring the author dead; the essay's title, in fact, poses a question about the author's existence as discourse, not its annihilation (he is asking, after all, *What is* an author?). Barthes's offering, however, requires a more attentive and close reading.

For Gallop, "to go back and reconsider the death of the author" (4) requires "a slow, detailed reading" (39), because, at its heart, *The Deaths of the Author* tests Barthes's provocative claims. The details are significant. To move slowly is not only a stylistic turn; it is, for Gallop, a theoretical imperative. When, for example, in *Sade, Fourier, Loyola*, Barthes calls for a "friendly return" to the author (not long after penning "The Death of the Author"), Gallop works through Barthes's seductive suggestion in order to deliberately account for his "friendly return" to the author's writing, death, and body.[2] Reading Gallop's beautiful and effective work, therefore, one becomes acutely aware of the critical significance "close reading" has, even if it has lost favor in the humanities. Thankfully, Gallop avoids this academic current when she proceeds deliberately, critically, and attends to Barthes's and others' writings with precision. In so doing, she realizes the authors' deaths as a *givenness* to life: "The author returns from the world of the text to life, but if the return is a return from the dead, the life returned to is not the author's but our life. The author returns to us" (39).

As I write these lines, two thoughts come to mind (I raise a third shortly). First, I wish to consider Gallop's returning author insofar as it evokes the Parousia, a second coming. What are the implications for raising a theological specter in this discussion? Second, what sets Gallop's argument apart from other readings of Barthes's noteworthy slogan? In other words, does her study resist the more reductive claims about the death of the author as such? She writes, and to repeat, "The author returns from the world of the text to life, but if the return is a return from the dead, the life returned to is not the author's but our life. The author returns to us." If "the author returns to us," is this not similar to the suggestion that "the death of the author" gives way to the reader, "to us"? As such, in what way does Gallop's close, slowly engaged, and *sensual* reading return the author to us in such a way that does not split the difference so neatly? The authors Gallop selects to sort through this task are in no small part crucial to reimagining the implications of death and the author/reader experience. They have all addressed this dynamic in one form or another. Although others explore these sensual and porous boundaries, Gallop provides a turn on the Freudian-Derridean mystic-writing pad through and upon which authorial traces remain and emanate.

Gallop, for instance, closely touches on the textual hauntings that Derrida and Spivak evoke. A key instance that both authors share is that they bring to life Marx in such a way that "treats [him] as a dead-but-still-going author" (16). Through the "dead-but-still-going," Derrida and Spivak resurrect the dead, or, more accurately, they revive the nondead. In Gallop's account, the author and reader for Derrida and Spivak are not dislodged from one another. Rather, the reader is entangled with the author, or with the one who is always already "dead-but-still-going" (Does a "post-Marx" moment really exist?). Spivak—who, as I write this review, is the only author about whom Gallop writes that she is "still with us"—grasps the anxiety of the "writing present." That is, Spivak urgently writes in such a way as to be perpetually catching up. Her endless endnote "updates" reveal "the exasperation, the sense of futility" that are crucial to the way we understand her "continual revision" (128). Spivak's writing is the critical wrangling with an aporia. Her "writing present is, to be sure, vanishing, but it is also, nonetheless, persistent" (128); it reaches for the possible in the impossible.

While this brings us back and around to the matter of second comings, the "per-sistency" *to write* (for which Derrida and Spivak are recognized) rings peculiarly queer. The theological Parousia effect is thus rendered perversely in *The Deaths of the Author*. Not insignificantly, Gallop's book "is a reconsideration of the death of the author in the era of queer theory" (5). The connection between "queer" and "theory" in *The Deaths of the Author* is "palpable" since the critical necessity to think theoret-ically for queers is not only phenomenologically essential but also politically crucial. Queer theory undoubtedly remains one of the few academic outposts where the stakes for life and death are not only critical to how one thinks about so-called LGBTQ progress; "queer theory" (more vitally, I think) wrestles with the limitations of lan-guage to express the inexplicable experiences that make queer lives *and* deaths indeed queer. The Parousia when offered through queer theory, therefore, does not merely evoke the second coming even in death—*nay, despite death and those who wish it dead,* queer theory comes again and again.

Gallop realizes this point saliently when she folds together the authorial shadows in the "continuing moments" that Eve Kosofsky Sedgwick, Craig Owens, and Michael Lynch share at once across and through their writing. At stake are precisely their (antic-ipated) queer deaths: Owens and Lynch will die from AIDS, Sedgwick from an "unex-pected diagnosis" of cancer (110). The hinge on which Gallop recounts Sedgwick and Owens's relationship is pivotal for how we envisage and render the writing about inexplicable queer desire (I think about "writing" here along the lines that Derrida draws, where *écriture* conjures cinematography, choreography, and so on). Sedgwick's "relation to Owens is in fact a relation of reading and writing" (94). They discover each other through books in a bookstore. Gallop's telling of this encounter is espe-cially tantalizing for my cinematic mind since "[Sedgwick and Owens's] relationship starts when Sedgwick reads an essay" by Owens in the bookstore. She reads in this public space that the "openly gay" writer "singles out [her] 1985 book *Between Men* for praise" in his essay "Outlaws: Gay Men and Feminism" (94). Through, as Sedgwick puts it, "this strange, utterly discontinuous, projective space of desire, euphemistically named friendship, lost at a distance, or even just reading and writing," the "touches of a body" resonate (quoted on 93).

Surprisingly, Gallop quickly brushes by (in one of the few hurried moments in the book) the bookstore *as* place and the "palpability" this holds for Sedgwick and Owens's relationship. Indeed, while Gallop reiterates temporality as central to the "writerly perspective on death," she neglects what is only hinted at in *The Deaths of the Author*: space. "*This strange and projective space of desire named reading and writing*" is but one of the few remarks on space (96; emphasis in original). The all-too-brief nod to space makes me wonder what Gallop thinks of Sedgwick's later insistence (and I choose this word carefully) in *Touching Feeling: Affect, Pedagogy, Performativity*, where she asks queers *not* to forget or to reject queer spatiality at the expense of queer temporality.[3] Like "the death of the author," "queer temporality" has reached saturation due to lusterless overuse.

Nevertheless, Sedgwick, Owens, Lynch, and Gallop find themselves engaged in memorializing one another through writing before, during, and after their deaths (Sedgwick for Owens, Sedgwick for Lynch in advance of his death, Lynch in advance of Sedgwick's death, and ultimately Gallop for Sedgwick while *The Deaths of the Author* is revised [114]). The "ironic temporality" that Gallops brings into play at multiple intersections in these queer authors' writings (*to and for one another*) is rendered by Sedgwick's oxymoronic phrase—in which she must make the gesture *to write*—"continuing moment." Writing is, in other words, anachronistic: "the printed word can't be updated instantly" (113). On the one hand, this is frustratingly true, particularly during the "continuing moment" when Sedgwick pens these comments (in 2000); she, like others, reflects on her writerly attempts to keep up with the shifting terrain on which the AIDS pandemic spreads. On the other hand, while this urgency to "keep up" is not dissimilar to the anxiety with which Spivak grapples in her writing, Sedgwick's "continuing moment" homes in on a queer aura that limns *The Deaths of the Author*:

> It is in the context of talking about AIDS that Sedgwick embraces the anachronism of the printed word. A decade earlier, it is in this context of mourning gay men dying young that Sedgwick come to value, not the "culture of the moment," not keeping up-to-date, but holding on to what

has passed. It is this experience of mourning, I suspect, that transforms her relation to the temporality of writing. . . . While the writer may go about revising and updating, the printed word is the province not of the writer but of the author. The printed word, necessarily anachronistic, is where the writer confronts her status as a dead author. (113–14)

Across time, the dead author's mark lingers, resonates, and queerly touches what has passed—for author and us.

Where does this leave us? To what extent does Gallop guide us through a new turn on "the death of the author"? To what extent does her reading make perverse both the literal stamping out (stomping out?) of the authorial gesture and its theological transcendence? Authorship—the malleable yet formidable creative dynamic where author and reader commingle—is, I argue, perceived by Gallop as the necessary work involved in expressing the seemingly inexpressible. Gallop's close readings in and around queer lives, the "fragments" that the "dead-but-still-going" author leaves behind, elegantly invite us into the traces, ghostings, and shadows that viscerally render the imbrication between the theoretical and the personal—a dynamic often disregarded in many academic circles.

"Taken together," Gallop writes, "our four chapters aim to revitalize the overly familiar death of the author so that we take it as both-theoretical-personal—so that we can take a fuller measure of its moving and unsettling effects on readers and writers, on reading and writing" (18). Queers have long known that Barthes's "The Death of the Author" was not meant as a guidebook to liberate the reader from the writer; it is, instead, an "unsettling" contribution. Such delusions of democratic grandeur have proven time and again to ignore the ideological trappings capitalism lays bare in the culture industry (Foucault spells this out most clearly with the "author-function" concept). Gallop, like queers before her, recognizes a more perverse and vibrant fantasy for Barthes's "death of the author." Again, hinging on a fragment, Gallop "linger[s]" on Barthes's "extraordinary and perverse fantasy: '*If I were a writer, and dead, how I would love it if my life . . . could travel outside any destiny and come to touch . . . some future body*'" (48; emphasis in original). She is "compelled by this fantasy" not because of "biography." Rather, she "glimpse[s]" a "slightly twisted, somewhat displaced fantasy of a reader's connection to the author," where the "fantasy of bodily touching" occurs (48). By writing Barthes (then Derrida, then Sedgwick, then Owens, then Lynch, and then Spivak), Gallop breathes life into the future-perfect dead authors that are never really dead as such in the first place.

The Deaths of the Author conjures a *corps de ballet* in which Gallop cinematically choreographs shadows and bodies so that in their performance they commingle. I am thankful for the invitation to dance.

Notes

1   Wollen, "Auteur Theory."
2   Gallop, *Deaths of the Author*, 30.
3   Sedgwick, *Touching Feeling*, 9.

ARCHIVAL PENETRATION

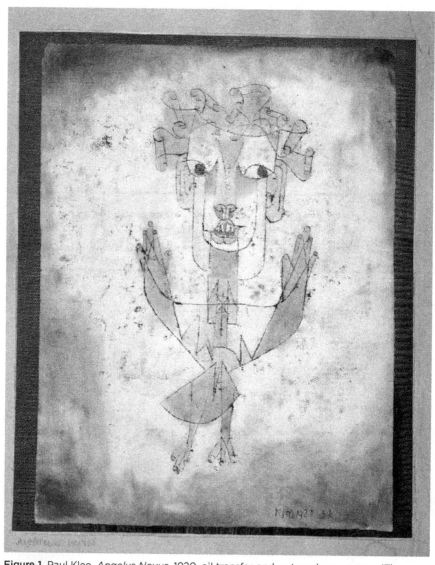

Figure 1. Paul Klee, *Angelus Novus*, 1920, oil transfer and watercolor on paper. (The Israeli Museum)

QUEER ANGELS...

4

A Klee painting named "Angelus Novus" shows an angel looking as though he is about to move away from something he is fixedly contemplating. His eyes are staring, his mouth is open, his wings are spread. This is how one pictures the angel of history. His face is turned toward the past. Where we perceive a chain of events, he sees one single catastrophe which keeps piling wreckage upon wreckage and hurls it in front of his feet. The angel would like to stay, awaken the dead, and make whole what has been smashed. But a storm is blowing from Paradise; it has got caught in his wings with such violence that the angel can no longer close them. This storm irresistibly propels him into the future to which his back is turned, while the pile of debris before him grows skyward. This storm is what we call progress.
—Walter Benjamin, "Theses in the Philosophy of History"

An archive of the cinema conjures the dream of historical reenactment. For some queer film historians, this dream-place has provided hope for "reclaiming" a historical past—a return to an originary site of knowledges where nonqueer writers have, consciously or unconsciously, neglected the dark crevices of homosexual activity. This essay, however, does not seek to reclaim a lost queer history. Rather, it looks to the ways that historical queers creatively re-presented (and took pleasure in) the remains of history. Their archive is a stash of tarnished gems that turn history into a work of art. Thus, the archive is not a place where history reveals itself as such. For these queers, it is a place where the debris of history aestheticizes the here and now.

Presenting the Homosexual!

The age of mechanical reproducibility—I speak here in particular reference to the cinema—coincides with the emergence of a representation of the body of the homosexual.

Revised from "Queer Angels of History: Take It and Leave It from Behind." *The Stanford Humanities Review: Inside the Film Archive: Practice, Theory, Canon* 7, no. 2 (1999): 150–65.

In 1895, the Lumière brothers first projected their Cinématographe films in public while Oscar Wilde's trials for "gross indecency" began. Not only did both these historical moments refigure the representation of the modern body, but, as Linda Williams has shown, the cinema initiated a process of visual archivization that organized and distinguished the normative body from the nonnormative.[1] In particular, the cultural trope of the homosexual came to be embodied in the figure of Oscar Wilde.[2] It was a body that was required to speak, to represent itself as a coherent "species" (to borrow Foucault's term).

Wilde, as the courts earnestly sought to prove, was unmistakably guilty of sodomy, buggery, or taking and leaving "it" from behind (soiled bed linen literally marked the spot).[3] Her Majesty's court also sought to prove that Wilde's physical presence solidified any gender confusion that more than a few leisured-class men may have considered when clarifying their own masculinity. Wilde's flagrantly aestheticized and "effeminized" body as well as his witty and excessive repartee undoubtedly stunned the banal upper classes. It was, however, more than words that shocked British society.

While lavishly toasted among London's West End during times of success, Wilde was to another degree turned away—clearly invited but never completely inside—by this social elite. (He was after all not only an Aesthete but Irish!) He was, in a sense, forever positioned both in and out, his backside turned toward Britain's privileged class, where he attained contingent and temporary admittance only through an uncertain glance over his broad, but effeminate, shoulders. Wilde's creative circles were always admiring yet disdainful.[4]

With Wilde's back finally forced in 1895 to turn away in shame from English society in light of his "act against nature," his body was publicly presented at once as a taker and a giver. This is to say that his simultaneous embrace, yet ironic refusal, of bourgeois commodity culture served to animate deliciously his drawing-room comedies. While delighting in the *divertissements* and sumptuous décor that housed his bourgeois acquaintances in London, Wilde was keenly aware of their displeasure—*their homophobia*—with the artist's presentation of self. In effect, Wilde lived in-between. As he immersed himself in middle-class excesses, he simultaneously digested it and then excreted it into his work of art (theater, books, and essays). In short, it was an act of taking middle-class culture from behind, while leaving it behind. The residual effect of this overaestheticized male body (the dandy!)—a demonstrative embodiment of consumption and refuse—served to represent "the" heterosexually identified homosexual for the better part of the twentieth century. But it also provided Wilde with the opportunity to rekey the cultural demands for that body's representation and the history that writes it.

The Historian as Liar

In 1883, upon Oscar Wilde's return to England from his extensive tour in America, he began to rethink his aesthetic association with John Ruskin's earthy aesthetic interests and his own notion of an organic and utilitarian socialist art movement. With the rapid rise of the industrial age, Ruskin's proletarian art-*cum*-Nature seemed short-sighted to Wilde. Wilde's turn toward High Aestheticism, however, was not simply a reversal of class sentiment. Between 1888 and 1895, Wilde produced a number of essays, short stories, and plays that displayed the vainglorious, yet dull and bloated, modern bourgeoisie who earnestly produced and consumed art in a purportedly reflective relationship between subject and object (i.e., *l'art pour l'art*). With all this producing and consuming going on, Wilde took great interest in the bourgeoisie's ability to disguise the modes of production that enabled a culture of consumption. Highly sensitive to bourgeois askance, Wilde undoubtedly recognized the hypocritical nature of their "realist" art and their claims for it as, in fact, Art.

His pivotal works of the period—especially the essays "The Decay of Lying" (1888), "The Critic as Artist" (1890), and the novella *The Picture of Dorian Gray* (1891)—came on the heels of three important experiences for Wilde: (1) his recent and extensive tour of America in 1882, (2) his very public and ongoing debate with John McNeill Whistler, and (3) the scandal that began in 1873 surrounding Walter Pater's book *Studies in the History of the Renaissance*. In the first, Wilde was awakened to the frenzied dichotomy attending American capitalism: masculinist common sense, on the one hand, and uncontrollable industrial growth, on the other. The latter proved to have castrating effects on the former (consider the hyper-manly Theodore Roosevelt, who took prompt action to shore up his masculinity when his colleagues referred to him as an "Oscar Wilde").[5] In the second, John McNeill Whistler, in his "Ten O' Clock" speech, asserted that only the artist (i.e., the painter *himself*) can understand and articulate the essence of a painterly work of art. The critic, and Whistler expected Wilde in particular to pay heed, "is an unattached writer [who] has become the middle-man in this matter of Art."[6] Wilde was no more than an obnoxious salesman (a venerator of the commodity) who was, not so politely, asked to shut up. In the final case, Pater (a mentor of Wilde) was charged by not a few with "a sentimental revolution [of art history] having no relation to the conditions of the actual world."[7] If Pater, however, was interested in the aesthetic impressions of the natural world rather than its phenomena, Wilde was inclined toward folding the two into each other.

What is central to Wilde's essays after 1888—and can be read in response to these cultural events—is his repudiation of Realism in art (painting, literature, history), which, as he saw it, placed the subject at a privileged yet deluded distance from the historical object. In "The Decay of Lying," Wilde blasphemously suggested not only that Life imitated Art; more radically, he insisted that Realism (i.e., Art imitating Life) in the visual and literary arts was a "complete failure." Its claims to "common sense," Wilde contended, ignored the necessary "translation" of Life and Nature into "artistic conventions."[8] As he saw it, claims for "Realism" as an aesthetic that equaled "real life" smacked of privileged idealism, bourgeois principles, and, mores couched as historical truth. In this way, traditional literature and painting, enhanced by bourgeois subterfuge, sought to bring the subject into conveyance with an elusive historical past that—aestheticized through Realism—served ideological premises that upheld progressive capitalism.

"Our historical sense is at fault," Wilde later writes when criticizing the tendency toward Realism in "The Critic as Artist." "Every century that produces poetry is, so far, an artificial century, and the work that seems to us the most natural and simple product of its time is always the result of the most self-conscious effort."[9] The Realist's assumptions that maintained the reflective distance between present and past, subject and object, was a sham. What history exists is only the "poetry" of each century. But how can the process, the "self-conscious effort," the very production of the work of art be displayed as a *process of work* and indeed, in the case of realist art, an act of middle-class deceit? For Wilde, in order to render the historical past, it was necessary to recognize what it in fact is: an aestheticized reproduction. The representation of history is the work of art at the hands of the artist. Wilde insisted, therefore, that the "natural and the simple" be exposed as the unfortunate decay of lying. The "natural and simple" (aligned with Realism) effectively disguises the deceit that is history. Hence, it is precisely the duty of the individual artist, according to Wilde, to disclose the process of production practiced in the making of the historical object in order to display its de facto artificiality. Because Wilde viewed the writing of history as a work of art—a presentation in the *here and now* in which artist, historical spirit, and work of art commingle—it is indeed the work of art, its *re*-presentation of historical subject as object, that is the mark of history itself. Since the artist's work involves the taking and leaving of bourgeois culture, the work of art—that is, *both in its labor and in its physical remains*—must be conceived more provocatively. In the spirit of fin de siècle *decadence*, the work of art must necessarily evoke the artist's individuality as, simply put, aestheticized debris.

To be sure, the individuality of the "individual" artist is not merely the "noisy" parade of autobiographical information (Wilde, "Critic as Artist," 1051); the artist's unique Self is the textual imbrication of the body, the work, and cultural spirit. The terms for Wilde's queer aesthetics thus only come to be through the formal concerns of the work (1054). This is why, in Wilde's view, Pater's art-historical writings offer such a "fine and exquisite piece of criticism" (1046). Under the "fanciful guise of fiction," Pater is a historian who, in his formal choice of narration, "can both reveal and conceal himself, and give form to every fancy, and reality to every mood" (1046). History is discoverable as such through aesthetic form.

Hence, Ernest (the conventional character of Wilde's dialogue) accuses Gilbert (the not so conventional, a.k.a. Oscar Wilde) of "do[ing] nothing but re-writ[ing] history" to suit his own aesthetic temperament. Gilbert responds, "the one duty we owe to history is to re-write it" (1023). To rewrite history—to dispel with "the details of history, which are always wearisome and usually inaccurate" (1021), signals the re-presentation of history as an aestheticized act of writing. History, in other words, is to be trusted in its untrustworthiness. It is a critical work of art that is invariably the passionate commingling of the spirit of the individual channeled through the formal conventions of art.

And so we come upon the Wildean work that Walter Benjamin called a "perfect and . . . dangerous book," *The Picture of Dorian Gray*.[10] Dorian Gray, the embodiment of youthful male beauty, becomes in Wilde's novella "the assertion of the absolute modernity of Beauty" (i.e., the dandy).[11] But the aura of the work of art, the nostalgia of youth generated through the Realist portrait, is already withering in Wilde's aestheticized objet d'art. Wilde reads Benjamin in advance by exposing the "loss of aura" always already at work in Realist art. Dorian's Faustian pact with the work of art, in which he stashes away his portrait in the attic, puts into relief Realism's deceit.[12] Dorian's rotting image of Self forcefully reminds the reader of their deluded faith in the "simple and natural." Life imitates Art just as Art imitates Life, a poisoned dynamic in which the boundaries between the double axes no longer hold. If the Realist painting unveils truth in *The Picture of Dorian Gray*—bodies rot toward death no matter how persistent we hope to ward it off—it is only because Wilde paints it as a lie.

At the point where the body of Dorian and his representation decays, Walter Benjamin and Oscar Wilde meet. The "perfect . . . and dangerous" book proved to be the youthful Benjamin's introduction to Decadence—a long and problematic encounter for Benjamin.[13] Fascinated by what he conceptualized as the withering aura in the age of mechanical reproducibility, Benjamin embraced willingly and unwillingly the "detritus of history" (as he termed it) hurled at his feet in the era of modernist progress. Dandies, flaneurs, and angels are the Wildean and Benjaminian tropes that, through this detritus, bewilder[14] and frustrate the terms for modern Realism.[15] Moreover, for Benjamin, Realism is acutely dangerous for the Jew and homosexual.

As cultural by-products, marginalized by bourgeois ideology, the Jew and homosexual *must* represent. Their bodies are demanded to speak, to be made visible. As Benjamin saw it, they are bodies necessary to fascist ideals.

Les Pochettes-Surprises du Gay Paris

In 1930, Benjamin had dinner with M. Albert (Proust's "counterpart" to Albertine). Following dinner, they visited the Parisian homosexual bathhouse that M. Albert operated; Albert, Benjamin recalls, sat at a podium "covered with bathing paraphernalia, pochettes-surprises, and admission tickets." Later, Benjamin exclaimed, "nothing can compete with the first sight of the man I had in the small homosexual bathhouse in the rue St. Lazare."[16] Indeed, "the first sight of the man," surrounded by the treasures with which M. Albert filled his bathhouse, was, for Benjamin, a pocketful of homosexual surprises!

But *les homosexuels pochettes-surprises* in which Benjamin found himself immersed were apparently in danger of disappearing. Shortly before his death, in a letter to Adorno, Benjamin, who was having "misgivings" about Proust's work, questioned Proust's relationship to his homosexuality and to his "race" (Proust's mother was Jewish). Benjamin suggests that a passage in Proust's *Sodom and Gomorrah* (a section concerning homosexuals and Jews) reveals "a deeply hidden . . . model of this basic experience for Proust: namely, the . . . experience of the assimilation of the French Jews."[17] The unfortunate circumstance in the storm of progress is the dangerous organizing principle around assimilation. Assimilation augured the loss of the irreducible individual, in which difference evaporated into the ether of sameness. For Benjamin, Proust's comparison between homosexual behavior ("complicity") and "the particular constellation determining the behavior of the Jews" (632) suggested the further constraining of the mobile (and, especially, urban) "constellation" of peoples.[18] To hold fast to assimilationist propriety, Realism reveals the greatest deceit: its hidden appeal to anti-Semitism and homophobia. In other words, to insist on the representation of identity (Realism *as such*) puts at risk the provocative contours of difference.

Benjamin rightly feared the ruse of assimilation, managed through the ideals of cohesive representation of race and sexual identity. He was fully aware that in delimiting the terms for representation, it played directly into the hands of fascist ideology. Here, Benjamin confronts the "perfect . . . and dangerous" world that Wilde creates in *The Picture of Dorian Gray*. In "The Work of Art in the Age of Its Mechanical Reproducibility," Benjamin argues, on the one hand, that the cinema has the potential to "shock" a complacent spectator (Benjamin applauds Chaplin for doing precisely this, as his "Little Tramp" figure disrupts and dishevels the superorganized world around him). On the other hand, the cinema traffics in images of bourgeois ideals precisely through "realistic images." The mass rallies represented in the films of Leni Riefenstahl, for instance, were particularly troubling for him. In the context of our discussion, such ideals toward Realism prove especially problematic in relation to gender. Benjamin rejected inelastically determined gender assignments that were/are categorized in modern "civilized humanity."[19]

Benjamin's queerness thus arrives on several planes. First, he likened the work of art to his own flaneur-like body, a mobile "work of art," a body unrepresentable as such, a materialized foil to bourgeois consumerism and hardened ideologies.[20] This is why, second, Benjamin refused to adhere to any political or creative doxology. He had no "credo" of communism.[21] As early as 1926, Benjamin declared to his friend Gershom Scholem, "God knows, you cannot count on me for a system (!) of materialism."[22] Even so, Scholem was befuddled by such remarks. He was especially taken aback by statements Benjamin made in an essay in *Zeitschrift für Sozialforschung*. "Is it intended to be a Communist credo?" Scholem inquired. "If not," he continued, "what actually is it? I have to admit that I don't know where you stand this year. Despite all the attempts, which you will recall, I have never succeeded—even in the past—in gaining a clarification from you as to your position."[23]

Benjamin responds to his friend with equal bewilderment: "[The] difficulty does not lie in the content of the information you request, but in the form of your request. You dress it up as a—perhaps rhetorical—question: 'Is it intended to be a Communist credo?'" Feeling what can only be read as an insult directed to him by his friend, Benjamin fires back in a letter dated May 6, 1934:

> Such questions, it seems to me, tend to absorb salt on their way across the ocean and then taste somewhat bitter to the person who has been questioned. I do not deny this in my case. I cannot imagine what really new things the essay in question could have taught you about me. It leaves me utterly amazed that you seem to want to find a summa—or a credo, as you call it—precisely in this text. . . . It should be apparent that we cannot maintain a correspondence in the manner of a controversy. And when items appear in the course of our exchange that suggest such a treatment, there is—it seems to me—no other course for its partners than to turn to the vivid image each carries in himself of the other. I believe that my image in you is not that of a man who easily and needlessly commits himself to a "credo." You know that my writings have certainly always conformed to my convictions, but that I have only seldom made the attempt—and then only in conversation—to express the whole

contradictory grounds from which these convictions arise in the individual manifestations they have taken. . . . That, among all the possible forms and means of expression, a credo is the last thing my communism resorts to; that—even at the cost of its orthodoxy—my communism is absolutely nothing other than the expression of certain experiences I have undergone in my thinking and in my life; that is a drastic, not infertile expression of the fact that the present [1934] intellectual industry finds it impossible to make room for my thinking. . . . And this practice—a scholarly one in the case of the essay you accuse—leaves the theory (the credo, if you like) a much greater freedom than the Marxists suspect. Alas, you seem to approve of their innocent ignorance in this case.[24]

What Benjamin recognizes at this moment (1934), during the rise of totalitarian fascism, is the equally doctrinaire positions held by some Marxists-communists. He is greatly concerned that in holding the line (as it were), the very ideals of communism all too easily echoed fascist praxis. Benjamin was a student of French history and philosophy, in which political ideals often found themselves strangled by authoritarian rule. He understood well, therefore, the implications that distinguished the republicanism of, say, Danton from that of Robespierre. His love for Baudelaire, Proust, and even Hollywood further anchored Benjamin's turning away from "credos" that serve to define communism, fascism, and culture of the bourgeoisie.[25]

Presenting his body, like Wilde, as a work of art, Benjamin—the flâneur—intimately experienced the extreme hazards that forced one to speak, to identify. If historical identity is unrepresentable as such, what, then, is presentable in twentieth-century art? What do we see? Feel? Think? Benjamin's angel of history offers a response.

Angelic Excrescence

In 1920, Paul Klee's painting *Angelus Novus* offered Benjamin an image that evoked the pleasure taken in historical debris (see fig. 1). Throughout the early 1920s, Benjamin so greatly admired both Klee and his work that he purchased *Angelus Novus* as part of his growing collection of books and paintings. Moreover, he intended to name his literary/philosophical journal *Angelus Novus*. Sadly, the journal never saw the light of day. In Benjamin's enthusiasm for the Klee work, he in 1921 composed a poem that weaved together an aesthetic bond between himself and the work of art.[26] Elsewhere in his letters, Benjamin folds himself into his newfound angel. Subject and object, body and work of art, "betake" themselves, Benjamin writes. He "hovers" with/as the

Angelus Novus, the work of art that comes to illustrate history as unrepresentable once and for all.[27]

Both Benjamin and Klee were troubled by the overdetermined nationalism brewing in Germany after its humiliating loss of World War I. Unlike Benjamin, however, Klee participated on the battlefield. He was a photographer on German airfields, where he was assigned to record images of the wreckage of airplanes when they crashed. Klee was fascinated by the mangled bodies and twisted steel left in the wake of the wartime event. For him, the crashes displayed the ironic effects of twentieth-century progress. Klee recounts the chaos on the airfield in a diary entry dated February 21, 1918:

> We were . . . on duty, again with the appropriate crash. . . . This weekend we have had three dead, one clobbered to death by the propeller, two came to pieces in the air! Yesterday, a fourth raced onto the roof of the repair hangar. Flew too deeply, caught into a telegraph pole, bounced once on top of the hangar roof, somersaulted and remained lying upside down, like a heap of rubble. People running from all sides, the roof at once black with mechanic smocks. Stretcher ladders, the photographer. A man disentangled and carried away unconscious. Yelling insults against spectators. First-class movie effect.[28]

In the Keystone Cops atmosphere of the German airfields, only the recording capability of motion pictures, for Klee, could possibly suggest the hysterical (in all senses) chaos of modernist movement attending the bleak comedy of the postcrash event.[29]

Klee did not make movies. He was, however, infatuated with the concept of flight and motion. His postwar paintings often suggest spinning, spiraling, and crashing birds, airplanes, and angels. In the modern age of progressive mechanical mayhem, Klee-as-angel could spin and spiral between the mechanical and human debris of twentieth-century social democracy.[30]

I think what Benjamin so admired about Klee's painting was, as one of Klee's critics pointed out, his "process . . . of ruin and new growth."[31] For Benjamin, Klee's paintings of angels suggested representation in ruins. Angels of history are caught in the whirlwind of modernist repetitive conditions that give life to "progress," a condition that can be best described as a condition of "ruin and new growth." This suits Benjamin's thesis of history precisely because it is a concept that realizes history as a flurry of events through which its effects fly within and against, somewhere in between, the nonmoving "storm" of social democratic progress. This, for Benjamin, is "homogeneous, empty time."[32] If Realism seeks to mythologize space and time as if they exist coterminously and teleologically, Wilde and Benjamin call out the deceit. Thus, *Angelus Novus*—the fractured work of art—distributes a kind of pleasure, ambiguous direction, and a debris-ridden representation that Benjamin embraced ("Which way is that angel spinning?" Sam Weber asks of Benjamin's angel).[33]

Klee's painting undoubtedly stimulated Benjamin's preoccupation with "the question of the relationship of works of art to historical life," because, as he saw it, "it is a foregone conclusion . . . that there is no such thing as art history."[34] Like Wilde, Benjamin realized that one cannot represent history as such. The queer angels of history, who endlessly spin yet are simultaneously caught, taking and leaving it from all sides, in the "single catastrophe" (social democracy), nonetheless re-present—as the objects and subjects of history—the corporeal excess left in the wake of cultural production. "We should be," wrote Benjamin in 1913, "the subject *and* object of culture."[35] Queer angels bewilder, rather than assimilate to, the strict parameters of twentieth-century representation.

Historical Perversions and Surreal Objets d'Art

If Wilde considered bourgeois history to be an aestheticized, if not fetishized, commodity, the Surrealists sought to aestheticize history as the impermeable domain of the unconscious. Benjamin fuses Aestheticism and Surrealism to make way for a queer "materialist" history. Surrealism was central to Benjamin's thinking immediately prior to his death in 1940. In fact, the trope of the Benjaminian angel found additional mobility in the Surrealists' philosophical tenets. Their "profane illuminations," as Benjamin called it, recast liberals' humanism and their purified angels. Instead, Benjamin gravitated toward the surreal angels that "liquidate the sclerotic liberal-moral-humanistic ideal of freedom, because they [the Surrealists] are convinced that 'freedom,' which on this earth can only be bought with a thousand of the hardest sacrifices, must be enjoyed unrestrictedly in its fullness without any kind of pragmatic calculation"[36] In these remarks, Benjamin's note on Surrealist "profane illumination" resonates with the philosopher's turn on "aura." For Benjamin, aura manifests at the point of correspondence with the work of art. Aura *is not* destroyed in the age of mechanical reproducibility. Rather, aura in the twentieth century is "profane illumination."

Benjamin's anxiety over the "loss of aura" in the work of art is not that it is destroyed; rather, aura in the age of mechanical reproducibility dilutes, decays, or liquifies. Aura is, in other words, transformed vis-à-vis mechanical means, by which the traditional (bourgeois) ideal of one-to-one contemplation of the work of art now expands (not without risk but "enjoyed unrestrictedly") to the masses with the giant movie screen. Herein lies the perils and/or possibilities for the transformation of twentieth-century aura: the mechanically reproduced image delivers either "monster rallies" that absorb the spectator into (fascist) ideals *or* avant-garde shock (montage) or Charlie Chaplin, who alerts the masses to (communist) ideals and praxis. John McCole tells us that Benjamin's "exuberant, defiant, and militant" rhetoric on this point reveals "aura as atavism, a mystifying haze [in which Benjamin's] advocacy of the technical instruments of [aura's] destruction constitute a moment in his work which can aptly be termed liquidationist."[37] In the aura's "liquefying" and "mystifying haze," we discover hope and danger. In other words, we discover something queer.

One can draw a direct line from Wilde's aesthetic traditions to André Breton's and his Surrealist friends' perverse "profane illuminations" to Benjamin's haze-ridden aura. With them, Baudelaire's poisonous poetry, Isidore Ducasse's (a.k.a. Lautréamont's) oft-violent poetic arrogance, Chaplin's pedophilic amours, Marquis de Sade's sexual *divertissements*, and Rimbaud's chilling *Saison en enfer* evoked a decadent experiential world in which the *flâneur extraordinaire* made himself "at home in venality itself."[38]

One more marginalized Surrealist figure crosses Benjamin's path, one who cannot be ignored for his queer sensibility that resonated across Continental culture: Georges Bataille. Benjamin, who attended the meetings at the Collège de Sociologie, was certainly intrigued by the Surrealist perversions held dear by Bataille (founding member of the Collège and librarian at the Bibliothèque Nationale).[39] Although Bataille found himself at the fringes of the Surrealist movement—basically because Breton had little tolerance for Bataille's aesthetic perversities, in which human fecal matter, punctured brown eyes, and the solar anus were so elegantly choreographed—he undoubtedly piqued the interest of Benjamin, who conducted research for his Arcades project at the Bibliothèque. Bataille's "risqué" collection of literature, buried in the vaults of the library, was a boon for Benjamin's archival research.[40] Ultimately, Bataille secured Benjamin's research notes during the Nazi occupation.[41] Considering Benjamin's rejection of categorizing art movements, he ably bridged Breton's doctrinaire terms for a dialectical unconscious with Bataille's revelations of historical shit.

By 1935, Benjamin told his long-standing friend Scholem that his work "represents both the philosophical application of surrealism—and thereby its sublation—as well as the attempt to retain the image of history in the most inconspicuous corners of existence—the detritus of history, as it were."[42] As early as 1931, Benjamin envisioned a "materialist" history that took into account, not unlike Wilde, the wasteful uses and abuses of bourgeois culture: "the strongest imaginable propaganda for a materialist approach came to me, not in the form of Communist brochures, but in the form of 'representative' works that emanated from the bourgeois side over the last twenty years in my field of expertise, literary history and criticism."[43] In recognizing history as effectively a representation of bourgeois excess, Benjamin's theses of history bear in mind that to write history, it is impossible, if not utopic, to ignore the headwinds of those cultural forces.

Benjamin, dodging, yet utilizing, both the debris and demands to represent and to disregard the "indispensable . . . rhythm of bourgeois life," acknowledges that he "has been shipwrecked, [and] carries on while drifting on the wreckage, by climbing to the peak of the mast that is already crumbling."[44] In this way, Benjamin is a key queer angel precisely because he understood the necessity to shock and scatter the terms for assimilation and complacency.

The Perversion of History

The sexual perversions gathered at the foot of Surrealism (celebrated by Breton when heterosexual, disdained when homosexual) offered a great deal of creative license for queer modernists.[45] By the 1950s, the debris of fin de siècle Aestheticism and French Surrealism made its way into the filmmaker Kenneth Anger's Hollywood archival treasures. In 1953, while in Italy, Anger crossed paths with the painter Pavel Tchelitchev, along with Tchelitchev's lover, the poet/impresario Charles Henri Ford.[46] Anger's interest in sorcery, magic, and men assuredly intrigued the precociously queer Ford and, especially, Tchelitchev. Anger long maintained his interest in surrealist and perverse imagery, which wended its way throughout his filmmaking career (consider the masturbatory dream sequences in his film *Fireworks* [1941] and, of course, *Scorpio Rising* [1963]). Folding Surrealism into his obsessive readings of the magician/occultist Aleister Crowley, Anger reveled in the aesthetic possibilities for sexual debauchery and magic(k)al sorcery.

Moreover, Anger and Tchelitchev shared a sexual and aesthetic fascination with bodily waste. Tchelitchev's series "Interior Landscapes" (1943–52) deploys imagery meant to aestheticize human innards. As early as 1946, Tchelitchev wrote the author/impresario Lincoln Kirstein that his formal concerns with the canvas had become "smearie."[47] For Tchelitchev to represent the body, he necessarily explored the phenomenological limits at which the artist's body imbricates itself with the work. For example, his large canvas *Phenomenon* (1936–38) prepares a stage upon which his world of friends and artists—Ford, Gertrude Stein, Edith Sitwell, and others—frolic in a rich palette of color and orgiastic sensuality. Set in the canvas's upper-right corner is a modernist glass building whose tower takes the shape of a tapeworm. It's no coincidence that a tapeworm lands in the vicinity of his dear friends; indeed, Tchelitchev struggled for years with this intestinal parasite, something not kept secret from his comrades. Its inclusion brings to bear the artist's refusal (inability) to conceive the artist's work of art as an experiential platform upon (*within*) which subject and object commingle. For queer artists, their bodies and their work fold into one another. The work of art *is* the lived world; it is a modernist world in which human waste and humans *as* waste intermingle. In this way, Tchelitchev's *Phenomenon* might be said to be of a piece with Klee's *Angelus Novus*. But there is something more (see fig. 2).

Anger's friendship with Tchelitchev was truly rewarding on so many fronts. During Anger's visit to Italy, their comradery gained intimate aesthetic currency as they exchanged queer pleasures and new forms of artistic expression. In fact, Anger's short film *Eaux d'artifice* (1953), in which fountains of water jubilantly ejaculate and dissolve into one another, was shot during his visit to Italy. The film is dedicated to Tchelitchev.[48] But the friendship ushered in another inquiry for Anger. If twentieth-century pursuits by artists and critics involved, yet again, wrestling with the limits of abstraction and Realist art, what aesthetic avenues were available to the queer pervert? Like Benjamin, the cinema appealed to Anger's delicious, sometimes malicious, mischievousness. And like Wilde, he heightened the aesthetic of lying and deception. He

Figure 2. Edith Sitwell, a friend and patron of the artist, looks upon Pavel Tchelitchev's queer cultural milieu in *Phenomena* (1938), at Tooth's Gallery. (© Science & Society Picture Library/National Portrait Gallery, London; courtesy of Daily Herald Archive/ Science Museum Group)

stole ideas and works of art for his own aesthetic ends (this before "appropriation" dazzled postmodern critics). Anger, literally, played with the devil.[49] This is queer history.

History as Gossip

Kenneth Anger grew up in Los Angeles, undoubtedly a spinning queer angel caught in the catastrophic debris of Hollywood representation. (He loved wearing the costumes designed by his grandmother, a Hollywood seamstress.) For him, it was precisely the excesses of Hollywood production that he viewed as the conditions of Hollywood history. *Kenneth Anger's Hollywood Babylon* makes this quite clear. As Anger saw it, a history of Hollywood has not much to do with the so-called factual details of history (those that Oscar Wilde had earlier swept away). Anger's history of Hollywood is made up of compilations of tabloid news stories, cocktail-party chatter, and junked movie paraphernalia.

It is worth noting the peculiarly queer Americanness of *Hollywood Babylon*. I don't mean to suggest some sort of queer-nationalist style. Yet certain aesthetic impulses may be traced to an array of artists who were, for the most part, living in the United States and who were invariably marginalized—*homophobically*—by consecrated American modernists (e.g., Clement Greenberg and his Abstract Expressionist acolytes). Anger, along with Tchelitchev and Ford's crew, resisted assimilationist strains in the American midcentury art scene. A key odd duck among the queer angels was Joseph Cornell. Like Anger, Cornell assembled his artwork by collecting images of movie stars and "found" objects from popular culture, objects he enshrined in lovingly decorated boxes. His love of Hollywood film, like Anger's, led him to making films or, one might say, remaking films from Hollywood leftovers. The films, of course, were dedicated to his angelic friends.[50]

Cornell is best known for his "shadow boxes"—filled with snippets of ballerinas' clothing (donated by dancers whom he had timidly desired and who were introduced to him by George Balanchine), photostat copies of photographs (*always a copy of a copy*) from his ever-growing files of newspapers, and clippings from magazines and books, bejeweled with pieces of glass—and his constructions were miniature shrines to the likes of Greta Garbo (1905–90), Hedy Lamarr (1914–2000), and Lauren Bacall (1924–2014). They were perversely delicate objets d'art offered in homage to the famous as well as the neglected. Along with Hollywood stars, Cornell dedicated boxes to forgotten nineteenth-century ballerinas or to birds, which he so tenderly admired (consider his 1955 film *Aviary*). Movie stars, ballerinas, and birds danced and flew through Cornell's reproduced world of caged *objets du jour*.

Indeed, both Cornell and Anger literally lived through the reproduced material that filled their mechanically produced existence in the twentieth century. Pieces of starlets' clothing, biographies, tabloid newspapers, comic books from used bookstores, and scraps of celluloid covered their walls and were stacked high on bookcases. Their homes in effect mirrored—nay, became—lived-in box-like shrines. While Anger lavished his apartment with "occult paraphernalia, homosexual and heterosexual pornography, tarot cards, and a blood-red decor," Cornell, in the dead of winter, spread birdseed across his kitchen table, positioned near an open window.[51] Birds flew in and out, imbibing in Cornell's offering. Echoing Klee's and Benjamin's mesmerizing dance with birds and other flying machines, Anger and Cornell immersed themselves in cultural debris in which interior and exterior worlds collided. Subject and object spun and created furiously.

When Anger filmed *Inauguration to the Pleasure Dome* (1954), he chose to shoot at the home of his friend, the Hollywood impresario Samson DeBrier. Casting sexual provocateurs, like Anaïs Nin, Anger hyperaestheticized DeBrier's space. As Dennis Hopper recalls, Anger created his set with a "labyrinth of materials: drapes, cloth, and things draped over everything, . . . old clothes that actresses had worn, pieces of sets, maybe a cup that somebody had used in a movie, stuff like that" (quoted in Landis, *Anger*, 72). The film, like the debris discovered in *Hollywood Babylon*—to be sure, like Anger's home—adoringly *re*presents Hollywood's historical refuse: queers, freaks, and perverts.[52]

Anger tells his unofficial biographer that writing *Hollywood Babylon* gave him "that particularly Hunnish pleasure in seeing your enemies fall to pieces in front of your eyes": "All I've had to do is sit back and wait to see the whole empire of Hollywood Babylon crumble into dust" (Landis, *Anger*, 94). The "pieces," the traces, are the remains for Anger that turn the archival collections of Hollywood into rubble, "into dust." Ashes to ashes, dust to dust, Hollywood remains refuse to entirely blow away. They linger in musty cabinets and in unkempt apartments. The remains pile on as they pass through memories and yellowed movie magazines. In short, they are the materials of a queer life. Anger's version of Hollywood history can be seen as the aesthetic connections between Aestheticism and Surrealism that throughout the twentieth century provided a queer conundrum: Can the "real" be represented as such? Hollywood—the land of the copy of a copy—gave queers the perverse satisfaction (*indeed, pleasure!*) in taking it and leaving it from behind.

The queer angel of history does not hover in the debris of history in search of historical beginnings once and for all; rather, and to follow Derrida, queers delight in the spinning debris because they burn with the passion to rewrite and to re-present the hope of history. For Derrida, we are "in need of archives . . . in one way or another, *en mal d'archive*." *Mal d'archive*: a fever, a burning compulsion to return to, to search for, the archive. Derrida continues, "It is to burn with passion. It is never to rest, interminably, from searching for the archive right where it slips away. It is to run after the archive, *even if there's too much of it*, right where something anarchives itself. It is to have a compulsive, repetitive, and nostalgic desire for the archive, an irrepressible desire to return to the origin, a homesickness, a nostalgia for the return to the most archaic place of absolute commencement."[53] For historical queers, the "irrepressible desire" to return, the *too-muchness* of it all, is precisely where pleasure in rewriting is discovered. In returning to the remains of an archive, queers well know that the "truth" of history is forever lost. But it is what is left behind that matters most for queer desire.

To be at once the subject and object of history, to be the produced and the producer, is to grab onto the debris of commodity culture. Wilde, *the* body that came to represent the modern homosexual, "rewrites" Realist history by aestheticizing it and, in doing so, reveals Realism's deceits. Through the "self-conscious" commingling of his body with the debris of cultural production, Wilde homosexualized history: for example, history as work of art. If the archive is the treasure trove of excessive historical material awaiting excavation, the queer body is at once the treasure and the archive. By recognizing Benjamin's perverse embrace of the "indispensable . . . rhythm of bourgeois life," queer angels likewise refuse to assimilate into established guidelines that demand them to represent once and for all. Instead, we bewilder the terms for historical origins not merely by taking pleasure in the production and wreckage of historical ideals (though we certainly do delight in it). Queers identify *as*, represent *as*, historical wreckage.

Queer thinkers and artists have long pursued the dilemma attending the complex crosscurrents at play in dialectical materialism. Is it possible for queers to subvert the vicious circularity that staunch materialists demand?[54] Sebastian Melmoth (a.k.a. Oscar Wilde), Walter Benjamin, and Kenneth Anger faced the representational trap set by historical traditionalists.[55] Yet, it is precisely this double bind that served queer transgression best, because it allowed for a reckoning with history. Queers quickly discovered, as we have seen, the historical value of waste and *pochettes-surprises*. This we call "camp." Jack Smith's *Historical Treasures*, Andy Warhol's screen tests and candy wrappers, John Waters's Divine melodramas, David Wojnarowicz's surrealist AIDS polemics and performances, Diamanda Galás's screeching operas, Bruce La Bruce's pornographic homage to Hollywood, and Ron Athey's freakish body tattoos and piercings spiral with the best of the early- and midcentury queer modernists. Faced with the insistence to represent in the age of mechanical reproducibility, queers practiced a perversion of dialectical materialism. Caught in the nowhere of representation yet always blasting in and out of every direction, the continuously spinning queer angels hope(d) and pray for the second coming.[56]

Notes

1   L. Williams, "Film Body." I'd like to thank Suzanne Nixon, Janet Staiger, and Andrew Hewitt for the many thoughtful discussions about this essay's topic. A version was delivered at the Society for Cinema Studies annual conference in April 1998.

2   See Cohen, *Talk on the Wilde Side*; and Sinfield, *Wilde Century*.

3   "A former housekeeper at the hotel, Mrs. Perkins, testified that there had been fecal stains on the bedsheets" (Ellman, *Oscar Wilde*, 460). Cohen, in *Talk on the Wilde Side*, also reports on the housekeeper's observation pertaining to the "conditions of the sheets" (178).

4   I am indebted to Andrew Hewitt for his thoughts on a homosexualized double move; see his "Sleeping with the Enemy."

5   Not by coincidence, Roosevelt was called an "Oscar Wilde" in 1882 by his fellow New York State assemblymen. Wilde's arrival in the United States in the same year provided fodder for Roosevelt's political rivals, who saw him as a young New York dilettante who lacked virile political know-how. To prove himself otherwise, Roosevelt (while Wilde returned to England in 1883) headed to South Dakota, hunted Buffalo, shed his New York aristocratic airs, and created a public-relations campaign unlike any ever seen in America (ironically similar to Oscar Wilde's) in order to present "Teddy Roosevelt," the cowboy. For an account of Roosevelt's "Oscar Wilde" moment, see Morris, *Rise of Theodore Roosevelt*, 162; and, for an elegiac critique of Roosevelt's public-relations campaign to shore up his manhood, see Bederman, *Manliness and Civilization*.

6   Whistler, "Ten O' Clock," 86.

7   Quoted in Donohue, *Walter Pater*, 57. See, further, Adam Phillips's introduction to Pater's work, to what is now called, to avoid cultural and historical confusion, *The Renaissance: Studies in Art and Poetry*. He points to a contemporaneous review that flatly warns that "[Pater's] book is not one for any beginner to turn to in search of 'information'" (viii).

8   Wilde, "Decay of Lying," 991. Further references to this work are cited parenthetically in the text.

9   Wilde, "Critic as Artist," 1020. Further references to this work are cited parenthetically in the text.

10 Benjamin to Herbert Belmore, June 12, 1921, in *Correspondence of Walter Benjamin, 1910–1940*, 16.

11 Wilde, *Picture of Dorian Gray*, 103.

12 I am reading the painting as Realist based on the cues given in the novella. The painting, as described in the story, appears to have the good fortune of being interesting merely because Dorian is the handsome figure represented. Otherwise, the painting simply has all the traits of a realist work of art: "the painter looked at the gracious and comely form he had so skillfully mirrored in his art" (Wilde, 18).

13 I write "problematic" because Benjamin remains indecisive as to how far a practice of perverse aesthetics might go. On the one hand, as Benjamin saw it, André Gide's *Corydon* has "hesitant and sanitized dialogue on love between young boys who . . . are all too lacking in Attic spice" (Benjamin to Scholem, February 19, 1925, in *Correspondence, 1910–1940*, 262); while, on the other hand (based on his support of André Breton's Surrealist ideas), Salvador Dali's version of aesthetic irony and playfulness invariably espoused pro-fascist sentiment that pushed the envelope past Benjamin's boundaries of "perfect . . . and dangerous." Most pointed, of course, is Benjamin's positing of the slippery slope that *l'art pour l'art* occupies in "The Work of Art in the Age of Mechanical Reproducibility": "'*Fiat ars-pereat mundus*,' says Fascism, and as Marinetti admits, expects war to supply the artistic gratifications of a sense perception that has been changed by technology. This is evidently the consummation of' *l'art pour l'art*. Mankind, which in Homer's time was an object of contemplation for the Olympian gods, now is one for itself. Its self-alienation has reached such a degree that it can experience its own destruction as an aesthetic pleasure of the first order. This is the situation of politics which Fascism is rendering aesthetic. Communism responds by politicizing art" (242). Wilde's "aesthetic pleasure," however, is not necessarily in toto bourgeois "destruction" of the object (as is the case with Pater and, as Benjamin sees it, Mallarmé [224]); rather, Wilde's Aestheticism, I think, provided Benjamin with a more complex perspective on "bourgeois history."

14 I replace my original term "confuse" with "bewilder" because I recall a discussion I had with Janet Staiger at the time writing of "Queer Angels." She queried if the term "confuse" was accurate for my argument. At the time, I was uncertain and kept it in place. I think a more accurate way to pose the after-*affect* of the dandy and flaneur—the modernist queer body—is "bewilderment." "To bewilder," I later discovered, was favored by James Baldwin in

his later novels. "Bewilder" suggests an unsettled experience in time and place, an experience grounded in memory, triggered by the materialized past (a souvenir). "Bewilder," as I see it, is not dissimilar to "uncanny" or *unheimlich*.

15   The Pre-Raphaelite Edward Burne-Jones, Wilde's friend who influenced his Aesthetic sensibilities, titled a painting of his *An Angel Playing a Flageolet* (1878). At the Burne-Jones recent retrospective at the Metropolitan Museum in New York (cat. no. 12), a curatorial notecard reads, "This watercolor reproduces an earlier design by Burne-Jones for stained glass. Angels were a favorite subject of the artist. Oscar Wilde reported a conversation with him in which Burne-Jones announced, 'The more materialistic science becomes, the more angels shall I paint; their wings are my protest in favor of the immortality of the soul.'" These protesting wings, as we will see, play an important part in a queer aesthetic tradition.

16   Benjamin to Gershom Scholem, January 25, 1930, in *Correspondence, 1910–1940*, 362.

17   Benjamin to Theodor W. Adorno, May 7, 1940, in *Correspondence, 1910–1940*, 632. Benjamin uses the term "race" in relation to his working through questions of anti-Semitism through a comparison of Judaism and Christianity. In a letter to Scholem, Benjamin observes, "a principle component of *vulgar* anti-Semitic as well as Zionist ideology is that the gentile's hatred of the Jew is physiologically substantiated on the basis of instinct and race, since it turns against the physis" (October 22, 1917, in *Correspondence, 1910–1940*, 99, emphasis in original). It is an important recognition on Benjamin's part since it brings to attention what today we refer to as "essentialism." For Benjamin, "vulgar" anti-Semitic and Zionist ideology is "physiologically substantiated" in identifying the other, their "race." Seen this way, and Proust brings this home for Benjamin, the assimilationist behavior of the homosexual and the Jew in bourgeois circles serves to conceal their difference, which, through this deceit, reaffirms anti-Semitism and, by extension, homophobia. It is not clear in his letter to Adorno if his later "misgivings" about Proust are because Proust ably (deceptively?) assimilated into gentile bourgeois culture (as homosexual and Jewish) or because Proust revealed his own self-hatred by raising concerns that the "other" was no longer recognizable, *identifiable* as such. In other words, would the other's nonassimilationist "race" and their behavior threaten his own assimilationist desires? Should their difference be made known by some slip or untoward gossip in Proust's bourgeois world, would it uncover his homosexuality and Jewish heritage by the mere slip of the other?

18   It is worth noting Susan Sontag's likening of a "creative" sensibility to a form of "self-legitimization" that is especially prescient for Jews and homosexuals, insofar as the "two pioneering forces of modern sensibility are Jewish moral seriousness and homosexual aestheticism and irony" ("Notes on Camp," 290). In Sontag's remarks, one notes Benjamin's concerns, in which a queer urban sensibility was at risk.

19   These concerns over pure representation can be traced to Benjamin's youth. As a young man, Benjamin was troubled by the cultural logic associated with rigid representations of corporeal identities. As early as 1913, for instance, Benjamin (age twenty-one) questioned medicalized gender assignments: "thus you should understand," he writes a friend, "that I consider the types, 'man/woman,' as somewhat primitive in the thought of civilized humanity." Benjamin to Belmore, June 23, 1913, in *Correspondence, 1910–1940*, 34.

20   Benjamin never really found a permanent home in which to reside. Shuffling from place to place, belonging nowhere, scattered between France and Germany, Benjamin undoubtedly identified with one who was only at home in the movement of the city. See, further, Benjamin, *Charles Baudelaire*.

21   Benjamin to Scholem, May 6, 1934, in *Correspondence, 1910–1940*, 439. Scholem and Benjamin's correspondence cited here is from 1934, one year prior to the publication of "The Work of Art in the Age of Mechanical Reproducibility" and most likely the period in which Benjamin was preparing the now-famous essay.

22   Benjamin to Scholem, May 29, 1926, in *Correspondence, 1910–1940*, 303.

23   Scholem to Benjamin, April 19, 1934, in *Correspondence of Benjamin and Scholem*, 107.

24   Benjamin to Scholem, May 6, 1934, in *Correspondence of Benjamin and Scholem*, 109–10.

25   In a different register, his resistance to ideological demands spilled over to his engagement with art and popular culture. For instance, he remained wary of modernist neologisms attached to works of art. In a lengthy letter to Scholem, Benjamin finds "cubism" as a term overgeneralized and unspecific; while Picasso's paintings leave "the impression of impotence and inadequacy," Klee has "obvious connections to cubism," yet, Benjamin says, "as far as I can judge, he is probably not a cubist" (October 22, 1917, in *Correspondence, 1910–1940*, 101). As a collector of philosophies, quotations, and books, Benjamin maintained an interest in art historical inquiry *and* interpretation because together they served well his numerous forays into the teachings and visual philosophies

of the Kabbalah, the Talmud, Surrealism, Messianism, Kafka, Proust, Charlie Chaplin, and Katharine Hepburn. In a letter to Greta Adorno (Theodor's wife), Benjamin informs his correspondent, "there is a lot of you in [Hepburn]" (July 20, 1938, in *Correspondence, 1910–1940*, 572).

26   "The Angelus calls himself angel / And quickly flees such strictures / For he does not tarry in the rooms / Of cunning sorcerer: Jews . . . / In his glory he betakes himself / He is bedded on stalks of roses / But he'd rather remain hovering" (Benjamin to Scholem, November 8, 1921, in *Correspondence, 1910–1940*, 194).

27   Benjamin to Scholem, November 8, 1921, in *Correspondence, 1910–1940*, 194.

28   Quoted in Werckmeister, *Making of Paul Klee's Career*, 112.

29   It has been rightfully brought to my attention that my terms—"hysterical (in all senses)"—indicates the etymological connection of "hysterical" to the womb. Though this is not the place to elaborate, a short digression is helpful. The hysteria—*the mayhem*—on the battlefield that Klee encounters, where bodies are torn asunder by a military apparatus, raises questions about which bodies are legally, morally, and ethically "allowed" to be dismantled. As early as 1697 in England, laws were put in place to bar intentional *maiming* of bodies ("mayhem" is etymologically linked here). In protecting the body as a whole, the law's intent was meant to assure "a person's ability to defend themselves in combat" (see Wikipedia, "Mayhem (crime)"). The law, albeit transformed over time, remains in place to varying degrees in the UK and the US. But laws that seek to defend the "whole" body from intentional "maiming" run up against matters that concern abortion and trans bodies. Here, women's and trans persons' choices to alter their body are still seen by some people as bodily "mayhem," illegal destruction of the body. In rereading Klee's (gleeful?) description of the crash site through the lens of "mayhem," one might entertain the idea that the violated bodies on Klee's "movie" set reveal the violently ironic undoing of juridical law that insists on the sanctity of the whole body, except in the service of combat. In relationship to trans bodies, see Velocci, "Standards of Care." I thank Andrew Katz for alerting me to the implications for "hysterical" and Cáel Keegan for our discussions on medical mayhem.

30   Klee thought of the Angelus figure as symbolizing "humanity, . . . which proves itself through destruction" (Werckmeister, *Making of Paul Klee's Career*, 80).

31   Werckmeister, 119.

32   Benjamin, "Theses on the Philosophy of History," 260–61.

33   S. Weber, "Mass Mediauras," 95.

34   Benjamin to Florens Christian Rang, December 9, 1923, in *Correspondence, 1910–1940*, 223.

35   Benjamin to Belmore, June 23, 1913, in *Correspondence, 1910–1940*, 35 (emphasis added).

36   Benjamin, "Surrealism," 189–90.

37   McCole, *Walter Benjamin and the Antinomies of Tradition*, 6.

38   Benjamin to Theodor W. Adorno, February 23, 1939, in *Correspondence, 1910–1940*, 598.

39   Alan Stoekel, introduction to *Georges Bataille*, xxi, xxvn18.

40   For a discussion of Bataille's relationship to Surrealism and his work at the Bibliothèque Nationale, see Polizzotti, *Revolution of the Mind*, 319–20. See also Benjamin to Theodor W. Adorno, August 2, 1940, in *Correspondence, 1910–1940*, 493–94.

41   Editor's footnote to Benjamin's final letter to Adorno, August 2, 1940, in *Correspondence, 1910–1940*, 639n.

42   Benjamin to Scholem, August 9, 1935, in *Correspondence, 1910–1940*, 505.

43   Benjamin to Max Rychner, March 7, 1931, in *Correspondence, 1910–1940*, 371.

44   Benjamin to Scholem, July 7, 1924, in *Correspondence, 1910–1940*, 245 ("indispensable . . . rhythm"); Benjamin to Scholem, April 17, 1931, in *Correspondence, 1910–1940*, 378 ("has been shipwrecked"). Benjamin's remarks are instructive when considering his understanding of materialist Surrealism. Consider Breton's version of a Surrealist existence in bourgeois society, from his second manifesto: "The terror of death, the cafés chantants of the other world, the shipwreck of sound reason in sleep, the crushing curtain of the future, towers of Babel, mirrors of inconsistency . . . these all-too-gripping images of the human catastrophe are perhaps nothing but images" (quoted in Etherington-Smith, *Persistence of Memory*, 381–82).

45   Polizzotti, *Revolution of the Mind*, 88–89.

46   Charles Henri Ford (1908–2002) and Pavel Tchelitchev (1898–1957) met in Paris in 1931. As lovers, they befriended the likes of Marcel Duchamp, Gertrude Stein, and Breton. In 1940, Ford and Parker Tyler (1904–1974) edited the first American journal dedicated to Surrealism, *View* (1944–47).

47   Tchelitchev continues, "there is more meaning in a soldier's shithouse where they clean on the walls their shitty fingers, much more, at least a shit-finger is a signature of a true phenomena, by his own secretion, so to say" (quoted in Kirstein, *Tchelitchev*, 111).

48 See Sitney, *Visionary Film*, 102.

49 On Anger's relationship with the Charlie Manson acolyte Bobby Beausoleil, the Hells Angels, and the vexed making of his film *Lucifer Rising* (1972), see Landis, *Anger*, 157.

50 Not surprisingly, when Tchelitchev died, Cornell made and dedicated a film to the painter. The film is titled *Angel* (1957) and was inspired by (of all things!) a neighborhood fountain in New York whose structure consisted of a decorative angel spouting streams of water. The gallery owner Alexander Iolas, summing up Cornell's not-so-innocent work, found both the artist and his debris-ridden artwork an act of necrophilia (Solomon, *Utopia Parkway*, 172). Film was a natural extension, then, of Cornell's necrophiliac aesthetic. His first film, *Rose Hobart* (1936), is not really his film at all. It is an act of thievery that pastes together the remains of Columbia Pictures' *East of Borneo* (1931). In it, Cornell recut and reused the film's "found" footage, which was headed for the trash in a New Jersey warehouse. The film is a spliced-together, fragmented compendium of close-ups of the film's star Rose Hobart (1906–2000). The film, when first shown at the Julien Levy Gallery, caused a small riot when Salvador Dalí (infuriated at being outdone by such a Surrealist masterpiece) overturned and smashed the projector (Solomon, *Utopia Parkway*, 89).

51 Solomon, 357; Landis, *Anger*, 117. Further references to this work are cited parenthetically in the text.

52 We see, of course, the waste of Hollywood in Anger's *Scorpio Rising* (1963): the once young, strong, and methodical Brando flashes on a television screen; James Dean posters tacked to the wall amidst a collection of comic strips and newspapers; images of Jesus Christ from a B-film version of the Passion juxtaposed with Nazi swastikas and SS uniforms.

53 Derrida. *Archive Fever*, 91 (emphasis added).

54 See, especially, Michael Warner's introduction to *Fear of a Queer Planet* and John Champagne's "Stop Reading Films!"

55 "Sebastian Melmoth" was the name Wilde adopted after his conviction, appropriately combining the martyred saint with Charles Maturin's eponymous *Melmoth the Wanderer* (1820). Maturin and Wilde were deeply indebted to the figure of the "Wandering Jew." After Wilde's imprisonment, he wandered, wounded by the course of events, through Italy and France. In doing so, he aestheticized the remains of his existence through a traditional figure for which wandering was its raison d'être. On this, see Ellman, *Wilde*, 523, 528.

56 See, further, Derrida, *Specters of Marx*, 180–81n2: "We should quote and reread here all these pages [of Benjamin's "Theses on the Philosophy of History"]— which are dense, enigmatic, burning-up to the final allusion to the 'chip' (shard, splinter: *Splitter*) that the messianic inscribes in the body of the at-present (*Jetztzeit*) and up to the 'strait gate' for the passage of the Messiah, namely, every 'second.' For 'this does not imply, however, that for the Jews the future turned into homogenous, empty time.'"

HIDE AND SEEK, OR, THE HISTORY OF DIFFERENCE UNDER ERASURE

5

When the *New York Times* reported on December 1, 2010, that the National Portrait Gallery in Washington, DC, "removed [David Wojnarowicz's video *A Fire in My Belly*] from an exhibition and *apologized* for its content after the video was criticized by the Catholic League and members of the House of Representatives for being offensive to Christians" (emphasis added), I was less surprised than I was in disbelief. After all, I am fully aware that the moral-cultural gatekeepers have not disappeared since Jesse Helms's heyday during the 1990s, when he paraded Robert Mapplethorpe photographs as the poisoned outcome of taxpayers' funding through the National Endowment for the Arts and the National Endowment for the Humanities. It soon became clear that Helms's appeal to the perversion of taxpayer money was merely a red herring that disguised his and America's trenchant homophobia and racism. It is worth noting that in this current state of affairs, taxpayer dollars are not at issue. According to Christopher Knight of the *Los Angeles Times*, the Portrait Gallery is privately funded. If the anxiety of losing institutional funding is no longer the reason that one censors, one can only assume that those who are put in charge of consecrating America's "Art" must fully subscribe to the moral doctrine dictated by Christians and their congressional lackeys.

My disbelief—and thus not my surprise—came about because this egregious act of censorship against *A Fire in My Belly* occurred on World AIDS Day, an event that once brought the art world to a standstill so that it might recognize the devastating losses AIDS wreaked on the creative worlds. The magnitude of these losses affected both artists and, as Fran Lebowitz has recently pointed out, the audience who, in myriad ways, gave life to the works of art. Moreover, World AIDS Day intended to remind the public about the aesthetic-political energies at work in AIDS activism, from large-scale

"Hide and Seek, Or the History of Difference Under Erasure." University of Illinois Press Blog (December 14, 2010).

protests at the National Institutes of Health to staged "die-ins" that blocked New York traffic. In other words, the political performances, the work of art, successfully raised consciousness about governmental inaction and apathy. Today, World AIDS Day is marked by Lady Gaga forfeiting Twitter so that she can "digitally die" and raise money for AIDS organizations and research. Apparently, Lady Gaga remained dead until a pharmaceutical businessman resurrected her on December 8, 2010.

My disbelief also took hold because on the day when the art world is meant to defend queer art and artists, to scream out against censorship, and to stand firm for the historical and contemporary artists who consistently and with fury announce the hypocrisy of Christian "love they neighbor" as AIDS ravages the globe, the National Portrait Gallery administration acquiesced to those who not only wish to erase the histories left in Wojnarowicz's wake but, more terrifyingly, seek to erase the histories that are yet to come.

Fortunately, protests have taken place across the country (albeit with very mediocre media coverage), and several very smart essays have been penned that clearly spell out the insidious decisions played out in Washington. The art historian and curator Jonathan Katz is speaking in several public forums about this spectacle, and a new generation of protestors, including Mike Blasenstein and Michael Dax, creatively and strategically "screened" *A Fire in My Belly* on their iPad outside the exhibit's doorway. Perhaps, and most importantly, Transformer—a Washington, DC, gallery—refused to bow to conservative venom and calls for censorship. Brilliantly, Transformer is screening Wojnarowicz's video in its storefront window on P Street. How gorgeous is that!

As such, the National Portrait Gallery's title for its exhibit—*Hide/Seek: Difference and Desire in American Portraiture*—is no longer a bon mot riddle. *Difference and [Sexual] Desire* is on full display at Transformer and across the world via the internet. Digital leaks are a wonderful thing. And while we have Wojnarowicz's portraits, such as *A Fire in My Belly*, to thank for electrifying a movement as well as history's remains, we must remember the Black queers who so importantly gave face to the range of sexual desire and political aesthetics that in no way can be understood only as white. Before, during, and after the NEH showdown in the later twentieth century, Richard Bruce Nugent, James Baldwin, Audre Lorde, and Marlon Riggs (among others) offered portraits of themselves that challenged homophobia and racism. When AIDS entered the scene, Riggs forcefully drove home the cultural linkages Americans made between homophobia and racism when his queer Black body with AIDS was (quite literally) put on display by Helms and Pat Robertson as the ultimate abject body for conservative Christians' agenda. As *Queer Pollen* shows, Riggs looked his inquisitors directly in the eye and challenged the greed and hate that left blood on their hands. It is time to revisit the lessons learned from Rigg's *Tongues Untied*.

It is my hope that *Queer Pollen* awakens the queer histories—across race, sexual difference, and desire—that have taken shape before, during, and (hopefully someday) after the era of AIDS.

PENETRATING EPSTEIN

Reviews of *Une vie pour le cinéma: Jean Epstein,*
by Joël Daire; *Jean Epstein: Critical Essays and
New Translations,* edited by Sarah Keller and
Jason N. Paul; and *Jean Epstein,* DVD Box Set

The Jean Epstein renaissance currently under way has yielded two significant books from both sides of the Atlantic: the French historian Joël Daire's *Une vie pour le cinéma: Jean Epstein* (La Tour verte, 2014) and the anthology *Jean Epstein: Critical Essays and New Translations,* coedited by the American scholars Sarah Keller and Jason N. Paul (Amsterdam University Press, 2012). Along with the *Jean Epstein* DVD box set distributed by Cinémathèque française and Potemkine films (2013), a range of fresh perspectives open onto the prolific filmmaker and writer. This review considers the new ways in which Epstein scholarship might be directed when drawing upon these critical interventions.

The return to Epstein coincides with—or perhaps is partially responsible for—the vibrant return to so-called classical film theory. Occupying center stage in the recent issues of *October* and *Screen,* and along with the writings of his contemporaries, Epstein's writings are revisited by young and senior film scholars alike. The results are inspiring, vigorous, and challenging when viewed against the backdrop of a period in film studies that some people have identified as "post-theory." Daire's and Keller and Paul's offerings are noteworthy in light of theory's resurgence because revisiting Epstein's life and creative output paves the way for revised ways to engage with the filmmaker's rich and diverse body of work. What is noteworthy and significant about these interventions is the different emphasis placed on the filmmaker by French and

---

"Penetrating Epstein: *Jean Epstein: Critical Essays and New Translations,* edited by Sarah Keller and Jason N. Paul; *Une vie pour le cinéma: Jean Epstein* by Joël Daire," *Sense of Cinema* 74 (March 2015), https://www.sensesofcinema.com/2015/book-reviews/penetrating-epstein-jean -epstein-critical-essays-and-new-translation-by-sarah-keller-and-jason-n-paul-eds-and-une-vie -pour-le-cinema-jean-epstein-by-joel-daire/.

American writers. Taken together, we discover in Epstein a complex figure, one whose ideas about cinema *and* its making remain critical for both contemporary film studies and, without doubt, queer studies.

In the preface to Keller and Paul's anthology *Jean Epstein: Critical Essays and New Translations* (hereafter *Critical Essays*), Tom Gunning quips that when he has mentioned Epstein's name in relationship to film studies, some interlocutors believed they misheard him to say "Eisenstein."[1] Gunning's point, of course, is that Epstein's name does not carry the resounding force of Eisenstein's. The Polish-born French filmmaker, however, has never been completely erased from theoretical discourse in the United States and, notably if not obviously, France. Gunning points out that the Keller-Paul collection "should be seen as a culmination rather than an entirely new project" (20). Nevertheless, the collection draws attention to unrehearsed areas of study in Epstein scholarship and teaching. Thus, as a comprehensive collection, *Critical Essays* more substantially anchors Epstein for the classroom curriculum and scholarly research.

Moreover—and another reason to underscore *Critical Essays'* contribution—Epstein's inclusion in academic literature and course outlines in the United States has been at best uneven in the history of film studies. Dudley Andrew, for instance, only gives brief mention to Epstein in his 1976 survey *The Major Film Theories*. Soon after, Stuart Liebman's dissertation ("Jean Epstein's Early Film Theory, 1920–22") and Richard Abel's invaluable two-volume anthology (*French Film Theory and Criticism: A History/Anthology, 1907–1929*) introduced significant and substantial translations of the filmmaker's writings. Alan Williams, in his historical overview of twentieth-century filmmaking in France (*Republic of Images*), notes the significance of Epstein's prewar body of work while swiftly bypassing his Breton period and any discussion about the director's investigation of film aesthetics and genre.

Liebman's and Abel's contributions cannot be underestimated since they make available both Epstein's intellectual engagement with film and his place within the critical debates in France about the cinema during the 1920s. Their adroit coverage of Epstein's writing sustained, if not resuscitated, the director's role in the discipline of film studies. For American readers, in particular, this work solidified the link between Epstein and his expansion of Louis Delluc's concept of *photogénie*.

To an extent, the translations in the 1980s assured that Epstein's modernist impulses survived the powerful wave of poststructuralism, semiotics, and psychoanalysis. But Epstein's thoughts on cinema also "survived" the paradigm shift because his theories easily crossed the threshold between "modernist" and "postmodernist." Epstein's theories profitably and seductively intertwine modernist/postmodernist theories, not unlike Deleuze's "body without organs"—*avant la lettre*. At the same time, it is worth bearing in mind that Epstein historically emerges along with the early twentieth-century modernist thinking that was articulated by the likes of Henri Bergson, Jacques Lacan, Jean-Paul Sartre, and Maurice Merleau-Ponty—all of whom parsed Freud, Husserl, and Heidegger.[2] Epstein thus emerges from within a specific cultural atmosphere in France, one steeped in debates over and theories of phenomenology, existentialism, and language. As the record shows, Epstein directly and indirectly responded to this intellectual dynamic in his writing and his filmmaking. A closer look at the subsequent gravitation toward "grand theory" and poststructuralism in film studies during the 1970s—theoretical approaches indebted to the "modernist" period—invariably reveals stark affiliation with Epstein's aesthetic and philosophical concepts. Jacques Aumont reminds us in *Jean Epstein: Cinéaste, poète, philosophe* that Epstein is "astonishingly close to certain intuitions" that, specifically, Deleuze penned several decades later.[3] It is certain that Epstein continues to remain relevant for twenty-first-century film theory and filmmaking.

Positioning Epstein beyond or outside these historical and theoretical contexts reveals a shortcoming, insofar as it features Epstein through a lens that magnifies his relationship to film as strictly avant-garde. In this way, the director has been either aesthetically isolated as a poetic modernist or lumped alongside avant-garde formalists or abstractionists. This focus is not necessarily wrong, but it is incomplete. Daire's biography restarts the way we envisage and discuss Epstein by problematizing and more accurately delineating Epstein's cinematic output. On this count, Daire is clear that to cluster Epstein with the likes of Viking Eggeling, Hans Richter, and Ferdinand Léger is to oversimply the filmmaker's contribution to the cinema, if not a particular brand of avant-garde practices with which Epstein is often associated (190). In other words, to fully grasp Epstein's unwavering commitment to his theoretical and aesthetic mission for the cinema, Daire reminds us that Epstein's engagement with the material world, and the movement within it, was not merely reserved for the avant-garde as such.

To a certain extent, both French and American scholarship has cemented the association, Epstein = avant-garde/art film. Yet, as Gunning and Aumont remind us, French scholarship has never entirely forgotten Epstein, and in doing so, French Epstein scholars have drawn broader perspective on the filmmaker. Even so, Daire is quick to point out that by 1949 French cinéastes and critics considered Epstein passé (197). With his death in 1953, however, French film criticism quickly revived their studies of Epstein, thereby yielding a more comprehensive portrait of the artist. Nonetheless, the more or less consistent attention paid to Epstein by the French suffers from a significant gap, one that I take up shortly.

Hence, evaluations and reevaluations of Epstein's work appeared in France soon after the director passed away from a cerebral hemorrhage. Notwithstanding Bazin's "silence" on the filmmaker (as Gunning refers to it), Alain Badiou applauded Epstein's "genius" in his essay "Cinematic Culture" (1957). Soon after, in 1963, Jean Mitry discussed Epstein's theory at length in *The Aesthetics and Psychology of the Cinema*, and in 1964, the journalist and prolific film critic Pierre Leprohon, with whom Epstein was familiar and on friendly terms, published his short monograph *Jean Epstein*. While Noël Burch believed that Epstein's ideas "strikingly foreshadow certain very contemporary concepts," he concluded that "his theories are a bit too far removed from actual practice to be really relevant." As mentioned, Deleuze, in 1985, drew upon Epstein's theories to carve out his concept of, in particular, the "time-image" in *Cinema 2*. Aumont's collection of essays *Jean Epstein: Cinéaste, poète, philosophe* appeared in 1998, and in 2008 Prosper Hillairet published a short and thoughtful book on Epstein's celebrated film *Cœur fidèle*.[4] Beyond academic publishing in France, Epstein's sister, Marie (a staunch cinéaste), worked tirelessly with Henri Langlois and the Cinémathèque to preserve her brother's cache of films, notes, drawings, and personal documents. It is in large part from this collection that Daire develops his biography and to which Franco-American scholars such as Christophe Wall-Romana turn.

Given the groundswell of interest in Epstein that is currently in play, Hillairet rightly asserts in his review of Daire's biography, "Spring 2014 was a privileged moment in the recognition of Jean Epstein's oeuvre." Indeed, along with Daire's biography, the Cinémathèque hosted a major retrospective of the director's work in April and May that included a vast repository of information on the archive's website.[5] Additionally, the museum, in tandem with Potemkine Films, released a marvelous DVD box set that includes fourteen films. The prints of *Six et demi, onze* (1928), *Finis terrae* (1928), *La glace à trois faces* (1927), and *La chute de la maison Usher* (1928) are masterfully and beautifully restored. The short "chansons filmée" *Les berceaux* (1931) reveals Epstein's generic range when placed alongside his grand-scale films made under the auspices of Albatros Films, including *Le lion des Mogols* (1924). The sound films shot in Brittany are invaluable inclusions in the collection since they invite the viewer to return to Epstein's theoretical compositions and realize the artist's conceptual designs in practice. *Le tempestaire* (1947), for example, is a fascinating and excellent example of the director's experimentations in cinematic sound, nonfiction filmmaking, and short storytelling. In the United States, the Museum of Modern Art's print of this particular film is of poor quality; happily the DVD now makes available the intricate cinematic designs that I was unable to detect when I first saw this film.

Moreover, the DVD provides access to the more difficult-to-see and grandiose productions Epstein made, as noted, for the studio, Albatros, that Russian émigrés had established in Paris. The DVD also makes available Epstein's own big-budget production of *Mauprat* (1926; the first film made under his own production company, Les Films Jean Epstein). Unfortunately, *Cœur fidèle* (1923) is not included here, which is a shame given both its central role in the director's oeuvre and its significant formal dimensions, which are crucial to view when attending to Epstein's film theories. Fortunately, the film was remastered and released in 2011 with English subtitles in both Blu-ray and DVD formats by Eureka Entertainment as part of the Masters of Cinema series. This package is elegantly designed and includes a booklet with Epstein's notes on the film's making as well as supplemental short, incisive essays.

With Daire's assistance, the Cinémathèque/Potemkine DVD box set also presents an invaluable booklet with commentary, a comprehensive filmography, and a selection of Epstein's drawings and writings. Smartly conceived introductions to the films, freshly recorded soundtracks for the silent works, inclusion of English subtitles, and interviews with the likes of Bruno Dumont, Viva Paci, and Wall-Romana make for a remarkable collection. The box set, therefore, allows the viewer to experience the incredible range of Epstein's filmmaking since it provides films from the multiple genres and environments (studio, nature) in which he worked: cine-poetry, large-budget studio productions, "les chansons filmée," and what Epstein's colleague Jean Benoit-Lévy referred to as "films de vie" (documentary, but something more—a recording of life in movement). With more than forty films made during his career and as more of his writings and films comes to light, it will become clear that film scholarship has merely scratched the surface of a critical investigation into the auteur's contributions.

The newly minted presentation of the films and fresh biographical details bring alternative perspectives on Epstein into relief and thus reboot what has become institutionalized knowledge about his filmmaking and theories. I do not wish to suggest that one construction of "Epstein" is ultimately better than the other. Yet, because distinct weight has been placed on Epstein's role as an avant-garde filmmaker-artist-theoretician, especially in the United States, Daire's biography and his new research introduce us to a more eclectic landscape on which to view Epstein's creative, diverse, *and* commercial offerings. Hence, while the widely seen *Cœur fidèle*, *La glace à trois faces*, and *La chute de la maison Usher* brilliantly resonate with Epstein's critical approach to cinema-as-art through his conceptualization of *photogénie*, it is necessary to give equal attention to the studio films such as *Le lion des Mogols* and *Mauprat*. The DVD box set should go some way in correcting the one-sided emphasis placed on Epstein. As the critical dimensions of Epstein expand with new research and as his cinematic experiments are revealed across a range of genres, we encounter a filmmaker whose singular enterprise anticipates and shadows the combined efforts of Pare Lorentz, Maya Deren, Vincente Minnelli, F. W. Murnau, and Jack Smith.[6]

This is why Daire's biography is important; it is vital that it be translated. The author goes to great length in highlighting Epstein's life as one that intersected with multiple milieus in the early part of the twentieth century. From his vexed relationship with Blaise Cendrars (37) to his long-standing professional and amicable relationship with Abel Gance (182), Epstein navigated the spirited debates on cinematic art that circulated among Parisian sophisticates while simultaneously bringing to the screen fast-paced costume dramas (such as the already noted adaptation of George Sand's novel *Mauprat* and the interminably long but richly developed *Les aventures de Robert MaCaire* [1925]). What is refreshing about Daire's study, especially given the critical discourse that emphasizes Epstein's role in avant-garde filmmaking, is his coverage of Epstein's studio work.

With access to Epstein's papers and other archival material offered by the Cinémathèque (Daire is the archive's "directeur du patrimoine"), the biography stitches together a complex weave of the aesthetic, intellectual, and financial concerns that informed Epstein's daily life. With Daire's biography, we now have a fuller account of Epstein's involvement with the French film industry. Indeed, Epstein was widely recognized and often cheered by critics from the popular press for his aesthetic sensibility and engaging narratives. According to Daire, recognition of his work by the public was extremely important to the director (191). The challenge for Epstein was how to harness aesthetic experimentation and his theoretical interests while drawing in a large and engaged audience. Hence, what one takes away from Daire's study is an image of a filmmaker who successfully, and with great aplomb, directed large-budget studio films, shot shorter-length "art" films, developed "education films" for a television series in the early 1950s about ballet ("Ballets de France," produced in concert with Benoît-Levy for an American audience), and—at the same time—published a lifetime's worth of major theoretical tracts on cinematic aesthetics that ranged from the poetic, *Bonjour cinéma* (1921), to the fully and richly conceived, *Le cinéma du diable* (1947). Daire's filmography and bibliography are thus tremendous assets—and an eye-opener—regarding Epstein's prolific output across media.

Daire's thorough chronological recounting of Epstein's life makes for an informative read. On the basis of vast amounts of documents, Daire details significant biographical episodes in Epstein's life: his studies in mathematics and medicine prior to making film; his commitment to socialism during the Occupation and earlier involvement with Ciné-Liberté (whose members included communists such as Léon Moussinac, socialists such as Germaine Dulac, and Popular Front icons such as Jean Renoir [152]); his dodging of creditors while forging alliances with new financial partners to build his own (failed) production company (106); and his near arrest by the Nazis in 1944 (the Red Cross, with which Epstein worked during the war, intervened to certify that he was not Jewish [165]). And, as Daire reminds us throughout, Epstein's sister, Marie, was never far from her brother during these events. Marie thus occupies a key place in Epstein's life and afterlife.

Yet, while all this biographical detail is extremely valuable and enticing, Daire only provides a passing glance on the filmmaker's homosexuality. The author tells us that the reason the subject is not fully addressed is because he did not wish to over-read the archival evidence. He argues that in his interpretation of the director's work and life, he is "careful not to extrapolate."[7] This is a surprising act of marginalization in an otherwise abundantly detailed book since it is difficult to divorce Epstein's intellectual engagement, cultural milieus, and creative practice from his homosexuality. It is even more surprising given that, in the late 1930s, Epstein penned *Ganymède, essai sur l'éthique homosexuelle masculine*. The work is housed in the archive and, happily, has been recently published in French by Les Presses du Réel, a project that has been guided by Daire's editorial skills.[8] In Daire's biography, however, he resists identifying the significance between Epstein's homosexuality and his creative practice.

In a brief and passing paragraph in the biography, he mentions Epstein's work on the *Ganymède* project and then states that, "in the same vein" and same time, the filmmaker began writing an essay on "sado-masochism [!]" With this quick aside, Daire misses a significant opportunity to draw attention to Epstein's coterminous thinking about cinema, homosexuality, and queer sexuality. These writings deserve more than a mere gloss since they not insignificantly coincide with the publication of key books and articles on film such as *Photogénie de l'impondérable* (1934). A link between a study on homosexuality and sado-masochism on the part of Epstein is, therefore, highly suggestive insofar as his thoughts for *Ganymède* and on sado-masochism offer insight into a queer filmmaker who elsewhere stressed the phenomenological possibilities of the cinematic experience. "Pain is in reach," Epstein declares in his essay, "Magnification."[9] Such a declaration, read against the backdrop of *Ganymède* and essays on sado-masochism, is truly provocative for film and queer theorists. Prosper Hillairet gets it right in his review of Daire's book, then, when he reminds us that Epstein's turn to *photogénie* is not dissimilar to—and difficult to separate out from—his homosexuality. The filmmaker's queerness, like his filmmaking, "exceeds reproductive sexuality, a sexuality to the limits, and as [Epstein] states elsewhere, cinematic *photogénie* exceeds the film itself."[10]

Curiously, Daire tantalizingly hints at the possibility of linking Epstein's intersected querying of homosexuality, masculinity, and cinema when he discusses Epstein's feature film *Mauprat*. According to the biographer, Epstein developed complicated structures of the "feminine" and "masculine" in the narrative, particularly as portrayed by the characters Edmée (Sandra Milowanoff) and Bernard (Nino Constantini) (83). Our introduction to Bernard in the film is indeed bewildering since, at first appearance, he appears to be a young woman who has desiring eyes for Edmée. In this way, Epstein opens the door to interpreting—as Daire indeed does—gender-play in a way that allows for something more than wanton "extrapolation" on the part of the critic.

The missing queer angle in the biography is additionally unfortunate because Daire relies on the very same archival documents when he expounds on Epstein's creative, political, and cultural milieus. In other words, these purportedly "nonqueer" circles undoubtedly overlapped with Epstein's queer milieu and simultaneously fostered his aesthetic approaches to cinematic form and content. For example, the gender confusion in *Mauprat* is startlingly queer and, of course, gorgeously constructed by Epstein's hand. But it is also constructed with what Daire calls the "joyous confraternity" that peopled the film's set (82). Daire's refusal to identify Epstein's queer world notwithstanding, it is no great leap to see that the director's creative circles were in fact just as queer as much as they were political. The creative milieu on the set of *Mauprat*, for example, included the set designer/photographer Pierre Kéfer, whose aesthetic touch soon guided the photographer Dora Maar's hand;[11] the presence of the queer surrealist René Crével; and the assistance of the future filmmaker Luis Buñuel (an intimate, of course, of the gay poet Federico García Lorca and the queer painter Salvador Dalí). And as Daire points out, Epstein also crossed paths with Jean Cocteau, Germaine Dulac, and Paul Poiret—a decidedly queer grouping with diverse and complex political positions. If it is valuable to recognize Epstein's relationship to political milieus (he sat comfortably with the communist Moussinac but not so comfortably with the fascist Paul Chack [161]), then it is equally valuable to recognize Epstein's queer circles.[12] In short, Epstein was no stranger to queer modernism and the malleable formations it assumed aesthetically, politically, and erotically. Since filmmaking was intimately involved in "joyous confraternity," his films invite a queer reading (consider, further, the cinematic *amité* of *Finis terrae*).[13]

For any number of reasons, scholarship developed under American auspices has more readily made way for a "queer" Epstein. The emphasis placed on Epstein as the filmmaker-as-artist and less the filmmaker-as-studio-guy may have something to do with the more inviting embrace of his homosexuality (this and a strong history of queer studies in the United States that is not readily accessible as a discipline in France). Sarah Keller and Jason N. Paul's collection of new essays and translations sets the stage for this particular pitch, in which one discovers Epstein's queer sensibility and its direct line to avant-garde cinema. It does this and a great deal more.

Keller remarks in her introduction to *Critical Essays* that while the feature films made during the height of Epstein's commercial success in the 1920s should not be "dismissed out of hand"—even though they "subscribe to more narrative-driven, sentimental scenarios"—the "bravado of the camera movement, which is in excess of that narrative information, shows again Epstein's commitment to subverting the hold of [that] narrative by letting its margins decenter it" (37). Yet, whereas Daire sees *Mauprat* as a dynamic, complex, and ostensibly queer studio film (the gender play that he notes in the biography), Keller sees the film as a "costume drama [that] lacks almost entirely the vigor described by Epstein about the effects of cinema on an audience" (38). Hence, whereas Daire revels in expanding on Epstein's commercial studio successes and their fusion of avant-garde aesthetics, Keller and the authors in *Critical Essays* focus their attention on Epstein's intellectual theories and making of cine-poetics via *photogénie*.

In bringing fresh perspective to Epstein's place in the avant-garde, Keller offers a comprehensive overview and thorough description of those films that highlight the director's aesthetic and theoretical principles. As one of the emerging young film scholars dedicated to rigorous analysis and possessing a crisp writing style, Keller sharply and ably traces the relationship among Epstein's poetry, writing, and filmmaking. Bridging close analysis of his films with the theoretical content and cine-poetic design of, for example, *Bonjour cinéma*, Keller solidifies Epstein's stature as a quintessential cine-modernist. Thus, she argues, *Cœur fidèle* and *La glace à trois faces* are major works because they—like his writings—"allow cinema's seams to show, [insofar as he] takes a sequence to a point of cinematic excess . . . and thereby calls attention to the process of picturing the world, emotional states, and intimate environments" (35). Like Epstein's cinema, Keller's enthusiasm for her subject is infectious.

Many of the works that follow Keller's introduction in *Critical Essays* are similarly compelling. As a whole, the new essays and the translations constitute a stunning collection of writings that secure Epstein's place as a cine-poet. Hence, Keller and Paul have assembled a magnificent range of essays that thoughtfully investigate the possibilities Epstein envisaged for the cinema-machine. Stuart Liebman's essay, "Novelty and Poiesis in the Early Writings of Jean Epstein," revisits his cinematic mainstay and locates the filmmaker within and, to a certain extent, against the language of the Russian Formalists. In "The 'Microscope of Time': Slow Motion in Jean Epstein's Writings," Ludovic Cortade works through the complex dimensions of slow motion as they are engaged in Epstein's theories of cinematic movement. Importantly, Cortade launches into a brief discussion that seeks to identify the "underestimated" connections between Bazin and Epstein (Gunning's remarks on Bazin's "silence" on the filmmaker notwithstanding). Cortade, via a review of the 1953 Epstein retrospective at the Cinémathèque, discovers a break in Bazin's silence on Epstein. Hinging on fragile but nonetheless critical evidence, Cortade's essay persuasively reveals the way Epstein haunts Bazin's thinking on slow motion and the materiality of the world. Again, essays such as Cortade's remind us of the Epsteinian threads that consistently weave through the history of film theory. Anchored with rewarding insights by Trond Lundemo, Nicole Brenez, and Rachel Moore, Keller and Paul's *Critical Essays* will prove to be a focal point for film curricula and breathe new life into film theory.

Finally, and to return to the sidelining of "queer Epstein" in the Daire biography and French criticism more generally, *Critical Essays* includes Christophe Wall-Romana's astute "Epstein's *Photogénie* as Corporeal Vision: Inner Sensation, Queer Embodiment, and Ethics." From the perspective of a queer scholar, I was pleased to encounter Wall-Romana's essay since it proves to be an antidote to the otherwise simple nods of acceptance or, alternatively, hasty dismissal of Epstein's homosexuality. As a recognized Epstein scholar (born in France, professor in the United States), Wall-Romana bridges the twinned aesthetic poles subtending Epstein studies that have been discussed here. He is thus a driving force behind the transformative attention granted the filmmaker. The scholar can be seen, for instance, in the aforementioned *Jean Epstein* DVD box set, where he discusses, in particular, the critical aspect of Epstein's homosexuality and why this identity is important to our evaluation of the films. Wall-Romana has also magisterially translated Epstein's *The Intelligence of a Machine* (2014) and published a major study on the director, *Jean Epstein: Corporeal Cinema and Film Philosophy* (2013). There is also word that he is translating Epstein's all-important treatise on homosexuality and masculinity, *Ganymède*. If true, this will be a major boon for film and queer studies.

For now, his cavalier essay "Epstein's *Photogénie* as Corporeal Vision" is precisely the springboard from which the relationship between Epstein's homosexuality and *photogénie* is provocatively addressed. "In the unique French mélange of respect of privacy and hypocrisy," Wall-Romana asserts, "nowhere had I read that Epstein was a homosexual, and no reference had ever been made to [Ganymède]" (58). For Wall-Romana, as well as Prosper Hillairet (to whom we referred earlier), to separate Epstein's homosexuality from the aesthetic form he critiqued and developed is to neglect a crucial component of his filmmaking and career. Epstein's "formulation of a self," Wall-Romana reminds us, belongs to a queer dialectic in its essential fluidity: "that is, between on the one hand narcissism and self-exploration, and on the other hand the dissolution or sublimation of the ego within a broader engagement with reality" (60). Here is queer movement. Here is *photogénie as* queer.

If Joël Daire's biography *Jean Epstein*, Sarah Keller and Jason N. Paul's anthology *Jean Epstein: Critical Essays and New Translations*, and the *Jean Epstein* DVD box set are taken together—and I believe this necessary—they make for required reading and viewing for scholars and cinéastes because they leave us with an array of entry points to further study Epstein's oeuvre. To my mind, these collections also present the following question: In what way might Jean Epstein's breadth of cinematic practice and intellectual engagement augur a critical intervention that sets the stage for new methodologies in the way cinematic form reveals the complexity of the queer auteur?

To be sure, spring 2014 was a "privileged moment."

Notes

1   Aumont similarly points to the homonymic aspect of the names "Eisenstein" and "Epstein" ("Cinégénie," 88).

2   Lacan—and his revision of Freud—was driven by a broad cross-section of debates that filled Parisian cafés. In the art world, André Breton and his surrealist companions placed Freud on their high-aesthetic altar. Epstein, no fan of Freud yet active in Parisian art scenes, was aware of the intellectual and creative environments in which these discussions disseminated. Indeed, to refute Freudian concepts such as the "unconscious" and instead to champion a phenomenological "subconscious," Epstein necessarily assumed the dialectal position he was required to hold when critiquing Freud. Lest we forget, Epstein studied medicine before turning to filmmaking. His concept of a bodily "subconscious" was decidedly *not* Lacanian "clinical" psychoanalysis, based on the "unconscious."

Along with Freud's standing among France's intelligentsia, Élisabeth Roudinesco points out that Saussure and Husserl prompted radical thinking during the period. Her magisterial work *Jacques Lacan* draws out the intricate intellectual connections and the key players in Paris's modernist circles who espoused these ideas. Her note on Lacan's work in the early 1930s, for instance, gives a glimpse into what the modernists were reading and engaging in the public sphere: "The year 1931 was a watershed for Lacan, for it was then that, starting from the basis of paranoia, he embarked on a synthesis of three areas of knowledge: clinical psychiatry, the teachings of Freud, and the second phase of surrealism. His remarkable knowledge of philosophy, and in particular of Spinoza, Jaspers, Nietzsche, Husserl, and Bergson, also contributed to the making of the great work of Lacan's youth: his medical thesis *De la psychose paranoïaque dans ses rapports avec la personalité* . . . appeared in the winter of 1932 and made its author a leader of a school" (31). To Roudinesco's shortlist of those who were grappling with the deep theoretical matrices unleashed by psychoanalysis and phenomenology, we can add the voices of Sartre, Bataille, and Heidegger (whose few essays published in France at the time nevertheless took on considerable force; see further, Roudinesco, 89). It is certain, based on Epstein's theoretical writings, that his queer modernist ideas were fueled by his readings and the cultural milieus in which these ideas circulated in France.

3   In Aumont's introduction to *Jean Epstein*, he gets quite close to naming Deleuze's theories on cinema as something less than original: "Or, à relire après les ouvrages de Deleuze, ils apparaissent comme étonnamment prochés de certain intuitions du philosophe, en des convergences de pensée troublantes" (But after rereading the works of Deleuze, [Epstein's writings] appear surprisingly close to some intuitions of the philosopher, with unsettling intellectual similarity; Aumont, "Avertissement," 7, my translation).

4   Badiou, "Cinematic Culture," 23; Mitry, *Aesthetics and Psychology of the Cinema*; Leprohon, *Jean Epstein*; Burch, *Theory of Film Practice*, 58; Deleuze, *Cinema 2*, 36; and Hillairet, *Cœur fidèle de Jean Epstein*.

5   La Cinémathèque Française, "Jean Epstein."

6   To be accurate, it could be said that Epstein and Murnau mutually anticipate each other. I am not familiar with literature that compares the two filmmakers, but provocative links might be made given their contemporaneity.

7   Daire's full apologia reads, "Du moins avons-nous essayé de recouper les informations, en n'hésitant pas à écarter des témoignages, y compris celui du principal intéressé, quand ils s'écartaient trop nettement de la réalité décrite par l'archive. Si nous avons parfois interpreté, nous avons eu le souci de ne pas extrapoler ou solliciter. C'est pourquoi certain aspects important de la vie d'Epstein resteront ici peu explorés, et en premier lieu la question de son homosexualité." (At least we have tried to cross-check information, not hesitating to exclude evidence, including that of principle interest, when it strayed too far from the reality described by the archive. If we have sometimes interpreted, we have been careful not to extrapolate or supplicate. This is why some

major aspects of Epstein's life will remain little explored here, and primarily the issue of homosexuality.) Daire, *Une vie pour le cinéma*, 15.

8   Along with Nicole Brenez and Cyril Neyrat, and with a preface by the French queer filmmaker Lionel Soukaz and an introduction by Christophe Wall-Romana, Daire has edited this important essay for the Epstein collection *Écrits complets, vol. 3, (1928–38); Ganymède, essai sur l'éthique homosexuelle masculine, Photogénie de l'impondérable et autres écrits.*

9   Epstein, "Magnification," 239.

10   Hillairet "Epstein, une vie de cinéma," 129.

11   The photograph *Le danseur Alberto Spadolini* (1935) was photographed by Maar at Kéfer's studio. The image is striking for the homoerotic sensibility it evokes since it conjures the contemporary work of George Platt-Lynes.

12   Peter Wollen elegantly demonstrates the creative energies and political implications that cultural milieus enable (see "Out of the Past").

13   Laurent Le Forestier's essay "Jean Epstein, un projet d'enquête: 'Le Cinéma du diable? . . .'" is intriguing to consider when placed alongside the affectionate friendship we see in *Finis terrae*. As Le Forestier points out, Epstein explored "l'influence des films sur les rapports d'amité et d'amour" as part of his project "Le cinéma du diable?" Le Forestier's essay raises a provocative issue around, especially, male French friendships (*amité*) and the cinema. In a larger project, I am considering the striking amorous comradeship expressed between male friends in France and the way their homoerotic intimacy is experienced—especially as part of an encounter with the cinema. For Jacques Derrida, *amité* was expressed vis-à-vis cinematic experience. See, for instance, Benoît Peeters's biography *Derrida*, where Derrida's "applied filmology" (i.e., going to the cinema) may be directly linked to his intimate friendships with Robert Abirached and Michel Monory. Although not related to the cinema, Louis Althusser describes a "theater" in which erotic love for his male companion Paul unfolds and that, in time, led the philosopher to wonder if he was "destined to become a homosexual" (*Future Lasts Forever*, 85).

IN EXCESS OF THE CUT

Peter Greenaway's *Eisenstein in Guanajuato*

One of my favorite books about Sergei Eisenstein is Léon Moussinac's *Sergei Eisenstein: An Investigation into His Films and Philosophy*. When I read it, my love for French cinema and my admiration for Eisenstein were fully rewarded. Not only was Eisenstein revealed as a figure reserved for the Soviet Boys' Club and their dedication to montage, but Moussinac also introduced me to an Eisenstein who, like me, reveled in the wide-ranging pleasures that the French arts offer: Balzac, Surrealism, Jean Cocteau, Blaise Cendrars, "the old houses, pregnant with their own histories" in the Marais, and the gilded halls of Versailles and Fontainebleau. Most importantly, Moussinac introduced me to an Eisenstein who "danced happily" with sailors while traveling in Saint-Tropez.[1]

What a find this book was for a gay graduate student in film and literature studies when, in the early 1990s, a vibrant dialogue in queer studies commingled with leftist debates that focused on the pro-choice movement and AIDS activism. Indeed, as I completed the work for my masters, concluding with a thesis dedicated to Derek Jarman's *The Garden* (1990), the intellectual and political air at the State University of New York at Buffalo was thick with modernist dreams in which aesthetics and politics furiously mixed. Jarman's aesthetic energies from this period (*The Last of England* [1987], *War Requiem* [1989], *The Garden*) coincided with those of another British auteur and art-school filmmaker, Peter Greenaway (*The Cook, the Thief, His Wife, and Her Lover* [1989] and *Prospero's Books* [1991]). In the same year that I finished my masters, Peter Wollen observed of the two filmmakers and the political climate that, although "they did not confront Thatcherism head on," their "strong visual style" gave way to "a less explicit artistic position within which their political anti-Thatcherism emerged."[2]

"In Excess of the Cut: Peter Greenaway's *Eisenstein in Guanajuato*" in *Los Angeles Review of Books* (April 15, 2016).

Although many reviewers compared the two, Jarman did not shy away from biting commentary about Greenaway's work. Jarman was particularly bothered by what Wollen refers to as Greenaway's "antiquarianism" and "lavish overindulgence" in *The Draughtsman's Contract* (1982).[3] This is a charge that Greenaway strongly contested, and as I saw it, his later *The Cook* more assertively aestheticizes "antiquarian" settings, elaborating a grotesque rendering of Thatcherite consumerist ideology, raising the stakes on his "political invective."[4] On whatever side one fell, however, the Jarman-Greenaway debates—aesthetically and politically—served graduate students well during the post-Reagan era.

If Jarman's and Greenaway's filmmaking raised the ante on aesthetics in response to political conservatism, my colleagues and I also brought Eisenstein into the cinematic challenge that both British filmmakers offered. With the Soviet filmmaker/theorist, we discovered more direct rhetoric to help us think through the relationship between theory and practice. With the anti-choice movement pressing down and friends and lovers dying every day, Eisenstein offered us ways we could get our heads around the aesthetic-political dynamic that we hoped would transform events in the late twentieth century.

Although we eagerly sought the same ideological ends, the films made by these three filmmakers held our attention through very different aesthetic and political means. As I reflect on it now as a gay film studies professor, I can see that the hotly contested debates that first animated Pudovkin's, Vertov's, and Eisenstein's commitment to montage were mirrored in the debates that I was part of in graduate school. Theories of montage, and the aesthetic distinctions embedded in these theories, invigorated us at every turn.

Yet, as the gay boy in that 1990s seminar room, I remained haunted by something particular and sentient about Eisenstein's theories of montage. We all concurred that Eisenstein was the king (certainly, for me, *the queen*) of montage. My friends, however, were invested in montage at the level of the cut. They were convinced that the cut was crucial for the "shock" it leveled upon the spectator. Montage-*as*-cut prompted the viewer to direct political action. But, as became clear, montage was something more than the cut for Eisenstein—something homosexual.

Indeed, I could not help but be erotically mesmerized by the images *within* the frame, images that were so intricately constructed by Eisenstein and on which he demanded we concentrate. His tightly framed, muscular, and chiseled young men in *Strike* (1925) not only lead the proletariat in protest against their not-so-attractive bourgeois factory owners but also jump naked into the sea to avoid the smarmy-looking spies who have been hired to rat on their political activities. The youthful vigor, yet sweet innocence, that give life to the sailors' faces in *Battleship Potemkin* (1926) are so determinedly etched into Eisenstein's frame that there is absolutely no question that they would ever be caught dead wearing the cursed pince-nez that belongs to the ship's malevolent doctor.

Beyond the sensualized bodies of the male proletariat, Eisenstein showcases the precision with which he approaches mise-en-scène. The excessive opulence that fills the halls of the Winter Palace in *October: Ten Days That Shook the World* (1928), for instance, forces a counterpoint to the hearty and dusty proletariat. In other words, he trained his camera lens on body *and* place. By doing so, he signaled the interdependence between image and cut. While my friends directed their attention toward Eisenstein's cut to secure a definition for montage, I, instead, zeroed in on his homoerotic and ultra-aestheticized mise-en-scène. Needless to say, one cannot do without the other.

This excess, in fact, is precisely "the area of magic as metaphor for the homosexual situation" that, in 1985, Derek Jarman astutely identified in Eisenstein's filmmaking.[5] Peter Greenaway's latest film, *Eisenstein in Guanajuato: Ten Days That Shook Eisenstein*, takes it upon itself to give cinematic expression to Jarman's phrase insofar as Greenaway's cinema aestheticizes Eisenstein's montage, broadly conceived, by concretizing Eisenstein's "homosexual situation." Folding cuts into mise-en-scène and mise-en-scène into cuts, Greenaway rewrites Eisenstein's "montage of collision" as the "montage of penetration." In short, he homosexualizes Eisensteinian montage.

Between 1930 and 1931, Eisenstein traveled to Mexico, where he, along with the cinematographer Edouard Tisse, shot truly magnificent images of the Mexican people and landscape, footage that would become the unfinished film *¡Que Viva México!* But *Eisenstein in Guanajuato* is not about the making of that film; rather, it concentrates on the ten-day period in Guanajuato when Eisenstein rethought the crucial relationship between cinematic montage and sexual desire. In Guanajuato, Eisenstein (Elmer Bäck) meets and falls in love with his Mexican guide, a comparative religion professor named Palomino Cañedo (Luis Alberti). "On October 25, 1931," Greenaway tells us, "the exact day of the fourteenth anniversary of the Russian Revolution," Eisenstein lost his virginity to Palomino. "And maybe it is no accident," he continues, "that his Guanajuato experiences take place in October, a month that sees the Mexicans celebrate their Day of the Dead and a month that supplies the title of Eisenstein's most expensive film, *October: Ten Days That Shook the World.*" Through the intermingling of events—falling in love, losing his virginity, rethinking the possibilities for cinematic form—the short visit to Guanajuato was nothing less than the "ten days that shook Eisenstein." The implications were tremendous.

If we are to believe Marie Seton, Eisenstein's biographer, the Russian filmmaker grew weary of montage as the be-all and end-all of cinema, especially once he traveled abroad. It seems clear that Eisenstein's travels to Europe, the United States, and Mexico provided him fresh perspectives on art and life.[6] As Greenaway sees it, "I always felt Eisenstein's first three films were very different from the last three—why? I think the answer to that is, when you go abroad, you become a different person."[7] To be sure, as Seton recounts, outside of his professional lectures at venues such as the London Film Society, Eisenstein chatted up friends in pubs and cafés, where it was reported that he "cynically" referred to his theories of montage as those that "he and his Russian colleagues had merely invented . . . to *cover up* the fact that half the time they didn't know what they were doing when they were obliged to work with short ends of film."[8]

If the rigors of montage were a "cover-up" for Eisenstein, were they only prompted by the limitations of film stock? Or, is it possible that montage as a "cover-up" was Eisenstein's "epistemology of the closet"? What masks did Eisenstein feel compelled to wear, as he became the international spokesperson for montage? It is well known, and many commentators have acknowledged as much, that Eisenstein was gay. Life in Paris and other queer European capitals certainly put at odds the masculinist "creative impulse" that drove his Soviet colleagues' theories of montage. Hence, while coming to terms with his sexuality, Eisenstein reworked his theories of montage. The coincidental linkage between montage and homosexuality should not be overlooked. It is critical to how we understand Greenaway's approach to making *Eisenstein in Guanajuato*.

While in London, Eisenstein informed Hans Richter that he had outgrown films, and with sound technology knocking on the historical door, Eisenstein recognized that montage must continually be revised to keep the cinematic experience alive.[9] Montage, in other words, did not exist in a "vacuum." In Europe, at the same time, to disguise his homosexuality from the prying eyes of the press, Eisenstein took refuge in what his Parisian friend, the filmmaker and theorist Jean Mitry, called "make believe." Eisenstein told Mitry, for instance, that he was married and that he was well versed in the social skills of the brothel. His dramatic anecdotes, however warmly received by his French companions, were considered overenthusiastic performances that in turn led his listeners to firmly believe that he "lived like a priest."[10]

Two distinct points are worth noting as we further contextualize and draw together—thanks to Jarman and Greenaway—the connection between Eisensteinian montage and Eisenstein's homosexuality. First, Eisenstein put a stress on "picturization" as a critical component to montage. Throughout his writings, he emphasized the synthesis of/between image and cut. Camera angles, mise-en-scène, actor-"types," the masks worn in Japanese Nō theater, the use of new technology, and other arts are the essential mechanics to Eisensteinian montage. If we are to understand montage comprehensively, it must be grasped as a multidisciplinary and multimediated concept.

Second, by declaring in no uncertain terms that Eisenstein's homosexuality coincides with his theories of montage, Greenaway vitally intervenes in the canon of film studies. By theatricalizing Eisensteinian montage as a cinematic theory that served as a "cover-up" for the filmmaker's homosexuality, Greenaway reveals the Eisensteinian "magical aura" as a concept of montage *in excess* of the cut.

Like Eisenstein, Greenaway sees the cinema as a great experiment. It is a medium through which a multimediated "synthesis" occurs. And the involvement of Greenaway and Jarman, like their cinematic idol, with other arts (painting, opera, installations, theater) makes for a cinema whose very aesthetic complexity challenges critics and audiences. The Eisensteinian triangle—Eisenstein, Greenaway, Jarman—is thus the queer-aesthetic catalyst that impels *Eisenstein in Guanajuato* because Eisenstein's theories of montage cannot be separated from homosexual desire. As Peter Debruge in *Variety* suggestively puts forth in his review of *Eisenstein in Guanajuato*, "It's a lot to take in."[11]

But "take it in" we must. Greenaway's *Eisenstein in Guanajuato* finally and homosexually penetrates the past of an adored, if not sacred, figure as well as the major concept with which he is directly associated. In this way, Greenaway's revision of Eisensteinian montage challenges the homophobia that has for so long circulated around Eisenstein as homosexual in film studies. Greenaway is firm on this point. When *Eisenstein in Guanajuato* was banned in Russia, he called out the homophobia that remains in place in the twenty-first century: "Putin," he unapologetically declared in his interview with Carmen Gray, "has encouraged homophobia." Yet, as he joyfully reminds us, *Potemkin* is a "delight" for queer theorists. And with Greenaway's "typically transgressive irreverence" (to borrow Gray's terms), his hyperaestheticized deflowering of Eisenstein brings home montage precisely as homosexual penetration.[12]

In the press release for *Eisenstein in Guanajuato*, Greenaway insists, "We are not in any way remaking a version of *¡Que Viva México!* but we have been only too aware of the significance of editing." The director, "only too aware of the significance of editing," makes clear that to make a film whose subject is Sergei Eisenstein is to make a film whose subject is montage. But if Greenaway is "only too aware" that a film about Eisenstein is necessarily a film about montage, and if Eisensteinian montage is expansive rather than enclosing, what formal direction does Greenaway take to fold back the "cover-up" that is no less than an open secret? How, in fact, does he homosexualize Eisensteinian montage?

Greenaway is equally aware that Eisensteinian montage cannot be divorced from Eros and Thanatos (a running theme in his own cinema). To rend montage from the clutches of the edit *as such* so as to enlarge the concept—aesthetically, cinematically, *and* homosexually—Greenaway "concentrated," as he notes in the press release, "on making the editing vocabulary noticeable *in the service of everything else the film needs.*" With twenty-first-century technology at hand and "long hours in the cutting room," *Eisenstein in Guanajuato* displays a panoply of neo-Eisensteinian technique: fast cutting sequences "to parallel Eisenstein's sometime manic desire to communicate," slow sequences to match the "languor of emotional pathos," still photographs paired with "very architecturally wide dioramas;" 360-degree pans, creating a "cinemascope triptych" to provide generous screen space for side-by-side images, and "a great deal of both 'visible' and 'invisible' green screening" in unexpected places, while, at the same time, "complying with Eisenstein's demand for under-lighting and back-lighting with use of grids and perforated shadows and deliberated 'moving-paintings.'" Indeed, it's a lot to take in. But there is more.

The cinematography and the editing are, it is important to recall, "in the service of everything else the film needs." Greenaway is clear that the terms in this film for Eros and Thanatos are directly linked to "Fucking and Death." They are "the two nonnegotiables," Eisenstein asserts in *Eisenstein in Guanajuato*. And if this nonnegotiable pairing holds true, Eisenstein's awakening to the nonnegotiability of "Fucking and Death" occurs precisely because Palomino homosexually fucks him in Mexico—the land that lovers embrace as the place of the living dead. In Mexico, Eisenstein learns, at the behest of Palomino, to "follow his cock" while on his death drive through Mexico, realizing both the making of a film and his sexual desire. (It is worth noting the unmistakable metaphor for this drive that opens and closes the film: Eisenstein enters and departs Guanajuato in a car.)

The scene in which Palomino penetrates Eisenstein is placed squarely midpoint in the film. Although filmed in a mix of shots, the sequence is predominantly shown in long take and in long shot. In avoiding a clichéd rapid montage that would pay awkward homage to the filmmaker, the long shot fully "picturizes" the bed on which Eisenstein fully and finally encounters fucking and death. The handful of close-ups that Greenaway inserts include those such as the "pure virgin olive oil" that Palomino pilfers from the restaurant where he and Eisenstein just dined. Once in the ultra-aestheticized bedroom, Palomino slowly and deliberately pours the elegantly lit oil down the director's back so that it gently pours through the crevice that divides Eisenstein's ass. Then, purposefully, Eisenstein's "guide" penetrates his lover. While doing so, Palomino discourses on the history of the "New" and "Old" Worlds. He regales Eisenstein with details about the impact of global migration and the origins of syphilis. He reminds his lover that like the Russian he now homosexually penetrates, Russia itself had lost its virginity through a bloody revolution in overly decadent surroundings. Here, in Mexico, and in luxurious long take, Palomino's cock provides the most significant cut for Eisenstein. Eisenstein bleeds. And as Palomino penetrates his lover, he remarks that, yes, of course, his cock severs the "capillaries in the sensitive anal interior sphincter." The cut, demonstrated in long take, reveals *"what matters,"* to recall a phrase from Mitry: What matters *"is the actual association, not the method by which that association is achieved."*[13] Eisensteinian montage and homosexual desire are folded into each other.

At this vital moment in film history, the emphasis on the Eisensteinian cut is now enveloped into Greenaway's deliberate long take. At age thirty-three—the age when Christ and Alexander the Great died—Eisenstein is cut at a critical moment in his life, cut on his body, and cut from the strictures of montage that have forbidden homosexual desire. The penetrative long take illuminates "the two nonnegotiables." Life, body, and cinema in the land of aestheticized Eros and Thanatos are now broadened and commingled in their conceptual possibilities.

In the final sequences of *Eisenstein in Guanajuato*, in the moments when Eisenstein is forced to depart those he has come to love (Palomino and Mexico itself), a parade of death masks takes place. Palomino and his family (he is married with two children) prepare for Eisenstein's exit. The singing children who walk alongside figures dressed in skeleton costumes bid farewell to Eisenstein. In reckoning with *the death drive*, with tears in his eyes, he tells his driver, "Drive away. This is the Day of the Dead. I'm a dead man. Drive slowly to the edge of town. This is a funeral cortège. And when you reach the edge of town, drive like the devil. I need to leave heaven in a hurry." Anticipating his slow yet ultimate rush toward death, Eisenstein places a death mask over his face, and the car pulls away from the pleasures heaven has given him.

In uncovering montage as something more than the cut, Greenaway transforms a crucial aspect of film theory. Eros and Thanatos—Homosexual Fucking and Death—release Eisenstein, if only for a short time, from the great montage "cover-up." But as things happen, one cover-up leads to another. Eisenstein invariably puts on a new mask. Nonetheless, it will be difficult to return to theories of montage as nothing more than the straight cut. With Greenaway's *Eisenstein in Guanajuato*, Eisensteinian montage is made to bleed.

Notes

1   Moussinac, *Sergei Eisenstein*, 43, 46.

2   Wollen, "Last New Wave," 49.

3   Wollen, 45.

4   Wollen, 47.

5   Ellis, *Derek Jarman's Angelic Conversations*, 65.

6   Seton, *Sergei Eisenstein*.

7   Gray, "Greenaway Offends Russia."

8   Seton, *Sergei Eisenstein*, 142.

9   Seton, 147.

10 Seton, 139.

11 Debruge, "Berlin Film Review."

12 Gray, "Greenaway Offends Russia."

13 Mitry, *Aesthetics and Psychology of the Cinema*, 176–77.

118 - Queer Imaginings

QUEER MODERNISM

The Cinematic Aesthetic of Vincente Minnelli

This essay follows through on James Naremore's important work on Vincente Minnelli and his study of the aesthetic and cultural movements in which Minnelli participated, especially in New York in the 1930s.[1] What I add here, however, is the queer inflection associated with these aesthetics that Minnelli imbibed and then carried to Hollywood. Although Minnelli married four times, had two children, and did not publicly identify himself as "gay," he certainly partook of a cultural milieu that was made up of a significant coterie of artists and critics whose aesthetic interests came to be marked as queer.

When Arthur Freed brought Minnelli to Hollywood in 1940, Minnelli's name didn't ring any bells at MGM, even though Minnelli brought with him an illustrious career as a theatrical director and costume and set designer from New York. In a memo to the studio executive Eddie Mannix, Cedric Gibbons, supervisory art director at MGM, expressed his concerns over Minnelli's hiring. The letter is worth quoting in full as it sets the stage for the creative tensions that Minnelli consistently encountered with Gibbons. It frames, at the outset of Minnelli's arrival at the studio, an anxiety that cuts across not merely an individual's position in relation to the Hollywood studio but also an anxiety as it intersects with contemporaneous notions of creativity and, as we shall see, with industrial modernity within the studio system. On April 2, 1940, Gibbons writes,

> For your information we have signed Vincent Manelli [sic], a New York stage designer. This was done through Arthur Freed. In speaking to Arthur on Saturday he told me about this man and said he was engaged as a dance director. I said, "Nothing Else?" And he said, "for ideas on dance numbers and

Revised and reprinted from "Queer Modernism: The Cinematic Aesthetic of Vincente Minnelli" in *Vincente Minnelli: The Art of Entertainment*, edited by Joe McElhaney. Detroit: Wayne State University Press, Copyright © 2009, 252–74.

musical settings, etc." I am afraid Eddie, that this will probably be another Harkrider-Hobe-Irwin-Oliver-Messel [sic][2] situation and if you remember you and I chatted at great length about this type of thing sometime ago—and I want to reiterate that I absolutely refuse to work under any conditions with any man designing settings unless he is brought through to me as a member of my department. The man may be the world's greatest genius. If he is, by all means give him my job. I find it tough enough as it is to work with the most sympathetic assistants I can secure. I do not feel that any of my men should take orders from anyone other than myself in the matter of set design, whether it be for musical numbers or the interiors of submarines. Do you think we need further experience in these expensive experiments? Not just the man's salary, but what he actually costs us. I, for one, had thought we had learned our lesson. Gibby[3]

Gibbons's sentiment toward Minnelli's arrival played itself out in a tension that underscored the relationship between Minnelli and the MGM Art Department for the next twenty years. At stake here was the way in which two men of modernist sensibilities struggled over the visual rendering of the burgeoning twentieth century. Minnelli's vision of modernity often worked at odds with that of Gibbons. In fact, Minnelli has called the MGM Art Department "a medieval fiefdom, its overlord accustomed to doing things in a certain way . . . his own."[4]

Both Minnelli and Gibbons were strongly influenced by currents of the international modernist movement, and both were decidedly set in their creative ways: Minnelli was a modernist within a genealogy of Whistler, Diaghilev, and Poiret, while Gibbons was a modernist in the efficient mode of Le Corbusier, Sullivan, and Gropius. Minnelli looked to the paintings of Van Gogh, the Impressionists, and the Postimpressionists, as well as the aesthetic/surrealist writings of Ronald Firbank and the fin de siècle sketches of Aubrey Beardsley.[5] He was an impeccable dandy/aesthete. He dressed, most often, in his favorite daffodil-yellow blazer and black turtleneck. His home in Beverly Hills was filled with art books, novels, paintings, and sketches (his earlier New York apartment interiors were also notably absent of any "streamlined" design).[6] His bookshelves were lined with the art books of Duchamp, Dufy, Renoir, Dalí, Matisse, and the not so modern Caravaggio, along with the writings of Flaubert, Baldwin, Bazin, and Freud. His bedroom walls, carpet, and bedding were saturated in deep-velvet reds.[7] The painting easel in his studio (overlooking his garden) always had a current work in process, just as his office desk always had the clutter of the research for his latest film project.

Gibbons's home, in contrast, sat at the edge of the California Pacific Rim in Santa Monica. Designed by Gibbons himself (with the MGM architect Douglas Honnold), it was considered the "ultimate Hollywood residence of the 1930s."[8] It embodied the cinematic in terms of the latest technology: "water sprinklers on the copper roof above . . . create the sound of rain, and a recessed light projector . . . [casts] the illusion of moonlight on a wall."[9] It was streamlined, white, and above all, "efficient." It is essential, writes Gibbons, that "the living room is as efficient as the kitchen and bathroom."[10]

Although this account of modernist creativity is simplified, it illustrates the palpable aesthetic tension Minnelli encountered upon his arrival. Gibbons's stress on the functional and efficient is clearly reinforced in his letter to Mannix. His concern with MGM's "expensive experiments" in his tightly run ship can only serve to disrupt the contained precision and functioning of his obliging (and obedient) department. His sense of ordered design and insistence on efficiency in business and creative design are hallmarks of a modernism flanked by the notion of utility and function. This efficiency shares an interesting relationship to the production and, if you will, the architecture of American masculinity in the twentieth century.[11] In effect, Minnelli's confrontation with Gibbons brought to bear the question of modernity's (not to mention Hollywood's) relationship to creativity and masculinity.

If the "efficient" architecture of the Bauhaus, Mies van der Rohe, and Le Corbusier was intended to unload the "effeminate" obstacles or "excess" that prohibited productive living, it was clearly in the service of allowing for a clean (and in keeping with the new era), functional, and machine-like space, something to which Gibbons aspired. To dehistoricize, for this modernist, meant to look forward because the historical carried the weight of a dead past that was found in such traditional media as architecture, furniture design, and the "realism" of Hollywood cinema.[12]

In fact, Gibbons, on the one hand, looked toward the day when "realism" could be abandoned from cinema so that "we may look for a setting which in itself will be as completely modern as is modern painting or sculpture."[13] As Peter Wollen remarks, "Modernism saw a teleology in the convergence of cubism with industrial techniques and materials and its development toward abstract art."[14] It is precisely the efficient modernist's aim to utilize the twentieth century's new technologies and machinations to rid the excess of everyday life so that "utility will supplant ornament."[15] Because ornament was viewed as effeminate, eliminating a decorative aesthetic reinforced a masculine, heterosexual art establishment. The virility of American creativity served to defend (male) artists from the charge of homosexuality. This rugged American cultural milieu found its apotheosis with the emergence of the American abstract artists after World War II, until Andy Warhol ("the swish") challenged it in the 1960s.

Minnelli, on the other hand, arrived at MGM armed with an extravagant and flamboyant eye for excessive detail. The set designs for his films became as bright and colorful as his window displays in Chicago and his stage designs in New York.[16] While Minnelli often found himself at odds with Gibbons's Art Department, Minnelli emerged victorious from these creative conflicts. Living in New York for nearly ten years before coming to Hollywood provided Minnelli with the opportunity to participate within a coterie whose urbane and often chaotic demeanor was shaped in a landscape far removed from the nascent spaces of Los Angeles. Unlike Los Angeles's sprawling terrain, New York's frenetic energies, fomented in contained spaces, yielded a very different aesthetic expression. It is precisely Minnelli's immersion within the excessive place of New York that inundated and informed his later work in Hollywood cinema.

New York was also a pivotal site for the exploration of the terms for American masculinity. As many scholars have shown, men in New York during the 1920s and 1930s were confronted with complex social intersections where masculinity, "effeminacy," creativity, and homosexuality found peculiar and exciting possibilities in their cultural entanglements.[17] It is the brilliance (and tension) of this social and creative excess that Minnelli saw and experienced that informed the visual extravagance he brought to the stage and screen. This extravagance—this campy rendering of the historical world onstage and in film—might be said to be Minnelli's aestheticized laugh at efficient masculinist modernity.

Minnelli's Masculinity and the Arts

It is a known fact that you are not a success on Broadway until legends spring up about you. Sometimes libelous, always exaggerated, these fantastic offsprings of envy and admiration are a mirror which reflects success. The Minnelli legends are legion.

—Shubert press release, ca. 1936

Indeed, Minnelli's creative atmosphere in New York was pressured within the conflicting historical discourses of American masculinity. It was a conflict that was long-standing and prescient for Minnelli. As Minnelli's fourth wife, Lee Minnelli, has pointed out, Vincente disliked the tough, jock sports "guy" and considered himself the Noël Coward type.[18] Minnelli's conflicted and sometimes peculiar concept of and relationship to masculinity established his ongoing creative reassessment of the contemporary scene of American gender and creativity.

Born in Chicago in 1903 but raised in the small Midwest town of Delaware, Ohio, Minnelli grew up in a Catholic French-Italian traveling theatrical family. At a young age, Chicago represented the bastion of nonprovinciality, and he soon set his sights on the urban promise of that city. While there, Minnelli worked as a window-display designer at Marshall Field's department store. Known for ornate and colorful window displays, Marshall Field's was a place where Minnelli encountered the new modernist art scene. His displays were usually of furniture, decorative accessories, and antiques. He considered his short stint as a photographer of stage celebrities dull and thought it not the medium in which he preferred to work. He attempted a brief (and failed) acting career, but most importantly, he continued to sketch, draw, and paint—he would always claim painting as his first love. As his collection of work grew, he gained an entrepreneurial sense for himself and subsequently landed a job with Balaban and Katz designing costumes for its stage shows.

Minnelli first became aware of, and took great interest in, the Fauves, the Impressionists, and the Surrealists (a movement that would have great import for his early work in Hollywood) through the Art Institute of Chicago. The works of Matisse, Duchamp, Ernst, and Dalí acted as early catalysts for Minnelli's visual imagination. Aubrey Beardsley's drawings so strongly impacted him that they resurfaced in Minnelli's own drawings (practically in a plagiarized form) for *Casanova's Memoirs*, which he illustrated when he first arrived in New York. Minnelli's absorption of the contemporary avant-garde scene was substantial; it served as an important element for his young, avid mind. For Minnelli, his admiration of Cézanne, Van Gogh, Renoir, and Dufy worked concomitantly with divergent forms of painting such as Cubism, Surrealism, and Impressionism. His intermingled aesthetics along with his childhood visions of Midwest Americana in such later works as *Meet Me in St. Louis* (1944) and *Some Came Running* (1958) reveal the diverse palette from which he worked. Inevitably, Minnelli became noted for his ability to fuse multiple genres that became the hallmark of his popular stage and film designs (see figs. 3 and 4).

Minnelli also began to read voraciously in Chicago. He discovered Joseph and Elizabeth Pennell's biography of James McNeill Whistler, which influenced his aesthetic understanding of form, composition, and color for the remainder of his career. It is instructive to consider Minnelli's relationship to his early readings of Whistler, as the artist not only embodied certain painterly principles (especially in terms of color) but was also identified as a "dandy" and "gentleman."[19] If the dandy was an enticing figure for Minnelli for its urbane and elegant ennui, Whistler would be the dandy extraordinaire because he was the dandy who, unlike the earlier dandies Byron and Baudelaire, created visually (and importantly in the medium Minnelli loved most). "I envied his childhood in the Russian court, his youth as a West Point cadet and starving artist in a Paris garret, his devotion to his distinguished wife."[20] The suffering-artist

Figures 3 and 4. Vincente Minnelli's decadent impulses revealed in the 1944 publication of *Casanova's Memoirs*, edited by Joseph Monét and drawings by Vincente Minnelli (New York: Willey Book Company, 1944). (Copyright © 1930 by Exotica Club, Inc.)

routine, however, was reaffirming imagery for the youthful (and not so wealthy at the time) Minnelli. Whistler's later remarks on poverty may have assuaged any feelings of remorse that he may have had during his brief lapses of financial insecurity: "it is better to live on bread and cheese and paint beautiful things, than to live like Dives and paint pot boilers."[21] And in this version of the gentlemanly and dandified aesthetic, where decorum was highly relished, both Minnelli and Whistler saw football as the demise of an elegant tradition. For Whistler, as the young cadet at West Point, he "resented each and every innovation [at this ceremonious institution], above all football."[22]

Hence, Minnelli discovered through the Pennells' book that to lack the popular American qualities of virile manhood was not necessarily a stroke of ill fate. Whistler's corporeality is described by a fellow draftsman: "I thought him about the handsomest fellow I ever met; but for some reason I did not consider him a perfect model of manly beauty—his mouth betokened more ease than firmness, his brow more reserve than acute mental activity, and his eyes more depth than penetration. Sensitiveness and animation appeared to be his predominating traits."[23] If Minnelli did not see himself measuring up to the dictates of American masculinity, he certainly was able to relate to the poetic American artist abroad whose temperament eschewed those manly characteristics in order to exercise a "sensitiveness" associated with creativity. Whistler's languorous ridings in hansoms, his "cool suit of linen, . . . his jaunty straw hat" worn in his youth, his one white lock in his curly black hair, and his "series of collars [that] sprang from the neck of the long overcoat . . . [and] extraordinary long cane" struck not only a sartorial performative image of the dandy but also a performative image of masculinity that appealed to Minnelli's concepts of creativity and gender.[24]

In this way, Minnelli embodied the historical discourse of the dandy-flaneur (e.g., George Brummel, Charles Baudelaire, Oscar Wilde, and, of course, Whistler). It is worth noting that Minnelli's alignment with Whistler over Wilde bespeaks a curious distancing from the dandy-aesthete who would come to be associated with the homosexual. The figure of Wilde, as Alan Sinfield has shown, linked the dandy-aesthete with homosexuality.[25] Minnelli may have dismissed Wilde over his favored Whistler (this, according to Minnelli, was because he took Whistler's side in the famous Whistler/Wilde debate of the nineteenth century).[26] But in the early part of the twentieth century, the visual weight of the Wilde trial was far from lifted. The embodiment of "sexual offender" in those who were seen as "creative," "artistic," or (to this day) "effeminate" allowed the middle class the opportunity to identify a physical scapegoat who would stand in for what one ought not be. It is not surprising, then, that Minnelli defended Whistler over Wilde in his memoirs. Like Wilde's "creative" contemporaries who tried to disassociate their dandified and aestheticized physical attributes from their "behavior," Minnelli (*only twenty-five years after Wilde's death*) was in the position to account for his "feminine traits" (and thereby adhere to standardized male/female, heterosexual binaries). This is not to defend Minnelli's fear of being identified with the charge of homosexuality but rather to provide a framework for the ideological underpinnings of the culture in which Minnelli functioned and negotiated as an American twentieth-century dandy-aesthete. Nevertheless, to be a dandy, to be a man performing within a creative cultural milieu, served to identify—and thereby warn—those guardians of manly middle-class norms of the presence of an "Oscar Wilde."

But Minnelli did not reject the Wildean aesthetic that ushered in camp. In fact, Minnelli embraced a camp aesthetic, historically following Wilde's aesthetic import—acknowledged or not. Minnelli is somewhat ironic when he states, "Waste was the cardinal sin. I had learned to recycle my experience in real life and applying them to my creative endeavors. I do it to this day."[27] The process of "recycling" is, of course, the reuse of disposed waste. There is, as well, a foretelling of decadence in this notion of "waste as the cardinal sin," in that it recalls the moral lasciviousness of Catholic ritual and cardinals so adored by Winckelmann and Wilde. The twentieth-century dandy, as Susan Sontag suggests, "has given rise to a certain kind of witty appreciation of the derelict, inane, *démodé* objects of modern civilization—the taste for a certain kind of passionate non-art that is known as 'camp.'"[28] This "appreciation of the derelict" is, then, an appreciation of historical debris that Minnelli highlighted in both his films and his lived world. More importantly, Minnelli's eclectic turn to queer-modernist aesthetics challenged the masculinist logic of modern art that, as we saw with Cedric Gibbons, insisted on a clean, functional line.

Lela Simone, music coordinator for the Freed unit at MGM, stated in an Academy of Motion Picture Arts and Sciences (AMPAS) interview, "Vincente [Minnelli] was not a man who was a dictator. He tried to do it in a soft and nice way. He worked in let's say . . . I don't know whether you will understand what I say . . . he worked liked a homosexual. I don't mean that nastily. I have nothing against homosexuals."[29] Citing this interview, Matthew Tinkcom has argued that Simone's view of "working like a homosexual" reveals that "labors performed by particular subjects, and not identities, can in some cases display the mark of the subject upon the product."[30] But what Tinkcom does not quote is instructive in that both the interviewer and Simone are confounded by her remarks. The interviewer clarifies Simone's response by asking her if she meant "his manner":

> SIMONE: It was soft.
> INTERVIEWER: Yes.
> SIMONE: You see?
> INTERVIEWER: And yet he was not?
> SIMONE: Ja.[31]

I would add that that "mark" to which Tinkcom refers, rather than displaying an inherent (repressed?) "homosexual" set of subject knowledges that surface "upon the product," actually articulates cultural anxieties ("And yet he was not?") associated with masculine creativity (i.e., "effeminacy" ["soft and nice way"] and homosexuality). As this (American) middle-class masculine anxiety persisted, Minnelli as the neo-dandy sought refuge from the vulgarities of this hypermasculine world by using his affinity for art in order to ironize, to situate within and against, and to bewilder (once again) this masculine anxiety. If he was to be constantly suspect, he would seek out the conditions in which he would feel comfortable exercising his creative talents. Declared or not, Minnelli participated in and visibly presented a homosexual aesthetic.

Small-Town Boys and Dandified "Hysteria" in Twentieth-Century New York

Aside from Minnelli's painterly interests in the Impressionists and Fauves, his fascination with Surrealism in Chicago prompted his readings, according to Minnelli, of Freud and Ronald Firbank. A subscription to the *New York World* introduced him to the city's sophisticated nightclub and party scene during the late 1920s, while *Vanity Fair* kept Minnelli current with New York's fashionable trends in literature, theater, and cinema. The *World's* heavily produced Sunday paper offered pages of photographs and editorials giving him a peek into New York's haut-couture society of stage, screen, and literature. *Vanity Fair* provided Minnelli with the forum for such eclectic figures as Carl Van Vechten, Gilbert Seldes, Colette, Vivian Shaw, Alexander Woollcott, Heywood Broun, and Cecil Beaton (who later worked with Minnelli on *Gigi* and *On a Clear Day You Can See Forever*). New York's reputation as being truly modernist spoke to Minnelli with great verve since it was a modernism that fit snugly with his aesthetic sensibility. Not only did the city offer a creative edge, but it was also (and it was well known) a culturally diverse city.

While Chicago presented Minnelli with a powerful introduction to the arts and urban living, it had, for Minnelli, "an impudent style with little class." Its lack of an urbane sensibility smacked of a certain manliness that suggested a "sleeves rolled up" mentality.[32] This observation of a rough and tough, socially rigid Chicago was bolstered by his subscriptions to the *New York World* and *Vanity Fair*. In these pages, New York was the "swellegant" counterpoint to Chicago's version of modernist urban culture. Minnelli's brief trips to New York for Balaban and Katz productions fueled his already charged desire to move. The recent Paramount Publix merger with Balaban and Katz made his move to New York possible. Paramount Publix's New York theaters would now stage grand vaudevillian-style shows in the tradition of the Balaban and Katz Picture Palaces in Chicago. Minnelli wanted in on the venture and soon found himself with a one-way ticket to New York.

For Minnelli, New York sophistication proffered a cultural milieu immersed in Noël Coward banter and elegant decadence. Now in New York, Minnelli was brought into the effluence of the city's unswerving energy. The roman à clef novels and essays sketched by Carl Van Vechten now came to life with an intensity that would indelibly mark Minnelli's work. Although Minnelli and Van Vechten do not, in their writings, ever mention if they directly encountered each other, their milieus overlapped, as did their interests in things culturally queer.

Van Vechten (b. 1880), another dandy-aesthete from the Midwest (Cedar Rapids, Iowa) who first moved to Chicago and found it dull, was the cornerstone of the New York social world in the 1920s. For Van Vechten, there were three "essentials" to art: "vitality, glamour, and imagination."[33] He was a photographer (with quite an impressive array of portraits), journalist, novelist, "manager" for budding talent, and gossip queen.[34] As Bruce Kellner suggests, "he was [New York's] leading dilettante."[35] Van Vechten invariably knew everyone who was anyone. His novels bespoke the campy decadence of sophistication that supported the glamorous world of New York's high society. Van Vechten's decadence was the blueprint (and imprint) of an American aestheticism that did not sit comfortably in the virile tradition of American art.

The composite of Van Vechten's transcontinental social arena included Gertrude Stein, Virgil Thomson, Parker Tyler, Pavel Tchelitchev, Alfred Stieglitz, Georgia O'Keeffe, George Gershwin, and Ethel Waters. Many of these figures were key in 1920s and 1930s New York social activity—and several of them, especially Gershwin and Waters, would later intimately overlap with Minnelli's world. Interestingly, Van Vechten's friendship with Waters and Gershwin was well established during the 1920s. Van Vechten would religiously attend their concerts as well as every social gathering in New York with them. Since it would be doubtful that he would miss any of Waters's theatrical performances (it's hard to imagine Van Vechten missing *any* performance in New York), he was most likely present at Minnelli's production of *At Home Abroad* in 1935 that starred Waters and Beatrice Lillie. When, shortly thereafter in early 1936, Van Vechten photographed Waters for his own personal portfolio, one can rightly imagine that the show (considering the calamitous offstage relationship that Lillie and Waters shared) was a topic of vibrant gossip between himself and Waters.

But Van Vechten's importance was not limited to his glowing coterie and extravagant personality. His writings on opera, dance, literature, cinema, and music generated an enormous current of aesthetic energy well into the 1930s. His attendance and ongoing critical support of Diaghilev's Ballets Russes in Paris paved the way for the dynamic dispersion of creative thought in New York. Van Vechten's commingling with the dandified audience of the Ballets Russes undoubtedly resonated with his personal design of the American twentieth-century dandy.[36] Later, Minnelli's design for the sets and costumes of *Scheherazade* at Radio City received successful critical review, as he utilized the "exotic" colors of Léon Bakst as they were, in one way or another, directly or indirectly interpreted and articulated by Van Vechten.[37]

Often unacknowledged or underestimated, Van Vechten's peripatetic wit and grace were in great part responsible for the impetus behind the Harlem Renaissance. His high-pitched charisma and dedication to many a budding career (especially, but not exclusively, to Langston Hughes and Countee Cullen) sparked white upper-middle-class interest in (and exoticizing of) Harlem artists and entertainment. Later, Minnelli attended the Harlem jazz clubs that were made popular by Van Vechten's prolific exposés of Harlem nightlife. Minnelli's friendships and experiences in Harlem were later brought to Hollywood when he made his first film, *Cabin in the Sky* (1943).[38]

Previously, in 1922, Van Vechten helped to launch Firbank's literary career into American notoriety. His fantastical/Surrealist fairy tales evoked the Aestheticism of Wilde and Proust, while, at the same time, Firbank liquefied his fairy-tale worlds into proto-Surrealist imagery. Firbank's literary style deconstructed the already contemporary notion of camp by further heightening the excess of camp's own strategy. At MGM, Minnelli's *Yolanda and the Thief* (1946) and *The Pirate* (1948) would unabashedly resonate with the excess of Firbank's fantastical aestheticism.

Central to Van Vechten's social and personal world was the painter Florine Stettheimer. As Van Vechten's close friend and social contemporary, Stettheimer had the financial wherewithal to disseminate the European art scene to Van Vechten and his New York compatriots as well as to personally introduce Van Vechten to such artists as Marcel Duchamp. Barbara Bloemink notes that as Stettheimer was "one of the few American artists privileged to have actively participated in pre–World War I European culture, she was an important carrier of that culture to a new location."[39] Like Van Vechten, one of her most important cultural deliveries was the ideas and imagery she discovered after her attendance of the Ballets Russes. She was in complete admiration of Bakst's colorful costume design.[40] This impression of the colorful, the ornate, and the decorative would spill over into her paintings, albeit in a finer line. Both Stettheimer's and Minnelli's paintings and sketches share an important contemporaneous aspect in that they both represent the body as influenced by the fashionable drawings of Ralph Barton.[41] I would add to Barton's offerings Edouard Garcia Benito's work in *Vanity Fair*. This modernist rendering of the body à la Benito speaks to a modernist androgyny that begins to articulate the dynamic dimension of American gender relations of the early twentieth century.

Although Stettheimer was championed by Van Vechten, Stieglitz, and her close friend Duchamp, her paintings never achieved critical or popular recognition during her lifetime. Although already a window-display predecessor to Minnelli at Marshall Field's (Stettheimer had designed windows at Wanamaker's in New York *and* Marshall Field's in Chicago), her set and costume designs clearly informed Minnelli's sense of design. In 1934 (at the age of sixty-three), however, Stettheimer's creative path took a monumental shift and "indirectly" crossed Minnelli's path with the opening of the opera *Four Saints in Three Acts*, with a libretto by Gertrude Stein and music by Virgil

Thomson and performed by an all-Black cast. *Four Saints* was to become a major avant-garde work of the period. As in her paintings, Stettheimer's set and costume designs for *Four Saints* were delicately ornate.

Minnelli remarks on this production in his memoirs, calling attention to the efforts of Stein and Thomson but not of Stettheimer. While it is not clear if Minnelli actually did see the premiere of *Four Saints* in Hartford, Connecticut (February 7, 1934) or its New York opening (March 1), he most certainly had read about it in the New York press, where not only was Stettheimer praised for her design work but also photographs of her sets and costumes were reproduced. Minnelli indeed referred to *Four Saints* as a "riveting surrealistic opera."[42] Its success (along with that of Harold Rome's revue *Pins and Needles*) would later convince Minnelli that "a surrealist revue would be viable."[43] In fact, to see the sets of his *Cabin in the Sky* is to see the echo of Stettheimer's designs for *Four Saints*. This is especially true in his use of white light placed against the white sets and costumes as worn by the all-Black cast.[44]

For Van Vechten, Stettheimer, and Minnelli, the cinema was the pivotal art of the twentieth century. All three were fascinated with the technical possibilities of movement with the new art. While Stettheimer leaned toward the European avant-garde movement in cinema, Van Vechten and Minnelli were unabashedly appreciative of Hollywood and the major European studio productions. For Van Vechten, his admiration of Clara Bow and Elinor Glyn pointed to his dandified embrace not only of a film such as *It* (1927) but also of his social position of having, and decadently enjoying, "it." In Minnelli's case, Jacques Feyder's *Carnival in Flanders* (1935) "embodied [his] fascination in art . . . with the artful detail and luminosity of the Flemish masters."[45] While this film clearly echoes the "Flemish masters," it is also laced with a bawdy irony that tickled Minnelli's taste for the debauch. Minnelli's unending accumulation of aesthetic possibilities from multiple media provided him with a vast set of knowledges that, as critics and reviewers often note, allowed him to bring together the traditional distinctions between "high" and "low" art.

Van Vechten's and Stettheimer's energetic support of *both* European and American artists sat in opposition to America's post-Armory-show sense of modernism, which looked to define a new and "pure" American art form devoid of European influence. Van Vechten's and Stettheimer's import of European art set the stage for a "queer modernism" that shared an international renown for its unsettling creative and moral decadence. These creative coteries, criticized for their association with eroticism, effeminacy, decadence, and primitivism, harbored a wellspring of artists whose sense of modernism did not look toward a pure "American" art form but rather toward a hyperaestheticized representation, a theatricalization, of the "functional" twentieth century. Like Van Vechten, Minnelli's identification as the "queer" dandy-aesthete provided him the opportunity to "camp" and, thereby, disorient standard social registers of cultural meaning.

Urban Sophistication

Van Vechten's and Stettheimer's (baroque) framing of New York's cultural and aesthetic milieu of the 1920s cannot be underestimated for Minnelli, in spite of Minnelli's apparent lack of direct personal and professional contact with them. The intellectual and creative groundwork laid during this period would ultimately stimulate the young Minnelli as he immersed himself in New York's high-paced dynamics. Van Vechten's and Stettheimer's ardent support of trans-Atlantic "Orientalist" visions of aesthetic pleasure registered with Minnelli as a way to transgress the social demands of virile and mechanical masculinity.[46] The excess of visual aesthetic pleasure was (is) that jouissance that the functionalist modernists had lost in their rigor toward efficiency. Van Vechten and Stettheimer would leave their marks on, and yield to, Minnelli's cultural arena of the 1930s. Minnelli's leap into New York's cultural scene provided him with, at once (and these are linked), the pleasure of visual excess and the opportunity to test and challenge the multiple questions of sexual and gender identity that any "queer" midwestern boy brings with him to the big city.

The contingent and discontinuous parameters of masculinity were nowhere more apparent than in New York. During the 1920s, the city was rapidly gaining a reputation (not necessarily a bad one) for its "pansy" population, drag balls in Harlem, bohemians of Greenwich Village, and supposed tolerance of decadent behavior in both the public and private spheres that many middle-class New Yorkers and non–New Yorkers endlessly enjoyed. New York, of course, also cradled an affluent (both creatively and financially) artist population. When Minnelli was finally brought to New York in 1931, he moved immediately into the Village, where the promise of creative and personal tolerance could be sought. Minnelli (bedecked as a composite of Whistler and Beardsley), according to *Esquire*, was "the incarnation of our preconceived notion of a 'Village type': flat black hat with a wide brim, loose collar and looser tie around his thin neck, a big portfolio of drawings under one arm and the cut of his long coat a triumphant marriage of Harlem and the Left Bank."[47] Minnelli certainly dressed the part, but he may very well have been somewhat disappointed with what was no longer the liberatory and bohemian Village he had once read about.

Minnelli would look back at this move in his memoirs as his step to "greener pastures."[48] But in the 1930s, New York was experiencing its own changes in its sociopolitical environment. While Repeal was inaugurated (December 1933), the Depression was sinking deeply into the New York economy. Jimmy Walker's graft-ridden city hall was out, while La Guardia's upright moralism was in, and the tolerance that queers had once enjoyed during the 1920s was seriously on the wane. In fact, as George Chauncey argues, Repeal actually reinforced the regulation of social conditions and social order. The introduction of a diligent law to New York's cultural milieu served to oppress those who were already socially marginalized. It is instructive to consider Chauncey's historical analysis of New York during the period of Minnelli's arrival, because it clearly puts into perspective the New York cultural conditions of creativity, masculinity, and homosexuality in which Minnelli lived. Chauncey argues that the 1930s ushered in New York's attempt to morally recuperate itself by eliminating the socially unwanted—especially "sexual perverts" and "social degenerates." With Repeal, the New York State Liquor Authority (SLA) was instituted to regulate places of ill repute. Sweeping raids took place at bars and restaurants, especially where homosexuals were "known" to congregate. What is interesting about these raids is the way in which the SLA identified homosexuals. The SLA undercover agents searched for "their campy behavior (or, as the agents called it, their 'effeminacy'), their use of rouge or lipstick, their practice of calling each other by camp or women's names, the way they talked or the fact that they talked about the opera or other suspect topics, or other aspects of their dress or carriage."[49] The "effeminate" creatures who were busted at these "known homosexual" bars were usually part of a lower- or working-class background. The middle class, under this state reign of terror, not only were able to avoid being arrested but also were the ones who were able to wear makeup, talk about opera, and "camp it up" across town at private and select cocktail parties. The satin-padded boundaries north of the Village and Times Square were filled with financially successful artists and theater folk who could afford to be "queer" within their protective and insular neighborhood.

This uptown milieu quickly became Minnelli's new coterie. His sudden dismissal in 1933 from Paramount Publix found him momentarily penniless and with rent due on his Village studio. In what Minnelli recalls as a "deus ex machina," he was hired by Radio City Music Hall, which provided him with a move uptown from "lower-class" lower Manhattan to the swank uptown location on East Fifty-Second Street where he would work and live for the next seven years. Hence, his move couldn't have been more socially apposite, as just west of Minnelli, Van Vechten resided at 150 West Fifty-Fifth Street, while Stettheimer dwelled at 182 West Fifty-Eighth Street. According to Chauncey, the streets of the East and West Fifties, "once given over to the homes of New York's wealthiest families," one observer noted in 1932, were "now filled with smart little shops, bachelor apartments, residential studios and fashionable speakeasies."[50]

This neighborhood in the early 1930s became the site for many successful writers and artists who "fled Greenwich Village" during its "decline." Max Eastman spoke of this new chic location as the home of "the *Smart Set* and *Vanity Fair* people."[51] While the "pansies" and "fairies" caroused just south of the neighborhood in Times Square, the middle-class "invert" spent time ("covertly") in the "elegant nightclubs" such as the Rainbow Room, which sat high above in the Radio City Music Hall/ Rockefeller Center complex (convenient for Minnelli's cocktail after one of those arduous and chaotic days at the Music Hall). Minnelli's social position (i.e., middle-class stage and costume designer during the Depression) allowed him to participate in the haute-couture society and, in effect, exercise his "feminine traits" in otherwise-hostile conditions for men who did not act masculine.

Once Minnelli began his work at Radio City, his New York career was quickly set in motion. The year 1933 marked the moment that Minnelli became a public persona. By 1935, Minnelli's social circles were swirling with the glamour of such figures as George Balanchine, George and Ira Gershwin, Pavel Tchelitchev, Dorothy Parker, Edouard Steichen, Paul Bowles, George Platt Lynes, and Kay Swift (who, according to Minnelli, named his salon on East Fifty-Third Street "The Minnellium"). In 1936, the Shubert organization offered Minnelli a job as director and producer of its musical revues. The Shubert press releases described his life as "gay, sophisticated, fantastic."[52] His body and behavior were well recorded in the *World Telegram*, *Vanity Fair*, and *Esquire*. Minnelli was known as "twenty-nine years old [his reported age ranged often around four years younger than he actually was], with black, carefully combed hair, brown eyes and agile hands."[53] He was "versatile" and "handsome." He was also endearing, as he was known for his shyness and gentle temperament; he understood the "value of the soft spoken word."[54] His attraction to Whistler decidedly acted as one of "the dominant forces in his life," not only because of Whistler's "oils and etchings" but also, following Whistler, because Minnelli "[thought] best when riding in a hansom through Central Park."[55] He is the stroller of the urban street: "Mr. Minnelli is a great walker . . . not only in Central Park, but along Fourth Avenue, where the old bookstalls are, in rummage shops and out of the way places. Why, treasures abound in these odd shops. Old prints, pictures of the theatre of fifty years ago, even strange fabrics . . ."[56] Minnelli was visibly identified as the dandy-aesthete, the flaneur—the man about town who took pleasure in the historical debris of the city.

But there must be an accounting for Minnelli's aesthetic and, thereby, unmanly preoccupations (not to mention his lack of a showgirl girlfriend, as some Shubert press releases revealed). If he takes dance lessons at Arthur Murray's ("but he keeps them a secret from his pals"), he also "plays indoor tennis because it's the best exercise he can think of. He's anxious to keep fit. He shies from any activity that might be considered effeminate."[57] As far as marriage is concerned, he "hasn't the time for courtship. . . . He is too busy looking at girls in the aggregate to spend much time on the one and only girl."[58] Undoubtedly, Minnelli's publicists went to great lengths to prevent being targeted as "effeminate" and, thereby, an "Oscar Wilde." These overdetermined treatises merely whitewashed Minnelli's creative sensibilities in order to sell tickets, recalling Whistler's sentiment, to the "rich, ignorant public" that loathes "effeminacy" and "softness" in a man.

While Minnelli was at the Shuberts (right before he left to fulfill his brief, but lucrative, contract with Paramount Pictures in Hollywood as "musical director"), he designed a scene for the production of *The Show Is On* titled "Jam Session," in which he employed the use of an eight-by-ten-foot rear projection screen. This screen hung above the stage, where revelers and musicians of a jazz nightclub were partying. On this screen was projected the close-up of a musician playing the trumpet. But the figure's head was not stationary. The image was a sort of hologram flashing and dissolving to the rapid rhythm of the music being played onstage. Minnelli pointed to this scene in an article he wrote for *Stage* in September 1936, where his writing style suggests the crosscurrent of theatrical hyperactivity during production of *The Show Is On*: "Some radio scout should hear Hoagie [Carmichael] whistling, singing, and talking simultaneously into a telephone. He demonstrates a song with full orchestral effects including vibraphone and hot fiddle. All this to a running commentary on audience reaction, possible lyrics, and statistics on eventual sheet music sales. . . . Another composer [enters]. . . . I'm looking for a certain kind of tune for this number called Jam Session. The number opens in one. . . . Oh, Lord, if I have to tell this story once more I'll start eating the straw off the floor."[59] In the bottom right-hand corner of this article is Minnelli's sketch for "Jam Session." The caption reads, "'Jam Session': 1936! Hysteria! Harmonic interlude involving the madhouse tactics of the aggravated music of today." But this was not the only remark (and rendering) of "hysteria" that Minnelli discussed at this time. In an undated press release from the Shuberts, a portion of a speech made by Minnelli to the "Fashion Group" is given: "The designers in the theatre today are at last on familiar ground. They are utterly in accord with their audience because their audience is part of the show. The barriers of foot-light and stage door have never been so nebulous. *The theatre and life have at last decided to meet on common ground, and that common ground—let's face it—is madness.* Never, I think, has satire in the theatre been so spirited—color so unrestrained, sophistication so genuine."[60]

It is clear at this point in Minnelli's career that he saw himself ("the designer . . . on familiar ground") *within* the commingling and bewildering visual representation that folded into the cultural world. Of course, what is striking about his surrealist vision and disposition is that "theatre and life" are fraught with "madness" and "hysteria." In his later Hollywood films (both musicals and nonmusicals), this "hysteria" and "madness" were filtered through his brand of surrealism, popular culture, and decorative art, which surfaced through the filmic frame precisely through those "nebulous barriers" that allowed for this back-and-forth relationship between the historical world and its representation. I would suggest that the hysteria of which Minnelli speaks is the masculine hysteria, the excess of masculine production, of the twentieth century—of which he was so sensitive (see fig. 5).

For Minnelli, the décor or mise-en-scène of the frame (of the stage or, later, of the film) was where the body (and most often the male body) was conditioned and manipulated by the spatial/temporal relationships that that body shared with the historical world. In other words, "theatre and life" are imbricated and immersed in

ttle less narrative
rse?
iays Dave Freed-
oaring sketch for
:r after dinner to
enact Abelard's
laugh as though
/ell, you'd better
ad, because you
veeks before the
ough it had been
le. . . . Ah, that's
y. It better be. I
od's *Mass* from

her coming up to the Studio the night before she sailed, dressed for evening and looking *that* pretty? She gave a solid two hours' performance, improvising things she would do in the show, and there wasn't five minutes of the whole thing that any producer would have wanted to cut. There's the answer. How to produce a good revue: First you get Bea Lillie. . . . Ah! dinner . . . and not a moment too soon. . . . Don't let me forget to call Century about the new arcs for the Spotlight Number . . . and, oh, did I tell you my new idea for the opening?

"Yes, three times—will you have another piece of steak?"

about that verse. Wouldn't you have thought Hollywood could leave us Ira, one of the really great talents of the theatre? . . . Here, Marion, are a few more pages for the script. If you'll endow them with the dignity of type, I'll make a scene for that cowboy song idea Howard Dietz has for Bea. . . . There's a boy who makes revue material an art. . . . Let's see. . . .

"The revue as an art form has become . . ."

I don't think I have anything there. . . . How will I ever get to that article? What a curious subject anyhow. How is the musical revue produced?

Will somebody tell ME?

ung blades drew the
h the lamp-lit streets.

Jam Session: 1936! Hysteria! Harmonic interlude involving the madhouse tactics of the aggravated music of today.

Figure 5. "Jam Session: 1936! Hysteria! Harmonic interlude involving the madhouse tactics of the aggravated music of today." (*Stage*, September 1936, 35)

historical activity, while the bodies, which are situated within this madness, are forced to negotiate the unstable and hysterical parameters of the frame in which they exist. In many a Minnellian case, hypermasculinized bodies are ironically placed within his overaestheticized frame. Onstage, for example, when Bert Lahr performed as a "delicate" woodsman in "Song of the Woodsman" (*The Show Is On*), the mise-en-scène literally exploded around him.[61] Later, in his MGM films, Gene Kelly's virility is pressed against the soft impressionism of Dufy in *An American in Paris* (1951); Robert Mitchum drowns in an overmasculinized house of cowboy boots, leather, and blood in *Home from the Hill* (1960); and young college studs nervously negotiate Minnelli's color patterns and dispersions in *Tea and Sympathy* (1956).[62]

But Minnelli's frenzied vision of creativity in theater and life is unequivocally "spirited" and gives way to an aesthetics of "color so unrestrained, sophistication so genuine." Minnelli's body, placed within this social "hysteria," became a discourse generated by him and with the New York press that labeled, defined, and protected Minnelli as the quintessential aesthete–cultural producer of the musical revue. It was his years in New York that publicly and, thereby, corporeally marked the tension between masculinity and creativity that would inform Minnelli's body as it intersected with his stage and film work for the rest of his career. His dress, his demeanor, his body, his home, and his workplace became discursive and visible sites that articulated the cultivated Minnelli within and against the efficient discourse of masculinity. His shyness, his artistic knowledge, his "agile hands," his deep love for color (especially red and yellow), his preference for tennis to keep fit would sit uncomfortably amid the contemporary conditions of American masculinity. This aesthetic and discursive terrain would repeat itself and identify Minnelli for the next fifty years. It is through this historical, queer modernist milieu, then, that one can begin to discern the multiple levels that served the queer-modernist architectonics that Minnelli later brought to Hollywood cinema.

Notes

1   See Naremore, *Films of Vincente Minnelli*, 7–50. I'd like to thank Joe McElhaney for the opportunity to revisit and revise this essay. His editorial suggestions are greatly appreciated.

2   John Harkrider was a costume and stage designer on Broadway and in films between 1925 and 1942. Oliver Messel was born in England, where he worked on sets and costumes for both the English and American stage and films. "Hobe-Irwin" is Hobe Erwin, who was an interior decorator in New York. He later worked in Hollywood for MGM and David O. Selznick.

3   Memo located at the Academy of Motion Picture Arts and Sciences Center for Motion Picture Study, Margaret Herrick Library (hereafter AMPAS), Special Collections Department, folder 18, MGM Art Department/E. J. Mannix File.

4   Downing and Hambley, *Art of Hollywood*, 59. Also quoted in Minnelli with Arce, *I Remember It Well*, 122.

5   See Naremore, *Films of Vincente Minnelli*; and S. Harvey, *Directed by Vincente Minnelli*, 25–35.

6   In a Shubert press release (ca. 1936), we are told that "[Minnelli] lives in a flat on E. 52nd Street which doesn't boast a single piece of chromium plated furniture." Shubert Archives, New York; see files regarding Minnelli and the programs he designed and produced.

7   I have been fortunate to see this collection firsthand through the gracious approval of Mrs. Lee Minnelli. Unless otherwise noted, all information ascribed to Lee Minnelli was recorded from personal interviews with the author during the summer of 1995.

8   Goldberger, "Hollywood House Worthy of an Oscar."

9   Albrecht, *Designing Dreams*, 91.

10 Gibbons, "Interior Decoration Vital Branch of Movie Making." Other sources that discuss Gibbons's dwelling and "architectural" design include Webb, "Cedric Gibbons and the MGM Style."

11 In *Ornament and Architecture* (1892), Louis Sullivan suggests that it "would be greatly for our aesthetic good if we should refrain entirely from the use of ornament . . . [because] we shall have learned . . . that ornament is mentally a luxury, not a necessity. . . . We feel intuitively that our *strong, athletic,* and simple forms will carry with the natural ease the raiment of which we dream" (quoted in Frampton, *Modern Architecture*, 51; emphasis added). Interestingly, recent renovation of Grand Central was discussed similarly: the station is said to be "getting a sex change," in that what was once "a temple to the manly cult of work" is now "[emerging] as a shrine to rituals associated with domesticity: dining, shopping and keeping up the house" (Muschamp, "Grand Central as a Hearth," 27).

12 "It is not possible to move forward and look backwards," writes Mies Van der Rohe; "he who lives in the past cannot advance" (quoted in Hochman, *Architects of Fortune*, xiv). The irony of the functional art/architecture of a modernist such as Mies was that often the living space he designed for an unburdened future became "uninhabitable," as in the case of his Farnsworth House of 1952, which was "located on the bank of a river that was

heavily infested with mosquitoes on summer evenings. Mies would not allow a screened porch, arguing . . . that to do so would have ruined the jewel-like design" (Hochman, 57).

13 Quoted in *Encyclopedia Britannica* and cited in Albrecht, *Designing Dreams*, 90.

14 Wollen, "Out of the Past," 17.

15 Wollen, 18.

16 Located at the Museum of the City of New York and the Metropolitan Museum of Art are several dozen sketches for Minnelli's Radio City Music Hall and Shubert productions: *At Home Abroad* (1935), *Hooray for What?!* (1937), and *Very Warm for May* (1939). Indeed, one of Minnelli's major conflicts between Gibbons and MGM's Technicolor adviser, Natalie Kalmus, was during the filming of *Meet Me in St. Louis*. Minnelli argued with Gibbons and Kalmus over the use of the colors red and green in a single shot (two colors, moreover, that Gibbons had forbidden to be used in his films). The decorative clutter of the Smith home also highlights the antithesis of the clean, functional line that Gibbons preferred. See Minnelli, *I Remember It Well*, 131–32.

17 See Chauncey, *Gay New York*.

18 Minnelli's effete and urbane demeanor is quite recognizable, for example, in his interview for *The Men Who Made Movies* (produced, written, and directed by Richard Schickel, 1973).

19 Many passages in Joseph and Elizabeth R. Pennell's book recount Whistler's work emphasizing the painter's palette, which was undoubtedly attractive to Minnelli's penchant for color. Whistler, according to the voluminous interviews conducted by the Pennells, insisted that "*colours should be arranged on the palette*" (*Life of James McNeill Whistler*, 1:50) and that precise "scientific methods . . . produce harmonious effects in line and 'colour grouping'" (1:222). For Whistler, "art is a science not because as some painters imagine, it is concerned with laws of light or chemistry of colours or scientific problems in the usual sense, but because it is exact in its methods and in its results as the science of chemistry" (2:8). Yet, at the same time, color disrupts a standardized viewing: "The artist must overload everything with strong contrasts of violent colours. His success with the rich ignorant public is assured if only he succeeds in setting his colours shouting against each other" (2:8). Clearly, Minnelli learned much from Whistler's science of art and color as well as how to sell to a "rich [if not] ignorant public."

20 Minnelli, *I Remember It Well*, 50. Minnelli highlights Whistler as "a pioneer in interior design, introducing blue and white décor and Japanese china to

London. He had an affinity for yellow [Minnelli's favorite color], painting walls of his house in its most sunny shading."

21   Pennell and Pennell, *Life of James McNeill Whistler*, 2:127. Generally speaking, Minnelli rarely fell upon financial hard times. His contract with the Shuberts in 1936 (*The Show Is On*) guaranteed him $3,500 to design "all scenery and costumes," $500 per week for staging the show's production (with a guaranteed minimum of $2,000), and 2 percent of gross weekly box-office receipts, as well as 2 percent of gross weekly box-office receipts if the show traveled abroad. Besides this terrific salary, Minnelli had "complete charge of the artistic phases of the entire production." Minnelli's contract is located at the Shubert Archive.

22   Pennell and Pennell, *Life of James McNeill Whistler*, 1:38.

23   Pennell and Pennell, 1:44.

24   Pennell and Pennell, 1:80, 300.

25   On the dandy, see Barbey d'Aurevilly, *Dandyism*; Baudelaire, *Selected Writings on Art and Literature*. On the dandy's historical association with homosexuality, see Sinfield, *Wilde Century*; Ellman, *Oscar Wilde*; and Cohen, *Talk on the Wilde Side*.

26   See Whistler, "Ten O'Clock."

27   Minnelli, *I Remember It Well*, 38; he also described *The Pirate* as "camp" in his memoir.

28   Sontag, "Happenings," 271.

29   Quoted in Tinkcom, "Working like a Homosexual," 24.

30   Tinkcom, 29.

31   "Oral History with Lela Simone," interview conducted with Rudy Behlmer, October 1990–January 1991, AMPAS, Oral History Program, 1994.

32   Minnelli, *I Remember It Well*, 51.

33   Kellner, introduction to *Letters of Carl Van Vechten*, 49.

34   And this was not only young talent such as Langston Hughes and Zora Neale Hurston but also older and forgotten writers such as Henry Blake Fuller. Van Vechten was also capable of raising the dead, as in the case of Herman Melville.

35   Kellner, *Carl Van Vechten and the Irreverent Decades*, vii.

36   The historical impact of Diaghilev's *Scheherazade* cannot be underestimated in terms of the New York art scene during the 1920s and 1930s (Van Vechten even named his cat Scheherazade). For a thorough and elegant description of the "dandy-aesthete" audience that attended the Ballets Russes in London and Paris after World War I, see Garafola, *Diaghilev's Ballets Russes*.

37   Minnelli reprimands a New York reviewer's ignorance for not recognizing his use of color and accoutrements for Earl Carroll's curtain in the 1931 *Vanities*, which were "particularly . . . inspired by Bakst and executed by Remisoff and Soudakin for the Ballets Russes" (*I Remember It Well*, 58).

38   See my *Manly Arts*, 165–211.

39   Bloemink, "Visualizing Sight," 71.

40   Sussman, "Florine Stettheimer," 43.

41   Minnelli, *I Remember It Well*, 50; Sussman, "Florine Stettheimer," 50.

42   Minnelli, *I Remember It Well*, 98.

43   Minnelli, 102.

44   Examples of Stettheimer's set designs from the production can be seen in Kellner, *Carl Van Vechten and the Irreverent Decades*.

45   Minnelli, *I Remember It Well*, 90.

46   Consider, for example, Minnelli's use of "trans-Atlantic Orientalist" visions in the "Get Yourself a Geisha" number from the around-the-world stage revue *At Home Abroad* (1935) or the chinoiserie décor of "Limehouse Blues" from the film *Ziegfeld Follies*. The eroticism, exoticism, and theatricalization of "Orientalist" pleasures in Western culture point to the decadent reappropriation of an otherwise Orientalist discourse that serves to manage and subjugate the Other. As Edward Said remarks in his discussion of Flaubert's "fascination with dissection and beauty" through Oriental culture, "the Orient seems still to suggest not only fecundity but sexual promise (and threat), untiring sensuality, unlimited desire, deep generative energies, [which] is something on which one could speculate" (*Orientalism*, 188). More concurrent with Minnelli at this time was André Breton's surrealistic favor of imagery of the "Orient," which contemporary conservatives saw as decadent and disturbing. See his "Legitimate Defense" (September 1926), in Nadeau, *History of Surrealism*.

47   Troy, "Never Had a Lesson," 99.

48   Minnelli, *I Remember It Well*, 56.

49   Chauncey, *Gay New York*, 344.

50   Chauncey, 303.

51   Chauncey, 303.

52   Eleanor Lambert, "Notes on Vincente Minnelli," unpublished, undated Shubert Theater press release. Lambert, a leading producer of fashion shows well into the 1970s, was a close friend of Minnelli while he worked in New York. Her influential involvement with the international fashion world had important creative resonances for Minnelli.

53 Birnie, "Chorine Thought and Was Wrong."

54 Lambert, "Notes on Vincente Minnelli."

55 Birnie, "Chorine Thought and Was Wrong."

56 Marion Hurwood, "The Show Is On," unpublished, undated Shubert Theater press release.

57 Birnie, "Chorine Thought and Was Wrong."

58 Lambert, "Notes on Vincente Minnelli," 3.

59 Minnelli, "Show Must Go On," 35.

60 Lambert, "Notes on Vincente Minnelli."

61 In John Lahr's biography of his father, Bert Lahr is described in this scene as costumed with a papier-mâché ax while "posed preposterously next to a scrawny tree. . . . He wore a checkered hunter's shirt and a toupee matted on his head. He began raising both hands delicately toward his chest and then unleashing an outrageous sound." In the meantime, Bea Lillie anxiously awaited her cue, when she could "throw boards, brooms, anything [she] could get my hands on" at the singing woodsman. Lahr, *Notes on a Cowardly Lion*, 163–64.

62 For an analysis of Minnelli's use of color in *Tea and Sympathy*, see my "Production and Display of the Closet."

THE CASE OF THE CERAMIC DILDO

Notes on Queer Historiography and Ramón Novarro's Remains

This essay, on the one hand, reviews a handful of texts (books, films, Los Angeles, stars) about the life and death of Ramón Novarro. On the other hand, it is a critical study of his biographer-historians, who, with some urgency, seek to ascertain and assertively "correct" the truth about the Hollywood actor's rise from immigrant to Hollywood stardom to a violent and homophobic demise. As such, I am concerned with Novarro's textual remains. Novarro is an odd duck, to be sure, and his place in film and queer history proves to be something of a problem for his biographers, who wish to rescue him from what they view as malicious and inaccurate representations of the actor's life and his violent death. What is one to do about historical accuracy when a Hollywood star, such as Novarro, whose own presentation of self—a titillating performance on- *and* off-screen—was nothing short of a deceptively charming performance? How does one, effectively, write about a queer Hollywood idol?

The rethinking of bio-historiography in relationship to Hollywood and its stars has developed along various scholarly trajectories through the lenses of queer theory and, more generally, gay and lesbian studies. Richard Dyer's *Heavenly Bodies* fuses the stars' "business of being an individual" with the way they "[embody] the social categories in which people are placed and through which they have to make sense of their lives, and indeed through which we make our lives—categories of class, gender, ethnicity, religion, sexual orientation, and so on."[1] Dyer's earlier work, *Stars*, presciently anticipates the gay pleasures in which he revels in the pages of *Heavenly Bodies*: Marilyn Monroe, Paul Robeson, and Judy Garland. But Dyer self-polices his own desire around his adoration for the star. In the final paragraph *Stars*, we read something of an apologia to the extent that Dyer describes and defends his (non-?)Marxist "delight" when lingering over the images of Monroe, Montgomery Clift, and Barbara Stanwyck. He is quick to mark his academic and political credentials: "I don't want to privilege these responses [beauty, pleasure, delight] over analysis. . . . I accept utterly that beauty and pleasure are culturally and historically specific, and in no way escape ideology." Nevertheless,

Dyer goes on to say that *Stars* and *Heavenly Bodies* are works that insist on a methodology that secures his vexed academic and queer impulses "that beauty and pleasure are culturally and historically specific."[2] The tricky matters that bundle historical specificity, beauty, pleasure, and queer desire are those I seek to address.

In the 1991 issue of *differences*, Jennifer Terry, in her essay "Theorizing Deviant Historiography," initiates the important question about form in relationship to queerness: What form does queer history take when it investigates "deviant subjectivity" (a moniker certainly associated with many movie stars, Novarro included)? Are traditional modes of historiography enough when giving life to queer subjectivity? Terry is clear that queer historiography "is not an alternative with its own glorious tumescence peopled by previously elided but not recuperated Others. Effective history [the term she uses to describe Foucault's methodological project] exposes not the events and actors elided by traditional history, but instead lays bare the processes and operations by which these elisions occurred."[3] Though Terry is interested in reconsidering "deviant subjectivity" as a "subject formation in relation to pathologizing discourses," she suggestively proposes queer historiography as "a way of conceptualizing and enacting subjectivities forged in process through multiple resistances to systematized homophobia. These subjectivities are neither static nor contained; they are effects in the history of the perilous present."[4] I am drawn, therefore, to ways to "conceptualize" and to "enact" the histories of queer subjectivities.

How does one write histories that pay attention to "subjectivities [that] are neither static nor contained"? In other words, what does queer historiography look like as we make our way through a "perilous" and homophobic present? When Dyer states (following his academic caveat in *Stars*), "I want to hang on to [beauty and pleasure] in some form or another," what form might his queer methodology take?[5] What possibilities exist for historical form when in the mode of "an other"? As my study proceeds, I take up these questions in light of the histories that now give shape to Ramón Novarro. Kenneth Anger, for obvious reasons, makes an appearance here since his *Hollywood Babylon* raises the ante on the industry's deviant stars and how one approaches these figures as queer subjects in, well, queer historical form. Anger is set side by side with Novarro's more recent and earnest biographers in order to illustrate a curious ("perilous") historiographical conflict that frames Novarro's biography. Perhaps less obvious for this essay's inquiry, but extremely significant for what it aims to suggest, are James Baldwin's theories on writing history, public figures, and Hollywood. Baldwin's concept of history provides a space in which a sensually erotic queer historiography takes flight.

Figure 6. Mischievous Ramón in *The Prisoner of Zenda* (1922).

Deviously Charming

I begin my study about Ramón Novarro with a few observations about the film roles he played throughout his career. I do this to underscore a titillating—if only coincidental—relationship between his images on the screen and the historical disseminations left in their wake.[6] What is striking about Novarro's film casting, and arguably a major reason for his success, is his devilishly charming characters. He is not so much the seductive Latin Lover who replaced Rudolph Valentino. Novarro's mentor and several-time director, Rex Ingram, initially thought this possible when he tailored Novarro's rise into stardom.[7] Whereas Gaylyn Studlar's research finds that Valentino's public persona "seemed to exemplify the epicene results of women's perverse search for a new model of masculinity that defied normative American models," men also thought he embodied a new "perverse" masculinity: the "pink powder puff."[8] According to André Soares, Novarro was not so threatening. Instead, Soares describes Novarro as the other "Latin Lover" in contradistinction to Valentino's sexually charged charisma. For him, Novarro was more impish; he personified "fun, not danger" (40). Novarro, in other words, struck simultaneous and paradoxical chords: boyish but savvy, ebullient yet earnest, heroic but humble, playfully naïve while sexually available.

In short, Novarro on the screen is decidedly deceptive; his is a delightfully alluring performance both—as it turns out—on- and off-screen.

Consider for a moment such charmingly deceptive roles as his most successful film of the 1920s, in which Novarro plays the eponymous lead in *Ben-Hur: A Tale of the Christ* (1925). In the film, Judah Ben-Hur assumes the role of "the unknown Jew" after his Jewish family's property is pillaged and his mother and sister are sent to a leper colony by the Romans. Under this anonymity, Ben-Hur confronts his former Roman friend (now archenemy) Messala (Francis X. Bushman), in the now-famous chariot-race sequence. A few years prior to making Ben-Hur, Ramón Samaniego (soon to be Novarro) met Ingram on the set of *The Four Horsemen of the Apocalypse* (1921). Samaniego was an extra in the film. Ingram believed the fresh talent could be sculpted for his own cinematic purposes; the director saw him as a "substitute for Valentino. There were the good looks, grace of movement, the Latin temperament, all allied to real acting ability" (O'Leary, *Rex Ingram*, 96). Still under his birth name, Samaniego worked with Ingram in the making of *The Prisoner of Zenda* (1922). The young actor was a hit as the devious villain, Rupert of Hentzau, who, with sharp legerdemain and precision, flipped a monocle from one hand directly into his eye. Later, again under Ingram's direction and with his new Hollywood moniker, "Ramón Novarro," the actor was cast in yet another role highlighted by a performance within a performance.[9] In *Scaramouche* (1923), Novarro plays André-Louis Moreau. Here, Moreau joins a traveling theater troupe, where he gains popularity as the "nameless clown," an identity that proves useful while he deceives his nemesis, the Marquis de la Tour d'Azyr (Lewis Stone), to win back the woman he loves, Aline de Kercadiou (Alice Terry, Ingram's wife), from the Marquis.

With Joan Crawford in the role of Priscilla Crowninshield, Novarro is cast in *Across to Singapore* (1928) as the mischievous younger brother, Joel Shore, who is wrongly accused of abandoning his older brother, Mark (Ernest Torrence), in Singapore. After escaping jail following his conviction on these false charges, Joel heads to Singapore to find his brother. Disguised as a sailor, wearing his brother's ill-fitting uniform, Joel enters a bar where Mark has been drinking heavily with other sailors. Seeing Joel in the baggy suit and not drinking with as much gusto as the others, one of the sailors looks at Joel and announces, "He's no sailor. He's a de-nurse girl!"

In a rather prescient act of duplicity, Ernst Lubitsch (not without dissent) cast Novarro as Crown Prince Karl Heinrich in *The Student Prince in Old Heidelberg* (1927). In the final scene, Heinrich is seen riding in a decorated carriage through the city streets with his new bride, who remains absent in the frame and to whom we are never introduced in the film. As Heinrich forces a smile to veil his grief over lost love, his marriage is presented as strictly a monarchial duty, a marriage of convenience. His conflicted facial expressions at once reveal the longing for his true love, Kathi (Norma Shearer), while ostensibly not letting his new queen know that he does not love her.

This pattern of doubled/duplicitous performances continued through the change-over to sound in the film industry, a transition that potentially spelled the end of Novarro's career due to his Mexican accent. Fortunately (sort of, as we shall see), his speaking voice, as well as his singing, carried well with the new technology (Ellenberger, *Ramón Novarro*, 80–85; Soares, *Beyond Paradise*, 128, 146–47). Many reviewers often applauded Novarro's new-era performances on-screen, as with the film *In Gay Madrid* (1930), where he "sings no fewer than six ballads, and all are pleasing."[10] *The Pagan* (1929), however, was illustrative of both Novarro's well-trained singing and the roles he came to typify. On the one hand, *The Pagan* was a silent film with synchronized musical numbers (similar to the form used in *The Jazz Singer* [1927]) that introduced Novarro's range of talent. The success of the film appeared to bode well for Novarro as sound technology took hold. In fact, the film's theme song, "The Pagan Love Song," became a hit and secured the actor's popularity for the time being.

On the other hand, *The Pagan* highlights the lengths to which Hollywood utilized Novarro as the "other." In effect, Novarro's roles were underscored by a performative duplicity that stretched across racial and ethnic identity (he was often cast as the "other": Arab, "native" Pacific Islander, American Indian, German, Austrian, Russian, Spanish, French). In *The Pagan*, an overtanned (i.e., Hollywood's makeup that signaled "mixed race") Henry Shoesmith Jr. (Novarro) rejects the constraints of Anglo-Saxon civilization for *une vie d'enfant sauvage*. He falls in love with a mixed-race native woman, whose surrogate father (Soares calls him a "ruthless white trader" [Donald Crisp]) blocks Henry's advances toward Tito (Dorothy Janis), the white man's "Christian duty" (Soares, *Beyond Paradise*, 142), because Shoesmith in no way demonstrates proper Christian values and lives as nature purportedly intended (a bit ironic given Novarro's well-publicized staunch Catholicism and his very public announcements about leaving the movies to enter the priesthood). The film's narrative conflict thus raises the vexed questions surrounding colonization and mixed-blood relations while managing them through the "natural" boy-meets-girl narrative. At the end of *The Pagan*, needless to say, all is well since it turns out that the two lovers' mixed-blood ethnicity is actually coequal; they are of the same stock, in other words. Thus, under Hollywood law, their love could be consummated with no worries of miscegenation.

And so it continued. Throughout the few remaining high points of Novarro's career during the 1930s, his charm and good looks took shape through misleading or misled characters: the Austrian Willi Kasder (Novarro) feigns illness and lies about familial ties in order to seduce a young woman, Helen Chandler (Laura Taub), in *Daybreak* (1931);[11] the young Russian lieutenant Alexis Rosanoff (Novarro) willingly deceives himself and tarnishes his honor because of his love for Mata Hari (Greta Garbo) in *Mata Hari* (1931); as a rogue Arab lover in *The Barbarian* (1933), Novarro suavely bids adieu to his many and simultaneously departing middle-aged, married, and Western-tourist mistresses while he efficiently pilfers their jewels; in *The Cat and the Fiddle* (1934), as the French composer Victor Florescu, he convinces (by lying) his American lover, the composer Shirley Sheridan (Jeanette MacDonald), that he no longer loves her and must leave her so that he can move on with his own career (in the film's diegesis, Florescu deceives Shirley because her manager convinces him that he is the stumbling block that holds back her quickly advancing career); as an American Indian in *Laughing Boy* (1934), Novarro tricks (by playing naïve) gullible American tourists, whom he coaxes into paying more for worthless trinkets. And because they fatuously exoticize the Indian, the American tourists are more than happy to pay up.

In a stunning act of poor management, MGM starred Novarro in the film *Huddle* (1932), in which the actor plays Antonio "Tony" Amatto, a second-generation Italian who attends Yale on a football scholarship. Imagine, Ramón Novarro, a football player. By the 1930s, Novarro's abilities to charmingly deceive began to wear thin. This was particularly the case when the screen illusion collided obtusely with his star-system persona and, ultimately, his "private" lived-world experiences, experiences that soon made their way into public discourse.

Later, with the best part of Novarro's acting career behind him, he took on two small but narratively significant roles. In 1949, he finally had the opportunity to make a Hollywood film shot in his home nation, Mexico. In Don Siegel's *The Big Steal*, he played the Mexican Inspector General Ortega. Under Siegel's direction, he continued the coy and mischievous roles that I have noted, this time alongside Robert Mitchum and Jane Greer in a film noir thriller. Here, Ortega portrays a police official who appears to only understand a fair amount of English, but as a "clever cat," he knows more than he lets on—language and otherwise. As he tells his assistant in the film, he is the cat who "lets the mouse go so that the freed mouse will lead the cat to where he can catch the mice." In 1960, when working with the well-known gay director George Cukor on *Heller in Pink Tights*, Novarro portrays De Leon, a ruthless business magnate who foolishly tries to double-cross his own hired assassin (Steve Forrest).

If Novarro's performances of deception began to wane but not entirely disappear from the screen, a similar acting role off-screen occupied him until his death. What perhaps turned out to be his greatest deception throughout his career (notwithstanding his sexuality, to be discussed in short order) was that Novarro often expressed no tremendous love for acting in film. He let it be known on several occasions that his true passion was singing: "Compared to music, the screen is so dissatisfying."[12] In effect, Novarro's performance on-screen was truly a projection of multiple illusions—for the audience, the studio, his colleagues, and what invariably became clear, himself.

Urban Migrations

Jose Ramón Gil Samaniego was born into a wealthy middle-class family in Durango on February 6, 1899. With Pancho Villa's revolution at their doorstep after 1913, the family was forced to leave their home. Between 1913 and 1918, the family escaped the revolutionaries via Mexico City and then, by 1917, El Paso, Texas. Ramón, with his younger brother, Mariano, arrived in Texas in advance of his family. Before the family reached El Paso, Ramón and his brother (apparently without informing their parents) headed west for Los Angeles because, according to Soares, "[Ramón] was intent on pursuing a show business career" (*Beyond Paradise*, 10). By 1918, however, the family's several years of turbulent movement came to an end when they were reunited in Los Angeles, where they finally settled (Ellenberger, *Ramón Novarro*, 5–10; Soares, *Beyond Paradise*, 1–11).

Later in Novarro's career, his national identity did not impair his rising stardom (though he was accused of communist activity by Joseph McCarthy, charges he ably sidestepped [Soares, *Beyond Paradise*, 200–201; Ellenberger, *Ramón Novarro*, 130–31]). This may be due, in part, to studio publicity that packaged him as "Spanish" and, as mentioned, an assortment of other nationalities in his films. It is a wonder that anyone in the United States knew he was Mexican. Nevertheless, as his career soared during the 1920s and began its descent through the 1930s, Mexicans revered him, and he, in turn, headlined events such as the one sponsored by the Mexican consulate in 1933 to aid storm victims in Tampico (Soares, *Beyond Paradise*, 198). In the 1940s, when Novarro hoped for a comeback, he announced that his return would begin with the Mexican film industry (Soares, *Beyond Paradise*, 237–38). He also embarked on a brief, but failed, career in directing as his acting work dwindled. The premiere for his directorial debut—*Contra la corriente* (*Against the Current*, 1936)—was planned for his hometown, Durango. It was the only film of a planned six projects that his newly founded company, RNS Productions, hoped to produce. According to Ellenberger, Novarro did not act in *Contra la corriente* but "appeared in a prologue in which he gave a tribute to Rex Ingram" (*Ramón Novarro*, 135).

Upon Novarro's initial arrival in Los Angeles, however, he encountered the xenophobia that mars the history of US immigration culture and policy. This history, as with so many things American, straddles contradictory elements. Soares importantly shows that, on the one hand, the influx of Mexicans across the border at the time of America's entry into the Great War (1917) was "especially welcome as cheap hard workers"; on the other hand, the American Southwest, "including the then largely WASP city of Los Angeles," had something of a "'Brown Scare,' as locals feared the invasion of poor, uneducated, brown-skinned Catholics into their communities" (*Beyond Paradise*, 13). Xenophobia, as it turns out, was further coupled with the "Red Scare" that, from the perspective of conservative American patriots, was aligned with labor organizations, organizations wedded to the industries in which many Mexicans found themselves working. Hence, by association, Mexicans were not only "Brown" but "Red." De facto, many Mexicans avoided "being targeted" by identifying as "Spanish" (Soares, *Beyond Paradise*, 13).

From the start, then, Novarro found himself occupying and negotiating the terrain of shifting identities. To be sure, his professional and personal biography is not dissimilar to the uneven and multiple histories of the place—Los Angeles—where he settled. "Under Spanish and Mexican influence," according to Lillian Faderman and Stuart Timmons, "the Gabrielino Indian village of Yang-na was gradually transformed into the city of Los Angeles" in the mid-nineteenth century through forced relocation or murdering of the Indian population.[13] While the area now known as Los Angeles was a "Mexican town of ranchos and cattle" during the 1840s, California's admittance into the Union in 1850 soon included a population composed of four thousand whites and thirty-seven hundred Indians (Faderman and Timmons, *Gay L.A.*, 9). The purge of the Indian population by white settlers was thus not complete, thereby creating a cross-cultural environment. This cultural mixing, of course, heightened tensions about morality and immorality.

What the early incoming missionaries, especially from Spain, found most offensive about their encounter with Indian villages was their "tolerance of same-sex marriage, cross-gendered behaviors, homosexual family life, and sexual fluidity" (Faderman and Timmons, *Gay L.A.*, 14). Nonetheless, a good number of Euro-American immigrants often disregarded their heritage of Christian piety and dogma by willingly participating in—indeed aiding and abetting—the manufacturing of Los Angeles's reputation as the "City of the Devils." By 1875, Los Angeles was perceived as "loose and lawless" and "ambivalent in its view of unconventional gender behavior" (Faderman and Timmons, *Gay L.A.*, 14–15). As any good student of queer, postcolonial, and film studies knows, the "incommensurability of cultural values and priorities" (as Homi Bhabha terms it) emerge with some force when containment corners a marginalized people through ideological and militaristic means.[14] Los Angeles is certainly a case in point since it is a site that clings to a magnificent duplicity; on the one hand, it packages an endless stream of white, heteronormative product, while, on the other hand, it enables a mixing of cultures that imbibe in perverse decadence and narcissistic gratification—cultures, ironically, that include individuals responsible for the ideological norms Hollywood relentlessly regurgitates.

Novarro's ancestry is drawn into this historical development of Southern California and the United States' conquest of the land. Hailing from Spain, the Samaniegos settled in "New Spain," which later gained independence as Mexico in 1821. The extended Samaniego family held large landholdings and, in some instances, was involved in the resistance against the American invasion during the 1840s (Soares, *Beyond Paradise*, 1–2). The significant loss of land, particularly the El Paso area in Texas, to the American government did not prevent the Samaniegos' rise into Mexico's middle class. Novarro's father opened a prosperous dental practice, while his mother avidly served the role as matriarch with an abiding and fervent dedication to Catholicism. "Before retiring to bed," Ellenberger writes, "each child would drop to one knee and receive [their mother's] blessing. Religion played an important part in Mrs. Samaniego's life, for she was devoted to St Francis and passed her love of God on to her children" (*Ramón Novarro*, 6). Mrs. Samaniego also instilled a love for the arts. By age five, Ramón studied piano and voice; by age six, he performed for family celebrations; and at age eight, he received a marionette theater that he used to entertain neighbors (Ellenberger, *Ramón Novarro*, 7–8).

Against the backdrop of revolution, however, Ramón's inculcation in the arts and religion met at a thorny intersection. As gunfire echoed outside the family home, Ramón at age fifteen asked himself whether he should become a priest or turn to music as a career. It seems that when he came across a program for the Metropolitan Opera "announcing Enrico Caruso and Geraldine Farrar in *Manon*," all spiritual and pious bets were off (Ellenberger, *Ramón Novarro*, 10). "Perhaps it was the devil tempting me. . . . I'm still not so sure it wasn't," Novarro later recounted (quoted in Ellenberger, *Ramón Novarro*, 10). Hence, for the remainder of his career, and like the city that ultimately made his fortune, Novarro found himself torn between the sins of the flesh (made so tempting within the creative urban milieu of Hollywood) and the absolution and redemption of those sins that religion (and Hollywood film) promised. Novarro maintained an experiential trajectory that repeated over and over; it was a life cycle that led him to acts of pleasure, then guilt, and then a quest for salvation and redemption through a return to the Church (whether through prayer or public announcements about joining the priesthood).

It is perhaps merely coincidence that the charmingly sly and duplicitous nature of the characters Novarro portrayed on the screen mimicked his intense self-deceptions. Whatever the case, the character images on the screen appear strikingly similar to how we might imagine Novarro's actions off-screen, actions that can only be described as an endless tug-of-war to conquer desire ("fort/da," in Freudian terms, if you will). Coincidence or not, the mirroring between screen and life in Novarro's case is quite remarkable, if not self-prophetic. In the mid-1930s, when his career came to a halt, he planned to finish a not-so-quasi-autobiographical play. It tells the story of a

> Mexican lad who yearns for great things. He is so ambitious, so eager to make good. Finally, after many, many years of struggle, he becomes a great motion picture star. Everything is at his command; the world is his. But the young star, knowing all this, learns later that life has more to offer than just the pleasure of living. He feels that now, with wealth and power, he can do things he always wanted to do. But the things he wanted to do become meaningless. For there is no motivation behind them; he finds himself doing them—and it is a tasteless, meaningless proceeding. And so, with all his material dreams fulfilled, the young star discovers that life is empty, hopeless. (Soares, *Beyond Paradise*, 209)

But, as Soares sums it up, Novarro "saw himself as a victim of—and not an active participant in—the Hollywood system" (*Beyond Paradise*, 210). Novarro is thus a case study for the desire to dust off archival treasures, to discover "the truth," "the Real." Yet, Hayden White reminds us, "historians necessarily disagree not only over the question 'What are the data?' but also over the form of the theories by which those data are constituted as 'problems' and then are 'resolved' by being merged with them to make up 'explanations.'" And, ultimately, to choose the way one "resolves" and "explains" the data is a "*moral* or *aesthetic*" choice.[15] What our case study—"Ramón Novarro"— offers is an analysis of moral and/or aesthetic choices when the data under consideration is queer.

Tearing at the Skin of History: Bathhouses, Hustlers, and Art Deco Dildos

What were the scenes of temptation and redemption in which Novarro participated (and then cast himself as victim or sinner, desperate to make penance)? With Novarro, it is difficult to pinpoint the tantalizing "whos," "whats," and "whens" of his queer affairs since, as William Mann puts it, he "shied away from reporters; his interviews were rare and always vague."[16] We do know that he was gay and managed to keep it under wraps (for the most part) until his violent death publicly exposed decades of secrets, innuendo, and uncertainties. Novarro's less-than-forthcoming responses in the press usually focused on the nuclear family he housed, cared for, and lived with throughout most of his career. More often than not, his love for music and singing and (as we discussed) his devotion to Catholicism took center stage in the contemporary recording of his life. In the short article he wrote for *Theatre Magazine* in 1928, he, in fact, bundles together his relationship with his family (his mother, specifically) and music. "Only my love of music," he writes, "brought forgiveness from my mother when, still, in my teens, I left home, in Durango, Mexico. I was goaded by the romantic search for fortune. My family was reassured only after I had announced that if I succeeded, it would all be toward my goal, music."[17] This bundling—music, mother, redemption—shadowed Novarro throughout his career.

This manufactured persona was all well and good; yet Novarro, along with his queer contemporaries of the time—the "out" William Haines and Nazimova as well as the reportedly "closeted" married couples with separate bedrooms, Cedric Gibbons and Dolores Del Rio, Edmund Lowe and Lilyan Tashman, and Rudolph Valentino and Natacha Rambova—posed something of a publicity problem. As William Mann points out, "If [William Haines] had been heterosexual, chief MGM publicist Pete Smith might have found his job a little easier, but not by much" (Mann, *Wisecracker*, 106). Indeed, Mann goes on to argue that the "myriad affairs and temper tantrums" of "straight" stars, such as John Gilbert and Mae Murray, were no day at the beach for those who managed the hypercontrolled image machine of Hollywood (106).

Regardless, the "homosexual angle" demanded some tricky maneuvering. In one sense, it appears that the gossip columnists were "in the know" about these stars' sexual proclivities; a tacit agreement took root between the studios' publicity departments and the press to keep such matters from the public. A quid pro quo existed since the press "depended on the largesse" of the studios' publicity mill and the studios certainly depended on the columnists to put their product in the best light (Mann, *Wisecracker*, 107). Hal Elias, Pete Smith's assistant at MGM, who toed the studio line, states, "We had our Bill Haines and our Ramón Novarros. . . . Those are the people who were discussed. Not negatively exactly—their so-called transgressions were considered important, but not in a negative sense exactly. They weren't condemned for it, let me put it that way."[18] At the same time, how were reporters meant to ask questions of these stars when they were fully aware of the "truth" that defined these stars' personal relationships? Moreover, the tacitly made "agreement" between the press and the studios was difficult to sustain: "Valentino lied. Novarro hid," Mann tells us (*Wisecracker*, 108). Haines, of course, was another story.

In fact, Haines—and not Valentino—is the main character in the tale that sets things rolling for Novarro's first precarious homosexual predicament. Given Haines's unapologetic stance regarding his homosexuality and his relationship with Jimmy Shields, this story is all the more revealing since it stands in as a representative event for the very different approach the two stars took (and that their subsequent biographers took) in scripting their lives. The rumor is this: In 1925, while Novarro was in the thick of the *Ben-Hur* debacle (the film was well past deadline and tremendously over budget), Haines invited Novarro to a bathhouse on Wilshire Boulevard. In an act of revenge, a fellow actor (one whom Haines once referred to with derogatory remarks) reported Haines and Novarro's sexual adventure to Louis B. Mayer. Mayer, purportedly not aware of Novarro's sexuality and all too aware of Haines's, was furious. Haines and Novarro were trotted out on Mayer's carpet and berated for the unacceptable behavior. Expectedly, Novarro kowtowed to Mayer's anger and demand to keep his private life private. Haines (just as expectedly) preferred to return to the bathhouses. "Reluctantly," Ellenberger concludes about this incident, "it was the last time that Novarro socialized with William Haines. From that point, he would try to make any rendezvous as private as possible, a practice he would follow to his death. He was not always successful, however, and would have other scrapes with Mayer and the law" (*Ramón Novarro*, 59).[19] But these "scrapes" had more to do with Novarro's turn to alcohol and his driving accidents after his career faltered in the 1930s.

Nonetheless, other rumors persisted about Novarro's homosexuality. His affair with Valentino is said to have taken place at the Alexandria Hotel, where "ritzy homosexuals . . . held soirees" (Faderman and Timmons, *Gay L.A.*, 36, 60; see, further, Ellenberger, *Ramón Novarro*, 14–15). Ellenberger tells us that beginning in 1927, Novarro kept a bungalow at Nazimova's "Garden of Allah," where queer activities were de rigueur given the actor's many lesbian affairs and gay friends (*Ramón Novarro*, 81). Though Nazimova's biographer Gavin Lambert does not mention Novarro in his book, it is most likely that the young budding star maintained the bungalow for his private trysts or for romantic evenings with the gossip columnist Herbert Howe, who "had become truly captivated by the heartthrob from Durango" (Soares, *Beyond Paradise*, 57).[20] At any rate, Novarro was aware of and participated in, albeit secretively, LA's queer culture during the 1920s.

Novarro's "rumored" homosexual encounters, affairs, and social dalliances raise a more complicated issue that puts contemporary queer historians at odds with one another. Though other rumors about Novarro, such as those just mentioned, get under some historians' skin, the most controversial rumor has to do with a gift Valentino's gave Novarro: a ceramic dildo. Ellenberger and Soares exemplify, to differing degrees, the historian's consternation over such undocumented events and pieces of evidence that have been cited as matter-of-fact (Mann, *Wisecracker*, 81).[21] Ellenberger and Soares go to some length in, first, distancing Valentino and Novarro from each other. Both refer to an interview from 1962 in which Novarro claims that he had only met Valentino once during his career (Ellenberger, *Ramón Novarro*, 15; Soares, *Beyond Paradise*, 20). This is not entirely true, as Ellenberger himself points out. A photograph exists from *The Four Horsemen of the Apocalypse* in which both actors share the frame with a large group from the cast. As an extra in the film, Novarro also dances in the background while Valentino tangoed (Ellenberger, *Ramón Novarro*, 15; Soares, *Beyond Paradise*, 26).

The matter that both biographers seek to dispel, however, is the "Art Deco dildo" that Valentino gave to Novarro "for his success in *Scaramouche*" (Ellenberger, *Ramón Novarro*, 15). For some queers, the dildoic objet d'art carries a long-standing fascination and gossipy credibility in its relationship to Novarro's murder, which took place on Halloween night 1968. The actor had invited—as he had on many occasions—two hustlers to his home. The night turned violent after the hustlers could not find a reported $5,000 that Novarro had stashed away. Novarro apparently pled for his life and recited the "Hail Mary" while he bled from his mouth after the boys rammed Valentino's gift down Novarro's throat. After trashing the house following their heinous crime, the hustlers fled. It took several days to make the arrest, and, of course (with the Manson murders competing for headlines), it caused quite a sensation.

Ellenberger, though less inflamed by the rumor of murder-by-ceramic-dildo than Soares, seeks to do away with the tawdry matter by turning to the deputy district attorney's statement, in which he insisted that no such objet d'art (ceramic or otherwise) was engaged as a weapon of choice. Soares, more vehemently, seeks to correct this "legend" that "apparently originated in 1975 with the publication of *Kenneth Anger's Hollywood Babylon*, a book filled with lurid and sensational stories, one of which has Valentino giving Novarro a black art-deco dildo that is later stuck down the actor's throat" by one of his killers (Soares, *Beyond Paradise*, 295). Armed with a battery of transcripts from the murder trial, Soares tells us that both "Paul and Tom Ferguson [the convicted murderers] angrily deny ever seeing such an object at Novarro's house" (295). He further depends upon a more recent biography of Natacha Rambova, from which he similarly pulls a quote from the Los Angeles prosecutor, who, again, insisted that no Art Deco dildo killed Novarro. Finally, Soares cites the coroner, quoted in the Rambova biography, to confirm that no dildo was "thrust down Novarro's throat" (295).

While Ellenberger grants that the legend of the dildo is apocryphal, he concedes that the (queerly) decadent pleasures associated with its salacious content ultimately supersede the authority of a materialist history that, once and for all, settles the record (see later in this essay). Soares, instead, waxes what can only be described as nostalgic for the studio-manufactured "Novarro," who was once "sold as the sensitive, philosophical, quasi-mystical film star. . . . For him to be chiefly remembered today as a perverted elderly homosexual killed by a sex toy that never existed is an injustice to both the complex individual and to the accomplished—and historically important—actor that was Ramón Novarro" (*Beyond Paradise*, 296–97).

Indeed. It is all the more clear, then, why the historian Anthony Slide in the foreword to Soares's book asserts, "With this biography, André Soares sets the record *straight*."[22] I do not wish to dismiss in toto the significance of material evidence and archival research that historians so rigorously assemble in order to recast prior "untruths" about their subject. There is something terribly ironic, however, in so earnestly setting the record "straight" when discussing a queer subject whose evidentiary remains are at best elusive and flimsy (this is, of course, the case for any figure put under the biographical microscope; an author's act of writing immediately renders the historical, as such, a failure of the "real"). Why should it worry Soares that "the dildo—more than *Ben-Hur, Scaramouche*, or *The Student Prince*—has been associated with the name Ramón Novarro for over a quarter century" (*Beyond Paradise*, 296)? Why is it better (more accurate?) to remember the "sensitive, philosophical, quasi-mystical film star" that MGM packaged and "sold" to its public (296)? Is it truly more valuable to consecrate the (reliable?) testimonies of state prosecutors and convicted murderers in order to contain the terms of history and pass judgment on its interpretation?

"Souvenirs Drenched in Blood"

It seems to me that "historian" Anger's approach to conjuring the tragic death of Novarro remains the most unrelentingly queer and, so, apt. This is to say, although Anger's recounting in *Hollywood Babylon* may employ what Soares refers to as "lurid and sensational" descriptions of the murder ("Here was a man dying, as he had lived, extravagantly, choked in his own blood"; Anger, *Hollywood Babylon*, 403), his Hollywood history expresses Anger's queer relationship with Hollywood and its scandals (his Hollywood history is, after all, entitled *Kenneth Anger's Hollywood Babylon*). "Two dumb beasts," Anger writes, "hustler brothers from Chicago, Paul and Tom Ferguson, chose October 31, Halloween, to play Death Angels for the sixty-nine-year-old Ben-Hur. All the boys wanted was his petty cash—$5000—which they'd heard from other hustler bums that Novarro kept hidden in his Hollywood Hills home. They tore the place apart, ripping to pieces the mementoes of his long career, which meant nothing to the greedy cretins. Souvenirs drenched in blood" (*Hollywood Babylon*, 403, 410). With this version, Anger does not plow through the voluminous "facts" (sixty-five hundred pages of transcripts) that Soares has gathered. To rehearse what he calls the "ghastly" murder, Anger, instead, plunges into the perverse pleasures of tabloid gossip and glamour that shaped the fantastical illusions about "Hollywood," the remains—*the texts*—in particular of a 1920s movie idol. How much different is Anger's writing from that of the tales the Hollywood apparatus and historians weave and reconfigure for a starry-eyed public? Are Anger's or Soares's historiographical methods so divergent from the publicity machine that manufactured the "historically important" *Ramón Novarro*? To what extent does the language of history, or what Hayden White refers to as "historiographical style," always already deceive the reader insofar as it purportedly satisfies access to "the truth" once and for all?[23]

Anger's methodology and style reveal precisely the trappings of the dream factory. To me, Anger evokes the "truth" of history insofar as it unveils history and biography as nothing more than an artificial exercise that grandly presents, packages, and neatly wraps its findings under the auspices of indisputable material truth. Anger's historiography points toward a methodology that intertwines with a long tradition of an aestheticized and embodied queer history. When Oscar Wilde, for example, defended Walter Pater from accusations that his *Studies in the History of the Renaissance* had "no relation to the conditions of the actual world," he argued that Pater's historical form is perfect precisely because it "can both reveal and conceal himself, and give form to every fancy, and reality to every mood." To be sure, Wilde praised Pater's writing of history since it fit snuggly with his own sense of an aestheticized historiography that necessarily did away with "the details of history, which are always wearisome and usually inaccurate."[24]

What, then, does queer historiography look like? Or, better, what does queer historiography *do*? Anger's recounting may employ what Soares refers to as "lurid and sensational" descriptions of the murder ("Here was a man dying, as he had lived, extravagantly, choked in his own blood") but he makes way for *his* queer relationship to Hollywood. For the queer historian, Hollywood history is a scandalously perverse one, not unlike the queer historian's own bodiliness. Anger reimagines a decadence that, in fact, the archival "data" suggests: Novarro found himself participating in not a few scurrilous activities. With his deviant queer eye, Anger-as-historian delivers a moral *and* aesthetic choice based on the "data" before him.

If, after a phone interview with Paul Ferguson in 1998 in which Ferguson confessed killing Novarro (thereby releasing his brother, Tom, from the crime), Soares concludes that the "fact that Paul has nothing to gain from assuming responsibility for Novarro's death gives credibility to his confession" (Soares, *Beyond Paradise*, 294–95), it does not necessarily follow that Anger's description of Novarro's death—so fervidly rejected by history's "straighteners"—is any less valid in its summation. Why is it necessary to dismiss the historical gossip manufactured by queers and for queers? Are we to applaud the authoritative gift that tells us that history is now straightened out, fait accompli, and teleologically set in stone once and for all because no reliable account proves a ceramic dildo ever existed? With Ferguson's confession and Soares's determination about the murderer's "credibility," does Anger's portrait of the "two beasts" no longer stand?

At the time of Novarro's death, a period riddled with assassinations, the eagerness to historically concretize public lives worried another queer, James Baldwin. When attempting to script a biopic about Malcolm X for Hollywood, he, not dissimilar to Anger, found himself struggling with star historiography. Baldwin ultimately looked askance at the currents that monumentalized great figures through turgid historical formats. He, instead, viewed history as a life-giving force; Baldwin did not want to be, in other words, "party to a second assassination" of X.[25] For him, it was neither possible nor desirable to entomb the dead and, therefore, the life force that that death inaugurated.

As a writer in search of a distinctive writing style that eschewed the portrayal of life and history as a strict cause-and-effect narrative (i.e., the Hollywood biopic), Baldwin hoped to locate a "new language" for cultural queerness.[26] This new language, which he continually experimented with and developed, sought to penetrate the violent inscription of the (white, heterosexual) historical as it tears into queer Black bodies and to expose the scars "engraved" on those bodies. Baldwin's eloquent vision for a new language brings to the surface at once the tender and violated skin of queer history. As such, Baldwin reworked the dominant language to express the ambiguities that ultimately shape the fragilely constructed contours of race, sexuality, and nation.

For all Ellenberger's concern about the ceramic-dildo tale, he aptly summarizes the discursive contours that surround Novarro's death: "There are many who still wish to believe this legend and the supposed relationship between the two Latin Lovers, and no amount of evidence will dispel that" (*Ramón Novarro*, 15). Alternatively, to breathe a sigh of relief, as Slide does because he believes the historical record has been set "straight," is rather discomfiting since it suggests that history need be or should be controlled and properly managed.

Who decides and for whom is it decided?

Teatro Intimo

Novarro's home, located at 2265 West Twenty-Second Street at Gramercy Place in the West Adams district of Los Angeles, was purchased around 1924. He landed this estate following his first successes with Ingram and Metro-Goldwyn, for which he was paid handsomely. According to Soares, Novarro involved himself with every detail of his first Hollywood-star home, where he lived with his family; he designed his oversized bedroom and bath in "a mixture of modern and traditional Mexican furniture decorated with religious artifacts, among them a crown of thorns" (*Beyond Paradise*, 66). With additional land secured on either side of the house, Novarro built a swimming pool and tennis court. If, recalling Mann's description of Novarro as the actor who avoided publicity by hiding from it, 2265 West Twenty-Second Street at Gramercy Place became the ideal hideaway, Novarro's compound, during the 1920s, served well as an escape from what he viewed as the illusory and perfunctory world of the movies. Perfectly enclosed with the relics of his past and immediate present—the religious to the modern, the marionettes given to him by his mother, the "secret" lovers he housed for extended periods, the crown of thorns that filled out his bedroom décor, and perhaps an unmentionable gift from a fellow heartthrob—Novarro earnestly hoped to satiate his transcendent creative energies while perfecting the multiple performances that were his trademark.

But the centerpiece of the house was El Teatro Intimo that Novarro built in 1926. Until his death, this room occupied the silent-film star's public image (until, of course, Kenneth Anger changed all that in 1975). The final sentence in the *New York Times* report on Novarro's death, for instance, stated, "In the large home he acquired at stardom's peak, he had a full-sized theater and often did marionette shows for his guests."[27] "Within its cream-tinted plaster walls," Soares describes, "the [sixty-five-seat] theater boasted an orchestra pit for twelve musicians, a stage for a company of thirty, overhead lighting, electrically controlled curtains, and underground dressing rooms" (*Beyond Paradise*, 116). The Hollywood star's home theater, however, neglected two objects of note: a projector and a movie screen. "In my Hollywood home," Novarro divulges in *Theatre Magazine*, "I have a theatre intime accommodating sixty guests. When people first see it, they invariably exclaim: 'Oh, a projection room in your home.' 'No.' I emphatically reply, 'pictures never enter this theatre.'"[28]

Hence, Novarro's "intimate theater," annexed directly to his and his family's living space, clearly announced, as noted earlier, the "movie star's" ambivalent sentiments toward his Hollywood career. Novarro made it perfectly clear that the theater "is for chamber music and other musical programs that [he] give[s] two or three times a year, called the Ramón Revue. . . . It is so delightful! So soul-satisfying!" With the construction of the theater, Novarro enabled himself to return to the very experiences that "brought forgiveness from his mother": music. For Novarro, music "is the most subtle, the most evanescent of all the arts."[29] Had Novarro expanded his imagination somewhat, he might have made similar claims about the shadows on the screen. Such imaginative possibilities did not cross his mind.

At Novarro's house, then, he successfully "compartmentalized" his life and "morals" (professional, family, and sexual), as Soares neatly puts it, while fusing them—at his own behest—with the Teatro Intimo. Soares's biography illustrates this commingling of disparate worlds with a marvelous photograph taken in 1933 at a "Ramón Revue" (*Beyond Paradise*, 117).[30] The snapshot is of Novarro's Hollywood world during the period when it began to crumble. In the photo, we see members of his family as well as his industry colleagues, including Cary Grant, Randolph Scott, Myrna Loy, Jeanette MacDonald, Irving Thalberg, Norma Shearer, Cedric Gibbons, Dolores Del Rio, James Whale, Gloria Swanson, Ray Milland, Adrian, Alice Terry, John Gilbert, and, most appositely, an ex-nun and a priest-to-be. The photo, in effect, reveals the elusive ideals to which Novarro so troublingly and desperately clung. It further suggests the myriad intermingling among lives and the at once possible and impossible historical knowledges that the photograph might yield. Since Novarro felt himself at odds with his Hollywood coterie and the art they produced (or didn't produce, as he saw it), why invite this world of philistines to witness a display of his "true" creative self? Who in this room slept with whom, and what creative energies were exploited and energized because of all this star-fucking? At the same time, why build this theatrical space to show off his mother's gifts (marionettes) and musical talent (another gift about which his mother insisted) to a group of people who, from Novarro's perspective, were not properly attuned to the finer arts or the sacred dimensions of family and religion?

At once a naïve and strategic actor on and off the screen, Novarro perfected a multivalenced performance in which duplicity proved to be the truth of who he was. The actor's Teatro Intimo, perhaps, most fully represents the dimensions of Novarro's queer Hollywood life. His theatrical—indeed, *theatricized*—space put on display Novarro's bewildered self. It was, in other words, the "safe space" where he, in disguised form, wrestled with his paradoxical ideals and desires. Ramón Novarro's beloved Teatro Intimo allowed for his performance of a queer self, beautifully and tragically rehearsed for all to see. Who, then, more mischievous than the likes of Anger to spin a yarn in which so many tales reveal the star's secrets, hidden gems, and disguised objects of temptation? As it turns out, Anger provides something more than "straightening" the facts. The queer historiographer aptly renders what queers have always performed so marvelously: the art of deception.

Notes

1   Dyer, *Heavenly Bodies*, 18. My thanks to Dan Humphrey and his colleagues for inviting me to present this work to students and faculty in the Film Studies program at Texas A&M.

2   Dyer, *Stars*, 184–85.

3   Terry, "Theorizing Deviant Historiography," 56.

4   Terry, 71.

5   Dyer, *Stars*, 185.

6   I'd like to thank Charles Silver at the Museum of Modern Art for arranging screenings and research material for this essay, as well as Joe McElhaney for making available his video collection. Moreover, I am grateful to Patrice Petro for her unwavering support for this essay when others had not seen its value.

7   The biographical information I cite may be found in the following works: O'Leary, *Rex Ingram*, 96; Ellenberger, *Ramón Novarro*, 24–25; Soares, *Beyond Paradise*, 42–43; Chávez, "Ramón Is Not One Of These." Further references to these works are cited parenthetically in the text.

8   Studlar, "Valentino, 'Optic Intoxication,' and Dance Madness," 27, 24.

9   The tale often told regarding the change from Samaniego to Novarro is that Novarro and the studio felt that his real name sounded like "ham and eggs" when Americans uttered it (Ellenberger, *Ramón Novarro*, 24; Soares, *Beyond Paradise*, 36). Earlier, Novarro dropped the accented *o* in Ramón. The first film to appear with the stage name "Ramón Novarro" was *Trifling Women* (1922; now considered lost).

10 "Novarro in New Talkie," 15.

11 The dialogue and action in *Daybreak*'s seduction scene, in which Kasder carries on a conversation with his love interest while running alongside her carriage, is worth noting. Helen says that he shouldn't "go around pretending to be people's cousin" to, in effect, seduce her: "I think you're perfectly depraved." Kasder then feigns illness and falls from the frame as the carriage continues on its way, causing Helen to be concerned about his health, which, in turn, leads her to invite him into her carriage. Miraculously, Kasder/Novarro quickly recovers.

12 Novarro, "From Screen to Concert Stage," 27.

13 Faderman and Timmons, *Gay L.A.*, 9. Further references to this work are cited parenthetically in the text.

14 Bhabha, "Freedom's Basis in the Indeterminate," 48.

15 H. White, *Metahistory*, 430, 433 (emphasis in original).

16 Mann, *Wisecracker*, 106. Further references to this work are cited parenthetically in the text.

17 Novarro, "From Screen to Concert Stage," 27.

18 Oral history, Margaret Herrick Library of the Academy of Motion Picture Arts and Sciences, quoted in Mann, 107.

19 Mann suggests otherwise and that Novarro and Haines entirely ignored Mayer's dictate. Haines's brother, Henry, told Mann that he remembered Novarro spending time at Haines's house in Santa Monica in the late 1920s (*Wisecracker*, 83).

20 See, further, Lambert, *Nazimova*.

21 Also, most infamously, Kenneth Anger in *Kenneth Anger's Hollywood Babylon*, 403. Further references to this work are cited parenthetically in the text.

22 Slide, foreword to Soares, *Beyond Paradise*, xi (emphasis mine).

23 H. White, *Metahistory*, 29.

24 See the revised version of my "Queer Angels . . . ," chapter 4 in this volume.

25 Baldwin, *No Name in the Street*, 11. Derrida strikes similar notes in "The Deaths of Roland Barthes."

26 Binder, "James Baldwin, an Interview," 208.

27 "Ramón Novarro Slain on Coast," 43.

28 Novarro, "From Screen to Concert Stage," 27.

29 Novarro, 27.

30 A complete guest list for this event can be found in Soares, *Beyond Paradise*, 350.

HOW DO WE LOOK SO FAR?

Notes toward a Queer Film Philosophy

I.

In *Elegy for Theory*, D. N. Rodowick teases out the diaphanous yet paradoxically opaque relationship between *theory* and *philosophy*. Rodowick argues that "the concept of theory has a long pedigree in the history of philosophy, where theory is often in contest or competition with philosophy." At the same time, theory and philosophy share a historical impulse toward meditation, contemplation. By the early nineteenth century, the intimate, commingled relation frayed when aesthetics and science (à la Hegel) arrived on the scene. The "boundaries [that mark theory, philosophy, aesthetics, and science]," Rodowick concludes, "are unstable, fluid, and often blurred and indiscernible or exchangeable." In short, "it may be that our relation to theory always has been, and perhaps always will be, contingent and historical."[1]

Similarly, Matthew Tinkcom reminds us, "Queer theory can thus be understood as asking questions that are historical and questions that are philosophical, and the two modes of question are interrelated and inform each other."[2] In his study that bridges theory and the film *Brokeback Mountain* (dir. Ang Lee, 2006), Tinkcom's remarks raise the provocative specter that haunts Rodowick's concept of theory: theory itself is nothing less than queer. In its very writing, queer theory—and, by extension, queer film theory—dramatizes the relation between theory and philosophy *as* supple, unsettling, troublesome, and "contingent."

As a mode of writing, queer (film) theory expresses the slippage between theory and philosophy, between the abstract and the material. *Écriture* cannot be overlooked for queer theorists. In a tradition stretching back to Oscar Wilde's aesthetic decadence (deconstruction *avant la lettre*), queer theorists delight in heightening theory, in making perverse, consecrated theoretical discourses that assert absolutes. Queer theory tears at the seams of discourse, where heteronormative ideology disappears into the crevices of language. Queer theory plays a game of hide-and-seek with hetero-ideology; it unmasks its partnership with language that asserts itself as common sense. Theory is therefore queer because it denaturalizes language. Queer theory lays bare the (heterocentric) device.

All along, queer theorists have embraced theory precisely because the language of theory is queer. It is performative. When theoretical language is referred to as "jargon," queer theorists, *like* feminists, remind their critics that to use commonsense terminology or a popular vernacular is to participate in the very logocentric discourse that forbids queer *écriture*.[3] And since, as Derrida reminds us, *écriture* extends itself beyond the limitation of the pen, (queer) film theorists write in relationship to a malleable art form—cinema.[4] For queer-film theorists, this is vital since it keeps in play queer theory, more generally, as a critically vibrant adventure.

What, then, does queer film theory propose? Is it enough for the queer-film theorist to state, "I will queer a film"? If so, what does such a "queer" activity involve? How does one know whether one has successfully "queered" a text? What film language—*ciné-écriture*—provocatively, *yet* "contingently," theorizes the relation between "queer" and film? And if queer film *écriture* is meant to keep things on the move, what are the risks for queer (film) theory becoming institutionalized in the halls of academia and, to be sure, popular culture? When, B. Ruby Rich announces in her essay "New Queer Cinema" that "queer [was] hot" at international film festivals during the early 1990s and that it showcased "art for *our* sake," did her newly minted categorization—"new queer cinema"—simultaneously signal its own death knell? What, on the one hand, are the implications when the enthusiasm for the "queer film phenomenon" successfully "[renegotiates] subjectivities, [annexes] whole genres, [and revises] histories in their image"?[5] On the other hand, what are the challenges when that enthusiasm is subsumed into deep pockets of consumer culture?

Indeed, it would be foolish to claim that queer (film) theory bypasses culture-industry ideology or to insist that it is immune to capitalist absorption. The culture industry breeds and reproduces itself through "radical" difference. It quickly and seductively packages cultural variations under the sign of the "new," brilliantly marketing identity difference as if it were a new model of automobile. Insofar as the culture industry depends on reproducibility through difference, it is driven by heteronormative ideology. This is to say, heteronormative and culture-industry ideologies work hand in hand since their fusion profits by the wish to sustain a progressive future. The "new" requires negation. How might queer (film) theory resist such appropriation? "Queer theory's opposition is precisely to any such logic of opposition," Lee Edelman argues; "its proper task [is] the ceaseless disappropriation of every propriety."[6] To be on the move, therefore, does not necessarily mean progress. Queer-film theory's movement is more akin to an unexpected pulsation or a disconcerting tremor.

The Archive. Representation. Deconstruction. Feminism. Psychoanalysis. Identification. Identity. Modes of address. Camp. And so on. Arguably, precisely because the cinema is a multimedia art form, it lends itself to wide-ranging methodological and theoretical investigations. In this way, cinema studies pairs well with queer theory's core commitment to interdisciplinarity. The cinema, however, provides something else for queer theory: movement. Because the heart of cinema's conceptualization sits squarely in its relation to movement, the idea of the cinematic benefits queer theory's "proper task [for] ceaseless disappropriation of every propriety." With queer film theory on the move, the aporia it invariably reaches is the fertile meeting ground where queer film theory discovers its critical energy. If, as Tinkcom rightly claims, "the condensation of the categories of lesbian-gay-bisexual-trans-queer into the now institutionalized abbreviation 'LGBTQ' . . . might seem to dissolve the differences among those names," then it is crucial to "[*derive*] *its energies*" at the theoretical impasse ("those very tensions," to use Tinkcom's phrasing).[7] Indeed, the aporia appears as the layover site where queer identities and queer thought gather and then move on. Queer film theory is thus a philosophical inquiry in which concepts unfold, disrupt, and regenerate because of uniquely erotic and political circumstances.

II.

From where does queer film theory launch? What are its activating and, to be sure, active antecedents? It is commonplace to mark Teresa de Lauretis's essay "Queer Theory: Lesbian and Gay Sexualities, an Introduction" as the work that introduced the term "queer theory." Her essay is also significant for its place in film and media studies. Published in the journal *differences* (derived from the proceedings of a conference held in February 1990 at the University of California, Santa Cruz), de Lauretis does not directly address film, which is nevertheless her academic métier. Instead, her essay focuses on the broader implications for academic queer theory. The essay asks how differing sexualities and gender identities might be theorized and "*imaged*"; it describes the work in the edited collection as "intended to articulate the terms in which lesbian and gay sexualities may be *understood and imaged as forms of resistance to cultural homogenization*, counteracting dominant discourses with other constructions of the subject in culture."[8] Coming from a highly regarded scholar in film and feminist studies, and by emphasizing a conceptualization of sexuality through imaging, de Lauretis's contribution to queer theory can thus be viewed as coterminous with her work in gender and cinema studies.

Indeed, de Lauretis's participation in an earlier 1989 conference at Anthology Film Archives in New York resulted in the publication *How Do I Look? Queer Film and Video*.[9] Focusing on the film *She Must Be Seeing Things* (dir. Sheila McLaughlin, 1987), de Lauretis forcefully argues that to reimagine cinematic looks—via the camera, the filmmaker, and the spectator—is to, in fact, queer the gaze.[10] Alex Doty notes in his review of *How Do I Look?* that de Lauretis opens "a search for queer desire, representation, and spectatorship as distinct from lesbianism (or gayness) expressed from within, or in relation to, various straight paradigms."[11] For de Lauretis, theorizing queer sexualities and gender cannot be "understood," therefore, without analyzing the way they are cinematically "imaged."

Although de Lauretis marks the entry of "queer theory" into academic parlance, identifying historical "firsts" is nevertheless a bit troublesome. She undoubtedly deserves recognition as the premier scholar who rigorously integrated and transformed feminist theory and queer theory into queer film theory. But an overview of queer-film philosophy would be remiss if it did not mark earlier queer-film theorizing, in advance of what we now refer to as queer film theory. Alfred Kléber (aka the filmmaker and theorist Jean Epstein) and the cultural critic Parker Tyler both conceptualized their own queer sexual desire as critical components to their film theories. And, like Epstein, Sergei Eisenstein redirected his homosexual impulses into his cinematic theories, which invariably wended their way into his filmmaking and drawings.[12] Germaine Dulac, Tami Williams points out, introduced queer sensibilities in her films through content and form, while Judith Mayne reveals the 1930s Hollywood director Dorothy Arzner through the lens of lesbian auteurism.[13]

Studies in camp are also a major precursor to queer film theory. Hollywood films are high on the list for scholars of camp, since it is through these texts that camp icons reigned supreme (Judy Garland, Bette Davis, Joan Crawford). Richard Dyer's *Heavenly Bodies: Film Stars and Society* (London: Macmillan, 1986) and anthologies such as *Campgrounds: Style and Homosexuality* (edited by David Bergman; Amherst: University of Massachusetts Press, 1993), with its assortment of early essays devoted to camp theories from the 1970s and 1980s, set the stage for concepts such as the "performative" that would soon appear in the pages of 1990s queer film theory.

Finally, it is important to note that "queer film theory" follows in the wake of conceptual frameworks designed by queer artists of color. Anticipating a later generation's use of language to express queer desire as mobile and malleable, queers of color engaged the cinema-*as*-place and cinema-*as*-concept so as to design a cinematic language that could blunt the presumptive whiteness that permeates the terms for sexuality. In the 1980s, for instance, Gloria Anzaldúa consistently turned to cinematic metaphors to channel her lived experience as a queer-feminist Chicana.[14] Earlier, James Baldwin experimented with cinematic language to render multiracial characters who discovered a sexual awakening in cinematic places (movie theaters in particular).[15]

The professionalization of queer theory as an academic enterprise, particularly in North America and the United Kingdom, took hold throughout the 1990s. In short time, academic presses—particularly Duke University Press and the quasi-academic press Routledge—poured queer volume after queer volume into university libraries, as well as independent and national bookstores. Edited collections were assembled that, in part or in whole, analyzed film through the vernacular of queer theory. Anthologies from the period that brought film and queer theory together include include *Inside/Out: Lesbian Theories, Gay Theories* (edited by Diana Fuss; New York: Routledge, 1991); *Queer Looks: Perspectives on Lesbian and Gay Film and Video* (edited by Martha Gever, John Greyson, Pratibha Parmar; New York: Routledge, 1993); and *Out Takes: Essays on Queer Theory and Film* (edited by Ellis Hanson; Durham, NC: Duke University Press, 1999). At the same time, numerous monographs authored by smart and eager queer theorists flooded the marketplace. Among the many monographs that supported the new discipline were key works that either reinvigorated or launched academic careers: *Now You See It: Studies on Lesbian and Gay Film* (by Richard Dyer; London: Routledge, 1990); *Homographesis: Essays in Gay Literary and Cultural Theory* (by Lee Edelman; New York: Routledge, 1994); *Bike Boys, Drag Queens, and Superstars: Avant-Garde, Mass Culture, and Gay Identities in the 1960s Underground Cinema* (by Juan Suárez; Bloomington: Indiana University Press, 1996); and *Uninvited: Classical Hollywood Cinema and Lesbian Representability* (by Patricia White; Bloomington: Indiana University Press, 1999).[16]

La fin du vingtième siècle proved to be a watershed moment for queer film theory. A perspicacious group of thinkers reconceived academic disciplines and, in doing so, revised—sometimes controversially—the long-standing principles to which traditional disciplines had become inured. In this way, queer theory captured the imagination of young doctoral candidates and newly minted junior faculty, as well as seasoned full professors. In many ways, film studies was the most inviting discipline for the queer-academic shake-up. Why? From its beginnings as a scholarly pursuit and, as noted earlier, because the cinema crosses multimedia platforms, the discipline maintained an "open-door" policy to its conceptual approaches. For many scholars, this is a draw, while for others, it identifies cinema's second-class status in academia. Moreover, cinema studies deal in an expressive art form that evaporates with its very presentation; nonetheless, it is an affective and materially realized art form. Because philosophy of queer theory reformulates theoretical language so as to express abstract, if not *inexpressible* as such, experiences around the materialization of queer sexual desire, queer film theory provocatively "images" the complexities of sexual desire. And though the philosophy of cinema that shores up queer theory is mired in heteronormativity and culture-industry ideologies, it has nothing to do with procreation and everything to do with pleasure.

Yet the excitement generated around queer theory and queer film theory occurred in direct relationship to political urgency: AIDS and a feminist movement at risk. The critique of "second-wave" feminists by "third-wave" feminists who emerged during the 1980s allowed for 1990s queer and feminist theorists to reconceive the historical and ideological terms for gender identity, sexual desire, and race. By fusing 1970s second-wave feminism (poststructuralism, psychoanalysis, and sexual difference) with 1980s third-wave feminism (cultural studies, race theory, and gender identity), a fresh eye was turned toward the theoretical terms for gender, race, class, and sexual desire. To be sure, the theoretical and political tenets associated with feminism served as critical tools for queer theory and, as it turns out, intersected with AIDS activism.

The stakes were—indeed, *are*—high. As the AIDS crisis unfolded during the 1980s, women's rights were simultaneously under threat. Conservative Republicans and Tories ignored or did little to fight AIDS, while anti-choice movements such as Operation Rescue in the United States blocked women's clinics and raised the volume on their homophobic rhetoric. Again, highlighting the critical link between historical materiality and the abstract conditions of ideology, feminists and queers took to direct action and theoretical concepts. On the streets and in the academy, scholars fended off bodies that blocked abortion clinics, while their comrades scattered the ashes of loved ones on the front lawn of the White House. (As I write these pages, texts and emails from the Human Rights Campaign [HRC] reaffirm its commitment to Planned Parenthood. Following years in which gay marriage drove gay and lesbian political interests—under the auspices of beltway organizations such as the HRC itself—the link between LGBTQ rights and women's reproductive rights is forced into the spotlight again, especially with the conservative Supreme Court falling into place as of 2018.)[17]

The implications for film and video theory were immediate during the 1980s and 1990s. Queer-feminist activists, like feminists before them, wrestled with content and form. What were the aesthetic/political consequences for queer filmmaking? Although content was relatively easy to agree on (people were dying, laws were passed to stymie women's rights), the matter over *how* to represent this content remained highly contentious.

III.

The central force that defines the philosophical currents that give rise to queer film theory is without question the political and cultural stakes raised around AIDS activism. By the time ACT UP was founded in March 1987, AIDS had taken its toll on gay men in the United States. The first cases were reported in 1981. By the end of 1984, 7,699 AIDS cases and 3,655 AIDS deaths were reported in the United States. By the end of 1987, as AIDS activism moved into full gear, the World Health Organization reported 71,751 AIDS cases in eighty-five countries, with an estimated five to ten million people living with HIV.[18] The impact on the gay community—across racial and class boundaries—precipitated a cinematic response that was as emotionally charged as it was politically driven. Collective queer mourning generated wide-ranging creative-media responses that were meant to shatter what had become the activist's mantra against government inaction: Silence = Death.

In a collection of essays titled *AIDS: Cultural Analysis/Cultural Activism*, the contributors considered the ways media representations of AIDS (video, the press, photography, and so on) were entangled in hetero-inflected discourse. The collection, edited by Douglas Crimp and published by MIT Press in 1987, opened the discussion on what counted as queer images.[19] What use of media at once expressed political acumen and collective and personal grieving, while signaling a break from hypermediated hetero-ideology? How was one to decipher "good" from "bad" queer images? Engaged this way, representations of the disease were revealed as spectacles shaped by homophobic ideology, in which—among other things—AIDS was stigmatized as the "gay disease." This did not mean, however, that a consensus was formed around "queer" representation.

Nevertheless, what was agreed on was that homophobia unconsciously and consciously permeated media institutions. Hence, because gay men practiced anal sex, AIDS was posited through a malicious cause-and-effect scenario: homosexual sex = transmission of AIDS. For all the political and scientific pushback that argued that HIV also spread through heterosexual sex and intravenous drug use, the homophobic narrative quickly cemented itself in the public's imaginary. Leo Bersani's radical essay "Is the Rectum a Grave?" (included in Crimp's anthology) forcefully ripped open the psychical dimensions behind heteromasculine homophobia, which framed the discussion around AIDS, HIV prevention, and government funding.

Crimp's important anthology went some way to greatly altering the terms for queer representation and aesthetic form. In an essay published soon after *AIDS: Cultural Analysis/Cultural Activism*, Crimp's "Mourning and Militancy" was another significant intervention. I quote this passage in full since it resonates with the cultural drives that gave shape to the creative energies surrounding AIDS activism, energies that politicized and aestheticized loss:

> Seldom has a society so savaged a people during their hour of loss. "We look upon any interference with [mourning] as inadvisable or harmful," warns Freud. But for anyone living daily with the AIDS crisis, ruthless interference with our bereavement is as ordinary an occurrence as reading the *New York Times*. The violence we encounter is relentless, the violence of silence and omission almost as impossible to endure as the violence of unleashed hatred and outright murder. Because this violence desecrates the memories of our dead, we rise in anger to vindicate them. For many of us, mourning *becomes* militancy.[20]

And yet the question remained: What does mourning *as* militancy look like in the work of art? How does one represent loss and anger through the filter of politicized identity? Filmmakers and video makers took the creative and intellectual challenge to the heart of their political activism.

The activists' cinematic and theoretical responses made for vigorous debate and a magnificent array of film and video. Indeed, the theoretical inquiry into what amounted to a proper political aesthetic for queer film became an international debate among queers. If agreement existed that *cinematic representations* of queers and HIV/AIDS were problematic in film (to say the least), arguments over *cinematic form* proved even more intense and acrimonious. While some film- and video makers turned to avant-garde traditions to shape queer images (Bertolt Brecht, Kenneth Anger, Jack Smith, Andy Warhol, and Barbara Hammer were exemplary), others relied on the generic and narrative norms associated with classical Hollywood or playfully toyed with them. On the one hand, Jean Carlomusto, Ellen Spiro, Alexandra Juhasz, Rosa von Praunheim, David Wojnarowicz, Gregg Bordowitz, Barbara Hammer, and the collective Damned Interfering Video Activists (DIVA-TV) took their political and aesthetic cues from feminist film theory, generic codes of documentary, and experimental filmmaking. On the other, queer filmmakers such as John Greyson merged Hollywood genre (including tropes from the musical) with experimental form in such films as *Zero Patience* (1993).

Queer theorists also took strong positions on the matter, especially where the "AIDS film" was concerned. Writing with hindsight in 2006, Chris Bell's and Robin Griffith's entries in the *Routledge International Encyclopedia of Queer Culture* demonstrate the theoretical tensions that were, and remain, active for what defines "queer cinema."[21] "To be sure," Bell writes, "there is often a vast difference between 'mainstream' films and 'independent' films about AIDS—the former frequently obfuscate issues of race, class and gender (see *It's My Party* [Kleiser, 1996] and *Long-time Companion* [René, 1989]), while the latter often foreground these very issues (*Tongues Untied* [Riggs, 1989])." In whatever form the films take, Bell argues, "the American AIDS film has worked as a tool for AIDS prevention as well as for compassion, encouraging the audience to act decisively in terms of support for the everyday necessities of people with the disease, as well as working towards stemming the tide of new HIV infections." He concludes, "In either case—as a form of mainstream, narrative entertainment or a call to action—the AIDS film has proven an important cultural response to the disease."[22]

Robin Griffiths's entry in the encyclopedia represents what he sees as a more nefarious ideological concern with, especially, American queer cinema. As such, and in his short essay, "New Queer Cinema, International," Griffiths holds out hope for international filmmakers against the tide of global capitalism and its absorption of queer cinema:

> Like the United States during the 1990s, queer filmmaking across the globe has evolved, albeit in multifarious ways, in response to both the AIDS crisis and the oppressive transcultural social representational regimes of a restrictively policed, mainstream, right-wing hetero-normativity. But rather than become absorbed into the cinematic cultural *Zeitgeist* of pre-millennial late capitalism, as did the likes of Todd Haynes, Gus Van Sant, *et al.*, international queer cinema has maintained its commitment to explore national and cultural specificity in its negotiations of queerness that resist both the universalist narrative of gay liberation/cultural assimilation and the commodification of a transnational queer culture, aesthetics, and politics.[23]

The jury remains out over what constitutes "accurate" queer images and, indeed, cinematic sounds.[24] Yet, perhaps, the jury *remaining out* is precisely that which "energizes" the aporia where queer film theory negotiates hetero-ideology and where it works to understand the images called "queer." The editors of *Critical Visions in Film Theory* make the case this way: "though film viewers are positioned by the gendered language and dynamics of desire deployed by the movies, they are also able to fantasize other possibilities."[25]

IV.

"Fantasy is the mise-en-scène of desire."[26] Laplanche and Pontalis's well-rehearsed axiom delivered the terms for feminist film theory in such a way as to open perverse, pleasurable, and problematic possibilities for analyzing narrative cinema. Because Hollywood is wrapped in ideological paradox, feminist-film scholars such as Elizabeth Cowie and Kaja Silverman resisted any oversimplified theoretical dismissal of the industry's firm commitment to narrative-driven cinemas. Instead, they placed their sights on Lacanian theory precisely for the paradoxes it unveils.[27] Not subscribing to a celebration of, nor a refusal to reckon with, the "culture industry," feminist-film scholars set out to grasp the ideological and psychoanalytical tensions that bear on the representation of women as well as their role as spectator.

By refusing hasty judgments on the spectacle—an event that purportedly confined women to the deleterious effects associated with the cinematic apparatus—the likes of Cowie and Silverman (and, as noted, de Lauretis) prepared the way for feminist-queer film theorists such as Lauren Berlant and Lee Edelman.[28] Edelman's deconstructive legerdemain, in *Homographesis* and *No Future*, uniquely reimagines the queer dynamic at work in classical Hollywood cinema. His sensual and playful penetration, his tearing into the queer seams at the outer reaches of *Laura* (dir. Otto Preminger, 1944) and *North by Northwest* (dir. Alfred Hitchcock, 1959), perversely delights in the phantasmatic where the "mise-en-scène of [queer] desire" unfolds. In Edelman's hands, Derridean and Lacanian *écriture* is choreographed in a magisterial *pas de deux*. He is, therefore, less concerned with "queer" representation than with the ways a text *fails* to abide the ideology of reproducibility. Edelman's theoretical snake dance charms the reader by drawing out a film's queer, disturbing textual spell.

Camp also makes its return through queer cinematic fantasy as unpacked through feminist psychoanalysis. By 2000, Brett Farmer reminded us that, first, a "gay camp reading emphasizes how the excessive female star-image recodes the star performance *as a performance*, a masquerade that does not correspond to the subjectivity on which it is played." In conjuring camp's historical imprint and fusing it with the language of feminist semiotic and psychoanalytic theory ("masquerade," "subjectivity"), Farmer complicates gay-male subjectivity. "In relation to issues of gender and sexual categorization," he concludes, "the effects of this gay camp reading of the star performance as artifactual masquerade denaturalize and destabilize hegemonic visions of gender as anatomically fixed and instead instate a polysemic scenario of gender ambivalence and queer transgressions." Second, echoing the remarks cited earlier by the editors of *Critical Visions in Film Theory*, Farmer emphasizes that camp readings "allow gay spectators not only to project and affirm their own psychocultural 'experiences' of sexual ambivalence and gender dissonance but also to articulate their own fantasmatic productions of regendered desire."[29] In effect, through the filters of camp and feminist psychoanalysis, Farmer critiques the idea that the masculine cinematic spectator is far from always heterocentric.[30]

The relationship between classic camp and queer theory, therefore, puts into relief the very paradoxical elements queer theorists highlight when studying Hollywood cinema. The "entertainment" industry is rendered queer precisely because it functions as ideological containment while, and precisely for this reason, it generates pleasure.[31] Interconnected as such, camp/queer theory during the 1990s redirected its critical light onto the perverse aesthetic and narrative turns that John Waters, Bruce La Bruce, and Cheryl Dunye bring to Hollywood's generic formulas. What is distinctive, with these three filmmakers, is that they illustrate the textual surface on unrevealed sexual, gendered, and racial desires that queer spectators often translate when "reading" Hollywood cinema. Recent *rereadings* of *The Boys in the Band* (dir. William Friedkin, 1970) through queer critical discourse and filmmaking confirm the point.[32] Whether described as "to camp" or "to queer," new textual and historical encounters occur. "The work," the "author-creator," and the spectator frolic with one another in Rabelaisian delight, yielding unanticipated readings of the text.[33]

Matthew Tinkcom's *Working like a Homosexual* astutely draws attention to this productively pleasurable force derived from Hollywood cinema. Through a Marxist reading, Tinkcom "explore[s] camp as a philosophy in its own right, one that offers explanations of how the relation between labor and the commodity is lived in the day-to-day by dissident sexual subjects who arrive at their own strategies for critique *and* pleasure."[34] Writing postmillennium, Farmer's and Tinkcom's books thus ushered in twenty-first-century queer film theory through fresh readings of feminist Marxism and Freudianism. Queer-film theorists thereby *make queer* their fellow feminists' work. To paraphrase remarks made by Thomas Elsaesser and Élisabeth Roudinesco (albeit in other, but nonetheless related, contexts), queer theorists bring plague to the Hollywood home by inviting Marx and Freud to the table.[35]

Indeed, it is seductive (and not incorrect) to surmise that feminists and queers embrace Continental philosophy, particularly as it is filtered through French postwar theory. Sudhir Hazareesingh suggests that the trademark for French thinking involves a love for "conceptual juggling acts [that] have produced delicious oxymorons and nourished yet another cherished feature of Gallic thinking: the love of paradox."[36]

Intertwining the critical discourses of camp and "grand theory" (often derogatorily dismissed as "pretentious") is certainly a "delicious . . . juggling act."[37] But there is something more. Queer-film theorists understand writing as a performative. It is an act deeply entwined with the bodies in which they live. Whether through Lacan, Foucault, Deleuze, or Derrida—to name only four highly recognized names—queer theorists toggle between the corporeal and psychical dimensions of pleasure and pain. They rigorously play in the unsettling crosshairs where Eros and Thanatos convene. And because the cinematic apparatus prompts sensual and decadent pleasure precisely through its phenomenon *as* apparatus, the cinema is a "desiring machine."[38] The cinematic apparatus thus enables a site for desire, or, specifically, it enables a site where desire may be imaged as the death drive. Queer theory is a theory of *jouissance*.

V.

In 1995, while at the "Lesbian and Gay History" conference at the Graduate Center at the City University of New York, Susan Stryker recognized a glaring omission about the panelists: "From my perspective, with a recently claimed transsexual identity, [the conference's "intellectual stars"] all looked pretty much the same: like nontransgender people. A new wave of transgender scholarship, part of a broader queer intellectual movement was, by that point in time, already a few years old. Why were there no transgender speakers on the panel? Why was the entire discussion of 'gender diversity' subsumed within a discussion of sexual desire—as if the only reason to express gender was to signal the mode of one's attractions and availabilities to potential sex partners?" Confronted by, at best, dismissal and, at worst, outright disgust by gay liberationists in the audience who hailed from the Stonewall era, Stryker listened to a diatribe from an activist who railed against "transsexuals" who believed they belonged to the "new queer politics." And because, the activist continued, "transsexuals . . . were profoundly psychopathological individuals who mutilated their bodies and believed in oppressive gender stereotypes and held reactionary political views," they were intent on "destroying" the gay and lesbian movement. For Stryker, this was an "iconic moment in [her] public life." She firmly responded that she "was not sick" and need not listen to such reactionary and oversimplified politicized noise. Stryker, however, was invigorated by the moment because she publicly presented a "new interpretation of gender diversity" to a queer audience.[39]

Ten years later (2005) and in the same auditorium at a conference titled "Trans Politics, Social Change, and Justice," Stryker heard again—*from the same liberationist, no less*—that "a new transgender hegemony" now pushed a "revisionist history of sexual liberation" that was "marginalizing and erasing experiences" of a generation that long struggled for gay and lesbian rights.[40] What stood out for Stryker at this point was what a strong force transgender studies had become in academia and in the political arena. Armed with ten years of trans scholarship, Stryker realized that trans studies not only developed a vast amount of critical and creative work but also confirmed for her that "transgender" pushed all the right political buttons. Hence, along with Stephen Whittle, Stryker published the first volume of *The Transgender Studies Reader*.

Things continued to move quickly. In 2013, Stryker, with Aren Z. Aizura, edited and published a second collection, *The Transgender Studies Reader 2*. The speed at which trans scholarship and activism moved forward was certainly "cause for optimism." At the same time, a "measure of caution" was necessary. Likening trans studies to the commodification of queer theory, Stryker and Aizura recall Teresa de Lauretis's 1994 disavowal of the very academic theory she named. The field, according to de Lauretis, was "a conceptually vacuous creature of the publishing industry." As the editors viewed it, queer theory "survived [de Lauretis's] disavowal." Indeed, marking the end of queer-theory history—as de Lauretis ostensibly does—is not much different than gay liberationists refusing entry for transgender culture and politics in the LGBTQ movement. In both cases, doors are effectively closed by those who assume a privileged position in discourse. For Stryker and Aizura, however, queer theory remains a "source of much of the important thinking on non-normative sexuality and deviant modes of life; it has been transformed by two generations of scholars who both creatively pervert it and contribute to its continuity as a framework for understanding the world." "Transgender studies," the authors offer, "should therefore actively participate in the proliferation and articulation of new modes of embodied subjectivity, new cultural practices . . . rather than becoming an enclosure for their containment."[41]

The two *Transgender Studies Reader* volumes are, therefore, invaluable and comprehensive collections that open queer theory toward unforeseen possibilities as well as necessary philosophical tensions and theoretical challenges. Film, however, does not find a significant place in these readers, and, to date, trans-film theory is still only discovering language to explore the critical dimensions that give rise to trans-cinematic content and form. In offering some preliminary thoughts on trans cinema, Helen Hok-Sze Leung in *TSQ* poses the primary question, "What counts as a trans film?"[42] The Stryker *Reader* volumes present a handful of trans readings of film. Judith Halberstam (aka J. Jack Halberstam in volume 2) focuses on matters of trans representation, plot, and narrative structure (i.e., "good"/"bad" representation).[43]

Eliza Steinbock delivers the most rigorous and promising conceptualization for trans/queer film theory in her essay "Groping Theory: Haptic Cinema and Trans-Curiosity in Hans Scheirl's *Dandy Dust* [1998]." Here, Steinbock draws upon a diverse palette of classic and feminist film theory in order to introduce a trans-film theory that bridges psychoanalysis and phenomenology. As such, she "[explicates] *Dandy Dust* in relation to Freudian notions of curiosity about sex difference [while underscoring] the difference between a haptic (and anal) curiosity and Freud's own optical (and penile) approach." Through psychoanalytic discourse, Steinbock writes that she is curious about Freud's case study "Little Hans." In her recounting of Freud's analysis, the little boy's desire for pleasure overrides his mother's admonishment when she discovers the boy playing with his penis. When caught touching himself, his mother scolds him and tells him that she will call for a doctor to "cut off [his] widdler." And then what will he "widdle with?" she demands to know. Hans, ignoring his mother's threats, tells her that his "bottom" will nicely suffice. For Steinbock, Hans cares less about what body part he fondles; he is more than happy to identify other sources of pleasure. In this way, he "pleasurably 'gropes' towards knowledge through the kinesthetic exploration of his own embodiment."[44]

The child's ambivalence toward genitalia and their hierarchical place in an erotic economy is precisely the point where Steinbock homes in on perverse trans-cinematic aesthetics that conjoin spectatorial perception. Following the film scholars Laura Marks, Vivian Sobchack, and Ann Rutherford, "Groping Theory" demonstrates the way two senses—sight and touch—facilitate a trans-cinematic experience. In "groping" for sensual knowledge, film "can orient spectators toward a haptic visuality." In doing so, it *reorients* the viewer, yielding unanticipated sensations. Rather than insist, as Freud does, that Hans's dismissal of the usual-genitalia suspects is "faulty perception," *transcinema* theory raises the stakes precisely on corporeal curiosity. As such, "the corporeally-involved spectator is poised to exploit the bodily pleasures of being touched by the folds of filmic space."[45]

In *Dandy Dust*, we are touched by the "transgendered arsehole," the unimaginable site for queer pleasure. To be "poised" and, thus, affectively "touched by the folds of filmic space" involves a particular turn on cinematic aesthetics. The film's director, Hans Scheirl, in other words, critically rehearses cinematic properties to explore opportunities that reconceptualize queer eroticism. *Dandy Dust*'s experimental form moves the spectator to and fro, "groping" for knowledge in their state of curiosity. The film's director "implores the viewer to open up the film, to try to assert meaning and infer connections." The dazzling cinematic imagery that augurs a radical trans cinema in *Dandy Dust* "manifests a body that cannot be said to be composed with any sense of finality, but always remains in a state of composing."[46] This, as Steinbock sees it, are the terms for "transgender politics" and, therefore, for trans cinema.[47]

But is this the final word on trans cinema? Is *Dandy Dust* the film that "counts" as a trans film? I am little concerned that Steinbock wishes to create a trans-cinema pantheon and breezily set aside "mainstream" films such as *The Crying Game* (dir. Neil Jordan, 1992), *Boys Don't Cry* (dir. Kimberly Peirce, 1999), or *Hedwig and the Angry Inch* (dir. Cameron Mitchell, 2001). More remains to be said. Kate Bornstein, for instance, turns the tables on representations that have accrued in trans cinema. She wonders what to make of the *non*trans character's "revulsion" toward trans bodies. In her critique of *The Crying Game*, Bornstein finds herself drawn to (*curious about*) the revulsion-as-desire we witness in these films. When the "straight" character, Fergus (Stephen Rea), encounters genitalia in the character of Dil (Jaye Davidson) that does not meet his expectations for gender identity and, thus, his sexual fantasy, Fergus's "vomiting," Bornstein reasons, "can be seen not so much as a sign of revulsion as an admission of attraction, and the consequential upheaval of this gender identity and sexual orientation. . . . The poor man's cognitive system had really been shaken up!"[48]

Beyond questions of representation, and as the terms for cinema transform (as they have always done), new language is required to rethink queer cinema. Changes in television viewing and programming coincide with how we might reconceive the cinematic in relationship to trans culture. While, on the one hand, the genre of the "television series" makes room for trans representation in such shows as *Transparent* and *RuPaul's Drag Race*, on the other hand, "television"-as-concept raises the theoretical ante on how we might rethink a trans cinematic. To be sure, "television" foregrounds complex theoretical propositions that, while taken up by new-media philosophers more generally, have not yet been explored by trans theorists. "Television," Samuel Weber notes, "does not merely allow the viewer to 'see at a distance' things that otherwise would be invisible. It *transports vision as such* and *sets* it immediately *before* the viewer. It entails not merely a heightening of the naturally limited powers of sight with respect to certain distant *objects*; it involves a transmission or transposition of vision itself."[49] Trans television theory is tantalizing for the ways one reimagines LGBTQ as a trans-mediated experience/event, a concept of identity on the move, an identity in "transmission or transposition."

A final word on trans cinema must be made about documentary filmmaking. This genre is as critical for transgender people and filmmakers as for many social movements, especially for the LGBTQ movement. From *Word Is Out* (dir. Nancy Adair, 1977), with its wide-ranging "coming-out" interviews with twenty-six gay men and lesbians, to *United in Anger: A History of ACT UP* (dir. Jim Hubbard and Sarah Schulman, 2012), with its wealth of archival footage and interviews, the genre's historical relationship to political engagement across civil rights movements has remained invaluable. The theoretical investigation into changing political and cultural land-scapes now continues for the trans movement. Tara Mateik's *Toilet Training: Law and Order in the Bathroom* (2004), for instance, merges experimental (certainly, playful) cinematic and televisual form with political and legal information regarding public-restroom use and the limitations placed on transgender people.

In short, these variations in cinematic aesthetics reveal the necessary tensions that Matthew Tinkcom encourages us to tackle when studying queer film. Queer film theory owes much to trans studies insofar as its puts into perspective the thrills and the perils that any avant-garde movement confronts. To what extent can queer film and queer film theory be said to be avant-garde? What queer critiques are available to filmmakers and film theorists to think conceptually and to think radically? To bring this essay to a close, I'd like to consider a queer-cinematic spectacle that invites both avant-garde and classical cinema as way to reroute possibilities for queer film theory.

VI.

Is queer film the neo-avant-garde? What theoretical concepts help to sift through the complexities that define avant-garde—let alone, *a queer avant-garde*? If, as we have seen, "queer film" quickly finds its way into consumer culture, what claims to radical-ness can "queer" maintain?

Following the publication of Peter Bürger's book *Theory of the Avant-Garde* in 1976 (translated in 1984), critics took the author to task for, among other things, his con-cept of "false sublation," in which Hegelian sublation is understood as the aesthetic tension between preservation and transformation. Bürger contended that the Hegelian paradox lent itself to the historical avant-garde, insofar as the movement's mission to dismantle bourgeois institutions of art, while revolutionizing praxes of everyday life, ultimately failed. Because the avant-garde's radical gestures reified the artist as a unique individual, and hence subsequently commodified "the artist," the avant-garde's critique failed. In effect, Bürger finds that the avant-garde's critique of the institution failed on two counts. First, the "category of individual production" was unable to negate "individual reception" (i.e., bourgeois autonomous, or contemplative, art). In this way, Duchamp's signature on the work of art served as "a kind of provocation that cannot be repeated indefinitely," whether as R. Mutt on *Fountain* (1917) or as Rrose Sélavy on the film *Anémic cinéma* (1926), or unmarked *as* a "Marcel Duchamp" yet delivered by the artist's hand as a gift for his patron, Katherine S. Dreier (*The Bride Stripped Bare by Her Bachelors, Even (The Large Glass)*, 1915–23). Once a provocation, the Duchampian gesture "no longer provokes; it turns into its opposite." The artist's signature does not "eradicate the idea of individual creativity, it affirms it, and the reason is the failure of the avant-gardiste intent to sublate art."[50] To be sure, spectators regularly line up for tickets to visit the Louise and Walter Arensberg Collection of Duchamp's artwork at the Philadelphia Museum of Art.

Nevertheless, according to Bürger, if Duchamp, the Dadaists, and the Surrealists failed to revolutionize the relation between art and life, "only in Brecht do we find elements of an aesthetic theory of engaged literature" and creative practice. Bürger cautions, however, that Brecht's avant-gardist practices emerged only after the critical "attack of the historical avant-garde movements" had been made. He further cautions, "one will have to take care not to adopt Brecht's and [Walter] Benjamin's solutions . . . and to transfer them ahistorically to the present."[51]

For many artists and critics who were raised on (often-reductive) theories of "postmodernism," Bürger's critical theory augured the end for any conception of a "neo-avant-garde." In responding to his critics' "attacks" and, thereby, resisting foreclosure on a possible history for a "neo-avant-garde," Bürger offers the following:

> We have to accept that avant-garde texts have become literature [institutionalized], *but we should also not lose sight of their originally intended effect, that is, to draw out the claim to authenticity in the seemingly most unserious products.* A nonpositivistic treatment of the products of the avant-garde would have to keep both perspectives in mind without playing them off against each other. The difficulty of fulfilling this demand underscores how far removed the avant-garde's impulse to transform real social relationships is from us today. This does not exclude, but rather includes, the possibility that the avant-garde could gain a renewed relevance in a future that we cannot imagine.[52]

Although this response was published in 2010, it is noteworthy that Bürger does not consider the politicized international art movements spawned by ACT UP. If a neo-avant-garde is to be defined for its sublation of the encounter between art and life, AIDS artists (from DIVA-TV to Gran Fury) indeed enacted provocative art/life praxis (recognizing their project as "a kind of provocation that cannot be repeated indefinitely"). AIDS activist art, Douglas Crimp and Adam Rolston asserted at the height of the movement, "[functions] as an organizing tool, by conveying, in compressed form, information and political positions to others affected by the epidemic, to onlookers at demonstrations, and to the dominant media."[53] The success of AIDS art made the movement highly visible, but, Crimp and Rolston ask, "visibility *to whom?*"

For AIDS activist artists, rethinking the identity and role of the artist also entails new considerations of audience. Postmodernist art advanced a political critique of art institutions—and art itself as an institution—for the ways they constructed social relations through specific modes of address, representations of history, and obfuscations of power. The limits of this aesthetic critique, however, have been apparent in its own institutionalization: critical postmodernism has become a sanctioned, if still highly contested, art world product, the subject of standard exhibitions, catalogues, and reviews. The implicit promise of breaking out of the museum and marketplace to take on new issues and find new audiences has gone largely unfulfilled. AIDS activist art is one exception, and the difference is fairly easy to locate.[54]

Seen through this filter, Bürger hints at something unexpectedly queer: "we should also not lose sight of their originally intended effect, that is, to draw out the claim to authenticity in the seemingly most unserious products." Bürger's remarks give pause because they evoke the specter of camp, something I could hardly equate with his "theory of the avant-garde." His glimmer of hope for a neo-avant-garde, then, gives purchase to a "renewed relevance in a future that we cannot imagine." To be sure, a queer avant-garde has imagined such a future precisely through an integration of art and life. From Wildean Aestheticism to Warholian Pop, the materiality of the body folds inextricably into and out of aesthetic practice. Here, just when radical aesthetics appear to stall, the aporia crackles with divergent and kinetic energies. As such, queer avant-garde practices surmount the aestheticized distance Bürger posits between Duchamp and Brecht. Arguably, Andy Warhol embodies and thus commingles Duchampian and Brechtian aesthetics, specifically through his queer cinematics.

It is well known, for instance, that Warhol conceived the Factory as a cinematic site. The Factory housed the "Superstars," about whom Warhol enthused: "Their lives became part of my movies, and of course the movies became part of their lives; they'd get so into them that pretty soon you couldn't really separate the two, you couldn't tell the difference—and sometimes neither could they."[55] If culture-industry cinema dissolves the political dimension for the "real," Warhol's queer-film practices brought into relief the imbrication—*the frisson*—that is life and art itself.

Herein lies the performative reimagining of the cinematic as queer praxis. Indeed, a history of queer art and artists involves the contradictory acts to at once preserve and transform—*sublation*. Variations on camp and feminist-queer theories have driven this particular critical and political turn from the end of the nineteenth century until our current time. To highlight queer sublation through a concept of the cinematic, I turn to Tara Mateik's cinematic performance *There's No Place . . .* (2011–).[56] *There's No Place . . .* is a long-term and ongoing project for the trans artist. It reconceptualizes L. Frank Baum's own long-term book-series project that unfolded over eighteen years (*The Wonderful Wizard of Oz*, 1900–1918). In this way, and like Baum's series, Mateik's *There's No Place . . .* takes on a sustained theme, where he engages queer and trans theory as artistic practice in which work of art, artist, and spectator are active forces in making queer canonical texts. With the project's launch in 2008, *There's No Place . . .* committed itself to transforming and making perverse the well-worn theme of "home." Immersed in "no place" that nonetheless inscribes itself as the ideological centerpiece for *every* place ("home"), Mateik's performance takes "home" on the road and presents it in a range of venues (galleries, theaters, and so on). In doing so, the mobile event space re-creates place for politically troubled/troubling bodies—African Americans, Latinos/Latinas, drag queens, and more. *There's No Place . . .* is the search for an ever-elusive but desired place called "home."

To keep the privileged site called "home" on the move, Mateik stitches together the cinematic adaptations of the Baum books (*The Wizard of Oz* [dir. Victor Fleming, 1939] and *The Wiz* [dir. Sidney Lumet, 1978]), along with multiple drag performances that continually revive life on the yellow brick road. Like Baum, Mateik extends and reworks the theme of "home," or the endless reimagining of an ideal place. Integrating Baum's "Wizard of Oz" series with the iconic camp films that followed on the books' heels, Mateik's queer lens rewraps the diverse media of literature and film through new-media technology, queer politics, and queer film theory. As the space between stage and audience collapse during the show, the spectators for *There's No Place . . .* participate directly. Along with the tech crew (camera people, sound and lighting technicians) and the actors, audience members join the scene. Each performance of *There's No Place . . .* is, therefore, never quite the same. While the performances conjure the fixed historical works (an MGM musical and canonical literature), they simultaneously put them under erasure, in the Derridean sense of *sous rature*.[57] In effect, the works are turned into texts. The works are, in other words, queered.

By pressing multimedia technology into service for *There's No Place . . .* , a multimediated queer body is envisioned. Mateik's aesthetic form, coupled with his own performance in the work, is thus critical. For example, Mateik's aesthetic concept involves drag queens lip-syncing so as to *re*perform an "original" recording of, say, Judy Garland speaking or singing. Not insignificantly, Mateik himself steps into the performance. He lip-syncs to audio recordings of director Sidney Lumet on the set of *The Wiz* as he instructs Diana Ross how to deliver the best possible Dorothy. In this way, Mateik *throws* the highly recognized and recorded voices onto the queer figures—including himself—who populate his films and performances.

In a queer theoretical context, lip-syncing carries historical significance (consider the renowned performance artist Lypsinka, who trots out the recorded remains of Bette Davis and Joan Crawford). Lip-syncing is historically noteworthy in queer culture and a critical attribute for camp performances. When, for example, a white gay boy hits the dance floor to dance and gesture in homage to a Black performer (such as Donna Summer, Beyoncé, or Diana Ross), queer cultural practice in relation to gender and race is made starkly queer. Brian Currid describes moments such as this: "queer performativity of that white boy in the disco is thus possible only inside the matrix of meanings that race and gender provide, while, in the practices of lip-syncing and dance, it comments on the racializing regime of gender by *ironizing its effects and queering its content.*"[58] Irony, humor, and sarcasm, along with the cutting bon mot, are rich and ample devices for the queer avant-garde. To queer is to make uneasy the "real." It is to disable—if only contingently—a culture of heteronormative constraint. By reincorporating and reenvisioning mechanically recorded voices, gestures, and images from movies and records, *There's No Place* . . . reveals the disjointed relation between original and copy (that is, the copy of a copy of a copy . . .). The queer cinematic "home" is where life and art remain indissoluble. In bringing queers "home," Mateik guides them into the sensual uncertainty of the aporia.

VII.

Looking back at my course outline for the seminar "Queer Culture, Theory, and Media," I am reminded that one topic or another is missing. Hence, in the outline, I include an apologia to my students and offer additional subjects for their studies in queer cinema and queer film and media theory. And here, again, I must apologize to the reader for my inattention to the "B"—bisexuality—that holds the center for "LGBTQ." "To a surprising extent," Maria San Filippo laments in her book *The B Word*, "bisexuality remains the orientation that dares not speak its name." The "invisibility" and "elusive quality of bisexual representation" in film, San Filippo rightly points out, is at once startling as it is anticipated. In other words, "cultural fascination-anxiety about bisexual desire and sexuality" is firmly maintained to uphold standards of monogamy—whether heterosexual or homosexual.[59] Monosexual relations thus simplify the terms for representing what is, in fact, an endless parade of sexual desires. American film, especially, finds it difficult to make human, abstract complexities cinematic.

Reluctantly, San Filippo identifies her own subject position as "queer bisexual." Perhaps "redundant," she nonetheless finds the malleability of the terms useful because it draws on flexible desires associated with "queer" while indicating the distinct areas of study necessitated by "the B word"—"bi-epistemology." Yet, because San Filippo's study concentrates on the limits of bisexual *representation*, the book's theoretical shortcomings await redress.[60] What rigorous approach to film theory might query bisexual desire through the relation between representation and cinematic form? Is a traditional narrative format an appropriate model for touching elements of desire that are not readily identifiable as such?

Queer-film theorists continue their philosophical journey so as to respond to these inquiries, keeping in mind that queer delight arises when asking penetrating questions, and not answering them once and for all. There is—*so far*—no place like "home."

Notes

1   Rodowick, *Elegy for Theory*, xiii, xiv, xii.

2   Tinkcom, *Queer Theory and "Brokeback Mountain,"* 6.

3   In an important edited collection of Lacan's writings, Juliet Mitchell flatly states the case about the use of language for feminist discourse (here, psychoanalysis): "Psychoanalysis should aim to show us that we do not know those things we think we do; it therefore cannot assault our popular conceptions by using the very idiom it is intended to confront: a challenge to ideology cannot rest on a linguistic appeal to that same ideology." In short, "easy comprehension" through language is an ideological ruse ("Introduction I," 4).

4   See Derrida, *Of Grammatology*, 9. On Derridean theory and cinema, see Peter Brunette's and David Willis's *Screen/Play: Derrida and Film Theory* and Tom Conley's essay "Site and Sound."

5   Rich, "New Queer Cinema," 17 (emphasis added), 15.

6   Edelman, *No Future*, 25.

7   Tinkcom, *Queer Theory and "Brokeback Mountain,"* 11.

8   De Lauretis, "Queer Theory," iii (emphasis added).

9   Bad Object-Choice Collective, *How Do I Look?*

10 "In *Four Fundamental Concepts of Psycho-Analysis*," Kaja Silverman explains in her book *The Threshold of the Visible World*, Lacan "insists emphatically upon the disjunction of camera and eye, but instead of deploying the camera as an independent optical apparatus, he uses it as a signifier of the gaze. The passage in which he introduces this metaphor locates the subject firmly within spectacle, and attributes to the camera/gaze a constitutive function with respect to him or her" (131). As it turns out, "the gaze would thus seem to be as old as sociality itself" (132).

11 Doty, review of *How Do I Look?*, 37. It is worth noting that although not cited in the issue of *differences* that de Lauretis edited, Judith Butler's seminal work *Gender Trouble* was published in 1990. Butler's well-known book, published in the year the Santa Cruz conference took place, is often recognized as the launch pad for queer theory more generally. Around matters of imaging queer sexualities, however, de Lauretis had already envisaged a paradigm shift for gay and lesbian studies in film and video.

12 See, for instance, Epstein's *Ganymède, essai sur l'éthique homosexuelle masculine*. Christophe Wall-Romana's introduction to *Ganymède* ("L'Homosexualité dans les écrits et les films de Jean Epstein"), as well as his essay, published elsewhere, "Epstein's *Photogénie* as Corporeal Vision: Inner Sensation, Queer Embodiment, and Ethics," importantly link the filmmaker's homosexuality with his filmmaking. For an elaboration on cinematic "pansexuality"—a book originally published in 1972—see Parker Tyler's *Screening the Sexes: Homosexuality in the Movies*. Eisenstein's film *¡Que Viva México!* is the most direct exploration of homosexual/homoerotic desire through his filmmaking, although *Strike* and *Battleship Potemkin* also hold their own in this regard. Peter Greenaway's film *Eisenstein in Guanajuato* drives the point home (on this, see my "In Excess of the Cut: Peter Greenaway's *Eisenstein in Guanajuato*," chapter 7 in this volume).

13 Williams, for instance, highlights Dulac's *L'Invitation au voyage* (1927): "heterosexual and homosexual longing, feminine passivity versus illicit desire, are set in opposition and rendered through metaphors of transport (taxi, ships, dance), orientalist exoticism (musicality, associative superimpositions), looking patterns (homosociality/homoeroticism, direct camera), authorial intertextuality, and rhythmic abstraction" (*Germaine Dulac*, 149). On Arzner, see Judith Mayne's *Directed by Dorothy Arzner*.

14 See Anzaldúa, *Borderlands/La Frontera*. For a discussion about and specific reference to Anzaldúa's use of cinematic language in *Borderlands*, see my *Queer Pollen*, 219–20.

15 See Gerstner, *Queer Pollen*, chapter 2.

16 My shortlist is obviously not meant to be comprehensive. Since libraries have fruitfully put digital-age technology to excellent use by creating resource guides by subject area, and to provide a current link to research, I include Fordham University Library's offering for studies in queer theory: http://fordham .libguides.com/c.php?g=354894&p=3004496.

17 It is with great sadness and anger that my return to this essay is coupled with the egregious harm the United States Supreme Court has done to a woman's rights and control of her body. The gutting of *Roe v. Wade* mars whatever remaining dignity the US had for its human rights record.

18 Be in the Know, "Origin of HIV and AIDS."

19 Originally published as an issue of *October* ("AIDS: Cultural Analysis/Cultural Activism," vol. 43 [Winter 1987]), the volume was republished with the same title through MIT Press in 1987.

20 Crimp, "Mourning and Militancy," 8–9.

21 The "Thematic List of Entries" in the volume provides a comprehensive list of film- and video-related topics that are useful signposts for the discussion here (in Gerstner, *Routledge International Encyclopedia*, xxiv–xxvi).

22 C. Bell, "AIDS Film," 29.

23 Griffiths, "New Queer Cinema, International," 426.

24 Two recent French films about the response to AIDS during the 1990s suggest that the way filmmakers confront this particular historical moment is still very much an ongoing debate. See Robin Campillo's *120 battements par minute* (*BPM*, 2017) and Christophe Honoré's *Plaire, aimer, courir vite* (*Sorry Angel*, 2018).

25 Corrigan, White, and Mazaj, "Introduction to Part 8, Sexuality and Gender in Cinema: From Psychoanalysis to Performativity," in *Critical Visions in Film Theory*, 708.

26 Laplanche and Pontalis, *Language of Psycho-analysis*, 318.

27 See Elizabeth Cowie's *Representing the Woman*. Silverman's contributions are many in this area. For now, see *The Acoustic Mirror*.

28 Along with Edelman's works cited earlier, see Lauren Berlant's *Desire/Love*. "For de Lauretis," Berlant rightly tells us, "the fetishistic 'perversion' of lesbian desire is productive, not destructive, of love" (41).

29 Farmer, *Spectacular Passions*, 150.

30 This is, of course, a critique of Laura Mulvey's cornerstone essay "Visual Pleasure and Narrative Cinema," in which the cinematic apparatus and its attendant spectator are always already male. Steven Neale and others questioned the concept that all men's desire could be simplified as the same (i.e., heterosexual). See Neale, "Masculinity as Spectacle."

31 Viewed this way, Foucault's import for queer theorists becomes strikingly clear. The relationship between power and knowledge, and discipline and punish, are the crucial tensions where the subject discovers pleasure. Foucault's

homosexuality, lived-world experimentation with sex, and death by AIDS made him, as David M. Halperin, puts it, "Saint Foucault" (*Saint Foucault*).

32 See Matt Bell's *The Boys in the Band: Flashpoints of Cinema, History, and Queer Politics*. His introduction to the collection is an invaluable overview of the decades-long transformation of the critical discourse around the play and the film.

33 The textual *ronde* described here derives from Bakhtin's concept of the "author creator": The work of art, he writes, is a "single but complex event that we might call the work in the totality of all its events [including] the giveness of the work, and its text, and the world represented in the text, and the author-creator, and the listener or reader" ("Forms of Time of the Chronotope in the Novel," 255).

34 Tinkcom, *Working like a Homosexual*, 4 (emphasis in original).

35 I play on, first, Elsaesser's subheading "Where Freud Left His Marx in the American Home" from his seminal essay "Tales of Sound and Fury: Observations on the Family Melodrama"; and, second, Roudinesco's opening statement for the preface of *Jacques Lacan*: "Jacques Lacan sought to bring plague, subversion, and disorder to the moderate Freudianism of his time" (xv).

36 Hazareesingh, *How the French Think*, 9.

37 While Hazareesingh reminds us time and again that paradox represents French thought *tout court*, he hastily dismisses Derrida's writing as a "dead end alley." This is especially unfortunate just as queer theory and cultural studies make headway in French academic settings. Many nonqueer writers miss the significance that Derridean *écriture* (as well as other texts by notables such as Lacan, Althusser, and so on) offers queers. We are, as the Black queer James Baldwin consistently confirmed, "in trouble with language again."

38 Deleuze and Guattari, *Anti-Oedipus*, 34.

39 Stryker, "(De)Subjugated Knowledges," 1–2.

40 Stryker, 2.

41 Stryker and Aizura, "Introduction: Transgender Studies 2.0," 6–7 (quoting de Lauretis).

42 In the premiere issue of *TSQ: Transgender Studies Quarterly*, Helen Hok-Sze Leung contributes a handy overview in the "Keywords" section that covers film. Smartly presented by subsections—for example, "Critically Trans," "Trans Auteurs"—Leung takes as her point of departure the "deceptively simple question," "What counts as a trans film?" Her outline in *TSQ* reminds us that the response is, indeed, not so simple.

43　In Halberstam's writing on film, they do turn to the work of feminist film theory, specifically psychoanalysis in relation to "suture." Because the terms "gaze" and "look" are often conflated in their writing, it is difficult to know where the corporeality of the look is distinct from the ideological implications of the gaze. Nonetheless, suture theory opens promising avenues for questioning the way cinematic form and representation entangle (if not disentangle) the relation between gendered body and ideology. See, along with the articles in the Stryker edited volumes, Halberstam, *In a Queer Time and Place*, chapter 4 ("The Transgender Look"); and Halberstam, "Skinflick."

44　Steinbock, "Groping Theory," 103.

45　Steinbock, 103.

46　Steinbock, 105, 112, 115.

47　The film *Community Action Center* (dir. A. K. Burns and A. L. Steiner, 2010), is noteworthy in this context. It is called a "sociosexual video," and we partake in sexual romps in which multiple variations of bodies and sexual pleasure take place. The Video Data Bank website joyfully describes the project: "This project was heavily inspired by porn-romance-liberation films, such as works by Fred Halsted, Jack Smith, James Bidgood, Joe Gage and Wakefield Poole, which served as distinct portraits of the urban inhabitants, landscapes and the body politic of a particular time and place. *Community Action Center* is a unique contemporary womyn-centric composition that serves as both an ode and a hole-filler" ("Community Action Center").

48　Bornstein, *Gender Outlaw*, 73

49　S. Weber, "Television," 115–16 (emphasis in original).

50　Bürger, *Theory of the Avant-Garde*, 52–53.

51　Bürger, 91, 90.

52　Bürger, "Avant-Garde and Neo-Avant-Garde," 705 (emphasis added).

53　Crimp and Rolston, *AIDS Demographics*, 20.

54　Crimp and Rolston, 19.

55　Warhol, *Andy Warhol Diaries*, 180.

56　Launched in 2011, *There's No Place . . .* involves a trilogy of multimedia performances and installation projects: *Army of Revolt, Friends of Dorothy (Judy Garland Screen Test)*, and *Friends of Dorothy (Diana Ross Screen Test)*.

57　In an important footnote, Derrida defines his understanding of *sous rature* this way: "It is a common error to equate the phenomenological reduction, 'putting out of play,' and the *sous rature*, 'putting under erasure.' . . . The distinction is simple: The gesture of bracketing implies 'not this but that,' preserving a bipolarity as well as a hierarchy of empirical impurity and phenomenological purity; the gesture of *sous rature* implies 'both this *and* that' as well as 'neither this nor that' undoing the opposition and the hierarchy between the legible and the erased" (*Of Grammatology*, 374–75n 34).

58   Currid, "Disco and Dance Music," 256 (emphasis added).

59   San Filippo, *B Word*, 4, 11.

60   San Filippo, 243. San Filippo has already expanded not only questions of bisexuality; her latest work, *Provocauteurs and Provocations*, explores the even-broader dimensions of sexuality and desire.

ON WRITING AND
CINEMATIC FRIENDSHIP

Figure 7. "Lovingly, Rose Sélavy . . ." *Rrose Sélavy (Marcel Duchamp)*, 1921. Photograph by Man Ray. Silver print 5 7/8″ × 3 7/8″. (Philadelphia Museum of Art/WikiMedia Commons)

QUEER TURNS

The Cinematic Friendship of Marcel Duchamp and Charles Demuth

For Peter Wollen

The emergence of Rose Sélavy in or around the summer of 1920 coincides with several key events for Marcel Duchamp: (1) Man Ray and Duchamp build their first optical machine, *Rotary Glass Plates (Precision Optics)*; (2) Man Ray and Duchamp record (with Man Ray's movie camera) these optical devices; and (3) Duchamp's patron, Katherine Dreier, purchases a hand-held camera for him since, according to Calvin Tomkins, he had "become curious about cinema techniques."[1] Rose comes on the scene, then, as a "cinematic blossoming" like the Bride in the *Large Glass*, who, Duchamp tells us, "basically is a motor."[2] Duchamp's conceptual turn to Rose Sélavy and investigation into "cinema techniques," I argue, is a significant "ideatic"—a term Duchamp admired—toward a more pleasurable and ambivalent form of autoerotic mechanical desire.[3] Indeed, when Duchamp later added the second *R* to *Rose* to evoke "eros"—*érotique*—it recalled the Lumières' 1895 film *L'Arroseur*, in which we see a sprinkler sprinkling his garden. But Duchamp's autoerotic interest in cinematic *technique* was not strictly beholden to representation.[4] The erotics of the Lumière film did not lie in seeing the sprinkler sprinkling as much as it lay in the film's title itself (a cinematic title that obviously conjures Duchampian onanistic possibilities). More presciently, Duchamp's erotic desire through film turned, in fact, on the turning of the camera projector's crank: "Why not turn the film?" Duchamp inquired.[5] As Annette Michelson reminds us, Duchamp's cinema is about—*if it is "about" anything*—the "cranking" of the apparatus.[6]

"Queer Turns: The Cinematic Friendship of Marcel Duchamp and Charles Demuth." *Marcel Duchamp and Eroticism*, edited by Marc Décimo. Newcastle, UK: Cambridge Scholars Publishing, © 2007, 105–15.

If Duchamp recognized the idea of cinema as a "return to the hand, so to speak," he, at the same time, turned the terms for gender performatives.[7] Duchamp thus guides the interrelationship between machine and body along an expanded exploration of motion, circles, secants, and trans-Atlantic travel between the queer creative coteries of New York and Paris. Hence, this essay attends to the queer social circles in which Duchamp slid in and out. It is within his movement across these circles that his perspectives on gender and cinema found their embodied and imbricated contours.

New York and Duchamp's Cinematic Turn on Gender

When Duchamp arrived in New York in 1915, he entered a city that Moira Roth identified as "futuristic and vulgar."[8] It was a city riddled with masculinist and Anglo-Saxon racism, where, for example, D. W. Griffith promoted *The Birth of a Nation* by trotting white horses saddled with Ku Klux Klan riders down Fifth Avenue. Not soon after, the antipacifist film *The Battle Cry of Peace* opened under the supervisory eye of Theodore Roosevelt. But Duchamp also arrived in a New York where an avant-garde in both white and African American circles fomented. Experiments in aesthetics often crossed explorations of gender, sexuality, and race among the participants of these creative circles. Not to be overlooked during this period was New York's dynamic discourse on the cinema, an intellectual discussion wrapped in a struggle to identify a sui generis national art form. Though the idea of American cinema was rapidly on a trajectory toward a standard model of narrative representation, it found rich aesthetic and intellectual engagement with critics and artists who intimately overlapped with Duchamp's New York milieus.

If American art was only to be found in its "plumbing and bridges" (as Duchamp claimed), it also revealed itself in the twentieth-century art machine, the cinema. Between 1915 and 1920, Duchamp encountered many of the young American film-makers and critics who spent time in the company of Walter and Louise Arensberg, Alfred Stieglitz, and Florine Stettheimer. Among them, Sadakichi Hartmann penned his 1912 essay "The Esthetic Significance of the Motion Picture" for Stieglitz's *Camera Work*. In 1915, Vachel Lindsay scripted his Whitmanesque philosophy of film in *The Art of the Motion Picture*. Here, Lindsay embraced the grandiose drama of D. W. Griffith, on the one hand, and anticipated Sergei Eisenstein's juxtaposition of dialectic, hieroglyphic images, on the other. The American artists Paul Strand and Charles Sheeler soon took up Lindsay's and Hartmann's theories to create in 1920 what is considered the first American avant-garde film, *Manhatta*.

By the time Strand and Sheeler made *Manhatta*, Duchamp was intimately aware of their cinematic concepts since Strand devised much of his photographic aesthetic from the Stieglitz coterie, while Sheeler developed his aesthetic interests through Duchamp's patron, Arensberg. Though sharp creative and philosophical differences identified these circles, their overlap was essential to what ultimately made its way into the Strand and Sheeler film. It is likely, however, that Duchamp found these early American avant-garde investigations about cinema enthusiastic but stale. Duchamp's penchant for "nonretinal" art and more intellectual-aesthetic pursuits had little to do with Sheeler and Strand's film, which was ultimately a derivative of European Cubist axioms of representation. Moreover, the filmmakers abided by Lindsay's film theory that relied heavily on poetic *meaning* and *the cut*. Duchamp's notion of cinema had little to do with either. *Anémic cinéma* (1925), for example, alternatively presents the juxtaposition of rotaries through dissolves (although edits are reserved to divide individual segments). The turning, wordless rotaries dissolve into rotating rotaries that display Rrose's puns. The playful spin of words thus appears through the dissolve, not through an edit.

Duchamp's move away from cinematic narrative and poetic editing is significant because his play with the cinema was not *anti*cinema as much as it was *non*cinema. Duchamp, in other words, did not participate in discussions about form and content that had earlier strangled the creative possibilities of painting and other arts. Rather, he embraced the concept of the cinematic itself. Duchamp was more concerned with the cinematic apparatus as a *mode of mechanical production*. Filmic recordings are simply by-products of the cinema machine, just as chocolate is the by-product of the chocolate grinder (see Duchamp's *Chocolate Grinder (No. 1)*, 1913), or gendered bodies the excess of the human culture machine (e.g., *Rrose Sélavy*). Cinematic blossoming is found, therefore, in the by-product or final discharge of production.

Man Ray's notes on his and Duchamp's first experiment with film highlight this concept of cinema. After recording the first images of their rotaries, the developing process proved disastrous when overdevelopment ruined the film and left, according to Man Ray, a "mass of tangled seaweed."[9] Duchamp was nonplussed over this outcome, while Man Ray was completely distraught. For Duchamp, the ends of cinematic production (i.e., representation) did not matter as much as the means that produced it. Indeed, while Duchamp may have admired the early filmic experiments of Jules Marey and Eadweard Muybridge, their scientific study of gendered bodies and corporeal movement simply used the camera machine *to represent* and to articulate a truth, to be sure, to frame it. (Duchamp's gender-unspecific *Nude Descending a Staircase* best illustrates his ironic and indifferent homage to Muybridge's cinematic cataloguing of mostly female nudes descending a staircase.)[10]

Instead, Duchamp's fascination with the machine more closely followed on his friend Francis Picabia's remarks that the machine is an extension of the body. In this way, he considered the camera machine an extension of bodily pleasure in which the cranking of the cinematic machine worked in concert with how we might crank the body. The cinema machine and Duchamp's thoughts on making cinema are, I suggest, linked to his own corporeality, a body of *différance* not predetermined, as he viewed it, by the dictates of gender subjectivity. Thus, the subjectivity of gender in Duchampian cinema, as Dalía Judovitz remarks, "is reduced to [the] circuit and relay of signifiers in motion, that is *Eros, c'est la vie* or *Rrose Sélavy*."[11] But if the relay of signifiers in motion defers production, it does not necessarily foreclose an erotic discharge. For Duchamp, to turn the cinematic crank, which, in turn, is to crank his body, is indeed a deferral of retinal production. To crank, however, did not eliminate production as such. The inevitable "mass of tangled seaweed" about which Man Ray anxiously wrote is more aptly realized as Duchamp's cinematic load, his aesthetic release of celluloid from his cinematic cranking. The tangled mess of celluloid, we might say, anticipates Duchamp's seminal load that he delivers in his 1946 *Paysage fautif.*

How might we trace Duchamp's autoerotic conception of cinema and its relationship to his understanding of gender and queer impulses?[12] Through which circles did he move to facilitate the production of a cinema and gender as a production delayed or differed, yet a production nonetheless? Certainly, his experiences in New York with a diverse group of folks, whose slippages in identity and aesthetic theory had much to do with the way his thoughts on cinema intersected with his musings on gender as well as religion, sexuality, nationalism, and ethnicity. (It is worth recalling that before he created his "feminine alter ego" in New York, Duchamp explored the idea of becoming Jewish.) As a human secant that crossed multiple social circles at several opportune points where youthful American moderns expressed their creative and cultural enterprises, Duchamp intermingled with New York's queer moderns, who meshed perversely with his bodily yet mechanical autoeroticism. Through these queer circles, it appears certain that Duchamp realized a transformed cinematic blossoming of gender as an assisted and embodied readymade, that is, Rrose Sélavy.

Queer Cranks

Who were these human by-products of the American cultural machine that Duchamp embraced and enabled him to explore his autoerotic and narcissistic pleasures that were equal to the cranking of the cinema machine? How might this cultural intermingling open up for Duchamp what Allen Weiss suggests is the "possibility of multiple, conflicting, sometimes ironic identificatory positions"?[13] Against the backdrop of supermechanized and virile America, Duchamp located the irony that such efficient apparatuses promised. For all the virile rigor it took to move commerce smoothly across its bridges (not to mention human waste through its plumbing), America also made way for the less-than-manly cultures and aesthetics of Charles Demuth, the Stettheimer sisters, Carl Van Vechten, and Marsden Hartley.

Much has been written about the Van Vechten and Stettheimer circles as well as Duchamp's participation in them.[14] Duchamp's appetite for ironic affirmation (or what we might consider one version of camp) was satiated by the flowery playfulness of the Stettheimer sisters, the arch rhetoric of Van Vechten, and the aesthetic debauch of Charles Demuth. Few have discussed, however, the place of the painter Demuth's relationship to and resonance for Duchamp. Both Duchamp and Demuth convened in New York salons held by the Stettheimers, the Arensbergs, and Stieglitz. They admired each other throughout their careers. Duchamp drew upon the painter's work and person in such a way that Duchamp's evocation of Rose Sélavy as well as his developing sense of the autoerotic finds a direct line to Demuth. Indeed, his relationship with Demuth proved to have a long-standing and charged effect on Duchamp's work and conception of gender.

Demuth was born in Lancaster, Pennsylvania, in 1883. Not only was he was known as the homosexual dandy about town who loved drink (an activity that appealed to Duchamp), but he was also considered frail; his health was in a constant state of deterioration (he walked with a limp and had diabetes, which eventually killed him). Demuth's body was fragile. According to some observers, his masculine, dark features were offset by his "delicate hands," which not only announced his homosexuality but served as the measurement of his aesthetic sensibility. Stieglitz particularly emphasized the correlation between Demuth's delicate corporeality and his "effeminate" art.[15] Duchamp might be viewed in a similar physical vein: dark, masculine features framed by a halo of effeminacy (delicate mouth; soft eyes; long, delicate fingers).

It is possible that Duchamp and Demuth first met in Paris at Gertrude Stein's salon before Duchamp left for New York in 1915. Nonetheless, they met straightaway on Duchamp's arrival to New York, most likely at the Arensbergs'. As Wanda Corn shows, they quickly became affectionate friends. In 1917, Demuth championed Duchamp's succès de scandale (the submission of *Fountain* to the Society of Independent Artists) by appealing to critics such as Henry McBride to take up R. Mutt's cause.[16] Between 1920 and 1923, Demuth attended the *Greenwich Village Follies*, where he greatly enjoyed the performances of the popular drag entertainer Bert Savoy. Duchamp may have accompanied his friend to see Savoy's performances, and, if not, he certainly would have heard about Savoy from Demuth or the press.

Significantly, Demuth enthusiastically commented on Duchamp's "movies," which gave him a "thrill."[17]

As drinking buddies who shared a fluid sense of gender in general and their gender identities in particular, Duchamp later recalled Demuth taking him to the "Hell Hole" or Golden Swan bar in the Village, where both reveled in what Emmanuel Cooper has called the "sleazy bar-room scenes" where "sexual transactions" likely took place.[18] Demuth's watercolor *At the Golden Swan* (1919) shows the two friends imbibing at the Hell Hole. In the painting, the chums sit toward each other, their gaze directed elsewhere, while they appear conjoined at the waist with their hands hidden. As we will see, Duchamp later recalls their friendship with his own work, which echoes another of Demuth's portraits that conjoins two friends.

At Webster Hall, Demuth introduced Duchamp to what Steven Watson has termed the "aphrodisiacal fantasies" that had been occurring since 1914 at the site's infamous costume balls.[19] Here, Duchamp met men in makeup and dresses, women in ties and short hair, revelers dressed in ambiguously defined gender costumes, and sailors who joined in sexual liaisons with their shipmates and assorted Others. What was most striking about these figures at Webster Hall and in the Village was the odd and ambiguous bodily markings that remained when traditionally gendered attire was not worn. In other words, the performances of mannishness or womanliness were always marred by gender imperfections (the beard ultimately revealed the man behind the woman's dress, or the breasts disclosed the woman behind the man's suit). The brilliance of these imperfections, the audacity not to be a pure man or woman, resonates clearly in Duchamp's Rrose (consider the trace of Duchamp's beard that seeps through the images of Rrose).

Though Tomkins dryly suggests that "Duchamp was not a convincing transsexual," it is important to note that Rrose was *not* meant to be a convincing anything.[20] Rrose is, as Marc Décimo reminds us, "both a woman and a man, while being neither."[21] Rrose, like the cavorters Duchamp encountered in Demuth's world *and* the celluloid in the camera, is the remains of cultural production. Rrose Sélavy is like all readymades: a discharge of autoerotic production. Lawrence Steefel tells us that Duchamp's erotic "discharge is intimately related to motion effects, so that the term 'lubricity' refers equally to slipperiness and fluidity of motion and to eroticism."[22] Rrose Sélavy is precisely the corporeal discharge of motion effects and eroticism, where the traces, the slippages of gender, reveal themselves at every turn. Rrose Sélavy is a body spent. If Rrose is "completely finished," however (as Duchamp once described the readymade), Rrose always returns for the sheer pleasure of re-turning.[23]

Demuth's "Good Seed"

In 1930, Demuth painted *Two Sailors Urinating* and *Distinguished Airs*. Both conjure ironic affirmation of masculinity translated as homoerotic experience. In Demuth's work, the activities of manly sailors are performed in a way not sanctioned by the regulations of the military or other social proprieties. Demuth's drawings also illuminate Duchamp's pleasure with cranking and circles; in fact, both drawings, like the earlier *At the Golden Swan*, demonstrate two men conjoined. Here, however, the men's hands are revealed, affectionately circular jerking while ostensibly urinating (*Two Sailors*) or participating in a circle jerk (*Distinguished Airs*).

In 1937 (two years after Demuth's death), Duchamp was commissioned by André Breton to design the doors for the gallery he was tending. Breton named the gallery Gradiva and commissioned Duchamp to design its entranceway door. Breton was pleased with Duchamp's glass-door design, which "silhouetted, as their shadows might, a rather large man and a noticeably smaller very slim woman, standing side by side."[24] On the one hand, Duchamp would have agreed with Breton's assessment of his figures on the door as "shadows." In his notes for the 1914 Box, for example, Duchamp speaks of "shadows cast by Readymades" that become a traceable extension or projection of the readymade. On the other hand, Breton's description of the shadows on the glass door remained narrow, particularly since his worldview rarely moved outside the heterosexual. Duchamp, of course, wanted little to do with the obvious (here, heterosexual coupling) that Breton thinks is present in his projected shadows. It is, therefore, worth looking from the "Other Side of the Glass," as it were. To look from an inverted position, where the door's image is reversed (similar to the way the cinema inverts its image when projecting its shadows), is to reveal a fresh Duchampian irony. When looking through the glass doors from the other side, the heterosexuals that Breton believes to be present are inverted. Indeed, the silhouette of the man and woman Breton imagines to be "standing side by side" may very well be, on the other side of the glass, the shadow of Demuth's American-sailor inverts cranking in a circular motion.[25] The shadows on the other side of the glass reveal, I suggest, an affectionate portrait that may be read as Duchamp's homage to his queer friend Demuth (see figs. 8 and 9).

Are the Gradiva doors the projected shadow of Duchamp and Demuth's affectionate friendship? By looking through the other side of the glass doors, we perhaps receive a glimpse into Duchamp's long-standing admiration for his friend. In 1949, Duchamp recognized his friend for "[planting] the good seed in America." In the short reflection he wrote for Demuth's posthumous exhibition catalogue at the Museum of Modern

"Queer pals! One good turn of the hand deserves another." *Above*: **Figure 8.** Charles Demuth's *Two Sailors Urinating*, 1930, watercolor and pencil on paper. (Photograph Courtesy of Sotheby's, 2014). *Below*: **Figure 9.** Duchampian inversion of Demuth's sailors? *André Breton and Oscar Dominguez Discovering the Trompe l'Oeil Entrance to the Gradiva Gallery, Just as It Is Being Installed by Marcel Duchamp*, 1937, black and white photograph, photographer unknown. (Image courtesy of Bridgeman Images; © Association Marcel Duchamp/ADAGP, Paris/Artists Rights Society [ARS], New York 2022).

Art, Duchamp remembered Demuth's "curious smile" and "incessant curiosity." He fondly recalled Demuth taking him, when he first arrived in New York, to the "Hell Hole" and Webster Hall. Duchamp further remarks that Demuth was an "artist worthy of the name, without the pettiness which afflicts most artists, worshipping his inner self without the usual eagerness to be right." Duchamp's praise of Demuth's nonaggressive narcissism sat squarely with Duchamp's love of the autoerotic and the good seed deposited. He concludes his remembrance of Demuth by stating that his "work is a living illustration of a 'Monroe Doctrine' applied to art; for today art is more the crop of privileged soils, and Demuth is among the first to have planted the good seed in America."[26] Demuth's "good seed," his creative discharge, spread among the trans-Atlantic circles like a perverse Monroe Doctrine that resisted the demands of European aesthetic hegemony. This good seed thus proved instrumental for the production of Duchamp's most provocative cinematic readymade: the American human discharge, Rrose Sélavy.

Notes

1   Tomkins, *Duchamp*, 229–30. I'd like to thank Jonathan Weinberg, James Maroney, Wanda Corn, Betsy Fahlman, Barbara Haskell, and Anna Miranda for their help locating and securing the Charles Demuth illustration for this essay.

2   Duchamp, *Salt Seller*, 42.

3   On the "ideatic," see Jay Bochner's "Eros Eyesore, or the Ideal and the Ideatic."

4   Although, as we know, he was fascinated with film performances by Chaplin as well as his own. Duchamp performed in several films including René Clair's *Entr'acte* (1924), Hans Richter's films *Dreams That Money Can Buy* (1947) and *8 X 8: A Chess Sonata in 8 Movements* (1957), and Andy Warhol's screen test *Marcel Duchamp* (1966).

5   Cabanne, *Dialogues with Marcel Duchamp*, 68.

6   Michelson, "*Anémic cinéma*," 65.

7   Cabanne, *Dialogues with Marcel Duchamp*, 68. Elsewhere, Duchamp is situated within J. L. Austin's theory of the performative, in Ades, Cox, and Hopkins, *Marcel Duchamp*, 152.

8   Roth, "Marcel Duchamp," 92.

9   Quoted in Marquis, *Marcel Duchamp*, 158.

10   Duchamp's other gender-play works include, of course, *L.H.O.O.Q.* (1919).

11   Judovitz, "Anemic Vision in Duchamp," 56.

12   Several writers have identified Duchamp's queer turn on his identity. See, for instance, Robert Harvey's "Where's Duchamp? Out Queering the Field,"

Paul B. Franklin's "Object Choice: Marcel Duchamp's *Fountain* and the Art of Queer Art History," Jerrold Siegel's *The Private Worlds of Marcel Duchamp* (198–99), and Christophe Wall-Romano's "'Cinematic Blossoming': Duchamp, Chess, and Infraqueer Mating."

13 Weiss, "Poetic Justice," 47.

14 See, for instance, Whiting, "Decorating with Stettheimer and the Boys"; and Sussman with Bloemink, *Florine Stettheimer.*

15 See Corn, *Great American Thing*, 193–239; Brennan, *Painting Gender, Constructing Theory*, 180–99.

16 Charles Demuth to Henry McBride, April 1917, in *Letters of Charles Demuth*, 5–6.

17 See Demuth's letter to Stieglitz regarding Marcel's "wonderful '*movies*'" (November 28, 1921, in *Letters of Charles Demuth*, 37); and later to Stieglitz about *Anemic Cinéma* (February 21, 1927, in *Letters of Charles Demuth*, 92–93). The quotation marks—in the originals—around the word "movies" are worth noting.

18 Cooper, *Sexual Perspective*, 116; see also Duchamp, "Demuth, Charles."

19 Watson, *Strange Bedfellows*, 228.

20 Tomkins, *Duchamp*, 231.

21 Décimo, "What's at Play in the Wordplay," 45.

22 Steefel, *Position of Duchamp's "Glass,"* 54–55.

23 Collin, "Marcel Duchamp Talking about Readymades," 37.

24 Polizzotti, *Revolution of the Mind*, 442.

25 Breton was notoriously homophobic, especially when in the US, and he referred to the queer American artists Charles Henri Ford and Parker Tyler's surrealist magazine, *View*, as *Pederasti Internationale*. On Breton's homophobia directed toward Ford and Tyler, see Polizzotti, 502–3; and my "Queer Angels . . . ," chapter 4 in this volume. For the record, Duchamp does not specify his glass-door couple's gender (Cabanne, *Dialogues with Marcel Duchamp*, 80).

26 Duchamp, "Demuth, Charles," 162.

MARLON RIGGS'S
TONGUES UNTIED

12

DVD Review

Lately, I've been startled or, at the very least, discouraged when the name Marlon Riggs is mentioned among students (as well as colleagues), as it evokes a shrug of ignorance or some vague recollection about a Black documentary filmmaker. Sadly, few are cognizant of the central place his work holds in twentieth-century film and Black-gay history. This cultural aphasia is especially disconcerting given the controversy Riggs triggered with his short film *Tongues Untied* (1989). The release of the film on DVD (distributed by Frameline, produced and remastered by Vivian Kleiman at Signifyin' Works) is a vital step in correcting this memory loss.

Tongues Untied is both a documentary and a work of poetry. Riggs was that unique figure who fused his roots in journalism with an embrace of the arts in general (and, for Riggs, this cut across dance, music, film, poetry, and so on). *Tongues Untied* and (arguably) the later *Black Is . . . Black Ain't* (1994) meld the qualities of reportage with an experimental aesthetic form that seeks to grasp the Black-queer experience. The rhythmic and repetitive structure of the chant of "brother to brother" that opens *Tongues Untied* sets the vigorous pace for Riggs's exploration of the complex dynamics of Black manhood and sexuality. Significantly, his experimental visual and sonorous concepts aesthetically rehearse the range and possibilities of same-sex love between Black men. *Tongues Untied's* direct and polemical appeal for "brother-to-brother" love (the "revolution," as Riggs pitches it here) grapples with the prescient issues of Black-on-Black homophobia, the seduction of white gay culture (and its attendant racism and homophobia), and the particularly painful political and lived-world experiences of AIDS for gay Black men. But it is Riggs's personal association with these issues that impresses on the viewer the struggle involved for Black gay men to articulate—indeed, *live*—their cultural identity. The message and the artistic enterprise Riggs undertakes here are trenchant and relevant to this day.

"*Tongues Untied* (1989): Review." *Cinéaste* 32, no. 4. Copyright © 2007 by Cineaste Magazine.

Figure 10. Marlon Riggs and friends on the set of *Tongues Untied*. (© Signifyin' Works; image courtesy of Frameline, San Francisco)

Originally conceived for film festivals (the film won awards in such places as Berlin and Los Angeles), *Tongues Untied* was broadcast on PBS's *POV*, which caused a national furor on the part of religious and political conservatives. Many Republicans and Democrats, Blacks and whites, gays and straights were outraged by what they saw and heard. The images of two Black men kissing, caressing, or simply dancing in the nude were/are, apparently, too much to bear for all cross-sections of the political, ideological, and racial spectra. Riggs, like his queer predecessor James Baldwin (especially in his novel *Just Above My Head*, in which the concept of Black "brother-to-brother" love is sexualized), unapologetically eroticizes the Black-male body with the ardent intent to claim that love between Black men is a revolutionary and, so, necessary act.

In addition, the political fiasco around *Tongues Untied* took shape at the crucial historical intersection of AIDS funding and federally funded art—the National Endowment for the Arts (NEA) specifically. With the likes of Senator Jesse Helms spearheading the homophobic bilateral attack on the dissemination of AIDS-prevention information and "homosexual" and "pornographic" art, Riggs (along with Tim Miller, Karen Finley, and institutions such as Frameline, Franklin Furnace, Centro Cultural de la Raza, and Visual AIDS for the Arts) took center stage as the American *poèt maudit*. The cultural row lasted for some time into the 1990s—*indeed, into the twenty-first century*—with devastating effect on moneys available for artists who didn't raise the flag for "American Art." Ironically, *Tongues Untied* became a weapon that Republicans used against one another during the 1992 presidential campaign. Pat Buchanan used a clip from the film to demonstrate how George H. W. Bush (!) was purportedly abusing taxpayers' dollars.

This newly mastered DVD package is thus an invaluable document not only for the crisp quality of the film's image and sound (meticulously prepared by Mark Escott of Berke Sound); the DVD also includes interviews with the director, the AIDS activist Phil Wilson, the cultural critic Herman Gray, the filmmaker Isaac Julien, and Juba Kalamka of Deep Dickcollective, all of whom bring perspective to the period in which the film was released. Julien's thoughts on the differences between his own work and that of Riggs are especially revealing given the British filmmaker's views on their concepts of class and aesthetics. The "Extra Scenes" from the film are most enticing and satisfying. The outtakes that producer Kleiman (who worked with Riggs on the original production) has selected are marvelous since we are allowed to see Riggs and poet-collaborator Essex Hemphill at work on the set. To hear these two artists rehearse together and direct each other's performance is a boon for any scholar interested in how the rich rhythms of *Tongues Untied* were achieved.

Though this DVD carries a heavy price tag, it is a worthy investment for academic and public libraries. *Tongues Untied* marks one of the most fractious periods in American art and politics during the twentieth century. Since the fallout of this moment remains with us today, this document is essential for lesbian, gay, bisexual, transgender, queer, and African American collections.

13

WITH "GAY ABANDON"

The Auteur as Homosexual Writer in the Twenty-First Century

"The recent pseudo-controversy over auteurism in the hospitable pages of *Film Quarterly* seems to have collapsed of its own weightlessness." Thus wrote a feisty Andrew Sarris in a riposte to the critique by Graham Petrie ("Tweedledum") and John Hess ("Tweedledee") in which they "assailed" auteurist principles in *Film Quarterly* as elitist and narrow. In his essay, "Auteurism is Alive and Well," Sarris argued, "Auteurism is not now and never has been an organized religion or a secret society. There are no passwords or catchwords. . . . It has never meant to be an exclusionary doctrine, nor a blank check for directors. It was stated at the outset that it was more the first step than the last stop in film scholarship." Indeed, "auteurism" opens itself to numerous methodological approaches. "After all," Sarris continued, "it depends on where one is writing, at what length, and for whom," yet it requires theoretical precision, unlike "the epithet 'auteurist' . . . flung about by Petrie and Hess with the same *gay abandon* with which the catch-all 'communist' is hurled at the outside world." Taken together, Sarris was insisting that "differing critical approaches can coexist. If not, it should be remembered that auteurism was born out of a passion for polemics."[1]

Sarris's vigorous defense of auteurism may take some readers aback given that a decade earlier he launched his not-too-timid rankings of Hollywood directors in his book *The American Cinema: Directors and Directions, 1929–1968*. I imagine his closing remarks are meant to remind the reader of the position from which he "polemicized" the cinematic value of Hollywood. It's a vital point, one on which auteurism has sustained itself in film studies and, from my perspective, one that remains a cornerstone for students when entering film studies and production programs.

"With 'Gay Abandon': The Auteur as Homosexual Writer in the Twenty-First Century." *Cinéaste* 45, no. 1 (2019): 24–29.

It is a point, to be sure, that has preoccupied my own research and cinematic interests for thirty years. When Janet Staiger and I first planned what would become our collection of essays *Authorship and Film* (2003), we were interested in the question of method as it related to auteur studies, or what by that time had become more and more recognized in North America as "authorship studies." In 1999, when our concept was developing, cultural studies in its broadest sense had taken firm hold in academia. Staiger and I participated in these academic areas and were thus interested in how queers, feminists, African Americans, Chicana/os, and others took on such a long-standing theoretical concept that, no matter how rigorously it was marked as "dead," returned again and again. To what extent is auteur studies only a polemic? If it is, in what way do fresh methodological approaches reinvent the concept? Nevertheless, it was clear to us that "every scholar (even those who subscribe to the 'death of authorship') speaks of going to a Robert Altman film."[2] The author's name may have changed (Nadine Labaki, Jordan Peele, Damien Chazelle), but the driving force to identify a name with going to the movies has not withered.

What methodological possibilities for auteurism await us on the scholarly horizon as new voices and filmmakers come on the scene? And how do cultural circumstances introduce reconceptualization of the auteur? It was a question that Staiger and I hoped to address in our collection by inviting a range of young and not-so-young scholars to reflect on ways that auteurism remained in play. Some ten years later, Cynthia Chris and I returned with the same burning set of questions in *Media Authorship* (2013). But because our disciplinary backgrounds were shaped differently, we sought to reframe the questions, particularly as new-media technology ramped up the stakes on how we define the artist behind the screen; moreover, we were interested in the implications for authorship precisely because of rapidly transforming technologies. Concerns over intellectual copyright and political activism were (are) important issues for us as we witnessed another dramatic shift in academia as "film culture" swiftly folded into "media culture."

At the same time, we held fast to our hope in auteur/authorship studies by resisting totalizing claims for its death. As we approached the theoretical concept for the collection, Chris and I were taken with what Roland Barthes referred to as a "friendly return" to the author. Barthes tantalizingly reminded us that his own polemic for "The Death of the Author" was nothing less than "la petite mort," a little death, an orgasm. We were drawn to Barthes's sensual invitation to rediscover "the pleasure of the text" through the auteur, a figure that Jane Gallop characterizes in Barthes's writing as an "[affirmation of] the reader's perverse desires." "Orgasm/*la petite mort*," we argued, "is not, in other words, death once and for all. The author's 'death' provides an opening for multiple interpretations and possibilities. These possibilities are the preferred model for authorship that we situate in this book."[3]

As it turns out, Chris and I (and, to be sure, Staiger and I) were echoing what Andrew Sarris had so urgently defended: "Auteurism was never meant to be an exclusionary doctrine." Perhaps we took on the concept with "gay abandon" (guilty as charged!), and we wrestled with distinctions between "auteur" and "author"; but—and I speak for myself on this count—it was difficult to ignore that auteurism permeates film and media studies in such a way that to abandon it *tout court* is disingenuous. Histories and traditions are not so easily cut off. In fact, such a response carries its own dangers. The language and terms we use to get at complex texts and world events maintain their currency precisely as—nay, because—they are revised and reengaged.

When Derrida was taken to task because he put into service a "watchword" ("apartheid") that the South African regime had jettisoned from its official national lexicon, he reminded his critics that in order "to struggle against this *historical* concept and this *historical* reality, well, then you've got to call a thing by its name."[4] By no means do I wish to conflate the catastrophe that is apartheid with auteurism. What I wish to underscore, however, is that to *insist-on-by-erasing* a historical concept by its name adheres to a flimsy faith in "progress" (and readers of Walter Benjamin are fully aware of the risks attending faith of this sort).

In whatever egoistic way Sarris claimed auteurism as an open-ended methodological model for film studies—and "Auteurism Is Alive and Well" is not short on promoting the author's own significance in the field—he is right to call out oversimplified and rote assertions that dismiss the concept once and for all. Is it not the case that "after all, it depends on where one is writing, at what length, and for whom"?

Writing and Twenty-First-Century Gay Auteurs

With Sarris's remarks in mind, as well as other authors with whom I have been engaged for some time, I'd like to expand auteurist concepts by considering three recent films directed by gay filmmakers. *End of the Century* (dir. Lucio Castro, 2019), *Sorry Angel* (*Plaire, aimer, courir vite*; dir. Christophe Honoré, 2018), and *Sauvage/Wild* (dir. Camille Vidal-Naquet, 2018) are made by so-called Generation X filmmakers. Castro (born 1975), Vidal-Naquet (born 1972), and Honoré (born 1970) are gay-identified filmmakers who turn to the cinema in order to present sexual desire from a perspective that arose during what Castro describes as a period of "in-betweenness."[5] It is a particular moment in coming to terms with AIDS. Honoré reminds us that his generation arrives from a "powerful historical context," and to ignore that "run[s] the risk of minimizing a generation's trauma, and not only for homosexuals." The affect for Honoré is that he views his cinema as one of "incompleteness" (*inachèvement*), a process of making work that must carry on.[6] Vidal-Naquet describes his first venture in feature filmmaking as making cinema hinging on "repetition" and "obsession" that yields "open endings."[7] These filmmakers, in other words, came to their sexual awakening during an unsettled period of AIDS (early to mid-1990s) in which their cinematic worldview resists easy answers or conclusions. It is a cinema on the move. And while AIDS complicated the way sexual pleasure was explored during the period (safe sex), the terms for sexual identity were also in flux. "Queer" emerged as a term to redefine gender and sexual identity, opening experiments in sexual practice to negotiate safe sex (or not). Castro's, Honoré's, and Vidal-Naquet's films thus emerge from an experience that not only put into question the limits for sexual desire but also enabled these men to reimagine homosexuality itself in cinematic terms.

What is striking, moreover, about these three directors who lived through this historical moment is that their films' narratives pivot on writers and readers, or writers of scenes. It is a provocative figuration that navigates the troubled path for homosexual desire because the writer on the screen merges with the auteur's own desire of in-betweenness and toward incompleteness. Foregrounding homosexual desire with AIDS thus raises the ante on personal relationships and self-identity. That the three directors draw upon an intensive interaction between literature and cinema is not necessarily unsurprising. Honoré, for instance, studied literature at the University of Rennes and has written numerous novels, essays, and children's books; Vidal-Naquet comes from a family of teachers and obtained a master's degree in literature with a specialization in nineteenth- and twentieth-century French literature; Castro actively participated in writing and poetry workshops in Argentina for more than nine years. Their literary influences are wide and give way to an approach to filmmaking that Honoré describes as cinematic literariness, a "way of making films in the first person—a mode of filmmaking that derives from literature."[8] Undoubtedly, cinematic literariness through the lens of auteurism harks back to André Bazin and his young acolytes' conceptual linkage between the novelist and the filmmaker. The auteurs discussed here continue and expand on this theoretical enterprise.

Our three gay auteurs are in fact cinephiles in the traditional sense in which the director's relationship to Alexandre Astruc's concept of *le caméra-stylo* (camera-pen) finds a direct line to the literary pen. This relation is coupled with the idea that their cinematic writing is firmly imprinted within the history of cinema. We should keep in mind that Castro, Honoré, and Vidal-Naquet view "traditional" concepts of the auteur and cinephilia as always in transition. For them, they are expansive realizations of the "first-person" filmmaker who grapples with the constraints set before them (culture, politics, the film industry, and so on). *End of the Century, Sauvage/Wild,* and *Sorry Angel* are thus indebted to the auteur-personal cinema associated with the likes of François Truffaut, Éric Rohmer, Jean-Luc Godard, Marguerite Duras, Rainer Werner Fassbinder, Alain Resnais, Michelangelo Antonioni, and Agnès Varda, who all worked against a homogeneous cinema in order to give often-radical perspectives on culture and politics that might otherwise go unnoticed. To these ends, Castro, Honoré, and Vidal-Naquet abide Varda's idea for dynamic "cinécriture," if not Astruc's mise-en-scène-inflected *caméra-stylo*.[9] For these filmmakers, Varda's and Astruc's concepts can no longer be simply rejected as out of date. They are concepts readily available for younger generations to refigure the terms for cinema within the cultural constraints they find themselves.

Writing Himself into the Film: Lucio Castro

In Lucio Castro's *End of the Century* (2018), we are introduced to Ocho (Juan Berberini), a hopeful writer on holiday, recently separated from a long-term partner. Along with his day job as a marketer for an airline in New York, Ocho writes poetry. Later, we learn that he had wished to leave business administration in order to study literature and to become a writer. As the film opens, we follow Ocho for more than ten minutes as he leaves the Barcelona train station, hearing only the ambient sounds and silences of the city. He arrives at his destination midway into his walkabout. Here, Ocho enters a sterile Ikea-esque Airbnb, where he discovers the bare essentials for his stay, including a few bottles of beer and a stick of butter in the refrigerator. While he settles in, Ocho leafs through several books placed around the apartment, whose banal decor is energized only by a balcony that overlooks a city street. From this perch, Ocho looks onto the tree-covered walkway below, one dotted by shops and lingering passersby. It is an ideal location from which to imagine the everyday narratives of the urban strollers, smokers, readers, and window shoppers. He soon spots a handsome young man wearing a Kiss T-shirt. We learn later that this is Javi (Ramón Pujol).

After a night's sleep, we again follow Ocho as he sets out onto the city's streets and heads for the beach. Javi reappears. Ocho, from his beachside blanket, sets aside the book he is reading to watch Javi take to the water. In short order, he does the same. No words are spoken between the men. They swim in parallel but never touch or communicate verbally. As they depart, because of their positions on the beach, they miss the opportunity to connect. Javi rides off on his bicycle, while Ocho resignedly returns to the Airbnb. Back home, Ocho retrieves a beer and heads to the balcony, where, yet again, Javi reappears wearing his Kiss T-shirt. This time, Ocho calls out, "Hey, Kiss!" Javi looks up and acknowledges Ocho.

With Ocho's utterance and Javi's recognition of his call into the film's narrative, Ocho's repetitive wanderings come to an end. His contemplative strolling breaks with the sound of his voice and gives way to the film's narrative interaction between Ocho and Javi. In effect, Ocho's "calling out" to Javi proves critical to the formal dimensions of the film because it resets the film's spatiotemporality, allowing cinematic fantasy and "real time" to blur. In this way, *End of the Century* is not unlike Otto Preminger's *Laura* (1944) in that the viewer is left wondering whether the encounter of the snoozing detective Mark MacPherson (Dana Andrews) with the eponymous character (Gene Tierney) is a dream element or an actual set of events. No obvious formal cues reveal whether Mark is dreaming or awakened in "real time" when Laura enters the scene. As Kristin Thompson reminds us in her analysis of *Laura* (*Breaking the Glass Armor: Neoformalist Film Analysis*), "the film itself refuses to aid us in deciding."[10]

Similarly, *End of the Century* provides no cinematic signpost for a break in time and space. What becomes clear as the film unwinds, and as we reflect on the film as a whole, is that the viewer for *End of the Century* watches Ocho the writer writing a story. Like *Laura*, the film "refuses to aid us in deciding" whether we are in the realm of "the real" or the creative imaginings of the writer/protagonist. As Ocho and Javi journey through the film together, Castro directs our attention to this very reading of the film. When the two men are seen walking through a museum, for instance, they pause before a large, epic canvas. Ocho turns to Javi and tells him, "I'm impressed by the amount of stories needed to paint something like this. Because at the time there was no way to record the event. Someone must have told the painter what the battle was like." Ocho is not only speaking to Javi but also speaking to and for Castro, who records the cinematic drama ("the battle") for the viewer. In this way, the film's auteur/painter (Castro) announces that we are watching his fantasy about a romantic epic peopled and told to him by Ocho and Javi (see fig. 11).

In an interview, Castro makes clear that he is drawn to literary and cinematic entanglements such as those we see in *End of the Century*. He is an avid reader of César Aira's writings, which revel in narrative disorientation, wanderings, and fantastical redirections (consider *The Hare*, 1991). When Castro reads, he reenvisions the place he occupies in "real time" as being the setting of the text: "I tend to experience the world as if I'm reading in real time what is happening to me." Reading, he continues, "gives me a slight sense of detachment to things. And I also write as if I'm reading, surprising myself with the words that appear (and I'm always the happiest when I'm writing)."[11] In this way, Castro embodies what Mikhail Bakhtin calls the "author-creator," whose work of art toggles between the "real and the represented world" so that they are "indissolubly tied up with each other . . . and in mutual interaction."[12] Like the other

Figure 11. Javi and Ocho impressed by the work of art, in *End of the Century*, directed by Lucio Castro.

directors taken up here, Castro models his own reading/writing experience as if underlining Barthes's well-worn phrase, "the birth of the reader must be at the cost of the death of the Author." And, yet, back again.

Cinematically, Castro's entangled writerly relations redirect our attention to Alexandre Astruc's *caméra-stylo*. The cinematic concept serves as the instrument that brings "happiness" to the writer, "surprising" himself and us, as he invites us into the experience of world-making. If Godard's auteurist cinema is, as Peter Wollen describes it, "a process of writing in images, rather than a representation of the world," then recent twenty-first-century gay auteurs such as Castro rehearse New Wave *écriture* to the extent that they infuse their cinéaste elders' aesthetics with seductive homosexuality, one haunted by the shadow of AIDS. Seen this way, *End of the Century* is the unspooling of an author's desire to write, to write cinematically, and to fuse "the real and the represented world" where auteur and spectator commingle, "mutually interact."

The Gay Auteur on the Move: Christophe Honoré

Like Castro, Christophe Honoré and Camille Vidal-Naquet realize—albeit quite differently—cinematic writerliness through a twenty-first-century lens that renders fraught homosexual desire through the eyes of gay filmmakers who came of age during AIDS. All three directors implement *cinécriture* strategies to reckon with their worldview, specifically as it is situated with loss and fear around AIDS. Like many of their predecessors' films from the twentieth century, the narratives in *End of the Century*, *Sauvage/Wild*, and *Sorry Angel* follow characters in tracking shots as they walk and dance or use 180- or 360-degree pans while characters sit and stare or read and write.

The mobile figure linked to a mobile *caméra-stylo* is especially prescient for gay auteurs' films. The queer figure-on-the-move—the writers-of-scenes—emerges with historical import. When, for example, Oscar Wilde assumed the pseudonym "Sebastian Melmoth," it was not only to hide from the insults he faced following his trial; Wilde aligned himself with the "Wandering Jew" character Sebastian Melmoth in Charles Maturin's novel *Melmoth the Wanderer* (1820).[13] In assuming this moniker, Wilde stressed his homosexual desire as an existence on the move. He is not alone. From Arthur Rimbaud's "worn-out shoes" in the poem "Wandering" to Allen Ginsberg's "best minds of my generation" in *Howl*, "who wandered around and around at midnight in the railroad yard," to David Wojnarowicz's assertion in *Close to the Knives: A Memoir of Disintegration* that "transition is always a relief," the literary portrayal of gay men's sexual desire revolves on and around movement.[14]

The homosexual wanderer is therefore not dissimilar to the homosexual cruiser, who seamlessly combines walking and dancing and who experiences sexual desire on the fly yet is deeply touched—indeed, moved by—his multiple encounters. Castro's, Honoré's, and Vidal-Naquet's films do not overlook the way cruising is choreographic (each of their films includes sequences of cruising). The cinema for queer filmmakers proves ideal for giving life to the history of lifelong wanderings that delight in ephemeral and homoerotic touch, in which transient and often incomplete satisfaction occurs (consider Fassbinder's *Querelle* [1982], Gus Van Sant's *Gerry* [2002], Chantal Akerman's *Je, tu, il, elle* [1974]). Wilde once said that smoking a cigarette was the ideal moment since it always leaves one completely unsatisfied. One always needs another cigarette. Smoking and cruising are not dissimilar.

For Castro, Honoré, and Vidal-Naquet, it is the choreographed, cruising camera that presents homosexual desire on the move. In their films, we see malleable desire embodied by writers who move through the world, who are effectively writing the scenes that unfold before us. No more beautifully is this cinematic literariness realized than in Honoré's *Sorry Angel*. Set in 1993, Honoré's film introduces two gay writers—Arthur (Vincent Lacoste) and Jacques (Pierre Delandonchamps)—who during the film's journey explore their sexual desires, romantic fantasies, and ultimate loss through AIDS. Arthur, the younger of the two, reads voraciously. Unlike the older, accomplished writer, Jacques, Arthur is a young university student building out the parameters for his place in the world. For him, reading books is not merely the wellspring of knowledge but also the means to learn how to live. His enthusiasm for books is shared with his young friends in the form of gifts to one another or in citing lengthy passages from authors in casual conversation. At the same time, Arthur's deep immersion in a literary world throws his and his peers' youthful existence into ambiguous disarray. Reading transforms their intimate relationships because reading books prompts new ideas, new worldviews. At one point, when book reading adversely alters Arthur's relationship with his girlfriend (Adèle Wisme), she literally throws the book at him because of his ever-shifting ideas about their relationship and his sexuality.

While Arthur and his young cohorts read, the established and well-trod author, Jacques, writes. His novels are successful. He is preparing a theatrical production during the time of the film. And given that he is dealing with the late stages of AIDS, he copiously details in writing his final wishes. With the disease, the spawning romantic relationship between Arthur and Jacques begins within the constraint of time. Their romance develops as a sexualized mentorship in which Jacques teaches Arthur how to write and Arthur rejuvenates Jacques's love for reading. But writing and reading—like the love between Arthur and Jacques (even in death)—remain entwined. They are inseparable and depend on each other.

In a key scene, Honoré presents Arthur and Jacques's intertwined relationship, in which matters of life and death hinge on the intricacies of reading and writing. From Arthur's dorm in Rennes, he takes a call from Jacques in Paris. In Arthur's bed is a young blond, Stéphane (Luca Malinowski), whom Arthur picked up while hitchhiking. A cross between a Nordic ideal and a painting that resembles a meeting ground between Caravaggio and Frans Hals (or something more literary, as we see shortly), Stéphane takes the opportunity to graze through Arthur's literary den. When Arthur leaves to take Jacques's call, Stéphane eyes Arthur's stack of nightstand novels resting atop a cinema magazine. On the table, we see the symbolically weighted copies of Umberto Sabo's unfinished novel about a relationship between an older man and younger woman, *Ernesto* (1953; published posthumously in 1975); Christophe Donner's novel *Giton*, about a romance between a younger and older man (1990); and Hervé Guibert's collection of poetic short stories *L'Image fantôme* (1981). Stéphane also looks upon the bedroom wall Arthur has covered with photos of Guibert (Honoré has made no secret that Guibert holds a central place in his recent thinking). Honoré's precise mise-en-scène shapes the contours of Arthur's most personal space, in which lovers pass through and through which Guibert's words and images fully resonate: "Writing is my faculty for love, my human faculty" (see fig. 12).[15]

With Stéphane left waiting, Arthur goes to his roommate's bedroom, where he speaks to Jacques. Jacques asks what literary type of blond is in Arthur's bed: Is it a "Whitman" or a "Vondelpark" blond? (Vondelpark houses a cruising area in Amsterdam familiar to gay writers, including Christopher Isherwood, among others). Not recognizing the references, Jacques walks Arthur through a gay-literary tradition of blonds, since the young writer "needs his library filled." His "youth and illusion" must discover ground

Figure 12. Stéphane fingers Arthur's bedside book collection, in *Sorry Angel*, directed by Christophe Honoré.

on which to express his enthusiastic desire. Attentively and eagerly, Arthur grabs paper and pen to take notes while Jacques explains the intimate exchanges—both literary and personal—that occur around Walt Whitman, Christopher Isherwood, W. H. Auden, Arthur Rimbaud, and Allen Ginsberg. Jacques's recounting from his vast literary readings creates an erotic and intellectual rush for Arthur, who urgently scribbles notes from Jacques's tutorial. The long-distance writing-and-reading moment between men enfolds when Honoré commingles the writer/reader intimacy into a singular cinematic space. On what appears to be a natural cut between the spaces of Rennes and Paris, where we hear and see Jacques continue to spin his tale of homoerotic literary desire, time and space have in fact converged to reveal Arthur resting between Jacques's legs in Paris. The passionate energy with which Jacques illustrates the network of blond desire across the gay literary canon is thus transposed cinematically so that love between Jacques and Arthur surmounts the limitations of distance and the finality of death. Honoré's cinematic writerliness puts into relief Arthur and Jacques's unparalleled intimacy, in which reader and writer, writer and reader, and their histories become one. The scene thus marks Arthur's joining into the literary history that Jacques unravels for him and to which they now both belong.

Writing Wildly: Camille Vidal-Naquet

Vidal-Naquet's *Sauvage/Wild* opens with a doctor writing notes about a patient who sits before him in an examination room. From all appearances—antiseptic exam room, harsh lighting, documentary-style camera movement—the doctor's notetaking is read as a legitimate exam procedure. That is, we look upon what is otherwise an innocuous setting in which the film's protagonist, Léo/Drago (Félix Maritaud), visits the doctor. It turns out, however, that the scene we witness is precisely that—a mise-en-scène of a fantasy (to paraphrase Laplanche and Pontalis). The doctor/patient relationship is soon revealed to be a performance. From the very outset of the film, then, Vidal-Naquet introduces relations between bodies as ones in which writing the scene plays a central role in exploring homosexual desire.

In interviews and public forums, Vidal-Naquet highlights that the actors in *Sauvage/Wild*—especially Félix—underwent rigorous choreographic lessons with professional dancers.[16] In rehearsing actors this way, Vidal-Naquet prepared the performers to work closely with the film's cinematographer, Jacques Girault (Castro and Honoré also choreograph the relationship between actors and cinematographer, Bernat Mestres and Rémy Chevrin, respectively). For Vidal-Naquet, Léo's cinematic body is knitted into the film's camera movement. During handheld sequences and long-take tracking shots, the camera and body are practically inseparable. The moving camera, thereby, attaches itself to Léo's wandering body, a body always preparing for its next sexual scenario. If, as Jacques Derrida and Eve Kosofsky Sedgwick remind us, performance, choreography, and cinematography are modes of writing, Vidal-Naquet's auteurist impulses serve to imbricate body and camera in the act of writing homosexual fantasies.[17]

The documentary-style camera work (precisely rehearsed by the director and his director of photography) draws out the complex paradox that is Léo's transient existence as a hustler on the street. Although he is a street-savvy young man, he is also naive, innocent. Not only does the camera observe Léo in his experiences, but the camera's attachment to its subject also suggests itself as a caring onlooker. It's a tricky position to achieve because while the camera caresses (to use Vidal-Naquet's description) Léo and watches over him, it simultaneously allows the boy freedom to choose existence on his own terms. The caring and observing camera in *Sauvage/Wild* echoes the cinematic world that François Truffaut offers us in *L'Enfant sauvage* (*The Wild Child*, 1969). Both films develop relationships between men in which feral, "primitive" existence and learned, "civilized" culture work in concert yet at odds with each other.

Doctors in *Sauvage/Wild* and *L'Enfant sauvage* take copious notes about their subjects. They inscribe into their journals the medical and scientific details that define the young queer men whose seemingly unstable existence requires language to make sense of it. Indeed, significant currency is given the doctors' writings and analytical readings of the "wild" boys' savage impulses. Yet the doctors in Truffaut's and Vidal-Naquet's worlds deeply care for their charges and, perhaps, question their own trappings of civilization. The hugs exchanged in both films between doctors and the boys illustrate the way visceral connections supersede intellectual codification.

In Léo's walking to and from the scenes in which he performs, he moves toward the new scenes yet to be written and, as it turns out, to be read. In an early critical scene, writing and reading overlap in the fantasy-making between john and hustler. It involves Léo's meeting with an older book collector. The scene illustrates a homoerotic dimension in which Vidal-Naquet brings together his immersion in writing and reading, which, moreover, directly bears on the auteur's cinephiliac queer imprint.

Met at a gay club, Léo's client is a widower who lives in a large, well-appointed apartment. While the client gently flips the pages of an old book, the first thing he says to Léo is that he "loves its grain." As he recounts his passion for collecting, the camera reveals the older man's overstuffed library shelves, upon which Léo gazes with doe-like eyes. It is clear that he is drawn to the warmth of both his client and the "grain" of the books that surround him. When the john hands a book to Léo and asks him to read, Léo holds the book, feels its paper, and then glances uncertainly at its pages. Does he not wish to read? Is he unable to read? Have the drink and drugs at the disco preempted any sort of reading whatsoever? He finally tells the client that he is a "bad reader." The man responds, "Never mind. We won't read tonight." Léo, Vidal-Naquet tells us, "is an excellent worker, but he's not good with words. He's good with his body." As such, reading and writing are only realized bodily for Léo (see fig. 13).

The scene yields one more act of writing and reading. Vidal-Naquet is deeply indebted to Hitchcock's cinema. Here, when the sexual encounter is cut short because the older man can no longer comfortably be penetrated, he tells Léo about his wife, Irène, who passed away. With her portrait looking onto the couple, Léo's client tells a story about how he would watch his wife before bedtime while she sat at her vanity table, brushing her hair. As we hear his recollection, the camera cuts to his scene of memory—the vanity with hairbrush and mirror in place. In doing so, Vidal-Naquet conjures Hitchcock's mise-en-scène in *Rebecca* (1940). Vidal-Naquet's camera records the two men, in bed, nestled together, as they write their scene, which incorporates literary traditions, past loves, and the cinema. Although the sexual act fails, hustler and john share the night together in gentle embrace. Reading, writing, and cinema fuse in Vidal-Naquet's cinema so that homosexual desire realizes itself in unexpected ways.

For Castro, Honoré, and Vidal-Naquet, character transformations are made possible because the bodies and cameras they put into service for their films intermingle so as to write scenes of desire. This is why *End of the Century, Sorry Angel*, and *Sauvage/Wild* are more readily seen as narratives threaded like a fine piece of string, vignettes held together by a series of moments in and of themselves. Psychological backgrounds

Figure 13. Without reading, *Léo* admires the grain of his client's book, in *Sauvage/Wild*, directed by Camille Vidal-Naquet.

are barely available, peripheral characters move in and out of the protagonists' lives, with some never to return, and the films' ambiguous endings suggest that the cinematic wanderers have by choice reached nowhere in particular with no permanency on the horizon. The trauma of historical circumstances from which Castro, Honoré, and Vidal-Naquet emerge (AIDS), and therefore their cinematic approaches to this trauma in relationship to homosexual desire, effectually opens writing and reading (the very essence of *la petite mort*) to reimagining the possibilities to live precisely because of this history.

Notes

1   Sarris, "Auteurism Is Alive and Well," 60–63 (emphasis added).

2   Gerstner and Staiger, introduction to *Authorship and Film*, xi.

3   Chris and Gerstner, introduction to *Media Authorship*, 8.

4   Derrida, "But Beyond," 163 (emphasis in original).

5   Castro's remarks were made at the premiere of *End of the Century* at the 2019 New Directors Series (Museum of Modern Art, March 30, 2019).

6   Gerstner, "NYFF Interview."

7   Gerstner, "Excellent Worker." *Sauvage/Wild* also premiered at the 2019 New Directors Series. Vidal-Naquet reiterated these comments during Q&A sessions at MoMA and Film Forum.

8   Correspondence with author, April 1, 2019.

9   See Astruc, "Birth of a New Avant-Garde"; and Conway, *Agnès Varda*, 122.

10   Thompson, *Breaking the Glass Armor*, 162.

11   Correspondence with the author, April 1, 2019.

12   Bakhtin, "Forms of Time of the Chronotope in the Novel," 254.

13   See Ellman, *Oscar Wilde*, 528.

14   Ginsberg, *Howl*, 9; Rimbaud, "Wandering," 47; Wojnarowicz, *Close to the Knives*, 62. Wojnarowicz makes an important "appearance" in Castro's film.

15   Guibert, *Mausoleum of Lovers*, 157. It is difficult to underestimate the significance Guibert's writing has for Honoré's cinematic conceptions. This is particularly true in the way ciné-literariness cuts across both artists' work: "As for me I write," Guibert notes, "without much regret, but I seethe with the cinema" (185). Honoré channels Guibert's queer creative spirit.

16   See Gerstner, "Excellent Worker."

17   See, for instance, Derrida, *Of Grammatology*; and Sedgwick and Parker, *Performativity and Performance*.

14

STRANGE DAYS

Christophe Honoré's Multimedia Trilogy

When *Plaire, aimer, courir vite* [*Sorry Angel*] premiered at the Cannes Film Festival in 2018 as an Official Selection in Competition, the filmmaker Christophe Honoré was asked if, following the success of Robin Campillo's *BPM: 120 battements* (the 2017 Grand Prix winner), a new film about AIDS was necessary. Honoré found the question curious and responded with another question: "Can we not talk about AIDS because another film has done so?" The cultural effect of AIDS and its impact on gay culture is, to be sure, difficult to "capture" in a single work of art. Honoré's latest trilogy—the novel *Ton père* (2017), the film *Plaire, aimer, courir vite* (2018), and the play *Les Idoles* (2018–19)—showcases precisely this effort to intervene on multiple fronts from his perspective as a French gay man.

Along with numerous accolades the press conferred on all three works, *Ton père* was a 2017 Prix Médicis finalist, and *Sorry Angel* won the prestigious Louis Delluc Prize in 2018, when it became an official selection for competition at Cannes. *Les Idoles* has only recently opened on the Paris stage, to rave reviews (including in the *New York Times*), after premiering in Lausanne, Switzerland, in 2018.[1] With the 2019 theatrical release of *Sorry Angel* in the United States (it had screened initially as part of the New York Film Festival in 2018), it is worth considering the film in relationship to the trilogy from which it derives.

As a filmmaker, novelist, and playwright, Honoré has said that creating a single work of art would limit his exploration of not only AIDS but also its impact on the French arts more generally. The trilogy, moreover, zeroes in on the impact AIDS has had on contemporary gay artists, especially those of Honoré's generation, born in the 1970s. *Sorry Angel*, therefore, holds center court in the trilogy that Honoré refers to as an "autoportrait." In the three works—as he has in his previous novels,

"Strange Days: Christophe Honoré's Multimedia Trilogy." *Cinéaste* 44, no. 2. Copyright © 2019 by Cineaste, Inc.

films, and theatrical productions—Honoré inserts himself in a history of French gay artists who, in this particular case, died from AIDS. The actor/director Cyril Collard (1957–1993), the dramaturg Bernard-Marie Koltès (1948–1989), the filmmaker Jacques Demy (1931–1990), the writer and journalist Hervé Guibert (1955–1991), the theater director Jean-Luc Lagarce (1957–1995), and the film critic Serge Daney (1944–1992) haunt the triptych.

When I met with Honoré in January 2019, after seeing his production of *Les Idoles*, he underscored that the trilogy as autoportrait is a "transmission." In this context, "transmission" emphasizes movement: movement of and between bodies, movement of blood and bodily fluids, movement of creative energies and ideas. In short, "transmission" involves a giver and receiver, an affective performance that touches its participants. Indeed, as many critics have noted, the trilogy is a moving experience that draws the spectator into a sentient encounter with French gay culture and history as they are linked with sexual desire and death. In conceiving the project in this way, Honoré situates himself as artist and spectator through a first-person dialogue with the other French gay artists who inform his work. The art historian Michael Baxandall in *Patterns of Intention* tells us that the artist "acts reciprocally on his culture [so that the work of art] becomes a serial and continually self-redefining operation, permanent problem reformulation," pointing out that the artist acts "as a social being in cultural circumstances."[2] And it is the homophobic "cultural circumstances" in France itself that triggered Honoré's "self-redefining operation."

Formed in 2012 by Catholics and other extreme-right-wing members, the anti-gay family organization La Manif Pour Tous (The Protest for Everyone) rallied hard to prevent gay and lesbian marriage. The group also pushed vigorously against gay households in which children are raised (*homoparentalité*). Their loud and very public protests against gay families directly affronted Honoré's life. As a gay father—and one who never shied away from claiming himself the "homosexual narrator" (as in his novel *Le livre pour enfants*, 2005) or from dealing with AIDS and gay men (as in both his novel and film *Tout contre Léo*, 2002) and homoeroticism (as in his film *Homme au bain*, 2010)—Honoré recognized an organization intent on curtailing choice not only for himself but also for an entire population of gay men and women. La Manif Pour Tous aimed its sights on containing sexual desire for all. Its movement jarred Honoré out of what he describes as his "blindness" to French homophobia.

The Novel

After Honoré's awakening to the ugly homophobia that surrounded him, his auto-portrait trilogy traces the contours of his life as a gay artist in that context. While we "hear" his voice across all three works (literally onstage in *Les Idoles*), his authorial voice within the autoportrait, echoing Baxandall, resonates "as a social being in cultural circumstances." In his novel *Ton père*, the gay-father figure invokes Honoré's experience to the extent that "Christophe Honoré, the gay father," shadows any French gay man who confronts chilling homophobia as he raises his child. The father figure in *Ton père* is at once personal as he is communal—and without burying his sexual desire, which *Ton père* openly acknowledges. *Ton père* instead delightfully, humorously, and erotically wanders through strategies that the father must navigate to, on the one hand, pick up his child at school while, on the other, necessarily sustain a life of sexual pleasure and creativity.

Ton père thus relaunches the "homosexual narrator"—"Honoré"—through freshly opened eyes. If La Manif Pour Tous was the impetus behind the trilogy in its placing homosexual desire and choice on the political chopping block, AIDS significantly permeates Honoré's approach to the novel's aesthetic and narrative design. In conjuring the names of artists and philosophers who died from AIDS—Koltès, Demy, and Daney, as well Derek Jarman (1942–1994) and Robert Mapplethorpe (1946–1989)—Honoré incorporates in the novel actual photographs of the artists who have passed. Their portraits create a montage across the novel that intermingles with Honoré's still-image photography presenting images of boys undressing or street views from his apartment. At the outset of the trilogy, *Ton père* introduces the project as a multimedia event. The novel thus marks the trilogy's task as one that reflects on the twenty-first-century gay father as a figure necessarily imbued with the histories and imaginative forces of the fathers who came before him. *Ton père*, as a consequence, refuses the limitations of the novelistic medium or of any given genre. Honoré's novelistic autoportrait introduces the concept of the trilogy, therefore, as a project of transmission committed to transformation across various media.

The Film

The second installment in the trilogy, *Sorry Angel*, folds out from *Ton père* rather than standing as a distinct filmic entity. This is not to suggest that each of the three works must be viewed as a whole—each can and does stand on its own. Yet, by looking at the three as movable and overlapping screens within screens or texts within texts, Honoré's concept may be more fully appreciated.

From the novel and the still photos it incorporates, Honoré turns to cinema, where AIDS and sexual desire intersect in complex ways. *Sorry Angel* follows the undergraduate years of a young gay man who studies at the University of Rennes—the campus where Honoré studied and where he found outlets for homosexual pleasure, at the same time as his creative energies developed. Reading books, going to the cinema and college pubs, and visiting the town's gay cruising sites became his wellspring of self-knowledge, just as they would for any gay student. Not unlike Honoré, Arthur (Vincent Lacoste) in *Sorry Angel* pursues sexual desire through the art that surrounds him at university. Books, film, and theater mix intimately as critical components to Arthur's homoerotic pleasures and his ambition to become a writer. The erotic heart of *Sorry Angel*, therefore, hovers around the process through which the arts—especially literature—give life to desire.

Arthur in fact meets the well-known, older, Parisian author and gay father Jacques (Pierre Deladonchamps) at the movies in Rennes, where Jacques is in town to direct a play. In the movie theater, the two men make eye contact during a screening of Jane Campion's *The Piano* (1993)—an appropriate film as backdrop for the encounter since *Sorry Angel* brings Eros and Art into constant play, as Campion does when uniting a woman's sexual desire with her beloved art form of music. The chance meeting in the cinema is doubly charged for Arthur and Jacques because the budding young writer and his older professional counterpart discover a profound connection, only to be undercut by Jacques's HIV status. Eros and Thanatos commence with the movies.

The stakes for "transmission" are heightened in *Sorry Angel* since the love that develops between Arthur and Jacques has no future other than death. But, for Honoré, the tragedy that is AIDS and the love it forestalls necessarily drive gay men to translate loss into creative and political practice (in whatever form that takes). It is, of course, nothing new to say that an artist is influenced by deceased authors who have come before. One of Honoré's treasured literary figures, J. D. Salinger, once asserted, "A writer, when he's asked to discuss his craft, ought to get up and call out in a loud voice just the names of the writers he loves. I love Kafka, Flaubert, Tolstoy, Chekhov, Dostoevsky, Proust, O'Casey, Rilke, Lorca, Keats, Rimbaud, Burns, E. Brontë, Jane Austen, Henry James, Blake, Coleridge. I won't name any living writers. I don't think it's right."[3] In calling out the names of those who have passed, Salinger—like Honoré—draws upon the creative impulses of the dead to infuse his own work, insisting on the living force of the dead. The artist cannot escape the dead or the historical leavings in their wake. During the height of AIDS activism, gay artists and intellectuals were remembered for reenergizing the (recent and not-so-recent) dead through aesthetic means (think David Wojnarowicz's conjuring of Rimbaud or Douglas Crimp's theoretical fusing of "mourning and militancy").[4] And, like Salinger, Honoré "call[s] out in a loud voice" those artists he loves. "I believe," Honoré has said in a *Film Comment* interview, "that when you write a book or make a movie, the people you would like to touch first and foremost are the people who made you want to write books or make movies."[5]

But for gay men, another set of troubling questions about the rapid and premature death of so many remain. What might these artists have accomplished? What might have we learned from their responses to our contemporary world? What would we have seen? Heard? Reenvisioned? What might Koltès, Guibert, Demy, Foucault, Jarman, Mapplethorpe, Marlon Riggs, and Keith Haring have given to an eager and younger generation of gay men? Their deaths proved to be a rupture all the more violent for artists, intellectuals, philosophers, and activists because unlike Foucault, who was able to march with Genet to protest prison conditions, or Haring, who was able to hang out and watch movies with Andy Warhol, gay men of Honoré's generation were not afforded these intimate encounters. They can only communicate with their elders through imagination. "I would have liked for my first film to be at a film festival," Honoré reflects in *Film Comment*, "where I came across Jacques Demy and he put his hand on my shoulder and said, 'Welcome little guy!'"[6] In returning to 1993 Rennes, Honoré's *Sorry Angel* evokes the enthusiasm of gay youth, as the relationship between a famous older writer and a developing younger writer reimagines his own longed-for real-life encounter.

In this way, *Sorry Angel* investigates a critical moment during the rise of AIDS. The disease psychologically and emotionally infiltrated Honoré's generation in ways quite different from those who were born ten years earlier. The film looks at a precise time and place in which a complicated transgenerational relationship takes place. Arthur, in his early twenties, and Jacques, in his midthirties, embody this phenomenon. But they also figure a larger set of circumstances present in the early 1990s. The generation of gay men in their twenties during the '80s was moved to the forefront of urgent political activism when mourning the loss of friends and lovers during an endless parade of death. Educating one another about "safe sex" and the science of the virus in their bodies formed a quick—albeit high—learning curve. By the early '90s, failed drug regimens to combat HIV appeared regularly, and thousands perished. At the same time, the campaign by AIDS activists around condoms and "safe sex" benefited a new generation of gay men. In many ways, the early '90s was an awkward and unsettling period to be a young gay man. Sexual desire and practice would not be the same for this group as it had been for the prior generation. Skin-to-skin pleasure was extinguished. Sex was framed by new rules, uncertainty, and anxiety. But desire is not equal to sex alone.

In *Sorry Angel*, Honoré plays out the disjointed transgenerational homosexual experience in which love between men is short-circuited at a critical point in the history of AIDS. On the one hand, the film is distinct from James Ivory's *Call Me By Your Name* (2017), in which pre-AIDS transgenerational love between men is romanticized through idyllic artistic traditions. On the other hand, Honoré's film differs from Vincent Gagliostro's *After Louie* (2017), in which the film's transgenerational relationship recounts a politically and aesthetically complex representation of love between men some twenty years after the full thrust of AIDS art and activism. Because *Sorry Angel* locates its narrative on the hinge between these two periods, Honoré trains his lens on a transitional moment. If *Call Me* and *After Louie* take place during clearly defined periods in gay history—pre-AIDS awareness and post-AIDS activism—both films deal in nostalgia (the latter politically, the former not so much). *Sorry Angel* occurs somewhere in between. Honoré's film takes stock of a moment of unknowingness in which the effect of AIDS cannot be cordoned off as "past" or "post-." For Honoré, 1993 is a peculiar and vexed moment for homosexuality.

When *Sorry Angel* draws to its close, Arthur is sitting near a public telephone in Rennes, awaiting Jacques's call from Paris. It's the call that never arrives because Jacques has succumbed to his illness. In that moment—1993—starry-eyed Arthur anticipates a future. It is a future in which Arthur looks forward to a range of hopes and dreams as a writer and gay man. At that moment, however, the gay man as artist begins his young career amidst the many around him who are transitioning to death.

Honoré, in 1993, also waited hopefully. While doing so, he came upon another gay artist who importantly influenced the trilogy.

The Play

When I first heard the English translation for *Plaire, aimer, courir vite* (*Sorry Angel*), I was disappointed. In fact, when Honoré first conceived the film, its working title was "Plaire, baiser, courir vite" (To please, to fuck, to run fast). It is a title, to my mind, that catches Honoré's playful mischievousness. The French title that finally prevailed nevertheless maintained the spirit of the work without annoying the censors. When I saw the production of *Les Idoles* at the Odéon-Théâtre de l'Europe in Paris, I rethought my take on the English translation of *Plaire*. Prompting my change of mind is what happens onstage when the curtain raises on this, the third part of the trilogy.

A figure not yet mentioned, though one who played a significant role in Honoré's realization of the trilogy, is the choreographer Dominique Bagouet (1951–1992). Honoré first encountered Bagouet's work when, as a student in Rennes, he traveled to Paris to explore its various art worlds and gay scene. He attended a dance performance of *Jours étranges* (*Strange Days*, 1990) and was taken with Bagouet's use of the Doors for the work's soundtrack. The choreographer wished to evoke his immersive experiences during the late '60s with the American band's unique sound. "I remember these sort of 'Beatnik nights' we used to spend lulled by Jim Morrison's warm voice,"

Bagouet recounts. "The atmosphere of these 'strange days' quite correspond to the distress of our adolescence which was looking for its own values in what became now a kind of mythology. This age also experienced ill-defined and obscure desires of revolt against norms and established codes."[7]

Bagouet's concept immediately took hold for Honoré. He was taken with *Jours étranges*'s remarkable choreography, in which dancers perform between staged silences and Morrison's mellifluous voice. Selected tracks from the *Strange Days* album ("Strange Days," "I Can't See Your Face in My Mind," and "When the Music's Over") give life to the dancers as they joyfully bounce around the stage, sensually envelop one another, and flutter their arms upward as if floating like angels. The dancing angels who appear toward the end of Bagouet's dance move effortlessly to "When the Music's Over." It is this particular angelic hovering and the Doors' number that echoes in *Les Idoles*. The play's opening is layered with the dancing angels and Morrison's singing, while Honoré's own voice is heard as he recalls the Sunday in 1993 Paris when he first saw Bagouet's *Jours étranges*.

Honoré explains in his notes to the play that his gay role models who died from AIDS invariably instructed his life, his loves, and his creativity. In experiencing their loss as well as the hope they left behind, "How," he asks, "do we dance now?"[8] As the third part of the trilogy, *Les Idoles* wrestles with this question by restaging life for his idols: the filmmaker Cyril Collard (1957–1993), Hervé Guibert, Jean-Luc Lagarce, Serge Daney, Bernard-Marie Koltès, and Jacques Demy. The play is not simply hagiography. Honoré does not shy away from the problematic histories his idols have with expressing their homosexuality (Demy's closeted history kept secure by his wife, Agnès Varda; Lagarce's admiration for the gay xenophobe Renaud Camus; Collard's rather large, if charming, ego). American figures such as Rock Hudson and Elizabeth Taylor are equally spotlighted for their significance while questioned for their awkward assertions about AIDS, especially in the French context.

But Honoré loves his gay French fathers. They are emotional, funny, intelligent, and giving. They are not short on opinions about how to deal with the politics of AIDS or, in fact, what "gay" ultimately means. They debate intensely such gay identities as "top," "bottom," and "versatile." "Versatile," in particular, throws the group into turmoil as they try to understand just exactly what it means. Fickle? Boring? Unstable? In this way, Honoré—as the omniscient voice in the room—devilishly toys with his idols' peccadillos. For instance, Demy (embodied by Marlène Saldana) strolls the stage in a fur coat, reviving Dominique Sanda's performance in his film *Une chambre en ville* (1982). When Demy decides it's time to perform on Honoré's stage—and he will perform dramatically as many times as he cowers in the corners of the stage—he sings and dances to "Les chansons d'un jour été" from *Les demoiselles de Rochefort* (1967). As Demy's joyous enthusiasm for his fabulous film and music intensify, we quickly become aware that Saldana wears absolutely nothing underneath her giant fur coat. Saldana's voluptuous body beautifully displays itself as the coat opens during her turns and flips onstage. She revels in her liberated body, which will nonetheless rewrap itself at the end of her performance. Saldana's dance fully expresses Demy's complicated relationship to his homosexuality.

This dance is but one example in *Les Idoles* of homage, which functions as an aesthetic trope in keeping with Honoré's concept of "transmission." As I've written elsewhere, Honoré's turn on homage is a queer rewriting, a form of camp in which *to camp* is a transformative act, at once loving yet critical.[9] If Honoré's work is heavy with homage, it is because he recognizes his debt to a history of artists, as well as his responsibility to critically transition their work into concepts of his own. Hence, *Les Idoles* transforms gender (Guibert is played by Marina Foïs, while Demy is performed by Saldana). Genres are also transformed, as musical tropes, drama, docu-fiction, and comedy overlap. Koltès's own desire to be transformed into his idol—John Travolta—takes place onstage through his compatriots' offering to re-create the making of *Saturday Night Fever* (1977). Honoré re-creates the making of the film, which is directed onstage by, of course, Cyril Collard and costars Serge Daney. While a camera shoots live Koltès's and Daney's reenactments of the film, a prerecorded version of their very same performance is seen from a different angle on an overhead screen. Screens transition into other screens, bodies transition into other bodies, and the past transitions into the present. It's a dazzling and overwhelming conceptualization of what Honoré calls "transmission." And as with all provocative camp, there is more.

With the theatrical setting, Honoré is provided another sensorial tool that is refused the other trilogy segments: smell. Although he consistently reaches to incorporate odors into his other works through language and cinematic technique, the theater is the one medium that allows Honoré to deeply involve the spectator's multiple senses. If the figures onstage recall in words the smell of fried fish in Foucault's apartment (Guibert) or a boy's cum, which "smells of warm rain" (Koltès), they also literally bring smell into the performance. *Les Idoles* opens with the actors lighting their cigarettes as they flutter onto the stage. The smell of smoke saturates the theater just as it surely filled the world of the figures resurrected onstage. Then, while *Saturday Night Fever* is (re)filmed, Demy offers his services as the set's caterer. As the shooting unfolds, the director now transitions into a cook, who whips up the Breton specialty—crêpes. The smell of frying dough lingers throughout the theater as cast and crew for *Saturday*

Night Fever imbibe Demy's delightfully prepared snack. Spectators for *Les Idoles* are treated sensually on so many fronts.

Les Idoles brings to a close the project that Honoré has brewed for more than twenty years. It took that many years, he has said, to digest the enormity of its subject matter and material. The trilogy does not deliver a complete or satisfactory recounting of lives lost because of AIDS. It does not achieve an explanation of why some men shy away from expressing their homosexuality either in their art or as men with children. It does not punish the political or artistic decisions made by those living during the most intense years of the AIDS pandemic. Instead, the trilogy fits snuggly within Honoré's term for his work as an artist: "incomplete." If, recalling Baxandall's comments that the artist employs upon his or her culture and history "a serial and continually self-redefining operation, permanent problem reformulation," we not only give space to Honoré's reimaginings but also open ourselves to a process of creativity in order to reimagine our own queer lives.

Notes

1 Cappelle, "On Paris Stages, Gay Artists Look Back."

2 Baxandall, *Patterns of Intention*, 73.

3 Slawenski, *J. D. Salinger*, 182.

4 See Wojnarowicz's photographic play with Rimbaud in his *Rimbaud in New York, 1978–79* and Douglas Crimp's "Mourning and Militancy."

5 Gerstner, "NYFF Interview."

6 Gerstner.

7 "Je me souviens de ces soirées à tendance 'beatnik' bercées par la voix chaude de Jim Morrison, le climat de ces 'strange days' correspondait parfaitement au désarroi de notre adolescence qui cherchait alors, dans ce qui est devenu une sorte de mythologie, ses propres valeurs et vivait aussi d'obscurs désirs mal définis de révolte contre les normes et les codes établis" (Bagouet, "Note d'intention du chorégraphe," 7).

8 Honoré, "Note d'intention"; translation by the author.

9 Gerstner and Nahmias, *Christophe Honoré*, 43.

SPECULATIONS ON THE ORIGIN OF THE WORLD

15

Notes toward Queer Feminism, Gustave Courbet's L'Origine du monde, and Christophe Honoré's 17 fois Cécile Cassard

To my father, for my mother

Jean Baudry asks, "But if cinema was really the answer to a *desire inherent in our psychical structure*, how can we date its first beginnings? Would it be," he continues, "too risky to propose that painting, like theater, for lack of suitable technological and economic conditions, were dry runs in the approximation not only of the world of representation but of what might result from a certain aspect of its functioning and which only the cinema is in a position to implement?" In considering the *cinema as a history of desire*—that is, the search for "lost satisfaction" through moving images—and, rather than tracking the "history of [cinema's] invention" as a teleological enterprise meant to satisfy desire once and for all, Baudry's query gives way to a more provocative aesthetic and theoretical turn on cinematic history. If it is "very possible that there never was any first invention of cinema," how might we nevertheless engage with the *history of the cinematic* as an impulse to satisfy desire? In other words, by shifting the terms for the history of cinema (one informed by empirical firsts) to a history of desire in which the idea of cinema always already served as a reach for "desire inherent in our psychical structure," we discover a malleable and psychically relational dynamic across the arts. If we consider painting, for instance, as something more than a "dry run" up to nineteenth-century cinematic technology, we quickly discover that painting, among other historical media, "have obviously produced their own specificity and their own history, but their existence has at its origin a psychical source equivalent to the one which stimulated the invention of cinema."[1] It is precisely to the "psychical source equivalent" of the other arts that "stimulate[s]" the cinema to which I turn for the work in this chapter.

Indeed, Christophe Honoré's *17 fois Cécile Cassard* foregrounds cinema's formal dimensions in such a way that invites the spectator into the history of the creative arts and, mutatis mutandis, the history of desire. As Honoré's first feature film, it draws our attention to the "desire inherent in our psychical structure" that paves the way for a career in film, theater, opera, writing in which we might ably explore Baudry's query into cinematic "origins." In this way, *Cécile* assumes a place in this theoretical discourse in relationship to feminist thought on woman's relationship to "origins." Woman, of course, bears the historical burden to represent the site of origins, a representation long desired by male artists—as we will see—in their quest to identify the originary moment. For Honoré, the mother-figure plays a critical role. For him, by marking Woman, the Mother, as the signpost for original meaning—the site for retrieving "lost satisfaction"—the mother-figure in *Cécile* navigates the ideological and psychical structures that, on the one hand, bar her determination of Self *as* Woman while, on the other, make way for unforeseen movement precisely because of the very constraints in which she exists. Yet, if *Cécile* finds itself situated within the framework of "sexual difference," the film, at the same time, unsettles the foundation on which those terms are established.

As an artist deeply immersed in the arts, Honoré recognizes the particularly recurring masculinist trope of "Woman-as-Origins." Attuned to patriarchal constraints that mark this historical representation, Honoré revisits the vexed sign Woman. In *Cécile*, he attends to the mother-figure as a woman on the move, *the searcher* for Self. Within the queer auteur's cinematic frame, woman and the mother-figure—often held as the artist's dream as sign of origins—discover mobility in body and language. Through movement, Cécile queries the very masculinist trappings and deceits that have come to define her as Woman. Crucially, Honoré returns to the representation of Woman through the lens of the "homosexual narrator," who envisages queer turns on the discourse of "sexual difference." In this way, the significance of such a turn will become clear not only for the promise *Cécile* holds for Honoré's future work; moreover, *Cécile* provides an opportunity to consider Baudry's provocative suggestion to consider cinema as not merely a technical apparatus launched in 1895. Rather, because Honoré's films are always situated in relationship to the other arts, it is possible to entertain a search for "a psychical source equivalent[s] . . . which stimulated the invention of cinema." To begin, a brief and narrow history of art and theory sets the stage.

A Cinematic Dry Run

Thus, I begin my study of Honoré's twenty-first-century film *17 fois Cécile Cassard* by tracing the history of Gustave Courbet's nineteenth-century painting *L'Origine du monde* / *The Origin of the World* (1866). To do so, however, is no more complicated than tracing the history of the "origin of the world" itself. It should come as no surprise, then, that the circuitous, if not confounding, trajectory this controversial painting takes should find it in the summer home of Jacques Lacan. Its peculiar historical silences, disappearances from view (*public and private*), discreet exhibitions, *and* multiple exchanges among various owners demonstrates nothing less than a Lacanian vocabulary checklist: purloined, veiled, return, repression, desire, lack, representation. No better terminology might be so well associated with a work of art whose aesthetic force conjures a will to knowledge, a desire for the return to beginnings—indeed, a wish to penetrate the origin of the world. As a work riddled with complex significance for feminist scholars, I launch my analysis of Honoré's *Cécile* with my own return to *L'Origine du monde* precisely because of the resonant discourses the painting generates for both scholars and artists who have drawn upon it to interrogate the ways that the work of art demonstrates desire, a desire for origins (see figs. 14 and 15).[2]

In a 1986 article in *October*, Linda Nochlin recounts her frustratingly endless quest for Courbet's *Origin of the World*: "Not only," Nochlin writes, "was the original *Origin* impossible to find, but the clues to its location seemed to be perversely, almost deliberately misleading, fraught with errors in fact." Her research for this longed-for work of art—as late as 1986—was riddled with "rumors" and art-historical gossip. Nevertheless, Nochlin's pursuit-*as*-pursuit resulted in a publication in a highly regarded, peer-reviewed journal and was subsequently anthologized in a book dedicated to her Courbet studies. Indeed, it was the search for a work of art whose only recourse to study (at the time of her writing) was "as a series of repeated descriptions or reproductions—an *Origin*, then, without an original."[3] What value is there for feminists such as Nochlin to publish on a work that is "impossible to find"?

Nochlin puts it this way: "In the case of Courbet's *Origin*, this ultimate-meaning-to-be-penetrated might be considered the 'reality' of woman herself, the truth of the ultimate Other. The subject represented in *The Origin* is the female sex organ—the cunt—*forbidden site* of specularity and ultimate object of male desire; repressed or displaced in the classical scene of castration anxiety, *it has also been constructed as the very source of artistic creation*." Not unlike our project here, Nochlin queries "the notions of origination and originality, . . . the founding notion that through the logic of research—i.e., the repetitive act of searching over and over again—one can finally penetrate to *the* ultimate meaning of a work of art."[4] And like Nochlin, we are concerned with our desire to return to this work—the "forbidden site, . . . the very source of artistic creation"—through a particular feminist lens in which male homosexual desire plays no small if not troubling role.

But why? Why should this very painting from 1866—unsigned yet distinctively marked as a "Gustave Courbet" by art historians and critics—continue to draw the

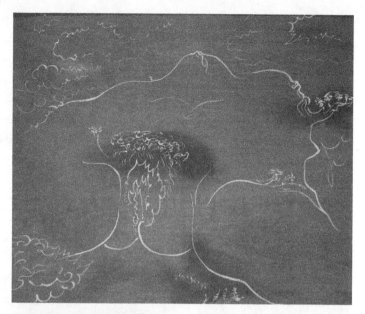

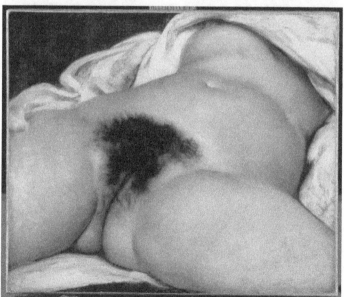

A visualization of Lacanian vocabulary: purloined, veiled, return, repression, desire, lack, representation. *Above*: **Figure 14.** André Masson, *Panneau-masque de "L'Origine de Monde," de Gustave Courbet*, 1955, oil on wood panel. (Banque d'Images, ADAGP/Art Resource, NY; © 2022 Artists Rights Society (ARS), New York/ADAGP Paris). *Below*: **Figure 15.** Gustave Courbet, *L'Origine du Monde* (*The Origin of the World*), 1866, oil on canvas. (Photo Hervé Lewandowski; Musée d'Orsay, Paris; © RMN-Grand Palais/Art Resource, NY).

attention of feminist scholars? Why should Courbet's painting—commissioned by a patron who wished to turn his sexual encounter with a prostitute into a work of art (or so the story goes)—continue to provoke? And, in fact, now that the work of art is on full display at the Musée d'Orsay—and now that *all* has been purportedly revealed (its transparent, glass sheath notwithstanding)—why should *L'Origine du monde* remain such a longed-for yet "forbidden" text? What does it mean to suggest that the work of art that lays before us is "constructed—[*confirmed with the artist's signature-brush-stroke*]—as the very source of artistic creation"?[5] And given the desire to return to *L'Origine* on the part of feminists, what are we to make of these returns when the return to penetrate origins is constructed cinematically and signed by a male-homosexual filmmaker such as Christophe Honoré? What does this return look like? What does it sound like? Is there a distinctive quality in the artist's style that marks the "very source of artistic creation" when the artist identifies as a male homosexual? Are the ideological and political stakes raised when the male artist identifies as nonheterosexual?

The questions are many. Not unlike Nochlin, our query has less to do with arriving at a conclusion about "where it all began" than it does with delighting in the scene of "origin," discovering an aesthetic through the search itself. To put a spin on Jean Cocteau, ontology has found a style.[6] Thus, we focus our attention on a (re)turn in which the site of origin unfolds cinematically through the mother-figure in *Cécile*, who exits her family (her child after her husband's death) and begins a journey in search of self. The film explores a woman's desire, manufactured by the gay boy or, to wit, "the homosexual narrator" and, more recently, the "gay father" (as Honoré identifies himself).[7] And, through the director's homosexual desire for a return to "origins," the film is signed by the auteur with a dedication, a gift *for* the mother. We will return to this not-insignificant offering.

Before concentrating on this specific effort, some brief historical remarks about Courbet's painting are in order. Our art-historical journey directs us—not without purpose—into the home of Jacques Lacan. We should add, at the outset, that Honoré *distances himself from psychoanalysis and, specifically, Lacanian theory*.[8] Nevertheless, to set aside Lacan in our discussion about *Cécile* would be to shortchange, theoretically, the "forbidden site of specularity" and its most significant acquisition in 1955, a purchase made by Jacques and Sylvia Lacan (Georges Bataille's ex-wife, née Sylvia Maklès). Moreover, to ignore the theoretical impulses that hardly originate (as it were) with Courbet's painting and Lacanian discourse would be to oversimplify the creative and psychoanalytic tools for feminist film theory enabled by Jacques Lacan (and, of course, Freud). The painting's historical handing off from one (hetero) male to another is not without provocatively psychic exchange value.

Although purchased by Lacan for his private collection in 1955, Courbet's painting—the original *L'Origine*—was not publicly revealed until June 26, 1995, at the Musée d'Orsay in Paris. Many reproductions were available from time to time. Tellingly, Lacan did not lend the painting to the 1966 exhibition *Courbet in Private French Collections*. The work did not leave his possession until his death in 1981, when it was turned over to the French minister of finance to settle estate taxes (*Elle* magazine referred to this return as a body "offered to the minister of finances"; a "fiscal secret," another scholar quipped).[9] Indeed, since its commission in the 1860s by the Turkish diplomat Khalil Bey, the painting was kept behind a veil—specifically, a green velvet veil in the case of Bey. Bey was an avid art collector, and *L'Origine* found a place among his large collection of landscapes. On select occasions, the painting was shown to dinner guests. "The last dessert," the art historian Shuli Barzilai imagines Bey claiming when he presented *L'Origine du monde* to his unsuspecting guests.[10] Once the Turkish diplomat's decadent joie de vivre caught up with him, however, *L'Origine* was sold to cover long-overdue accounts.

In 1910, the work of art landed in the possession of Baron Francis Hartvany of Budapest. He made the purchase from the Bernheim-Jeune Gallery, where, Barzilai recounts, "it was held in a double-locked frame."[11] What image covered the desiring objet d'art? A landscape titled *Le Château de Blonay*. The covering image presented to the viewer was that of a "castle in the snow," a minor effort purportedly painted by Courbet or his assistant. During World War II, Hartvany, a Hungarian Jew, hid his enormous art collection in a Budapest bank under the name of a Christian friend. He then fled to Paris. The painting was subsequently ignored by the Nazis and then claimed by the victorious Soviets. Apparently, one other person, Émile Vial, owned the painting during the period between Bey's ownership of it and when Hartvany took possession. Mark Hutchinson smartly connects Vial's ownership of the work to Marcel Duchamp, who, Hutchinson contends, crossed Vial's path on several occasions. Duchamp will soon make a not-inconsequential return to our narrative. Nevertheless, covered by seemingly innocent landscapes—*double locked*—meant to protect *L'Origine* during its undercover travels, the work of art landed once again in the French countryside, where it partook in the mise-en-scène of Lacan's summer home, where psychoanalysis reigned supreme.

Élisabeth Roudinesco—Lacan's meticulous critical biographer—tells us that by time the Lacans purchased Courbet's painting, the "castle in the snow" landscape had disappeared. Since, as Roudinesco claims, Sylvia "thought the picture so scandalous it ought to be kept hidden," she insisted that another cover be created. Unsurprisingly, and since our story focuses itself within the Lacanian household, the commission to veil *L'Origine* was granted to a family member. It is worth noting at this point that the Lacans' intimate circle not only was composed of highly recognized intellectuals and artists (Claude Lévi-Strauss, Michel Leiris, Marguerite Duras, and—yes—Duchamp) but was also composed of family, *by law*. Sylvia's older sister, Rose, married the painter André Masson in 1934. Even Maurice Merleau-Ponty's friendship with Lacan took on what Roudinesco calls a "family aspect": Merleau-Ponty's wife was a close friend of Sylvia—the couples vacationed often with each other. When all was said and done, however, the painter in the family, Masson the *brother-in-law*, was charged with replacing the lost cover for *L'Origine*. Masson delivered to his in-laws "a wooden cover" that, according to Roudinesco, is a "superb panel reproducing in abstract form the erotic elements of the original. A secret mechanism made the panel slide back to reveal the Courbet, but most of the time it remained hidden."[12]

"Masson's *panneau-masque*," as Barzilai describes it, "while following the contours of the original, is thus ingeniously styled to evoke a landscape."[13] Once again, a select audience was permitted access to *L'Origine* only after the owner unhinged the secret mechanism so as to pass through the "ingeniously styled" landscape, a veil now offered at the hands of the brother-in-law who, by blood and other intimate bonds, was associated with the Lacans, the Batailles, and the Merleau-Pontys. What do these landscape coverings both reveal and conceal?

Figure 16. Gustave Courbet, *The Source of the Loue*, 1864, oil on canvas. (The Met Museum, H. O. Havemeyer Collection, Bequest of Mrs. H. O. Havemeyer, 1929)

Figure 17. Gustave Courbet, *A Brook in the Forest*, 1868–77, oil on canvas. (The Met Museum, Gift of Ralph Weiler, 1967)

As it turns out, Courbet's "very source of artistic creation," the "forbidden site," shares its existence with a series of protective, if not provocative, landscapes he painted around the same time as *L'Origine du monde*. And as if in uncanny homage, the landscapes, which ultimately covered *L'Origine*, overlap each other in tantalizing ways. Painted during the same period, Nochlin points out, Courbet's landscapes strike a familiar note with the *centerpiece* of our discussion.[14] We are reminded, for instance (and among others), of *The Source of the Loue* (1864), *A Brook in the Forest* (1868–77), *Grotto of the Sarrazine near Nans-sous-Sainte Anne* (1864), and *The Source* (1868). With *L'Origine* historically and squarely situated between *The Source of the Loue* and *The Source*, it is difficult to ignore what Nochlin highlights in these closely aligned canvases as "the veritable black hole at the heart of the image, pulling us into dark, mysterious depths" (John Updike once referred to the "veritable black hole" in *L'Origine* as the "matted Rorschach blot").[15] There are, Nochlin continues, "other issues of meaning inscribed in [Courbet's] landscape series" that are, "first of all, . . . the historical association of such natural sites with the female body, preferably the nude female body."[16] Courbet's large-scale work *The Painter's Studio: A Real Allegory Summing Up Seven Years of My Artistic and Moral Life* (1855) most explicitly proves the point. Here, Courbet's nude female model is transposed by the male artist's hand with the stroke of his brush—*an exchange between the woman's body and canvas*—into a landscape (see fig. 18).

Later, the Lacans' dinner guest Duchamp pulled back—ever so ironically and chillingly—the curtain on Courbet's "veritable black hole," where he created a three-dimensional landscape that at once conceals and reveals a woman's mutilated torso. The landscape that shields yet promises entry to *L'Origine* is, as Duchamp presents it, a peephole, a keyhole, onto the trauma that is "l'origine du monde." His *Étant donnés* (1946–66) appears, therefore, as a knowing participant within the elaborate art-historical game of hide-and-seek (one wonders to what extent Lacan's and Masson's seductive shielding inspired the ever-prankish Duchamp). Duchamp's work of art is, again, a participant in the history of coverings that veil the cut, that pose the woman's torso in the purportedly protective landscape.[17] At the same time, *Étant donnés* reveals the historical artistic trope as a horrifying *mise-en-abyme* in which landscape and the woman's body fold, violently, into each other. The peephole provides, also and of course, a handy metaphoric segue for our adventures in the search for cinema's origins. But one more pit stop is necessary in our travels with Courbet before we turn our sights on Christophe Honoré's "very source of [cinematic] artistic creation" (see figs. 19 and 20).

Figure 18. Gustave Courbet, *The Painter's Studio: A Real Allegory Summing Up Seven Years of My Artistic and Moral Life*, 1854–55, post-restoration, oil on canvas. (Photo: Patrice Schmidt; Musée d'Orsay, Paris; © RMN-Grand Palais/Art Resource, NY)

Figure 19. Duchampian wooden doors-*cum*-peephole. Marcel Duchamp, *Étant donnés:* *1° la chute d'eau, 2° le gaz d'éclairage . . .* (*Given: 1. The Waterfall, 2. The Illuminating Gas . . .*), 1946–66, mixed media. (Image courtesy of the Philadelphia Museum: Gift of the Cassandra Foundation, 1969, 1969-41-1; © Association Marcel Duchamp/ADAGP, Paris/ Artists Rights Society (ARS), New York 2022)

Nochlin's prolific studies on Courbet touch on a number of provocative areas for feminist art historians. One key area, and useful in our concerns with the cinema, is her study of Courbet and movement. The desire to represent movement and its psychical dynamic, noted earlier in Baudry's rethinking about cinematic history, well precedes the cinematic apparatus. Indeed, the desire on the part of the artist to represent movement—to manufacture the illusion—is dependent on the artist's desire *to see himself move.* And so, Nochlin demonstrates, it is with Courbet, who, like so many artists throughout history, "envisioned themselves as marginal creatures, restless voyagers, at home nowhere on the face of the earth."[18]

Courbet, in the spirit of "The Wandering Jew" who inspired his creative energies, carefully integrated his romantic impulses as the "restless voyager," roaming the earth's landscape and transposing his movement into such works as *The Meeting* (1854). If in 1855 *The Painter's Studio* "sums" up Courbet's past male "artistic and moral life" (his free-spirited movement as artist), it also anticipates the male artist's desire for movement, in which he "pulls us into dark, mysterious depths."[19] The male artist's

Figure 20. . . . through the peephole. Marcel Duchamp, *Étant donnés:*
1º la chute d'eau, 2º le gaz d'éclairage . . . (*Given: 1. The Waterfall, 2. The*
Illuminating Gas . . .), 1946–66, mixed media. (Image courtesy of the
Philadelphia Museum: Gift of the Cassandra Foundation, 1969, 1969-41-
1; © Association Marcel Duchamp/ADAGP, Paris/Artists Rights Society
(ARS), New York 2022)

"artistic and moral life," therefore, are inseparable as he (and we must insist on this
gendered attribution) moves restlessly and desiringly toward "l'origine du monde."
In this way, male artists historically perceive themselves intermingled with—if not
as—the work of art. (It will become clear that Oscar Wilde, the sodomite, complicates
the terms discussed here for the relation between artist and work. Wilde's homosex-
ualizing the work of art is not far removed from the way Honoré is considered here.)

Artists are thus privileged Romantics who are forever mobile; they knowingly guide the viewer-reader into the deep, black hole where they promise to reveal "other issues of meaning."[20] An artist's landscape is at once his palette and the site for privileged, masculine movement.

I emphasize this point about the ostensibly (hetero) male-gendered artists and mobility because women are rarely represented *in movement* by nineteenth-century (male) artists. In fact, they are often rendered in repose, or asleep . . . *and* in the nude (whereas sleeping men are presented fully clothed, and if not sleeping, they are on the move). Courbet, Nochlin notes in her critique of Michael Fried in her study, "feels free, like many male artists, to 'merge corporeally' with some of the female objects of his representation [as in *The Painter's Studio*]." Nochlin disagrees. If Courbet "merge[s] corporeally," it is only to present her as the sign, "Woman," "the passive Other to the artist's active subjecthood."[21] Courbet's relationship to Woman through the work of art, in other words, maintains the romantic male-artist ideal. He remains outside the frame; he is the maker of meaning. Courbet's turn on realism is especially noteworthy since it is an aesthetic that purportedly allows the male artist to step outside the work. The male artist, it was understood, transcended his work and, to be sure, himself. Seen this way, Courbet's masculinist objectivity reveals his artistic claim that pure truth is at hand, *by his hand alone*, which delivers the viewer deeply profound meaning.[22]

In comparison, one might consider Oscar Wilde's decadent aestheticization of the work of art. He enfolded distinctions between object and self. In angering fin de siècle eager realists, Wilde cut the artist's bravura that claimed realism as truth. For Wilde, the work of art is a lie, and, mutatis mutandis, the artist is a liar.[23] And if realism upholds masculinist privilege for the likes of Courbet and others, Wilde's aestheticism discomfortingly *feminized* both artist and work of art. Courbet, Nochlin rightly concludes, "depicts himself as fully and unequivocally phallic" with his "dominating brush."[24] And, we might add, the "dominating brush" provides the means to secure the purported distance between artist and work. Wilde—the flamboyant dandy extraordinaire—instead literally wore his work of art, thereby folding body and art, Self and Other, into each other.

What do we do, then, with the active "homosexual narrator," gay father, and queer auteur of contemporary French cinema and other media art forms, Christophe Honoré? To what extent does his embrace of multiple art forms expand cinema's capacity to keep things on the move, to penetrate the "mysterious depths" from which life begins and ends, and to settle on any simple definition of desire? With Honoré (a figure not entirely different from Oscar Wilde, the nineteenth-century "homosexual narrator" *and*, similarly, gay father), we might ask, What are the implications for the twenty-first-century sodomite, Honoré, when he delights in "merg[ing] corporeally" with his cinematic creations? Pointedly, what are the implications when the homosexual artist seeks to merge, aesthetically, with what Jane Gallop defines as the "monstrous mother"?[25] Or, in fact, how might the queer auteur lead into what Cáel Keegan calls the "bad future" (to this we will return). Finally, to what extent does Honoré's queer cinematic search for origins—*his desire*—trouble the historical limitations set for woman in a masculinist world?

"The Aim of All Life Is Death"

Honoré's desire, I argue, is usefully read through Freud's assertion in *Beyond the Pleasure Principle*: "If we are to take it as truth that knows no exception that every living things dies for *internal* reasons—*becomes inorganic once again*—then we shall be compelled to say that *the aim of all life is death*."[26] In this way, Honoré's cinematic dance with Eros and Thanatos brings to light a host of complex questions that circulate around the body of the queerly gay-boy auteur, the mother-figure, and the cinema: Is it possible to aesthetically penetrate—*differently*—"l'origine du monde" when directed by the hand of the homosexual narrator? If so, how does Honoré's *caméra-stylo* penetrate differently—politically, theoretically, aesthetically—than Courbet's "dominating brush"? And where is Woman in all this? Is it true, as Jacqueline Rose contends, that "Woman is excluded *by* the nature of words, meaning that the [phallic] definition poses her *as* exclusion"?[27] What are the implications for "Woman's" return to art-historical nature—the landscape, the "nature of words"—if in fact she is excluded *by* its very nature (recall Courbet's *Painter's Studio*)? What old and new theoretical operations are available to interrogate (male) homosexual desire as a return to *l'origine du monde*? And to what extent does the history of feminist theory allow for yet delimit queers and woman in assuming their active role in the search for origins?

Honoré's film *17 fois Cécile Cassard* is dedicated in the following way: "à mon père, pour ma mère" (to my father, for my mother). Generous offering to one's family notwithstanding, Honoré's dedication in this, his first feature film, signals what proves to be a central trope in his filmmaking in which he explores the conundrum marked as "sexual difference." To work through the tricky business of "sexual difference" that feminists took to task and reaffirmed in the 1970s and to interrogate its limits *and* possibilities, the theoretical terms I wish to engage here in studying the figure of woman-as-mother require thoughtful critical analysis of what has come before and what future conceptualizations await us. To do this, I put into relief feminist theory on sexual difference (especially in regard to the writings of Luce Irigaray) in order to speculate on the queer openings those theories compel us to address in the twenty-first century.

Announced up front in Honoré's *Cécile* through the film's dedication, sexual difference is cinematically marked. It thus introduces a film that is meant to signal the gay auteur's relation to the (m)other. On the one hand, the film is offered *to* his father, who passed away when Honoré was a boy. The cinematic gift is thus given *to* the father from a distance, in memory of him, with gratitude *to* him; it is a gesture extended *out toward* the father. The film made *for* his mother is, on the other hand, a gesture that marks the unique parameters of the "original relation" between mother and child. To make *for* his mother is more than a gift *to* the memory of a relationship with the Other (the father). In making the film *for* his mother, Honoré as queer auteur offers a cinematic gift *for* her, hoping to reunite himself into the integral relation with the (m)other. And while his offering to father and mother suggests giving from afar, the stakes *for* giving at a distance in the mother-gay-son relation are considerably higher. To borrow from Jean-Paul Sartre, Honoré's cinematic offering to his mother makes queer "the proof of the Other" that the gay boy desires.[28]

Honoré's cinematic dedication brings into relief the relationship between body and consciousness and, thus, renders his place "within the original relation with the Other."[29] Luce Irigaray's writing, in particular her critique of Sartre's concept of the "original relation" as gender "neutral," serves to introduce a way to think about the gay male's relationship to—indeed *for*—the (m)other. My study, therefore, queries the existential relation between gay-male subject and (m)other and the intimate place the cinema (or, as will be discussed, the "manufactured object") occupies in this relation. Because Irigaray takes to task Sartre's assertion that the "original relation" is gender neutral, Irigaray reminds the reader that the search for the "original relation"—"*the proof of the Other*"—involves a bodily imbrication of mother and child. She further reminds us that this phenomenological relationship, one couched in sexual difference, does not foreclose its unique psychical dimensions. By articulating the gender specificity overlooked in Sartre's theoretical position, Irigaray directs us toward a rewarding, if problematic, point of entry when studying Honoré's cinematic gift "for" his mother and, thus, his desire for the original relation. At the same time, Irigaray runs up against the criticism that her arguments stray dangerously close to essentialism.[30] Yet, by complicating the terms for sexual difference, Irigaray disarms her critics insofar as she bridges the biological and psychical dimensions that come "to represent" Woman through complex ideological discourses that not only define Woman as such; more importantly, Irigaray demonstrates that these material and abstract ideological intersections give way to possibilities for woman's self-determination.

Finally, and no less importantly, Irigaray's arguments prompt us to consider Kaja Silverman's studies invested in the "female authorial voice."[31] Here, Silverman's reclaiming for women's and the *auteur's* voice in cinema enables a study of the gay-male auteur as a figure operating "inside" *and* "outside" the dynamic of the text (here, as we will see, the *choric fantasy* comes to light). Through these theoretical turns, I argue that Honoré's gift *for* his mother complicates empirically based understandings of sexual difference because it aestheticizes—*thereby queerly homosexualizes*—the symbiotic and gendered "original relation" between gay-boy subject and (m)other.[32] But it does something more. Honoré's search for origins through his body of work unfolds through multimediated worlds in which figures classified by sexual difference (*and racial difference*) are transfigured by the auteur's queerly reimagined terms when desiring the original relation.

The Cinematic Womb

Following *17 fois Cécile Cassard*'s dedication ("to my father, for my mother"), which marks sexual difference at the heart of the text, we enter a cinematic womb. Here, and in abiding Freud's claim that "the aim of all life is death," Honoré introduces the original relation as the site for birth and the site from which the process of death begins. The cinematic world is thus announced, thematically, as a world interested in returns, the cyclical dimension of life and death (see figs. 21 and 22).

With the film's dedication faded from the screen, we hear hollow vibrations, a sound seemingly emanating from a chamber or tunnel. As the cavernous sound sustains, we cut to an extreme close-up of a child, appearing tightly curled as he wiggles within the gently carved, fluid-filled cinematic frame. The child—whose name we will soon learn is Lucas (Johan Oderio-Robles)—moves himself toward the camera so that his

à mon père, pour ma mère

Figure 21. "to my father, for my mother." *17 fois Cécile Cassard*, directed by Christophe Honoré.

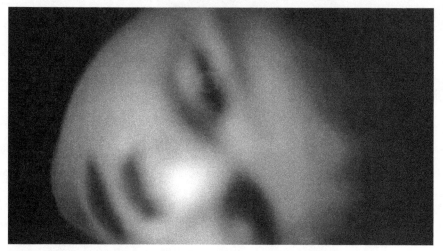

Figure 22. "I'm beginning to imagine that people can die." *17 fois Cécile Cassard*, directed by Christophe Honoré.

face fills the frame. We hear him utter, "I'm beginning to imagine that people can die." The child recognizes from within the original relation the inextricable relation between birth and death. The film's opening images and sounds, therefore, set the stage for what Kaja Silverman refers to as the "*choric* fantasy," a concept that envisages a cinematic reimagining of the "original relation" between mother and child—the "*choral* womb."[33] Reading the cinematic fantasy this way is significant for the way we conceive queer-feminist possibilities when analyzing cinema, particularly when aestheticized by a queer auteur.

Following the moment when life begins and death is anticipated—*the trauma of birth*—the film's narrative follows the child's mother, Cécile Cassard (Béatrice Dalle), who we learn at the outset has lost her husband to a fiery car accident.[34] Left with three-year-old Lucas (the child to whom we are introduced in the cinematic womb), Cécile wrestles with her sudden and psychically changed world. Her world, in which patriarchal culture and language—"the Symbolic," to say it quickly—dictate familial structures *for* family, *for* woman, and *for* motherhood, is abruptly altered. This is not to say that the dead father's largesse does not come in handy. In recognizing that the "father's tools" are useful when dismantling and reconfiguring the "father's house," Cécile affords herself the privilege to be—recalling Nochlin's reading of Courbet's ability to be in no place and all places at once—"at home nowhere on the face of the earth." With the patriarch's financial capital made available, Cécile's mourning prompts her desire to move on. She leaves Lucas with a close friend and begins an uncharted journey that leads her from Tours to Toulouse.

The story is told in seventeen vignettes (hence the title), and we follow Cécile on her journey as she wanders through the French landscape, albeit constrained by gender regulations. She moves through Honoré's cinematic world as if pushing the boundaries of the film's mise-en-scène. In other words, a woman's freedom *to choose* in the film involves an active pushing *out of* and *reaching for a beyond* the frame. On the one hand, Honoré's mother drives, walks, dances, gambols, and swims across the profilmic space. Her movement disrupts, pushes against, limitations set by the frame. On the other hand, Honoré directs her movements *as search*. Cécile reaches *beyond* the frame, to press against the complex ideological choices set before her. To reach for the beyond-the-frame, moving to and for, Cécile takes on the psychical and ideological struggles that define her as "Woman," as "mother," in order to penetrate the constraints of the material world.[35]

In *Cécile*, the geographic shift (from Tours to Toulouse) inaugurated by her husband's death startlingly changes the terms for sexual difference—*her identity as Woman*. Honoré moves Cécile cinematically from place to place and squarely situates Cécile in an altered world, one peopled only by men. The disproportionate sexual difference she encounters in her travels at once reveals the very language that sets the terms for this difference while opening Cécile to new critical pathways in which she discovers herself.

With *Cécile*, I argue, Honoré presents a woman's *emplacement*—"incessant replacement"—to render the ways in which she occupies the mother-figure.[36] Indeed, Honoré's film makes available unexpected possibilities, for Woman, in a masculinist world. In *Cécile*, Honoré provocatively envelops—*sonorously and visually*—the mother-figure within patriarchal discourse, where she must confront, at every turn,

Figure 23. Cécile on the move. *17 fois Cécile Cassard*, directed by Christophe Honoré.

the challenges set before her. Once Cécile leaves her child in Tours, she thus confronts masculine privilege head-on. Her move to Toulouse puts her directly within a world of men and male desire, heterosexual and homosexual. It is a sharply aestheticized world where sexual difference is demarcated along gender lines. In body alone, Cécile must resist the masculinist hurdles set before her. Her movements, her gestures, her relationships with and against men demonstrate Cécile's self-determined navigation within the constraints set by cinematic landscape.[37] If Honoré frames the landscape through which Cécile moves, it is Cécile who manages the contours of the landscape's terrain through self-determined gestures and decision-making. Yet, if Honoré's mother-figure sets herself free from the constraints of the patriarchal order, is she still not encumbered by the ideological forces that define sexual difference?

A Mother's Touch

In Irigaray's critique of Sartre, she unhesitatingly claims sexual difference as the centerpiece for understanding the existential bond between mother and child. For Irigaray, the mother-child relationship is particularly complex for the woman-daughter relation because a woman's instantiation of Self—as Woman—is always already inscribed within the language of the Father. Woman's existence in the world is thus marked at the outset by lack: "Woman always speaks *with* her mother, man speaks in her absence. . . . This *with* has to try to become a *with self.*" Because the "girl-subject" occupies a uniquely intimate bodily experience with the mother's corporeality, the mother-daughter relation is significantly different from the mother-son relation because "the girl-subject" . . . "does not exert mastery, except perhaps in her silence, her becoming, her overflowing. The girl-subject does not have objects as the boy does. It splits into two in a different way and the object or *the goal is to reunite the two by a gesture, to touch both* perhaps so that birth is repeated, so that no unconsidered regression occurs, so that the self is kept whole or, sometimes, upright. *Women do not try to master the other but to give birth to themselves.*"[38] The object had by boys but not had by girls allows the "girl-subject" to in fact "reunite" subject and object without "exerting mastery" over the Other via an external object. Boys thus only *touch the Self-Other original relation from a distance.* The girl-subject, "*by a gesture, to touch both* [*Self and Other*], . . . *give birth to themselves.*" Seen this way, the girl-subject *acts as one* with the (m)other. She has not the need to manufacture an object "to give birth to themselves." The concern for the boy-subject, therefore, is that to discover the original relation, he must manufacture the object *for* the m(o)ther in order to reunite himself with the original relation.

In critiquing the patriarchal terms for sexual difference and the original relation, Irigaray's refusal of the original relation as "neutral" seeks to reclaim woman's central role when coming to terms with origins as such. For Irigaray, the boy-subject necessarily must "exert mastery" over objects for a return to the original relation because sexual difference puts him at a distance from the "original relation." Women's "mastery" of *and in* the world ("her becoming, her overflowing") involves "absolute need . . . not for the penis or phallus but for the chance to be born to themselves, to be free to *walk*, walk away and walk back, however it pleases them."[39] Mastery of Self-*as*-Woman, according to Irigaray, necessitates the will *to choose*. Women choose to move, "to walk," in whatever way pleases them or through that which they desire. Thus, Woman's mastery of Other and Self requires freedom to move. To neutralize, as Sartre does, shortchanges women's movement because Sartre's claim veils itself in patriarchal discourse and privilege. To reframe "the question of the sexualized determination of that [purportedly neutral] scene," the veil that shields woman and only reveals her at the behest of men's pleasure must necessarily be removed once and for all.[40] (We find ourselves curiously in men's historical veiling and unveiling of Courbet's *L'Origine du monde*.) In doing so, Irigaray envisions women's control of their bodies *for itself*. This is why the mother-daughter relation holds central court for feminists such as Irigaray, since, from their perspective, mother-daughter as Self-Other diminishes man's privilege in the original relation. Yet, if Irigaray effectively reprivileges woman's role in the original relation, is she merely keeping in play the patriarchal language of "sexual difference"? She argues otherwise.

In Irigaray's paper "Body against Body: In Relation to the Mother," she claims that motherhood is a privileged but "wounded" site. She is a gendered body entrapped within the psychical and phenomenological contours of the "phallocratic economy," an economy through which "our society and our culture operate on the basis of an original matricide."[41] But in order to impede "matricide" and the grave circumstances it portends for women and culture as a whole, it is necessary, according to Irigaray, to restore sexual difference to the "original relation." This can be done, she argues, once the terms and implications for the "placental couple" are expanded. In rethinking the couple as such, a complex integrated life that nourishes the mother-child relation is discovered (this is particularly true for the mother-daughter relation, *between women*).[42] If, as Irigaray suggests, it is "our task is to give life back to the mother" through the "couple's" bodily commingling, the woman's body and her relation to the original relation are no longer framed by patriarchal discourse.[43] In other words, Irigaray argues for a reset of the terms, *the language*, that define sexual difference. Sexual difference is no longer fixed along binaries established at the point of origination, in which the original relation is rendered "neutral." Instead, the "placental coupling" embedded in the original relation is now the site from which women reclaim the language for Self. Yet, as queers are readily aware, this is not the end of the gendered story.

Push, Draw, Lean

To what extent can patriarchal constraints be redrawn, reimagined, through radical feminist and queer theory? Is it possible to resist heteromasculinist ideologies without reasserting or engaging in the very strategies we critique? For Irigaray's part, she understands that feminist theory involves chipping away at Sartre's taken-for-granted claims that the original relation is gender neutral. Irigaray concedes that the philosophical concept of the "we-subject" that composes the "original relation" is difficult to extricate from long-held heteromasculinist language in which the mother-figure is viewed as the vessel that completes man's desire for the reproduction of self. Yet, Irigaray holds firm to the idea that the "original relation" is not merely metaphysical, allowing for patriarchal transcendence. For her, the abstract desire for origins must be materially coupled since the original relation carries very different implications for the girl-subject and the boy-subject.

In Irigaray's view, the boy-subject remains bodily and ideologically distanced from the mother. He does not have the privilege of experience between women, between mother and daughter. He must necessarily thrust himself outward to discover any notion of Self. This is only achieved in his relationship to a "manufactured object." Whereas the girl-subject requires no mastery of an external object in her becoming Woman because she is always already imbricated with/as (m)other, the boy-subject's *becoming* takes place through displacement, transference. The boy-subject necessarily "exerts" himself *toward* the "manufactured object," or an "image of transcendence," to reach for the m(o)ther: "I am to turn, push, draw, lean," Sartre asserts.[44] The boy-subject must, in other words, necessarily "draw" himself into—"manufacture" *for* himself and *for* the (m)other—in order to rediscover the original relation. On this point, Irigaray and Sartre on the same page.

Hence, the boy-subject's relation to self/(m)other is directed elsewhere, or through the "turn[ing], push[ing], draw[ing], lean[ing]" on to the "manufactured object." In effect, Irigaray contends, the boy-subject's appeal for recognition by the Other reduces him to "*any body.*" "I, thus, become an '*any body*' which only my intention *towards* you can help me *to overcome.*" Irigaray refuses this Sartrean position: "I am sexuate, I am not neuter, anonymous, or interchangeable."[45] But by insisting on what "*I am*" and what "*I am not,*" Irigaray finds herself perilously close to delimiting language in ways not dissimilar to Sartre. If the "any body" conjures the "neuter," it thereby proves not dissimilar to Sartre's language of the "neutral." By firming up the binary codes for sexual difference, Sartre and Irigaray maintain hardened positions in relation to gender and sexual difference. Is it possible, instead, to reclaim *"any body-ness"* as precisely the terms with which we might come to, in fact, terms for *queer sexual différance* (to put a Derridean spin on it)? If becoming "any body" provides a gateway for queer "intention towards" the Other and thus seeks to overcome (or, at least, to make messy) the demand *to be* as such, I wish to suggest that Honoré's relationship to the cinematic "manufactured object" *for* the mother puts into play a queer handling of sexual difference or of, indeed, "any body."

The Language of Sound and Light

With our historical and theoretical dimensions presented, we may return to the film so as to mine its cinematic reimagining of the original relation with its emphasis on its presentation as a gift *for* the mother. To analyze the following sequences in Honoré's *Cécile*, it is useful, therefore, to remind ourselves of the theoretical bridges we have thus far constructed in *Queer Imaginings: On Writing and Cinematic Friendship*. In returning, revising, and reconfiguring creative practices and feminist and queer theories through the lens of queer auteurism, I have sought to devise a film theory in which a monstrous mother-figure (à la Gallop) liberates the patriarchal constraints of sexual difference toward a "bad future." If we have encountered the body of the homosexual auteur within these constraints, then a move must be made that expands homosexuality toward its own queer possibilities. Hence, it is necessary to reengage the limits of Irigaray's concept of sexual difference in order to, first, identify the homosexual's relation to the (m)other. From here, fresh possibilities emerge that press sexual difference toward a queerly manufactured transfiguration of the original relation.

In this context, and as I have suggested earlier, the "manufactured object" through which the boy-subject may reach toward the "original relation" is the cinema. Honoré's cinema as "manufactured object"—an object of exertion that depends on a *process of making for the (m)other*—serves as the aesthetic gesture, the conduit through which the homosexual narrator reaches for memory, *for loss*. The cinema materializes his outward exertion—*the draw, the push, the lean*—for the (m)other. The manufactured object gives aesthetic form to his desire, a failed enterprise that nonetheless repeats itself prolifically in the case of Honoré.

What does the failure to satisfy desire look like? How do we describe Honoré's cinematic failure to integrate with the (m)other? We—as James Baldwin admits in another context—"are in trouble with language again." Indeed, it is precisely the trouble with *la langue* with which we must contend. And in making perverse the return to origins, it is worth bearing in mind that, in French, *la langue* may be translated as "language" and as "the tongue": the "mother tongue." How we recall this translation is not insignificant for Honoré's filmmaking.

As noted, in *Cécile Cassard*, Cécile's geographic shifting about within France, movements prompted by her husband's death, unexpectedly alters her relation to sexual difference. Cécile's cinematic movement into a world of all men—movement prompted by her existential hinge between life and death—situates her in the crosshairs where she must confront sexual difference. Once in Toulouse, she finds herself only among men (straight, gay, and so on). She "is excluded *by* the masculinist nature of words." But Cécile, it turns out, gets the final laugh at the expense of the nature of things and the men who determine such things.

During Cécile's cinematic movements, she brushes against this all-male world, a mélange of men who clamor for her attention. The men mark her as friend, as surrogate mother, as object of sexual desire. Her quick friendship with a gay young man, Mathieu (Romain Duris), alternates between friendship and a mother-child relation. As we will come to expect in Honoré's later films, such a dynamic is riddled with sexual and incestuous tension, both at the surface and beneath the skin. Cécile and Mathieu's relationship is also significant because the narrative turns on Mathieu's longing for a stable, family-style relationship. Cécile—*woman, mother, lover*—refuses his demand as it is pitched through the patriarchal language that contains her. Cécile is less interested in the gay man's pursuit to recapture idealized familial traditions.

Mathieu is but one type of man caught within heteropatriarchal discourse who crosses Cécile's path. Two teenage boys, early in the film, swoon over her at a bar. They follow her and join her in her hotel room. The occasion only rises to playful flirtation, seductive looks and glances, as the boys ultimately fall asleep. Although Cécile's gaze makes available both sexual and maternal desire, the scene further escalates the complex place that the mother-figure navigates when pressed into an all-male world. Nevertheless, Cécile successfully sets the terms for the way the boys act on their desire for her as both maternal nurturer and object of desire.

Later, when Cécile walks the darkened streets of Toulouse, she is followed by a stranger whom she had encountered earlier in a cemetery. With the stranger, a sexual encounter occurs in which Honoré explores the limitations of language, particularly for women in a masculinist world. As the sensual dance unfolds between Cécile and the stranger, she kisses him through the sweater that she has pulled over his head. She veils his mouth, preventing him from speaking. On a cut, we see him on his knees, his face buried in her crotch, performing cunnilingus. With his tongue—*la langue*—he extends himself toward her, *for her*. Because of the pleasure she experiences, Cécile's cannot speak; she can only emote pleasurable groans and sighs. Language fails. Although tongue-tied, she nevertheless discovers ways to express. Indeed, no words can convey the sentient delights made by the tongue that pushes and leans toward irretrievable origins, toward death, and thus the inexpressibility that gives rise to pleasure principle—this is to say, *jouissance* (see figs. 24 and 25).

Here, Cécile's body pressed against the wall, *la langue* of the patriarchy proves at once to contain her while allowing for pleasure, albeit with some indifference to the man's advances. Yet both Cécile and the stranger are at a loss for words. For a moment, *la langue maternelle* and *la langue étrangère* "speak" the same language. Through the sexual encounter, in other words, the sound of *les langues* commingle. The stranger's tongue leans into, pushes itself toward his imagining for a return to the original

Figures 24 and 25. *17 fois Cécile Cassard*, directed by Christophe Honoré.

relation. His desire draws him toward the site from which all knowledge is purportedly held under lock and key. Cécile, held in tension within the patriarchal aporia, takes pleasure in the stranger's striving. At this cinematic point of linguistic ambiguity, Cécile finds herself at a turning point upon which *la langue* hinges on pleasure within constraint, a vexed point for the reckoning with Self and Other.

As Cécile walks away from the stranger's tongue, leaving him with his desire, and as gentle snow falls in Toulouse's chilly winter air, she pauses at the tunnel's exit. With her back turned toward us, she stands silently in a moment of reflection. Her pause at the end of the tunnel allows the spectator to take stock of Cécile's journey and the men who have crossed her paths: her husband and son in Tours, her newfound male acquaintances in Toulouse, and her friendship with Mathieu. Thus, from the cold blue atmosphere of winter that envelops her, and looking outward, Cécile exits the frame. The sonorous hum that filled the chilly scene from winter—a sonorous resonance not unlike the noise we hear from within the cinematic womb that opens *Cécile*—soon contrasts with the film's final sequence, in which we find Cécile snuggled with Mathieu within the red-orange warmth emanating from the crackle of a summer campsite fire.

Hence, in the warmth of the final scene in *17 fois Cécile Cassard*—along the river—Mathieu tells Cécile that he longs to have a child with her. He enthuses, again, at the prospect of reproducing new life with the woman who appears all things to men, above all mother to *his* child: "I promise, once you are ready, I will give you a child." Cécile rejects his offer—nay, she rejects what amounts to Mathieu's gift for himself ("*I*

Figure 26. Cécile embraces herself as Self/(M)Other, in *17 fois Cécile Cassard*, directed Christophe Honoré.

will give you . . ."). Nevertheless, they spend the night together, spooned, cuddling in such a way that again holds in tension the desire between mother and child, woman and man, and the look and the gaze. To recall our earlier discussion in this book's introduction, where I discuss Bataille's "potlatch" as a process of gift-giving that involves an exchange predicated on one-upmanship (the competition for who can give the better gift), Cécile outdoes her male competitor. In other words, her cinematic journey has brought into focus *for herself* the operations by which men seek to utilize women in their futile quest for origins. In short, Cécile's always-bettered gift is for herself.

In the morning, the campfire's embers smolder. Cécile awakens and walks away from the sleeping Mathieu, then makes her way to the river. Here, in the final moments of the film, Cécile's embraces herself, her body, *as* Woman. She stands on the bank of the river, hugging herself, wrapping herself with Self/(M)Other. At the river's edge, the mother-figure's tongue, *sa langue*, that is always already on the tip of her tongue, belongs, as Irigaray reminds us, to her body. *La langue* is uniquely hers. Her two lips, in movement with *la langue*, allow the mother-figure-*as*-Woman to speak *for herself* at the source of all life. In *Cécile*, Woman returns her body to the four elements that give life to existence—earth, fire, water, and air. Immersed in the fluid scene in which all life originates, Cécile's *la langue*, her two lips, no longer lose touch with themselves in rebirth of her becoming. Finally, alone with "nature's" four elements, she looks directly into the camera. In addressing the cinematic apparatus, *la langue de Cécile* is revealed as silent laughter (see fig. 27).

Figure 27. *La langue de Cécile*, in *17 fois Cécile Cassard*, directed by Christophe Honoré.

Possibilities

Honoré, the male-homosexual auteur, appeals to the "original relation" through an exertion, a gesture, a sensuous encounter with movement and sound in which his relation to the manufactured object hopes for a queer intermingling of Self and Other. Sartre calls this "option" *the possible*. Yet "the possible in terms of a subjectivity which would be what is . . . is on principle doomed to failure." It is worth quoting (perhaps necessary) to quote Sartre at length on the dialectic folds he offers with regard to "the possible" and its successful failure for the subject:

> But it is true that the possible is—so to speak—an option on being, and if it is true that the possible can come into the world only through a being which is its own possibility, *this implies for human reality the necessity of being its being in the form of an option on its being.* There is possibility when instead of being purely being and simply what I am, I exist as the right to be. Property right appears only when someone contests my property, when already in some respect it is no longer mine. The tranquil enjoyment of what I possess is pure and simple fact, not a right. Thus if possibility is to exist, human reality as itself must necessarily be something other than itself. This possible is that element of the For-itself which by nature escapes it qua For-itself. *The possible is a new aspect of nihilation of the In-itself in For-itself.*[46]

Irigaray's resistance to the "nihilation" between "in-itself" and "for-itself" is the significant break she makes with Sartre, insofar as Irigaray's adherence to sexual difference—to be "sexuate"—reclaims the mark of Being as such: "For-itself" *as* Woman. If Sartre sought to trouble idealist Absolutism (what he refers to as the "In-itself") by giving ground to the Self-Other relation (the "For-itself"), he did so at the expense of Woman by holding fast to the neutrality (naturalized masculinist privilege) of the original relation. Irigaray, in her response to Sartre, opens the possibility of Woman-as-Mother toward what she identifies as a Self-Other "coupling" *between woman,* between mother and daughter.

Irigaray's theories on sexual difference emphasize the will *to choose* as crucial for woman's self-determination (Woman-as-Self). Yet her theoretical reimagining around masculinist neutrality and positions on choice proves limited in scope, as do most theories as they age and are (hopefully) refined by future scholars. One such scholar to open the future is Cáel Keegan. Keegan persuasively acknowledges the critical usefulness in drawing and expanding upon the history of cinematic texts and critical theories that have come before. Keegan thus "pushes, draws, and leans" into and against the formidable ideological constraints, and not only those that contemporary scholars face; he puts into perspective the constraints that earlier feminists and queer scholars contended with. If Irigaray wrote from within particular historical constraints in which Sartre's supercharged patriarchal privilege defined the "neutrality" of the original relation in which sexual difference was consecrated along hetero-naturalized lines, is it possible now to eke out lines of queer—more saliently, *trans*—flight from both Irigaray's and Sartre's theoretical oversights? And, if so, to what extent must we bear in mind our own (unforeseeable) theoretical shortcomings in the here and now? Perhaps it is worth borrowing and revising Irigaray's dismissal of the "any body."

In whatever way it is presented, the *neutral* "any body" that emerges via Sartrean and Irigarian thought remains beholden to the binary structures inherent to sexual difference, hetero "male/female." Introducing Keegan's concept of "trans care" into our analysis of Irigaray and Sartre in relation to Honoré's *Cécile Cassard* invites new options and possibilities in our work involved in expanding theoretical language toward free will of the Self. By following Keegan's lead, "trans care" in critical analysis unsettles "good/bad" axes on which a good deal of queer analysis relies. Keegan reminds us that reductive negation delimits queer desire. To think beyond—*not merely negate*—sexual difference, it is necessary to identify the language that comes to define it in order to revise and to desire something more. I suggest, following Keegan, what we might call *sexual différance*: "a trans politics of abolition requires the desire for something else, something as yet outside of the available systems of classification, something that might make nearly everyone feel . . . *bad*."[47] Just as Irigaray pushed against Sartre's twentieth-century "available systems of classification," twenty-first-century queers—*queer auteurs*—must desire "something else" while keeping in mind the debris deep rooted in systems of classification, *la langue*. This is why every political and aesthetic intervention "might make nearly everyone feel . . . *bad*."

To "feel bad," to feel ill, is to feel queer. To feel bad is to recognize the ideological constraints as the sine qua non for a queer existence. In feeling bad, queers desire to move outward; we manufacture a world never quite complete, *reunited*, so as to re-create once again. "Truly embracing badness," Keegan goes on, "means moving beyond a politics in which cisgender people grant the least disruptive form of transgender identity a marginal amount of inclusion. It means, instead, pursuing a world in which the distinction between cis and trans cease to exist altogether, because the systems enforcing binary sex and gender are dismantled."[48] In moving through what Baudry calls a "desire inherent in our psychical structure" (a "desire for something else"?), we call again on Linda Nochlin's deep pleasure in her search for origins, *l'origine du monde*. The desire to search thus requires pushing outward, exerting oneself, through a thicket of ever-unwieldly language/*la langue* shortcomings. It requires that we recognize desire as a joy in feeling bad because in our dissatisfaction, we are compelled to keep on the move.

With all this said, how do we return to a study of Honoré's cinematic "draw[ing]" *for* his mother that arguably positions the gay-boy subject who cannot reproduce or, in fact, "give birth to [himself]" as only the girl-subject can. If the gay-boy's desire for the (m)other is "doomed to failure" because the original relation, as Irigaray poses it, must refuse the boy-subject, the homosexual boy finds himself vexed precisely because, as Lee Edelman would have it, he cannot reproduce Self as *ideal* Other.[49] For Edelman, this is the very definition of queer.

If the male-homosexual auteur can never be *with* the (m)other once and for all, his becoming Self through his work of art is a perverse and delightful exertion toward failure. To fail involves the gay boy's *queer intention toward* the "original relation" *for* the (m)other. Cinema is his "thrust" *forward* insofar that it *queerly homosexualizes* by aestheticizing—*makes artificial*—the "original relation." Honoré makes no claim to discover the original relation through the body of the mother-figure in *Cécile* or in any of his works. Instead, the manufactured object, *Cécile*—his first film in 2001—prepares the way for how we envisage the "homosexual narrator's" pivot toward a queer auteur. The pivot is made all the more clear and provocative in Honoré's recent theatrical work, in which the genders of iconic figures are transfigured. Marlène Saldana, for instance, dons a thick fur coat to become Jacques Demy, while Marina Foïs embodies Hervé Guibert's homo-frisson in *Les Idoles*. In *Le Ciel de Nantes*, sexual difference collapses in Honoré's queerly transformed family. His brother, Julien Honoré, takes on the role of the Honoré matriarch. More provocatively, *Le Ciel de Nantes* spotlights France's racist impulses by imbruing the purported whiteness of the French family with racial impurity. In the play, the "homosexual narrator" (that is, Christophe Honoré) is doubly queered, made impure when the Arab actor Youssouf Abi-Ayad embodies Christophe. Honoré's troubling of racism also appears in his operas such as *Cosi fan tutti*.

For Honoré, transfigured bodies dance toward desire. His films and theatrical productions—the manufactured objects—transform bodies and their relation to others. Honoré's mediated figures *choose* language and movement as the way to give life to queer desire. Queer imaginings such as those of Honoré are precisely renderings of desire to embody, *if not penetrate*, the Other. His queer imaginings are given for the mother with love, ever from a distance.

Coda

Honoré's dedication that opens *17 fois Cécile Cassard* is marked "for" the (m)other. The dedication inaugurates a cinematic gesture—*l'écriture de l'auteur*—through light and sound that "draws" Honoré into the manufactured object through the *choric fantasy*. If he is reunited with the original relation, it is indeed from a distance, which is precisely a queer's relation to origins. Quite different from Courbet's "dominating brush," where the distance between artist and work of art serves to objectify and constrain Woman while reaffirming his privileged position in the Self/Other relation, Honoré's *caméra-stylo* instead invites movement for women on their terms. He illuminates the challenging pleasures women take in discovering language for herself. At the same time, his *caméra-stylo* pens a broader language of Self, a queerly *trans*formed Self. Honoré's manufactured body of work yields possibilities for the "any body" and thus toward desire, or what Keegan calls the "bad future."[50]

Notes

1. Baudry, "Apparatus," 307 (emphasis added). I am deeply grateful to Sarah Keller for her patient and rewarding review of this essay.

2. Although I primarily make my case through critical scholarship, artists have deeply influenced my thinking about cinema and desire. Consider the performance artist Deborah de Robertis's display of self as a mirror of Courbet's *L'Origine* (May 29, 2014, Musée d'Orsay). About her performance and following other feminist turns to the painting, de Robertis states, "There is a gap in art history, the absent point of view of the object of the gaze. In his realist painting, the painter shows the open legs, but the vagina remains closed. He does not reveal the hole, that is to say, the eye. I am not showing my vagina, but I am revealing what we do not see in the painting, the eye of the vagina, the black hole, this concealed eye, this chasm, which, beyond the flesh, refers to infinity, to the origin of the origin" (Sutton, "Artist Enacts 'Origin of the World' at Musée d'Orsay"). For video of the performance, see Vartanian, "Performance Artist Does the Impossible."

3. Nochlin, "L'Origine du Monde," 76.

4. Nochlin, 76 (emphasis in original).

5. Nochlin, 76.

6. Referring to Josephine Baker, Cocteau declared, "Eroticism has found a style" (see E. White, *Flâneur*, 75).

7 Quoted in Gerstner and Nahmias, *Christophe Honoré*, 13. See Honoré's novel *Ton père* for an "autoportrait" of the homosexual father and life with a child.

8 Conversation with the author, March 2017.

9 Quoted in Barzilai, *Lacan and the Matter of Origins*, 13.

10 Barzilai, 13.

11 Barzilai, 13.

12 Roudinesco, *Jacques Lacan*, 184.

13 Barzilai, *Lacan and the Matter of Origins*, 16.

14 Nochlin, *Courbet*, 200.

15 Nochlin, 199; Updike quoted in Lewis, "Lip Service."

16 Nochlin, *Courbet*, 199–200.

17 If feminist artists such as de Robertis found herself drawn to Courbet's painting, other (hetero?) male artists similarly evoked Courbet's centerpiece. Balthus purportedly uttered, "Je fais du Surréalisme à la Courbet" (I do Surrealism in the style of Courbet; quoted in Nicholas Fox Weber's biography *Balthus*, 361). As Alan Woods seductively points out, Balthus's nude-woman pose is "often a pose of display; relatable, in the Western tradition with its taboos and teases in the female nude" ("Now Let Us Look at the Pictures," 201). Indeed, Bertrand Bonello's contemplative gaze in Antoine Barraud's film *The Portrait of the Artist / Le dos rouges* (2014)—a male artist's look that zeroes in on the female model's genitalia that Balthus, "teasingly," displays in *Alice dans le miroir* (1933)—underscores the force that the desire for origins, as rendered on the female body, occupies in the work of art. See also Bruno Dumont's Duchampian and Courbet-esque imagery in *L'Humanité* (1999).

18 Nochlin, *Courbet*, 43–44.

19 Nochlin, 199.

20 Nochlin, 199.

21 Nochlin, 171.

22 See Gerstner, *Manly Arts*.

23 Wilde, "Decay of Lying."

24 Nochlin, 171.

25 In the essay "The Monster in the Mirror," the always-provocative Jane Gallop draws a comparison between the mother-child relation (specifically, mother-daughter) and the critic-text relation. "This is the specific dilemma of the literary critic," Gallop contends, "for the critic produces a text that is at once a reading and a text. Literary criticism is always double, both text and reader, *mother and daughter*. . . . The literary critic is that kind of monster"

(20; emphasis in original). "Actually," Gallop continues, "just as any text is also a reading, any mother is also a daughter, also an individual struggling for autonomy, trying to untangle herself from the mothering web. . . . The problem is that the term *mother* is already confusedly double. The apparently singular term means both one of the parts *and* the whole monster" (21; emphasis in original). I am offering a queer turn on Gallop's comparison between critic and text, i.e., mother-child relation (specifically, mother–(gay) son relation).

26 Freud, *Beyond the Pleasure Principle*, 32 (emphasis added).

27 Rose, "Introduction II," 49.

28 Sartre, *Being and Nothingness*, 339.

29 Sartre, 337.

30 Judith Butler has famously critiqued the essentialism that underlines the binary logic that defines sexual difference. Butler argues that by holding firm to these terms, "a monolithic as well as monologic masculinist economy" is reaffirmed (*Gender Trouble*, 13). Feminists such as Irigaray and, subsequently, Kaja Silverman complicate the "monolithic" conceptualization attending sexual difference in a psychoanalytic discourse.

31 See chapter 6 in Silverman's *The Acoustic Mirror*.

32 See the Honoré interview in Gerstner and Nahmias's *Christophe Honoré* on the relationship between gays and cinema.

33 See Silverman, *Acoustic Mirror*, 101–6.

34 Barzilai places emphasis on Otto Rank's controversial book *The Trauma of Birth* (1924), because Rank "repeatedly falls on the pivotal influence of the mother rather than the father in human development" (*Lacan and the Matter of Origins*, 25). To be sure, Rank insists that his project is to "reinstate the high estimation of woman which was repressed simultaneously with the birth trauma, and we can do this by freeing her from the weight of the curse on her genitals" (Barzilai, 37). As Barzilai views it, Lacan's preliminary writings—prior to his signature work, in which the unconscious is *like* a language—similarly privilege the mother over the father's import in the family romance. In *Les complexes familiaux* (1938), Lacan (like Rank before him) questions the significance of castration anxiety (à la Freud) and whether the concept of *sevrage* (separation at birth and from weaning) is more crucial: "In Lacan's redelineation of the concept of castration, the dread of irreparable loss, of separation from a highly valued object—a dread not merely fantasized but actualized during the weaning process—first emerges in relation to the mother. Castration anxiety

is born with the moment of birth, with the primal passage from the womb into the world" (Barzilai, 31).

35 The mother-figure's movement is not only significant in Honoré's *Cécile*. Women's movement is central to his cinema more generally. We see travel made by women in the films *Ma mère* and *Non ma fille n'ira pas danser*, in which mothers in particular continuously move (on) from their familial obligations. From seaside to nightclubs, from city to country, and from country to country, Honoré's women are unable or refuse to sit still. In *Les bien-aimés*, for instance, women literally choose the shoes that move them from France to Czechoslovakia, over bridges, and ultimately across historical space and time. Crucially, Honoré moves women cinematically. Along with traditional tracking shots, the director uses jump cuts to link historical periods (*Non ma fille* and *Les bien-aimés*); dissolves that merge women's walking across maps in *Les bien-aimés*, thereby recalling Truffaut's use of the dissolve in *La sirène de Mississippi* (1969); and adaptations of other media to move space and time (consider *Ma mère*, in which Honoré moves the novel's location from France to the Canary Islands; Steven Shaviro, for one, was not pleased with such a move. See "Come, Come, Georges," 56).

36 I follow Samuel Weber's concept of "emplacement": "The notion of emplacement, then, collects and assembles the various ways in which everything, human beings included, is 'cornered' (*gestellt*) and set in place. But since the places thus set up are the result of emplacement, they can never simply be taken for granted. Places must continually be established, orders continually placed. As emplacement, the goings-on of modern technics thus display a markedly ambivalent character: they arrest, bring to a halt, by setting in place; but this placement itself gives way to other settings, to the incessant re-placing of orders through which new places are set up and upset" ("Upsetting the Setup," 72).

37 The Oulipian Marcel Bénabou tells us in his essay "Rule and Constraint," "Constraint is thus a commodious way of passing from language to writing. If one grants that all writing—in the sense both of the act of writing and the product of that act—has its autonomy, its coherence, it must be admitted that writing under constraint is superior to other forms insofar as it freely furnishes its own code" (41).

38 Irigaray, "Gesture and Psychoanalysis," 99 (emphasis in first quote original; emphasis in second quote added).

39 Irigaray, 100 (emphasis in original).

40   Irigaray, "Power of Discourse," 73.

41   Irigaray, "Body against Body," 20, 11.

42   Debra Bergoffen argues that, for Irigaray, "sexual difference is the question of the couple" ("Irigaray's Couples," 151) and thus offers an "alternative understanding of couples" insofar as the "couple (the placental couple, the mother-daughter couple, the heterosexual couple), whether or not it is the site of what patriarchy calls sexual difference, is the site . . . where desire and difference are either nourished or repressed" (153). And though Irigaray emphasizes the mother's nourishing body as one in which the "daughter-mother" relation is privileged, it is certain, as Bergoffen stresses, that the mother's nourishment—in order to disrupt the "phallocratic economy"—necessarily gives life to all bodies to which the mother gives life (151).

43   Irigaray, "Body against Body," 18.

44   Quoted in Irigaray, "Daughter and Woman," 38.

45   Irigaray, 39 (emphasis added).

46   Sartre, *Being and Nothingness*, 75 (emphasis added).

47   Keegan, "On the Necessity of Bad Trans Objects," 35–36 (emphasis in original).

48   Keegan, 36.

49   See, for instance but not exclusively, Edelman, "The Part for the (W)hole," in *Homographesis*, 60–61.

50   Keegan, "On the Necessity of Bad Trans Objects," 36.

INTERVIEW WITH THE NEW ZEALAND FILMMAKER PETER WELLS

16

A note on my interview with the director: From 1999 through 2000, I served as Lecturer at the University of Otago in Dunedin, New Zealand. It was my first professional gig as a newly minted PhD. It was a move for me and my partner (as well as our two dogs!). The experience was thrilling and challenging. The time was well spent since it afforded me the opportunity to publish a handful of essays and complete the manuscript for my first book. Writing about American masculinity from my perch in New Zealand was unexpectedly rewarding. The essay I coauthored with Sarah Greenlees (a graduate student at the time), "Cinema by Fits and Starts: New Zealand Film Practices in the Twentieth Century" (*Cineaction* 51 [2000]: 36–47), serves as a useful reference point for several of the texts referred to in this interview. My tenure in New Zealand also afforded me the warm acquaintance with the author and filmmaker Peter Wells. Peter was more than generous with his time. His gay sensibility—intellectually and erotically bound up with his relationship to his country—remains a unique voice in queer cinema. His film *Desperate Remedies* (1993) is a beguilingly beautiful work of cinema. Later, my essay "Ricordi! Peter Wells, Memories of a Queer Land," published in Ian Conrich and Stuart Murray's anthology *New Zealand Filmmakers* (Wayne State University Press, 2007, 121–31), more fully explores Peter's rich and diverse oeuvre and thus his contributions to his "strangely normal" world of New Zealand. Peter Wells died February 18, 2019, at the age of sixty-nine.

Peter Wells is a New Zealand writer and filmmaker. He has made short, feature-length, and documentary films. His films were the earliest films to introduce gay subject matter to New Zealand, with works such as *A Death in the Family* (which dramatized responses to AIDS and won the Blue Ribbon Award at the American Film Festival), *Desperate Remedies* (1993, a lavish queer production cowritten and codirected with Stuart Main), and *A Taste of Kiwi* (a short film that homosexualizes the overdetermined New Zealand national pastime, rugby). His writing has garnered such awards as the New Zealand Book Award for Fiction. He has contributed immensely to bringing queer literature and filmmaking into New Zealand culture. As coeditor of *Best Mates: Gay Writing in Aotearoa New Zealand* (1997), Wells unearthed the rich history of queer writing in the country. His stories have been anthologized widely, both nationally (*The Oxford Book of New Zealand Short Stories*) and internationally (*The Penguin Book of Gay Short Stories*). Two of his stories have been made into films, *One of Them!* and *Memory and Desire*. He is currently working on a short film with the filmmaker Garth Maxwell that revels in the splendor of bare feet. The following interview with Peter Wells was conducted during summer 2000 in Auckland, New Zealand. The interview was transcribed by Lisa Wilkie.

DG: When you're making a film, how hard do you work at trying to get the mise-en scène to perhaps speak "disguised power"?

PW: Well, each film has its own sort of territory and landscape. *Desperate Remedies* was part of a very high surface world—

DG: —and very well planned out, I would guess, in terms of the mise-en-scène.

PW: We did a lot of scripting.

DG: Did you use storyboards?

PW: Yes, and Stewart [Main] had a big book, a marvelous book really, which was like a visual dictionary where we used to paste in images that we liked from Hollywood films or ads or anything that kind of caught your eye and would clue the people working on the film into the sort of "mindspace" that we wanted the film to have.

DG: The film certainly creates a fascinating "mindspace" for the viewer as well. In many ways, that film, for one coming from America, resonates with that Hollywood camp sensibility. I kept thinking about Lana Turner in *Green Dolphin Street* (1947) and those scenes where she's walking through the port town of Wellington in the mid-nineteenth century.

PW: The fact that we had to make *Desperate Remedies* on a relatively small budget meant being more extreme in the way we visualized it.

DG: Because of budgetary constrictions?

PW: Yes. We didn't have a budget to do a kind of a grand naturalistic sort of *Picnic at Hanging Rock* [dir. Peter Weir, 1975] type film or a Merchant-Ivory period-type film.

DG: Do you think you would have wanted to do that that type of film?

PW: I don't think any of our other films, the films that Stewart and I made together, were particularly naturalistic anyway.

DG: Yeah. I never got that feeling with your short films either. There was always something artificial there. Merchant-Ivory is so cleaned up. I guess that's why some people call that "quality cinema."

PW: Yet there was nothing within the script itself that meant that it couldn't have been a naturalistic film. Funnily enough, some people say the dialogue is stilted and artificial and not the landscape.

DG: I was thinking that the dialogue in that film fits with the artificiality of the relationship between Lawrence Hayes [Kevin Smith] and Dorothea Brook [Jennifer Ward-Lealand].

PW: It was interesting with the dialogue. I never realized until after the film that a lot of those Hollywood costume pictures actually had extremely slangy dialogue.

DG: Completely. There's a weird thing with those old Hollywood films because in order to give the sense of "period," Hollywood would have the actors assume a British accent for the upper classes, while the lower classes would have an American accent that resembled some weird amalgam from the Midwest or New York City. But your film also seems to register a New Zealand anxiety or uncertainty about the landscape. It seems that New Zealand films turn to the landscape as an important aesthetic of both the country and its idea of national cinema. There's a particular artificiality about the way it is represented in *Desperate Remedies*.

PW: Probably for Pakēha people [white settler]. The sort of country we really do live in, or its translation into language and art and things like that, was actually quite a late arrival in terms of perception. Pakēha only started to work out a way of representing the landscape in the 1930s and 1940s.

DG: Yet even Rudall Hayward [an early New Zealand filmmaker who began making films in the 1920s and continued well into the 1970s] and, later, John O'Shea started to look at the national perception of the landscape. O'Shea, I think, does some of that in his musical *Don't Let It Get You* [1966] probably one of my favorite New Zealand films!

PW: Yes, but even in literature as well. It's not a given what the countryside is like or what the landscape is really like. It's like there's no one way of particularly showing it, and I think each filmmaker to a certain extent just reinvents it as a "thing." So there's the sort of Jane Campion *Piano* landscape, which to a certain extent comes from a Vincent Ward landscape in *Vigil* [1984], for instance.

DG: Yes, but Ward's landscape is even darker. I know that this is probably anathema to say, but Campion's film appears to me have a Merchant-Ivory quality, whereas Ward's film might be likened to a perverse Bergman-esque sensibility. The world gets very dark in his films.

PW: Also, the strange thing about New Zealanders, as with Australians, is that although the two countries have a predominantly rural self-image and myth, most people actually live in cities and have always lived in cities and have come from cities, so there's a kind of weird displacement there between cultural myth and lived experience. I mean, I'm not from the country. Stewart's not from the country. We're suburban boys from a city!

DG: Do you think, though, that there's a connection between a sense of identity and landscape that filmmakers feel the need to deal with in some way in New Zealand film?

PW: Yes. I think when you go and film in the countryside, to a certain extent it's a very made-up landscape. A film which Stewart and I never made (but which possibly influenced Vincent Ward a little bit) was a film set up north in the gumfields, where Yugoslav people came in the 1890s. We wrote a film which was all very bleak and very muddy and very wet. Many years later, I met

Vincent at an awards ceremony, and he said to me something like, "That was a tremendous script you wrote. What happened to it?" I said, "Nothing," and we both laughed.

DG: So his film got made.

PW: A completely different film [*Vigil*]. But there were certainly parallels between the sort of dark and uncomfortable vision, basically quite a hostile vision of the country—the landscape as monster.

DG: Indeed, when I look at the body of New Zealand film work since the Film Commission period [the Film Commission was established in 1978 to fund production and promote New Zealand film], the films tend to give a sense of the landscape as being somehow hostile—a "monster." It's a force to be reckoned with, even the cityscape.

PW: But that's probably part of the whole thing of how Pakēha people feel to a certain extent; they have to come to terms with being where we live. I don't think that future generations will feel that nearly so much, but certainly past generations had to because basically we are European by background.

DG: What's the change you see coming, or becoming, with the new generation of filmmakers in New Zealand?

PW: Well, I think there's a much greater acceptance of New Zealand being its own particular place with its own particular destiny, part of which has come about, ironically, through these films and books.

DG: So you see a fomenting of a new culture that's not just British or American?

PW: Yes.

DG: Do you see, then, an interesting blurring that brings together different cultures in New Zealand that keep moving and not becoming, in some sense, "pure" but perhaps more aesthetically and politically fluid and mobile?[1] The diversity of South Pacific and Polynesian cultures is undoubtedly changing New Zealand's landscape.

PW: Yeah. It's a strange thing because on one level we have a much greater weight of international media on us now, but that's always been very powerful in New Zealand anyhow.

DG: Very much so. American and British newsreels, as well as Hollywood film, have always been here.

PW: And they were so powerful because it was the only news we kind of got, you know. If you consider that you don't have any contact with the rest of the world apart from Hollywood dramas, then you're going to have a particularly extreme view of the rest of the world and how we perceive ourselves.

DG: Gordon Mirams, the New Zealand film critic and censor during the 1940s, wrote in 1945 that if there's anything you can call a New Zealand culture, it's Hollywood culture. So as early as 1945, a New Zealand critic is saying that if we're going to understand ourselves, we need to in some way understand how it is that Hollywood has done what it has done to our culture and, more importantly, how we participate in it. Cultures seem to have the uncanny ability to both embrace *and* resist cultural dominating forces like Hollywood or whatever it might be.

PW: When I was doing research on the Civic Theatre [in Auckland], I talked to all these women who had worked in the picture palace, so cinema was in their blood. And, of course, when the American soldiers arrived, they found it very difficult to separate the movies from real life. To them, they were characters out of a film who just walked into their lives; they thought they were tremendously glamorous and things like that. Some of them married these men, and some went back to the US with them. And then, of course, they found the reality of some of their lives was extremely tough. It was a terrible shock because you know behind the cinema image was an economic and social reality which was very different.

DG: As you mention this, I'm thinking two things: one is, again, the Film Commission body of work, where there is a peculiar, if not disturbing, look at the effects of Americanization in New Zealand: *Heavenly Creatures* [dir. Peter Jackson, 1994], *Constance* [dir. Bruce Morrison, 1984]. These appear to me as films trying to understand the implications of this dream-life that Hollywood manufactured and, then, how New Zealanders receive these images and ideologies. But I am also thinking how the "terrible shock" may have been provocative for queer New

Zealand filmmakers. It seems that an important part of queer cinema here is that the filmmaking is a perversely aestheticized presentation of the lived experience of the filmmaker in relationship to all this Hollywood stuff. It's the messiness you were talking about earlier. It's like, "Here comes Lana Turner, and here comes Elizabeth Taylor, and maybe today I'm feeling a little bit like, you know, Susan Hayward" or something. For me, this campy queer messiness comes out in your films, for example. Is this maybe the weird Americanization/Hollywoodization [that has become] a part of the queerness of New Zealand filmmaking?

PW: Well, it's hard to generalize; definitely *Desperate Remedies* was the most obvious one.

DG: And it's not only Hollywood Americana you draw upon for *Desperate Remedies*. The film even looks to *Senso* [dir. Luchino Visconti, 1954] in many ways.

PW: Yes, we watched *Senso*, which I love.

DG: Yes, it's a wonderful film and, yet again, another piece of queer tradition in the cinema.

PW: With *Desperate Remedies*, when we talked to the actors about what we were trying to do with the film, part of the feeling we were trying to achieve was of Pakēha people in some sort of blockade. They were in a blockaded town really. I drew on some historical examples of the Land Wars in New Zealand [1845–72], which took place, as you know, at exactly the same time as the Civil War in the States. The setting of *Gone with the Wind* was in our mind [dir. Victor Fleming, 1939]. In New Plymouth, which was really the epicenter of the Land Wars, Pakēha people had to withdraw from their farms and bury whatever they had that was valuable. They just withdrew into town, but the town itself became quite blockaded. They got very, very low on food, and people got sick; it was a whole sort of weird kind of world. That was the way I actually saw the town of Hope in *Desperate Remedies*, though the film is really more hyper-hysterical rather than hyper-historical.

DG: The hyper-hysterical seems to be an aesthetic you bring to more contemporary issues such as rugby. What has been your experience with making films like *A Taste of Kiwi* [1990; this short film juxtaposes footage from actual rugby games with gay pornography]. It is an excellent example of queering the national sport. What sort of response do you get—did you get—with the film?

PW: It is interesting because with *Desperate Remedies*, we were lucky. We were protected, so to speak, by its "overseas success." It was picked up by Miramax, so the locals couldn't unload on it in the way they do when a film only has to rely on a New Zealand audience's taste. *A Taste of Kiwi* always had a good response really. But then it's never been "officially" through the censor, although now it could probably pass the censor. At the time, it would never have been passed. It only ever came on in cinemas in a guerilla way, where it was just suddenly on— unannounced—which made it even more kind of astonishing because it's so flirtatiously hard core! I mean within a New Zealand context, where the All Blacks are some sort of Gods—*to have them rooting each other!*

DG: Yes. There certainly is this privileged place for the rugby player in New Zealand. It's so great to see the "gods" eroticized *and* homosexualized.

PW: The film has had a funny history really because I showed it in sort of an uncut Super 8 form, and a very well-meaning teacher from a Catholic school had brought all his sixth form—fifteen- and sixteen-year-olds, star students—along. And, of course, I felt sorry for him really because it probably put him in a really difficult situation.

DG: What happened?

PW: There was a shocked silence and a lot of red faces. But this reminds me of a school of physical education in Dunedin, actually, which asked for the film. I don't know what they thought it was. I asked the lecturer how it was received, and he said with a great sense of shock, after nobody said anything, someone then said, "Can we watch it again?" Of course, it's pretty frantically cut, which I think adds to the eroticism. It gives it a "Did I see that?" quality, which throws the viewer into it much more. After all, the staple of porn is the long and, to me, usually boring shot. At other screenings, though, people nearly always laugh incredulously.

DG: To me, that film is such a good old-fashioned shock and dose of fabulous sexuality.

PW: I would love to have it on—*if one could only get it on*—during a football match like on national television. It'd be great!

DG: I guess *Taste of Kiwi* really raises the issue of censorship in New Zealand. I find it fascinating teaching in New Zealand as a film and media scholar. For example, when I want to show Andy Warhol or something from the underground, there's a couple of responses I always get. One is, "Why would you want to show Andy Warhol films?" Someone at one of the New Zealand censor boards, in fact, asked, "Isn't that just entertainment?" There's this idea that there wouldn't be any "academic" value to watching Warhol.

PW: It's a kind of Puritan viewpoint, isn't it?

DG: The other curious issue that arises around these films is that once we use these films for "education purposes," it still has to go through the censor. The concern for the "common good" almost seems very authoritarian. The thing that I found interesting in your article ["Frock Wars! Wig Attacks! Camp as a Strategy in *Desperate Remedies*," University of Auckland, 1997] is how you had to get by issues of censorship through a use of the visual. What do you think about censorship issues in New Zealand?

PW: Well, I think censorship at the point we were making *Desperate Remedies* operated on many different levels, one of which was ostensibly a commercial level. You know, if you make a film that was too overtly lesbian, it would be not marketable, and that was a very, very strong pressure on us really because you've got to remember that the script goes before the Film Commission, which is made up of only, I think, one professional filmmaker, and the rest of the people are from the general community. There was someone who was literally the head of something like the Carpenters' Union or the Masterbuilders' Union of New Zealand. In fact, he turned out to love the film and really loved the script. It was one of those really surprising things that you never really expect. But you realize your script is actually going almost to members of the general public, and when you meet with them, they have the right to talk to you about what's in the script. This process is never expressed in terms of censorship, but it's expressed in terms of "we don't think the narrative works so well here" and things like that. We were under enormous pressure not to divulge that the two women were lesbians until the very end of the film.

DG: Yes. The film potentially suggests an ambiguity in the women's relationship since there's the Kevin Smith character, who throws a wrench into it.

PW: But interestingly enough, and that's the difference between the written word and visual images, in the script you could get away much longer with the idea of it not being very clear what their relationship was. But in fact image-wise with the film, it's such a heightened hysterical world anyway, and the looks between the women are so charged and things like that, that I think the audience fairly early in the piece really *does* realize that the two women have a very strong relationship.

DG: So you did have to make a decision about the way the film looked cinematically so as to address an issue that might not be able to be articulated verbally. How were you able to erotically charge those looks between the two women in the making of the film?

PW: I think the challenge to visually render the erotics of the relationship did interfere with the filmmaking to a certain degree. There was a certain point in the film where the two women are standing in their negligees; the crew were begging us to have Jennifer and Lisa kiss. Looking back, they probably were right, but it was such a tremendously thought-through and fraught thing!

DG: The pressure of censoring the lesbian kiss, then, was more a combination of indirect or roundabout pressures via the Film Commission and ultimately channeled through the producer. Did you confront any problems with the male nudity and the boarding-house scene?

PW: No, because that wasn't where their anxiety was. In the script, those scenes weren't written as being that; it was just written as being an early morning in the boarding-house type scene. The same situation happened with the sort of buggery scene, you know, the male fucking scene. I mean that was not in the written script at all, so you can slip these little things in. Our producer, James Wallace, maintained a point of view that the script was predicated on the two women's relationship not being revealed. He felt it was important that the two women were not identified as lesbian until the very end. This was a constant tension on the set about how much we showed. James's point was that we had signed documents with the Film Commission which legally meant we had to shoot the script they had agreed to. Stewart, who had worked as an editor, knew that all sorts of things can happen in the editing of a film, and he wanted *more*: *more sex*. We had a few screaming matches. James and Stewart did anyway.

DG: Wow! Once you had the final cut, though, did it have to go once again before a review board?

PW: No, no.

DG: That's really interesting.

PW: Yes, I know it is. I think it's not a very well thought-through thing. Fortunately, now, I think it's written into contracts that the Film Commission have the, *sort of*, say about final cut.

DG: It's very much like the old Hollywood Production Code from the 1930s.

PW: Yes.

DG: It's a fascinating contradiction in New Zealand in terms of how the country deals with homosexuality. By law, my partner and I were able to come over here and receive legal status as a homosexual partnership. Yet, on the other hand, when you're making a film like *Desperate Remedies*, there remains an unspoken censor in culture that controls and mitigates what's considered good for culture or not good for culture. There is a gap between the law and cultural acceptance.

PW: Yes, and also what is commercial—"commercially viable"—was what the producers and Film Commission were always talking about. It was never expressed to us in terms of censorship, ever really. It was, in a way, a much more difficult thing to deal with in that it came across as "we're talking to you primarily in terms of the commercial potential of the film, and if you make this film *too* lesbian or *too* homo, you will limit your audience." So it's another—it's a kind of an interesting rephrasing of censorship.

DG: It's a bit discomforting when censorship is paradoxically packaged as "free speech" in free-market culture.

PW: I couldn't agree more. And, of course, the irony was that lesbian filmmaking was just on the cusp of breaking through commercially, so in the end, it turned out that the so-called commercial pressures were in actual fact the product of cultural narrowness. It's curious being queer in New Zealand because in some ways, just as with film, we are partly American invention, but then we're not at all. We're the product of a peculiar and unique mix of other things: the freedom which comes from distance, isolation; the strangeness which comes from making things up yourself, from distorted images which are received in a cargo-cult way; and I guess our Scots and English genes, with a touch of Irish thrown in, trying to coexist with a Polynesian warrior culture which has been here since at least the twelfth century. Our major document [the Treaty of Waitangi, signed between Pakēha and Māori in 1840] is the product of nineteenth-century evangelical guilt. So a kind of gothic sensibility seems pretty normal here. I think people discern this strangeness in New Zealand film. Of course, to ourselves, we are almost insanely normal. There's a clothing label here that is found on these elegant and beautifully made lounge-lizard clothes. It is called Strangely Normal. That's us!

Note

1 At the time Peter and I met, a widely seen advertising campaign—"New Zealand—100% Pure"—ran nationally and internationally.

LETTER TO SAM

A note on this correspondence: My dissertation committee at UCLA was led by Stephen Mamber and was composed of Peter Wollen, Vivian Sobchack, Catherine Lord, and Samuel Weber. Since filing the document for my doctorate, I was fortunate to keep in touch with committee members in varying degrees; all have been supportive. One of my committee mentors, Sam Weber, kindly kept a fairly regular volley of friendly emails with me as my thoughts on Derrida, Benjamin, and Freud developed. In those interactions, ideas were exchanged, along with suggested readings and film viewings. As such, they proved of incalculable value for my thoughts on queer cinema (ideas that may not always be in accord with his). Sam was always quick to respond, as he was always happy to find time to grab a coffee when I was in Paris. His correspondence encouraged me to write and think in unimaginable ways. For that I am grateful. During my sabbatical in 2014–15, I deeply immersed myself in the "big books" stacked up on my desk. As it often happens, intense readings and viewings lead to a burning desire to write. Reading Thomas Piketty's celebrated *Capital in the Twenty-First Century* alongside Benoît's critically engaged biography of Jacques Derrida prompted the following email to Sam. If I were to title this "essay," I would name it "Homo-aporia: Notes on Capital and Queer Cinematic Friendship." Finally, it is worth noting that, when I wrote my dissertation, Sam was the person who instructed me in how to attach a document to an email. It seems appropriate that our relationship sustained itself these many years via email, in which attachments readily flew back and forth. What follows is my email sent to Sam on August 25, 2014.

Hello Sam,

I hope your summer has been delightful. Mine has included the added pleasure of anticipating sabbatical.

Along with completing an essay for an upcoming collection on *The Boys in the Band*, I read several books, two of which included Thomas Piketty's *Capital in the Twenty-First Century* and Benoît Peeters's *Derrida*. Your spirit hovered as I read these works, and for this reason, in part, I write. When I finished reading *Derrida*, I rewatched Amy Ziering Kofman and Kirby Dick's documentary *Derrida* (2002). These summer texts moved me to write you with some thoughts about "economies" of queer desire, cinema, and friendship (especially between men). I'm hoping to stitch together what these works offer (and, as it turns out, *neglect*) with an eye toward the tricky intimacy men *of all sorts* share in these economies (I'm calling it a "homo-aporia"—we shall see!).

I begin with a caveat: the notes are somewhat clumsy (I think I just wrote a short paper!). By the end, I am working through ideas about the implications for cinematic technique, "homo-aporia," and mutatis mutandis the friendship between men.

Please feel free to skip to the bottom, where I address a brief practical matter or two. The bulk of this email corresponds with a dialogue I had with you in my head. Apologies if it rambles . . . it's a work in progress.

Piketty's book, as you know, took the US by storm this spring. I was happy to see the conversation stretched on matters of income equality. The author makes important links between class and race, but, as feminists recently highlight in *The Nation*, he misses an opportunity to discuss gender as it plays into the global economy. I learned much about economic theory; the book has certainly changed the terms for the debate.

One reason I bought Piketty's book was in fact driven by my interest in his final footnote (I had seen it in a preview on Amazon). In it, Piketty queries why French Marxists such as Louis Althusser and Alain Badiou never engage the positivist terms for their critiques of capitalism. The note reads, "When one reads philosophers such as Jean-Paul Sartre, Louis Althusser, and Alain Badiou on their Marxist and/or communist commitments, one sometimes has the impression that questions of capital and class inequality are of only moderate interest to them and serve as mainly a pretext for jousts of a different nature entirely."[1] I was so pleased to come across this note because my plans have been to return to Sartre's and Althusser's work. I had just read Badiou's book *Cinema* for a presentation I delivered on post-'68 French cinema, so his work was fresh in my mind. Derrida's omission from Piketty's note further intrigued me (but that is discussed below).

In any case, Piketty's note was useful insofar as it raises the following: To what extent is Piketty's uncertainty about and discomfort with Althusser et al.'s "Marxist and/or communist commitments" thinking in "a different nature entirely"? What, then, is the "nature" of Piketty's study? On the one hand, his review of racism and poverty is invaluable, while, at the same time, it is also remarkably androcentric, as the feminists point out.[2] But the androcentrism involves something more: heterocentrism. His acknowledgments that open the book neatly indicate just from where this particular "energy," as he calls it, derives to write: "Finally, thanks to Juliette, Déborah, and Hélène, my three precious daughters, for all the love and strength they give me. And thanks to Julia, who shares my life and is also my best reader. Her influence and support at every stage in the writing of this book have been essential. Without them, I would not have had the energy to see this project through to completion."[3]

Hence, from front to back, and back again, I found myself asking whither queer "Marxist and/or communist commitments" and the State Apparatus in the twenty-first century? Indeed, Piketty goes on at great length about the implications for inheritance, particularly as a familial device that enables capital to compound itself. Yet, and given the heightened debate in France about "homoparentalité," it is odd that gay-parent adoptions and the reconfigured (French) family are not taken up. The possibilities for such transformation are at play and do pose unthought-of questions about inheritance and so forth. Do these potentially queer shifts augur new models in a capitalist economy? Does the queer family offer innovative forms of exchange? What are new forms of queer inheritance? To what extent does homoparentalité rethink inheritance distribution when kinship is reconfigured? What might these malleable relations look like under the terms of twenty-first-century capitalism?

Yet not all the philosophers that Piketty critiques fare any better in terms of heteromasculinist assumptions. For instance, Badiou's recent discussion about desire and "the language of money" unwittingly suggests a queer radical approach to a culture of exchange without identifying his theory as, well, queer. In an interview on BIOECON TV's *Occidente: Portraits, Visions*, *and Utopia*, Badiou asks whether or not alternative forms of exchange can take place through a "noncompetitive model." He argues, the "unlimited desire for money," encouraged through the "the fiction of money," needs to be creatively rethought, specifically, by artists.[4] It is their job to offer new concepts of exchange that begin with a rethinking of human relationships. For Badiou, to reestablish relationships in which a "deep sense" and a "deep truth" of love exists, artists must generate new fictions of desire in order to facilitate unimagined forms of exchange. Badiou emphasizes, however, that "deep" love must resist "absolutist" impulses (monogamy?); he suggests the term "friendly" to describe these relationships. As he sees it, a reconfigured relationship is "not exactly that of the passion of love, but it is a way that lets us let the other [*les Autres*] come close, share, that is not immediately dominated by judgment, by condemnation and competition. I would propose some kind of universal friendship."

When I heard Badiou's enthusiastic imaginings for new forms of desire and "exchange," I anticipated some sort of gesture, on his part, to gay culture. Badiou's neglect on this count is surprising given his cinephilic credentials. He is aware of Fassbinder's, Pasolini's, Vallois's, Rippleh's, and Denis's films, in which radical desire is *cinematized* as queer corporeal exchanges. But as the great champion of Godard ("Mention Godard First!" he insists), Badiou's relationship to cinema involves little challenge to sexual desire beyond heterosexuality.[5] Badiou's organizing of the cinema as an art form that is resonant for radical politics and love is one determined by strict lines for form and content. This became clear to me when I read his angry response to Jacques Demy's queer musical-opera *Une chambre en ville* (1982).[6] Combining the musical genre with a workers' protest narrative was incompatible, if not incomprehensible, for Badiou. Demy's film is a brilliant queer vision of a new economy!

Thus, Badiou's remarks on love and cinema got me to thinking about what kind of love *queers* capitalist models of normative relationships of love without reproducing the heterocentric terms that support them. My response: cruising. Cruising in public space (not necessarily the gay bar) responds to Badiou's new language of exchange since cruising involves brief and immediate sexual encounters. Cruising is a movement, a loose choreography, in which desire is reproduced and exchanged but yields nothing more than desire. It seems an ideal version of "universal friendship" that Badiou calls for. And when one thinks of each director noted above (and I include Honoré), their cinematic choreography of bodies is "not exactly that of the passion of love but it is a way that lets us let the other [*les Autres*] come close, share, that is not immediately dominated by judgment, by condemnation and competition." Call me gay, but this sounds an awful like cruising.

And this is where Derrida steps in . . .

For me, reading Peeters's *Derrida* kept questions of queer form and content, queer friendship, and queer cinematics in play. Derrida is unquestionably the elephant in the rooms arranged by Piketty and Badiou. I wonder, for example, what Piketty thinks of Derrida's *Specters of Marx* (2006)? Badiou, we are told by Peeters, was pleased to see its publication, even though he and Derrida didn't see eye to eye.[7] In this way, and since the film *Derrida* did so well, I wonder what Badiou makes of Derrida's attention to eyes and hands as he describes them to the film's directors? The interview sequence in which Derrida discusses eyes and hands is so beautifully erotic. When he speaks, I am seduced. He is aware of his contemplative language and its associative gestures that draw the viewer to gaze into his eyes and onto his hands. We are cinematically touched while we look, while we cruise.

Hence, after reading the biography and watching the film, I became all the more aware of Derrida's erotic engagement with the world (but, to be honest, I always thought he was sexy). In your interview with Derrida, for example, you succinctly mark Derrida's erotic presence when you relay your first encounter with the not-yet-confident philosopher: "Only gradually did he free himself up, inventing a public persona for himself and a form of erotic identity that he made his own" (Peeters, *Derrida*, 190). For me, Derrida's invention of a "public persona" as an "erotic identity" is a *queer* erotic identity because it is so provocatively cinematic, so seductive. The relationship between his body and the cinema is confirmed throughout the biography.

I was so excited, for instance, to see that Derrida loved going to the movies with friends "to do some applied filmology." As a young boy, it "represented an extraordinary form of travel" from life in Algeria (Peeters, *Derrida*, 27). From the start, then, Derrida's "friendly relationships" are bundled and made moveable with the cinema. "Applied filmology" is nothing less than a cinematic friendship, a cruising of sorts. It's so fantastic! To my mind, cinema—or the cinematic experience—was crucial to his writing as a boy and, later, as a public intellectual.

In this way, his letters to Michel Monory are invaluable for how we might think about cinematic friendship between men in relationship to Derrida's concentration on eyes and hands (Peeters, *Derrida*, 41). A link may be made between the cinematic touch that Derrida offers in the film's interview, noted above, and Derrida's signature on the notes he wrote Monroy. As Peeters points out, the significance of touch in the correspondence that the intimates shared played a major role in Derrida's early thinking. Derrida, for example, describes his longing to touch his friend when they are at a distance from each other: "Just six weeks to wait; then we'll go out, we'll go for walks together again, we'll think and feel together; together we will keep silence, too, between long, long private discussions; for then we will tell each other what letters cannot say. Will we have any moments of peaceable, trusting joy, Michel? I almost feel I am no longer capable of this without you, but will I be so with you?" (Peeters, *Derrida*, 46).

When deeply saddened and depressed, he shares his tears with Michel: "I am not able to produce anything other than tears. . . . Weeping over the world, weeping for God. . . . I am almost at the end of my tether, Michel, pray for me" (Peeters, *Derrida*, 46). Combined with his intense relationship with Michel and his deep readings (recently, here, Sartre's *Nausea*), Derrida tells Michel, "I no longer know what nature—or the natural—is, I am painfully amazed by everything" (47).

What Peeters and the excerpt from the letters illuminate is a deep passion, a deep love shared between Derrida and Monroy. What we see, in effect, is a relationship of a "different nature entirely." Such a relationship as this is thus difficult to grasp—to be seen—by some. As I see it, Derrida and Monroy point to the sort of relationship Badiou calls for as a "universal friendship." I would add, it is a stunningly queer relationship. The correspondence, in other words, displays an exchange between men that is different from the way Eve Sedgwick defines the "homosocial." In her view, homosociality entails proximity between or among men while, at the same time, maintaining a distance from one another so as to avoid the appearance of homoeroticism, or homosexual desire. Derrida and Monroy's relationship, on the other hand, insists on articulating and giving full appearance to their intimacy, which is, in truth, extremely erotic. Their untiring desire to touch each other is unambiguously sensual. Their (heterosexual? homosexual?) friendship is something of a *homo-aporia*—a sentient intimacy between men? an ambiguous desire for men?—since it is *less but more* than homosocial.

Homo-aporia is more seductive than homosocial because, ultimately, homosociality bears the imprint of homophobia. Homosexuality, alternatively, asserts its homosexuality as its raison d'être. Hence, what other forms of male-to-male sensuality are identifiable in which relations between men straddle the "fictions" of homosociality and homosexuality? Yet, if homo-aporia is a more apt term because it describes a desire that shuttles between male-to-male sensuality and sexuality, is the term vibrant enough to be thought of as radically queer? What are the limits of homo-aporetic touch? To what extent do Derrida's *writerly* hands touch Monroy? To what extent do Derrida's eyes caress Monroy? What happens when Monroy looks back at Derrida? Does the term "homo-aporia" open new possibilities for how we think about the friendly exchange between men? Or does it desexualize the dynamic and, so, dequeer the friendship?

Derrida's link between eyes and hands thus remains promising if we couch this exchange as cinematic. Seeing and touching/handling are indeed critical to a cinematic experience. Whether watching, writing about, writing for, or making film, eyes and hands are vital to the cinematic enterprise. And in "inventing a public persona for himself and a form of erotic identity that he made his own," Derrida, I believe, engages himself cinematically. In other words, his "public persona" is not dissimilar to a movie screen; Derrida's "erotic identity" facilitates an erotic exchange between author and reader/ spectator. Seen this way, Derrida, like the movie screen, opens us up, as Boyd McDonald tells us, to cruising![8]

Hence, although it is obvious to say that Derrida engages me erotically through his writing, his erotic form of writing, moreover, deeply moves my thinking about and my relationship to queer cinema. This has happened in complicated and surprising fashion. At first, I was confounded when Derrida rejects Godard (Peeters, *Derrida*, 434; Godard is Badiou's darling after all). To presume a connection between Derrida and Godard is, in short, too obvious, too modernist. Derrida, as he does, raises the ante on cinema when we hear that he favored *The Godfather*!!! At first, such a claim is just as confounding as his refusal of Godard's influence. But Derrida's pleasure "in [doing] some applied filmology" involves a form of "applied" writing. As a cine-writer, Derrida redirects a history of the auteur in a specific way—a way that Godard ultimately refuses. I think Derrida resuscitates Alexandre Astruc's auteurist concept *la caméra-stylo* in rewarding and queer ways. Derrida, ever so briefly but importantly, points to this possibility when in *Of Grammatology* he identifies cinematography as a mode of écriture.[9]

To remark Astruc's *caméra-stylo* as cinema's writing instrument is to raise the stakes on mise-en-scène in the pro-filmic sense. But it also raises the stakes on auteur theory. While the classical underpinnings of the theory pit montage and mise-en-scène against each other (I realize this is reductive, but think Bazin and Eisenstein), I think it valuable not to dismiss the importance of montage but recognize the way it elevates the significance of mise-en-scène (to my mind, Bazin and Eisenstein may not have been that far apart about this cinematic dynamic).

Derrida reminds us of something more. (In this light, it would be so interesting to present Bazin, Eisenstein, and Derrida side by side for a seminar reading). Cinema's signature—cinematography and montage—comes about through a direct engagement with the director's eyes and hands.[10] We might suggest, therefore, that Derridean film theory, *cine-écriture* (as Varda has put it), emphasizes the "putting in the scene" *at one's hand* and *through one's visual perspective*. In this way, the auteur's mark sets in motion the sensual cinematic experience, an experience launched by their touch and their look. Derrida sums up cinema this way: "In cinema I like there to be an intelligence that isn't that of knowledge, or intellectual in quality, but of the way it's directed" (quoted in Peeters, *Derrida*, 434).

What does this have to do with *The Godfather* and Godard? With queer friendship? Godard's ultimate emphasis on form—montage—to conquer reductive narrative meaning as such runs the risk, if my line of thought holds here in terms of Derrida's position, of establishing an absolutist cinema. Godard, I think, wrestles with this when he is working with the Dziga Vertov Group. Coppola (in the example cited by Derrida), however, rigorously "directs" narrative *and* form so that the subtlety of "intelligence" permeates all aspects of the film's making. *The Godfather* is at once intelligent while pleasurable without the pretense of "knowledge" (Woody Allen is as problematic as Godard is for Derrida; Peeters, *Derrida*, 433–34). *The Godfather* is quite the erotic experience as well—on multiple levels.

To conclude this unexpected—and perhaps taxing—exegesis, it occurs to me that the venomous critiques leveled against Derrida about his writing are ultimately homophobic or, rather, queer-phobic (Peter Dews's book *Logics of Disintegration* is recently on my mind). I think this to be true because the homosocial boys' club to which these critics belong is threatened not only by Derrida's theoretical threads; moreover, Derrida's cinematic *écriture* is *too* erotic. It is writing of a "different nature entirely." His writing calls attention to writing as erotically charged, which destabilizes the aggressive heteromasculinist groupings aligned with the likes of Terry Eagleton, Dews, et al. Their critiques remind me of those that Vincente Minnelli (and the musical genre, more generally) regularly receive. Derrida's "friendly" economy for relationships can be unsettlingly queer business, especially for not-so-queer men!

There is more to say, of course, but I'll stop here. I will only point out that Derrida struggled with his own heteromasculinist limits. When asked in the film *Derrida* which of his favored philosophers he considered his "mother-philosopher," Derrida was stumped. Nevertheless, he admitted to the threshold he could not cross (at least he admitted it!) and was sensitive to the implications for what it was he could not envisage. And, yet, mothers and queer culture are its own story.[11]

[*Ex post facto*: Perhaps had Piketty considered Derrida's Marxist turns, he would have imagined—*awakened to?*—a queer economy for the twenty-first century.]

We are still planning to be in Paris over Thanksgiving. I hope you have some time to meet.

Thanks for reading my note—either in part or in its entirety. I was so moved to write after engaging all these texts this summer . . . and you were on my mind as the person to whom I should address my thoughts.

Hugs,
David

Notes

1   Piketty, *Capital in the Twenty-First Century*, 655.
2   See, for instance, Geier et al., "How Gender Changes Piketty's *Capital in the Twenty-First Century*."
3   Piketty, *Capital in the Twenty-First Century*, viii.
4   See bioecon tv, "Bioecon TV Presents Alain Badiou."
5   Badiou, "Reference Points," 1.
6   Badiou, "Demy Affair."
7   Peeters, *Derrida*, 511. Further references to this work are cited parenthetically in the text.
8   McDonald, *Cruising the Movies*.
9   Derrida, *Of Grammatology*, 9.

10   In a new essay, I have since rethought my somewhat overdetermined posi-
      tion here on Godard's auteurist impulses since seeing his film *The Image Book*
      (2018). The film, for me, brings into focus Godard's emphasis on the montage/
      mise-en-scène relationship as indissoluble. See Gerstner, "Women's Hands,"
      482–84.

11   On this, see my essay "Speculations on the Origin of the World," chapter 15
      in this volume.

IN MEMORY OF PETER WOLLEN

David A. Gerstner and Matthew Solomon

I wrote this memoriam with my long-standing colleague and friend Matthew Solomon. We remain grateful for Peter's gifts of knowledge and wide-ranging approaches to cinema.

Peter Wollen and auteur theory are (*often and rightly*) spoken in the same breath. But like the theory with which his name is indelibly stamped, his wide-ranging scholarly and creative practice make way for yet-unexplored intellectual experimentation. Peter was not ahead of the curve; he made the curve. On December 17, 2019, Peter passed away, leaving a legacy of extraordinary writing (*écriture* in the broadest terms) for the students he mentored and those yet to come.

Born in 1938 in London, Peter came of age postwar, in which his cinephilia merged with his political formations. Taken together, his career in writing and filmmaking ushered in a period of creativity in which the ideological complexities that marked the 1960s and 1970s found provocative contours in his work. He first turned to journalism writing for the *New Left Review*. Already delighting in a playful yet deeply committed voice regarding cinema, he wrote under the nom de plume Lee Russell (we can hear Peter's lovely chuckle as we write these notes). His 1964 essay "Howard Hawks" hints at his subtle and unique talent to grasp the paradoxical dimensions that gave rise to the pleasures of cinema in a despairing world. In this essay, the Hollywood director's long-standing theme in which "danger" and "fun" intertwine reveals what would prove to be Peter's subsequent concerns with the cinema: "Danger gives existence pungency," Russell/Wollen writes. Hawks's world is one of "nihilism," in which the moment action occurs, danger arises. "This nihilism," Peter continues, "in which 'living' means no more than being in danger of losing your life—a danger

"In Memory of Peter Wollen." David A. Gerstner and Matthew Solomon. (SCMS website, December 2019).

entered into gratuitously—is augmented by the Hawksian concept of having 'fun.' The word 'fun' crops up constantly in Hawks's interviews and scripts. It masks his despair."[1] Writing against the backdrop of postwar London, where the energies of a new creative spirit were launching against the backdrop of a traumatized world, Peter introduced a way of seeing in which he easily choreographed Hawks, Alfred Hitchcock, John Ford, and Gene Kelly with Jean Renoir, Jean-Luc Godard, Michelangelo Antonioni, and Ken Russell.

Peter was never one to separate making films from researching and writing about films. He cowrote the script for Michelangelo Antonioni's *The Passenger* (1975) with Mark Peploe and adapted *Friendship's Death* (1987) from one of his short stories. He was partner to a number of critical and creative collaborations that combined theory and practice, which for him were always inevitably imbricated. Among the most notable were the six films he codirected with Laura Mulvey between 1974 and 1982, which constitute perhaps his most significant and radical contributions to cinematic form and feminist filmmaking. In the wake of Mulvey's 1975 essay "Visual Pleasure and Narrative Cinema," they concentrated their cinematic efforts on exploring the language of cinema as it reinforced patriarchal ideology and masculinist pleasure, perhaps most notably in *Riddles of the Sphinx* (1977), which fused avant-garde art practice with feminist theory to develop a cinematic language that challenged and refused patriarchal film form.

One of Peter's major contributions to the study of cinema and/as art was careful attention to the creative milieus in which filmmakers and artists have worked, which allowed him to make unexpected connections while rendering historical contexts in palpable detail. And while Peter won the SCMS Career Achievement Award in 2006 for his remarkable scholarly work, the award, in our minds, recognized the way he dazzled his students when sharing his wide-ranging research interests, which orbited around "cinema and the other arts" (the title of a graduate seminar he offered regularly at UCLA). The topics he chose to investigate in his writing and teaching were unusually diverse, ranging from painting and photography to dance and fashion. Peter was the author of books, screenplays, reviews, and poems, but the historical-critical-theoretical essay was perhaps his preferred form. His essays are generative and reward rereading. Whether he is reflecting on the children's books of the author-animator-director Frank Tashlin, on the auteurist politics of Michael Curtiz, on Louise Brooks's distinctive hairstyle, on early hip-hop ("rapping takes disco leaps ahead," he noted in 1982),[2] on the often-overlooked mechanics and chemistry of the film laboratory, on the panopticism that Louis XIV enabled through dance, or on the unsettling postcolonial modernity that riddles a cricket match, the attentive reader not only discovers astute observations about *how and why* we experience the world as we do but also encounters a tantalizing choreography of ideas and material practice in which "fun" and "despair" become startlingly clear. Although a number of his writings have not yet been collected or republished, many can be found in *Readings and Writings: Semiotic Counter-Strategies* (Verso, 1982), *Raiding the Icebox: Reflections on Twentieth-Century Culture* (Indiana University Press, 1993), *Paris/Hollywood: Writings on Film* (Verso, 2002), and *Paris/Manhattan: Writings on Art* (Verso, 2004). The titles of these last two collections point to Peter's prescient interest in "world cities" as nexuses for transnational cultural, political, social, and economic exchanges. Such exchanges defined both his intellectual and his personal biography.

Never himself pursuing a doctorate degree despite advising numerous PhD students, Peter maintained a commitment to his and their writing. As with his own writing, he encouraged an accessible style to reach an intellectually curious readership. His contributions to *Sight & Sound* during the 1990s are fine examples that play with form and sparkle with acumen. He never forsook *criticism*, insisting that critical judgment and discernment were an important part of the critic's and, indeed, the artist's job. For him, criticism and scholarship were inseparable and must necessarily inform each other.

Those who knew Peter will recall his infectious laugh, his boundless curiosity, and the generosity of his staggering intellect. He challenged us. He supported our desires to learn and experience the world in unanticipated ways. In our sadness, we feel nonetheless lucky since he leaves behind a body of work that has only just begun to be taken up with rigor and pleasure.

Notes

1   Russell, "Howard Hawks," 84.
2   Wollen, "Semiotic Counter-Strategies," 212.

BIBLIOGRAPHY

Abel, Richard, ed. *French Film Theory and Criticism: A History/Anthology, 1907–1929*. Vol. 1, 1907–1929. Princeton, NJ: Princeton University Press, 1988.

Abelove, Henry, Michèle Aina Barale, and David M. Halperin, eds. *The Lesbian and Gay Studies Reader*. New York: Routledge, 1993.

Ades, Dawn, Neil Cox, and David Hopkins. *Marcel Duchamp*. London: Thames and Hudson, 1999.

Adorno, Theodor W. *Aesthetic Theory*. Translated by Rolf Tiedeman. Minneapolis: University of Minnesota, 1997.

Ahmed, Sara. *Queer Phenomenology: Orientations, Objects, Others*. Durham, NC: Duke University Press, 2006.

Albrecht, Donald. *Designing Dreams: Modern Architecture in the Movies*. New York: Harper and Row, 1986.

Althusser, Louis. *The Future Lasts Forever: A Memoir*. Translated by Richard Veasey. New York: New Press, 1992.

———. "Ideology and Ideological State Apparatuses (Notes toward an Investigation)." In *Lenin and Philosophy, and Other Essays*, translated by Ben Brewster, 127–86. New York: Monthly Review, 1972.

Andrew, J. Dudley. *The Major Film Theories*. Oxford: Oxford University Press, 1976.

Anger. Kenneth. *Kenneth Anger's Hollywood Babylon*. New York: Dell, 1975.

Anzaldúa, Gloria. *Borderlands/La Frontera: The New Mestiza*. San Francisco: Aunt Lute Books, 1987.

———. "Speaking in Tongues." In *This Bridge Called My Back: Writings by Radical Women of Color*, edited by Cherríe Moraga and Gloria Anzaldúa, 165–73. Watertown, MA: Persephone, 1981.

Astruc, Alexandre. "The Birth of a New Avant-Garde: La Caméra-Stylo." In *The New Wave*, edited and translated by Peter Graham, 17–23. New York: Doubleday, 1968.

Aumont, Jacques. "Avertissement." In *Jean Epstein: Cinéaste, poète, philosophe*, edited by Jacques Aumont, 7–8. Paris: Cinémathèque francaise, 1998.

———. "Cinégénie ou la machine à remonter le temps." In *Jean Epstein: Cinéaste, poète, philosophe*, edited by Jacques Aumont, 87–108. Paris: Cinémathèque francaise, 1998.

Badiou, Alain. "Cinematic Culture." In *Cinema*, translated by Susan Spitzer, 21–33. Cambridge, UK: Polity, 2013.

———. "The Demy Affair." In *Cinema*, translated by Susan Spitzer, 64–66. Cambridge, UK: Polity, 2013.

———. "Reference Points for Cinema's Second Modernity." In *Cinema*, translated by Susan Spitzer, 58–63. Cambridge, UK: Polity, 2013.

Bad Object-Choice Collective, eds. *How Do I Look? Queer Film and Video*. Seattle: Bay, 1991.

Bagouet, Dominique. "Note d'intention du chorégraphe." In *Jours étranges: Chorégraphie de Daniel Bagouet*, 7. Lyon: Les Carnets Bagouet, 2015. http://www.lescarnetsbagouet.org/pedagogie/Dossier_JoursEtranges.pdf.

Bakhtin, Mikhail. "Forms of Time of the Chronotope in the Novel." In *The Dialogic Imagination*, edited and translated by Michael Holquist and Caryl Emerson, 84–258. Austin: University of Texas Press, 1981.

Baldwin, James. *The Fire Next Time*. New York: Dial Press, 1963.

———. *If Beale Street Could Talk*. New York: Vintage Books, 2002.

———. *No Name in the Street*. 1972. Reprint, New York: Vintage International, 2007.

Barbey d'Aurevilly, Jules. *Dandyism*. 1897. Translated by Douglas Ainslie. New York: PAJ, 1988.

Barzilai, Shuli. *Lacan and the Matter of Origins*. Stanford, CA: Stanford University Press, 1999.

Bataille, Georges. "The Notion of Expenditure." In *Visions of Excess: Selected Writings, 1927–1939*, edited by Alan Stoekel, translated by Alan Stoekel, Carl R. Lovitt, and Donald M. Leslie Jr., 116–29. Minneapolis: University of Minnesota Press, 1993.

Baudelaire, Charles. *Selected Writings on Art and Literature*. Translated by P. E. Charvet. 1972. Reprint, London: Penguin, 1992.

Baudry, Jean-Louis. "The Apparatus: Metapsychological Approaches to the Impression of Reality in the Cinema." In *Narrative, Apparatus, Ideology: A Film Theory Reader*, edited by Philip Rosen, 299–318. New York: Columbia University Press, 1986.

Baxandall, Michael. *Patterns of Intention: On the Historical Explanation of Pictures*. New Haven, CT: Yale University Press, 1985.

Bederman, Gail. *Manliness and Civilization: A Cultural History of Gender and Race in the United States, 1880–1917*. Chicago: University of Chicago Press, 1995.

Be in the Know. "Origin of HIV and AIDS." Accessed July 26, 2022. https://www
.avert.org/professionals/history-hiv-aids/overview.

Bell, Chris. "The AIDS Film." In *The Routledge International Encyclopedia of
Queer Culture*, edited by David A. Gerstner, 28–29. London: Routledge,
2006.

Bell, Matt, ed. *The Boys in the Band: Flashpoints of Cinema, History, and Queer
Politics*. Detroit: Wayne State University Press, 2016.

Bénabou, Marcel. "Rule and Constraint." In *Oulipo: A Primer of Potential Literature*,
edited by Warrant F. Motte, 41–46. Normal, IL: Dalkey Archive, 2008.

Benjamin, Walter. *Charles Baudelaire*. Translated by Harry Zohn. 1976. Reprint,
London: Verso, 1989.

———. *The Correspondence of Walter Benjamin, 1910–1940*. Edited by Gershom
Scholem and Theodor W. Adorno. Translated by Manfred R. Jacobson and
Evelyn M. Jacobson. Chicago: University of Chicago Press, 1994.

———. "Surrealism." In *Reflections*, edited by Peter Demetz, translated by Edmund
Jephcott, 177–92. New York: Schocken, 1986.

———. "Theses on the Philosophy of History." In *Illuminations*, edited by Hannah
Arendt, translated by Henry Zohn, 253–64. New York: Schocken, 1986.

———. "The Work of Art in the Age of Mechanical Reproduction." In
Illuminations, edited by Hannah Arendt, translated by Henry Zohn, 217–52.
New York: Schocken, 1986.

Benjamin, Walter, and Gershom Scholem. *The Correspondence of Walter Benjamin
and Gershom Scholem, 1932–1940*. Edited by Gershom Scholem. Translated
by Gary Smith and Andre Lefevere. Cambridge, MA: Harvard University
Press, 1992.

Benzaquen, Susan, Robert Gagnon, Cora Hunse, and John Foreman. "The
Intrauterine Sound Environment of the Human Fetus during Labor."
American Journal of Obstetrics and Gynecology 163, no. 2 (1990): 484–90.

Bergman, David, ed. *Campgrounds: Style and Homosexuality*. Amherst: University of
Massachusetts Press, 1993.

Bergoffen, Debra. "Irigaray's Couples." In *Returning to Irigaray: Feminist Philosophy,
Politics, and the Question of Unity*, edited by Maria Cimitile and Elaine P.
Miller, 151–72. Albany: State University of New York Press, 2007.

Berlant, Lauren. *Desire/Love*. Brooklyn, NY: Puntum Books, 2012.

Bersani, Leo. "Is the Rectum a Grave?" *October* 43 (Winter 1987): 197–222.

Bhabha. Homi. "Freedom's Basis in the Indeterminate." *October* 61 (Summer 1992):
46–57.

Binder, Wolfgang. "James Baldwin, an Interview." *Revista/Review Interamericana* 10 (Fall 1980): 326–41. Reprinted in *Conversations with James Baldwin*, edited by Fred L. Standley and Louis H. Pratt, 190–209. Jackson: University of Mississippi Press, 1989. Page numbers refer to the reprint edition.

bioecon tv. "Bioecon TV Presents Alain Badiou at Occidente: Portraits, Visions and Utopia." Vimeo, 2012. https://vimeo.com/43703770.

Birnie, William. "A Chorine Thought and Was Wrong." *World Telegram*, November 14, 1936, 3.

Blair, Sara. *Harlem Crossroads: Black Writers and the Photograph in the Twentieth Century*. Princeton, NJ: Princeton University Press, 2007.

Bloemink, Barbara. "Visualizing Sight: Florine Stettheimer and Temporal Modernism." In *Florine Stettheimer: Manhattan Fantastica*, edited by Elisabeth Sussman with Barbara Bloemink, 69–95. New York: Whitney Museum of American Art, 1995.

Bochner, Jay. "Eros Eyesore, or the Ideal and the Ideatic." In *Debating American Modernism: Stieglitz, Duchamp, and the New York Avant-Garde*, edited by Debra Bricker Balken, 99–113. New York: American Federation of Arts, 2003.

Bornstein, Kate. *Gender Outlaw: On Men, Women, and the Rest of Us*. New York: Routledge, 1994.

Boston, Richard. *Boudu Saved from Drowning*. London: BFI, 1994.

Brault, Pascale-Anne, and Michael Naas. Introduction to *The Work of Mourning*, by Jacques Derrida, 1–30. Chicago: University of Chicago Press, 2001.

Brennan, Marcia. *Painting Gender, Constructing Theory: The Alfred Stieglitz Circle and American Formalist Aesthetics*. Cambridge, MA: MIT Press, 2001.

Brunette, Peter, and David Wills. *Screen/Play: Derrida and Film Theory*. Princeton, NJ: Princeton University Press, 1989.

Burch, Noël. *Theory of Film Practice*. Translated by Helen R. Lane. Princeton, NJ: Princeton University, 1973.

Bürger, Peter. "Avant-Garde and Neo-Avant-Garde: An Attempt to Answer Certain Critics of *Theory of the Avant-Garde*." *New Literary Criticism* 41 (2010): 695–715.

———. *Theory of the Avant-Garde*. Translation by Michael Shaw. Minneapolis: University of Minnesota Press, 1984.

Butler, Judith. *Gender Trouble: Feminism and the Subversion of Identity*. New York: Routledge, 1990.

Cabanne, Pierre. *Dialogues with Marcel Duchamp*. 1967. Reprint, New York, Da Capo, 1987.

Cappelle, Laura. "On Paris Stages, Gay Artists Look Back." *New York Times*, January 17, 2019. https://www.nytimes.com/2019/01/17/theater/christophe -honore-les-idoles-returning-to-reims-french.html.

Champagne, John. "'Stop Reading Films!': Film Studies, Close Analysis, and Gay Pornography." *Cinema Journal* 36, no. 4 (1997): 76–97.

Chauncey, George. *Gay New York: Gender, Urban Culture, and the Making of the Gay Male World, 1890–1940*. New York: Basic Books, 1994.

Chávez, Ernesto. "'Ramón Is Not One of These': Race and Sexuality in the Construction of Silent Film Actor Ramón Novarro's Star Image." *Journal of the History of Sexuality* 20, no. 3 (2011): 520–44.

Chris, Cynthia, and David A. Gerstner. Introduction to *Media Authorship*, edited by Chris and Gerstner, 1–18. New York: Routledge, 2013.

Chude-Sokei, Louis. *The Last "Darky": Bert Williams, Black-on-Black Minstrelsy, and the African Diaspora*. Durham, NC: Duke University Press, 2006.

Clarke, Cheryl. "The Failure to Transform: Homophobia in the Black Community." In *Home Girls: A Black Feminist Anthology*, edited by Barbara Smith, 190–201. 1983. Reprint, New Brunswick, NJ: Rutgers University Press, 2000.

———. "Lesbianism: An Act of Resistance." In *This Bridge Called My Back: Writings by Radical Women of Color*, edited by Cherríe Moraga and Gloria Anzaldúa, 128–37. Watertown, MA: Persephone, 1981.

Cleaver, Eldridge. "On Becoming." In *Soul on Ice*, 21–36. 1968. Reprint, New York: Dell, 1992.

Cohen, Ed. *Talk on the Wilde Side*. New York: Routledge, 1993.

Collin, Philippe. "Marcel Duchamp Talking about Readymades." In *Marcel Duchamp*, edited by Museum Jean Tinguely, 37–40. Olstfildern, Germany: Hatje Cantz, 2002.

Collins, Lisa Gail. "The Art of Transformation: Parallels in the Black Arts and Feminist Art Movements." In *New Thoughts on the Black Arts Movement*, edited by Lisa Gail Collins and Margo Natalie Crawford, 273–96. New Brunswick, NJ: Rutgers University Press, 2006.

Collins, Lisa Gail, and Margo Natalie Crawford, eds. *New Thoughts on the Black Arts Movement*. New Brunswick, NJ: Rutgers University Press, 2006.

Combs, Rhea Lynn. "Exceeding the Frame: Documentary Filmmaker Marlon T. Riggs as Cultural Agitator." PhD diss., Emory University, 2009. https://etd .library.emory.edu/concern/etds/gt54kn56x?locale=en.

Conley, Tom. "Site and Sound." *MLN* 121 (2006): 851–61.

Conway, Kelley. *Agnès Varda*. Urbana: University of Illinois Press, 2015.

Cooper, Emmanuel. *The Sexual Perspective: Homosexuality and Art in the Last 100 Years in the West*. London: Routledge, 1994.

Corber, Robert J. *Homosexuality in Cold War America: Resistance and the Crisis of Masculinity*. Durham, NC: Duke University Press, 1997.

Corn, Wanda. *The Great American Thing: Modern Art and National Identity, 1915–1935*. Berkeley: University of California Press, 1999.

Corrigan, Timothy, and Patricia White, with Meta Mazaj, eds. *Critical Visions in Film Theory: Classic and Contemporary Readings*. New York: Bedford/St. Martin's, 2011.

Cowie, Elizabeth. *Representing the Woman: Cinema and Psychoanalysis*. Minneapolis: University of Minnesota Press, 1997.

Crimp, Douglas, ed. *AIDS: Cultural Analysis/Cultural Activism*. Cambridge, MA: MIT Press, 1987.

———. "Fassbinder, Franz, Fox, Elvira, Erwin, Armin, and All the Others." *October* 21 (Summer 1982): 62–81.

———. "Mourning and Militancy." *October* 51 (Winter 1989): 3–18.

Crimp, Douglas, and Adam Rolston. *AIDS Demographics*. Seattle: Bay, 1990.

Currid, Brian. "Disco and Dance Music." In *Gay Histories and Cultures: An Encyclopedia*, vol. 2, edited by George Haggerty, 255–57. New York: Routledge, 2012.

Daire, Joël. *Une vie pour le cinéma: Jean Epstein*. Grandvilliers, France: La Tour verte, 2014.

Davis, Angela. "Black Nationalism: The Sixties and the Nineties." In *The Angela Y. Davis Reader*, edited by Joy James, 289–93. Malden, MA: Blackwell, 1998.

de Baecque, Antoine, and Serge Toubiana. *Truffaut: A Biography*. Berkeley: University of California Press, 1999.

Debruge, Peter. "Berlin Film Review: 'Eisenstein in Guanajuato.'" *Variety*, February 16, 2016. http://variety.com/2015/film/festivals/berlin-film-review-eisenstein-in-guanajuato-1201430972/.

Décimo, Marc. "What's at Play in the Wordplay: A Rendezvous Not to Be Missed." In *Marcel Duchamp*, edited by the Museum Jean Tingeuly, 45–49. Olstfildern, Germany: Hatje Cantz, 2002.

de Lauretis, Teresa. "Queer Theory: Lesbian and Gay Sexualities, an Introduction." *differences: A Journal of Feminist Cultural Studies* 3, no. 2 (1991): iii–xviii.

Deleuze. Gilles. *Cinema 1: The Movement-Image*. Translated by Hugh Tomlinson and Barbara Habberjam. 1986. Reprint, Minneapolis: University of Minnesota Press, 1989.

———. *Cinema 2: The Time-Image*. Translated by Hugh Tomlinson and Robert
  Galeta. Minneapolis: University of Minnesota Press, 1989.
Deleuze, Gilles, and Félix Guattari. *Anti-Oedipus: Capitalism and Schizophrenia*.
  Translated by Robert Hurley, Mark Seem, and Helen R. Lane. Minneapolis:
  University of Minnesota Press, 1983.
Demuth, Charles. *Letters of Charles Demuth, American Artist, 1883–1935*. Edited by
  Bruce Kellner. Philadelphia: Temple University Press, 2000.
Derrida, Jacques. *Archive Fever: A Freudian Impression*. Translated by Eric Prenowitz.
  Chicago: University of Chicago Press, 1995.
———. "But Beyond . . . (Open Letter to Anne McClintock and Rob Nixon)."
  Translated by Peggy Kamuf. *Critical Inquiry*, Autumn 1986, 155–70.
———. "The Deaths of Roland Barthes." In *Philosophy and Non-Philosophy Since
  Merleau-Ponty*, edited by Hugh J. Silverman, translated by Pascale-Anne
  Brault and Michael Naas, 259–96. New York: Routledge, 1988.
———. *Dissemination*. Translated by Barbara Johnson. Chicago: University of
  Chicago Press, 1981.
———. "Loving in Friendship: Perhaps." In *The Politics of Friendship*, translated by
  George Collins, 26–48. London: Verso, 2005.
———. *Of Grammatology*. Translated by Gayatri Chakravorty Spivak. 1974.
  Reprint, Baltimore: Johns Hopkins University Press, 2016.
———. *Specters of Marx: The State of the Debt, the Work of Mourning, and the New
  International*. Translated by Peggy Kamuf. New York: Routledge, 1994.
———. "The Taste of Tears: Jean-Marie Benoist (1942–1990)." In *The Work of
  Mourning*, edited and translated by Pascale-Anne Brault and Michael Naas,
  105–10. Chicago: University of Chicago Press, 2001.
———. "Tympan." In *Margins of Philosophy*, translated by Alan Bass, ix–xxix.
  Chicago: University of Chicago, Press, 1982.
Dews, Peter. *Logics of Disintegration: Poststructuralist Thought and Claims of Critical
  Theory*. London: Verso, 2007.
Donohue, Denis. *Walter Pater: Lover of Strange Souls*. New York: Knopf, 1995.
Doty, Alexander. Review of *How Do I Look? Queer Film and Video*, edited by Bad
  Object-Choice Collective. *Film Quarterly* 46, no. 1 (1992): 36–37.
Downing, Patrick, and John Hambley. *The Art of Hollywood*. London: Victoria and
  Albert Museum, 1979.
Duchamp, Marcel. "Demuth, Charles: A Tribute to the Artist." In *Catalogue for
  the Charles Demuth Exhibition at the Museum of Modern Art, New York*.
  Reprinted in *Salt Seller: The Writings of Marcel Duchamp*, edited by Michel

Sanouillet and Elmer Pererson, 162. New York: Oxford University Press, 1973.

duCille, Ann. "The Occult of True Black Womanhood: Critical Demeanor and Black Feminist Studies." *Signs* 19, no. 4 (1994): 591–629.

Dyer, Richard. *Heavenly Bodies: Film Stars and Society*. London: BFI and Macmillan, 1986.

———. *Now You See It: Studies on Lesbian and Gay Film*. London: Routledge, 1990.

———. *Stars*. London: BFI, 1979.

Edelman, Lee. *Homographesis: Essays in Gay Literary and Cultural Theory*. New York: Routledge, 1994.

———. *No Future: Queer Theory and the Death Drive*. Durham, NC: Duke University Press, 2004.

Ellenberger, Allan R. *Ramón Novarro: A Biography of the Silent Film Idol, 1899–1968*. Jefferson, NC: McFarland, 1999.

Ellis, Jim. *Derek Jarman's Angelic Conversations*. Minneapolis: University of Minnesota Press, 2009.

Ellman, Richard. *Oscar Wilde*. New York: Vintage, 1988.

Elsaesser, Thomas. "Tales of Sound and Fury: Observations on the Family Melodrama." In *Imitations of Life: A Reader on Film and Television Melodrama*, edited by Marcia Landy, 68–91. Detroit: Wayne State University Press, 1991.

Epstein, Jean. *Ganymède, essai sur l'éthique homosexuelle masculine*. Paris: Independencia Éditions, 2014.

———. "Magnification." In *French Film Theory and Criticism: A History/Anthology, 1907–1929*, vol. 1, edited by Richard Abel, 235–41. Princeton, NJ: Princeton University Press, 1988.

Eribon, Didier. *Insult and the Making of the Gay Self*. Translated by Michael Lucey. Durham, NC: Duke University Press, 2004.

Etherington-Smith, Meredith. *The Persistence of Memory: A Biography of Dali*. New York: Random House, 1992.

Faderman, Lillian, and Stuart Timmons. *Gay L.A.: A History of Sexual Outlaws, Power Politicos, and Lipstick Lesbians*. New York: Basic Books, 2006.

Farmer, Brett. *Spectacular Passions: Cinema, Fantasy, Gay Male Spectatorships*. Durham, NC: Duke University Press, 2000.

Field, Douglas. "Looking for Jimmy Baldwin: Sex, Privacy, and Black Nationalist Fervor." *Callaloo* 27, no. 2 (2004): 457–80.

Foucault, Michel. *The History of Sexuality: An Introduction, Volume 1*. Translated by Robert Hurley. New York: Vintage Books, 1990.

————. *The Order of Things: An Archaeology of the Human Sciences.* Translated by Alan Sheridan. New York: Vintage Books, 1973.

————. *Remarks on Marx: Conversations with Duccio Trombadori.* Translated by James Goldstein and James Cascalto. New York: Semiotext(e), 1991.

Frampton, Kenneth. *Modern Architecture: A Critical History.* 1980. 3rd rev. ed. London: Thames and Hudson, 1992.

Franklin, Paul B. "Object Choice: Marcel Duchamp's *Fountain* and the Art of Queer Art History." *Oxford Art Journal* 23, no. 1 (2000): 23–50.

Fregoso, Rosa Linda. *The Bronze Screen: Chicana and Chicano Film Culture.* Minneapolis: University of Minnesota Press, 1993.

Freud, Sigmund. *Beyond the Pleasure Principle.* Translated by James Strachey. New York: Norton, 1961.

Fuss, Diana, ed. *Inside/Out: Lesbian Theories, Gay Theories.* New York: Routledge, 1991.

Gallop, Jane. *The Deaths of the Author: Reading and Writing in Time.* Durham, NC: Duke University Press, 2008.

————. "The Monster in the Mirror: The Feminist Critic's Psychoanalysis." In *Feminism and Psychoanalysis*, edited by Richard Feldstein and Judith Roof, 13–24. Ithaca, NY: Cornell University Press, 1989.

Garafola, Lynn. *Diaghilev's Ballets Russes.* Oxford: Oxford University Press, 1989.

Gates, Racquel. *Double Negative: The Black Image and Popular Culture.* Durham, NC: Duke University Press, 2018.

Geier, Kathleen, Kate Bahn, Joelle Gamble, Zillah Eisenstein, and Heather Boushey. "How Gender Changes Piketty's *Capital in the Twenty-First Century*: A Roundtable." *Nation*, August 6, 2014. https://www.thenation.com/article/ archive/how-gender-changes-pikettys-capital-twenty-first-century/.

Geller, Theresa L. "The Cinematic Relations of Corporeal Feminism." *rhizomes* 11/12 (Fall 2005–Spring 2006). http://rhizomes.net/issue11/geller.html.

Genet, Jean. *The Thief's Journal.* Translated by Bernard Frechtman. New York: Grove, 1964.

Gerstner, David A. "An Excellent Worker: An Interview with Camille Vidal-Naquet." *Cinéaste* 44, no. 4 (2019). https://www.cineaste.com/fall2019/excellent -worker-camille-vidal-naquet.

————. *Manly Arts: Masculinity and Nation in Early American Cinema.* Durham, NC: Duke University Press, 2006.

————. "NYFF Interview: Christophe Honoré." *Film Comment*, September 28, 2018. https://www.filmcomment.com/blog/nyff-interview-christophe -honore/.

———. "The Practices of Authorship." In *Authorship and Film*, edited by David A. Gerstner and Janet Staiger, 3–25. New York: Routledge, 2003.

———. "The Production and Display of the Closet: Making Minnelli's *Tea and Sympathy*." *Film Quarterly* 50, no. 3 (1997): 13–26.

———. *Queer Pollen: White Seduction, Black Male Homosexuality, and the Cinematic.* Urbana: University of Illinois Press, 2011.

———, ed. *The Routledge International Encyclopedia of Queer Culture.* London: Routledge, 2006.

———. "With 'Gay Abandon': The Auteur as Homosexual Writer in the Twenty First Century." *Cinéaste* 45, no. 1 (2019): 24–29.

———. "Women's Hands and the Cinematic Cut: The Work of Montage in *Man with a Movie Camera*, *Klute*, and *The Piano*." In *The Oxford Handbook of Film Theory*, edited by Kyle Stevens, 482–504. New York: Oxford University Press, 2022.

Gerstner, David A., and Julien Nahmias. *Christophe Honoré: A Critical Introduction.* Detroit: Wayne State University Press, 2015.

Gerstner, David A., and Janet Staiger. Introduction to *Authorship and Film*, edited by Gerstner and Staiger, xi–xii. New York: Routledge, 2003.

Gever, Martha, John Greyson, and Pratibha Parmar, eds. *Queer Looks: Perspectives on Lesbian and Gay Film and Video.* New York: Routledge, 1993.

Gibbons, Cedric. "Interior Decoration Vital Branch of Movie Making." *World*, June 29, 1929.

Gibson, Catrin. "Authentic Love and the Mother-Child Relationship." *Sartre Studies International: An International Journal of Existentialism and Contemporary Culture* 23 (2017): 60–79.

Ginsberg, Allen. *Howl.* San Francisco: City Lights Pocket Bookshop, 1996.

Goldberger, Paul. "A Hollywood House Worthy of an Oscar." *New York Times*, November 6, 1980, C10.

Goldstein, Richard. "'Go the Way Your Blood Beats': An Interview with James Baldwin." In *James Baldwin: The Legacy*, edited by Quincy Troupe, 173–85. New York: Simon and Schuster, 1989.

Gomez, Jewelle. "But Some of Us Are Brave Lesbians: The Absence of Black Lesbian Fiction." In *Black Queer Studies: A Critical Anthology*, edited by E. Patrick Johnson and Mae G. Henderson, 289–97. Durham, NC: Duke University Press, 2005.

Gray, Carmen. "Greenaway Offends Russia with Film about Soviet Director's Gay Love Affair: An Interview with Peter Greenaway." *Guardian*, March 30,

2015. https://www.theguardian.com/world/2015/mar/30/peter-greenaway
-sergei-eisenstein-in-guanajuato.

Griffiths, Robin. "New Queer Cinema, International." In *The Routledge International Encyclopedia of Queer Culture*, edited by David A. Gerstner, 424–26. London: Routledge, 2006.

Grosz, Elizabeth. *Volatile Bodies: Toward a Corporeal Feminism*. Bloomington: Indiana University Press, 1994.

Gubar, Susan. "What Ails Feminist Criticism?" *Critical Inquiry* 24, no. 4 (1999): 878–902.

Guibert, Hervé. *The Mausoleum of Lovers: Journals, 1976–1991*. Translated by Nathanaël. New York: Nightboat Books, 2014.

Halberstam, Judith. *Female Masculinity*. 1998. Reprint, Durham, NC: Duke University Press, 2006.

———. *In a Queer Time and Place: Transgender Bodies, Subcultural Lives*. New York: New York University Press, 2005.

———. "Skinflick: Posthuman Gender in Jonathan Demme's *The Silence of the Lambs*." *Camera Obscura* 3, no. 27 (1991): 36–53.

Halperin, David M. *Saint Foucault: Towards a Gay Hagiography*. New York: Oxford University Press, 1995.

Hanson, Ellis, ed. *Out Takes: Essays on Queer Theory and Film*. Durham, NC: Duke University Press, 1999.

Harper, Phillip Brian. *Are We Not Men? Masculine Anxiety and the Problem of African American Identity*. New York: Oxford University Press, 1996.

Harvey, Robert. "Where's Duchamp? Out Queering the Field." *Yale French Studies* 109 (2006): 82–97.

Harvey, Stephen. *Directed by Vincente Minnelli*. New York: Museum of Modern Art and Harper and Row, 1989.

Hazareesingh, Sudhir. *How the French Think: An Affectionate Portrait of an Intellectual People*. New York: Basic Books, 2015.

Hemphill, Essex. Introduction to *Brother to Brother: New Writings by Black Gay Men*, xv–xxxi. Washington, DC: Redbone, 1991.

Henderson, Mae G. "James Baldwin: Expatriation, Homosexual Panic, and Man's Estate." *Callaloo* 23, no. 1 (2000): 313–27.

Hewitt, Andrew. "Sleeping with the Enemy: Genet and the Fantasy of Homo-Fascism." In *Gender and Fascism in Modern France*, edited by Melanie Hawthorne and Richard Golsan, 119–40. Hanover, NH: University Press of New England, 1997.

————. *Social Choreography: Ideology as Performance in Dance and Everyday Movement*. Durham, NC: Duke University Press, 2005.

Hillairet, Prosper. *Cœur fidèle de Jean Epstein: Le ciel et l'eau brûlent*. Crisnée, Belgium: Yellow Now, 2008.

————. "Epstein, une vie de cinéma." *Journal of Film Preservation* 91 (October 2014): 126–29.

Hochman, Elaine S. *Architects of Fortune: Mies Van der Rohe and the Third Reich*. New York: Weidenfeld and Nicolson, 1989.

Honoré, Christophe. "Note d'intention." Theatre-Contemporain.net. Accessed July 23, 2022. https://www.theatre-contemporain.net/spectacles/Les-idoles/ensavoirplus/idcontent/89269.

————. *Ton père*. Paris: Mecure de France, 2017.

Horkheimer, Max, and Theodor W. Adorno. "The Culture Industry: Enlightenment as Mass Deception." In *Dialectic of Enlightenment: Philosophical Fragments*, translated by John Cumming, 94–136. New York: Continuum, 1993.

Internationale Situationiste Students. "On the Poverty of Student Life: Considered in Its Economic, Political, and Psychological, Sexual, and Particularly Intellectual Aspects, and a Modest Proposal for Its Remedy." University of Strasbourg, 1966. http://library.nothingness.org/articles/SI/en/display/4.

Irigaray, Luce. "Body against Body: In Relation to the Mother." In *Sexes and Genealogies*, translated by Gillian C. Gill, 9–21. New York: Columbia University Press, 1993.

————. "Daughter and Woman." Translated by Monique M. Rhodes and Marcoi F. Concito-Monoc. In *To Be Two*, 30–39. New York: Routledge, 2001.

————. "Gesture and Psychoanalysis." In *Sexes and Genealogies*, translated by Gillian C. Gill, 90–104. New York: Columbia University Press, 1993.

————. *I Love to You: Sketch for a Felicity within History*. Translated by Alison Martin. New York: Routledge, 1996.

————. "Power of Discourse." In *The Sex Which Is Not One*, translated by Catherine Porter, 68–85. Ithaca, NY: Cornell University Press, 1985.

James, Joy. Introduction to *The Angela Y. Davis Reader*, 1–28. Malden, MA: Blackwell, 1998.

Jařab, Josef. "Black Aesthetic: A Cultural or Political Concept?" *Callaloo* 25 (Autumn 1985): 587–93.

Judovitz, Dalía. "Anemic Vision in Duchamp: Cinema as Readymade" In *Dada and Surrealist Film*, edited by Rudolf E. Kuenzli, 46–57. Cambridge, MA: MIT Press, 1996.

Kaplan, Cora. *Sea Changes: Essays on Culture and Feminism*. London: Verso, 1986.

Keegan, Cáel. *Lana and Lily Wachowski*. Urbana: University of Illinois Press, 2018.

———. "On the Necessity of Bad Trans Objects." *Film Quarterly* 75, no. 3 (2022): 26–37.

Keller, Sarah. *Barbara Hammer: Pushing out of the Frame*. Detroit: Wayne State University Press, 2021.

———. Introduction to *Jean Epstein: Critical Essays and New Translations*, edited by Sarah Keller and Jason N. Paul, 23–47. Amsterdam: Amsterdam University Press, 2012.

Keller, Sarah, and Jason N. Paul, eds. *Jean Epstein: Critical Essays and New Translations*. Amsterdam: Amsterdam University Press, 2012.

Kellner, Bruce. *Carl Van Vechten and the Irreverent Decades*. Norman: University of Oklahoma Press, 1968.

———. Prolegomenon to *Letters of Carl Van Vechten*, vii–xvii. New Haven, CT: Yale University Press, 1987.

Kinsley, Michael. "Donald Trump Is Actually a Fascist." *Washington Post*, December 9, 2016. https://www.washingtonpost.com/opinions/donald -trump-is-actually-a-fascist/2016/12/09/e193a2b6-bd77-11e6-94ac -3d324840106c_story.html.

Kirstein, Lincoln. *Tchelitchev*. Santa Fe, NM: Twelvetrees, 1994.

La Cinémathèque Française. "Jean Epstein." Accessed July 26, 2022. https://www .cinematheque.fr/cycle/jean-epstein-117.html.

Lahr, John. *Notes on a Cowardly Lion*. New York: Knopf, 1969.

Lambert, Gavin. *Nazimova: A Biography*. New York: Knopf, 1997.

Landis, Bill. *Anger: The Unauthorized Biography of Kenneth Anger*. New York: HarperCollins, 1995.

Laplanche, Jean, and J. B. Pontalis. *The Language of Psycho-analysis*. Translated Donald Nicholson-Smith. London: Karnac and the Institute of Psycho-analysis, 1988.

Le Forestier, Laurent. "Jean Epstein, un projet d'enquête: 'Le Cinéma du diable? . . .'" *Ciné-Ressources*. Accessed July 25, 2022. http://www.cineressources.net/ ressources/JeanEpstein_unprojetdenquete.pdf.

Leprohon, Pierre. *Jean Epstein*. Paris: Seghers, 1964.

Leung, Helen Hok-Sze. "Keywords." *TSQ: Transgender Studies Quarterly* 1, nos. 1–2 (2014): 86–89.

Lewis, Gail. "Audre Lorde: Vignettes and Mental Conversations." *Feminist Review* 34 (Spring 1990): 100–114.

Lewis, Helen. "Lip Service: Why Vagina Is the Perfect Word." *New Statesman*, August 28, 2013. http://www.newstatesman.com/books/2013/08/lip-service -why-vagina-perfect-word?page=3.

Liebman, Stuart. "Jean Epstein's Early Film Theory, 1920–22." PhD diss., New York University, 1980.

Lorde, Audre. *Sister Outsider: Essays and Speeches by Audre Lorde*. Berkeley, CA: Crossing, 1984.

Lorde, Audre, and James Baldwin. "Revolutionary Hope: A Conversation between James Baldwin and Audre Lorde." *Essence*, December 1984, 72–74, 129–30, 133.

Maeda, Kazuo. "Prenatal Life in the Mother." *Journal of Health and Medical Informatics* 6, no. 177 (2015): 1–4.

Mann, William J. *Wisecracker: The Life and Times of William Haines, Hollywood's First Openly Gay Star*. New York: Viking, 1997.

Marks, Laura. *The Skin of the Film: Intercultural Cinema, Embodiment, and the Senses*. Durham, NC: Duke University Press, 2000.

Marquis, Alice Goldfarb. *Marcel Duchamp: The Bachelor Stripped Bare*. Boston: MFA, 2002.

Mast, Gerald. "Projection." In *Film Theory and Criticism*, 2nd ed., edited by Gerald Mast and Marshall Cohen, 299–305. New York: Oxford University Press, 1979.

Mayne, Judith. *Directed by Dorothy Arzner*. Bloomington: Indiana University Press, 1994.

McBride, Dwight A. "Can the Queen Speak? Racial Essentialism, Sexuality, and the Problem of Authority." *Callaloo* 21, no. 2 (1998): 363–79.

———. "Straight Black Studies." In *Black Queer Studies: A Critical Anthology*, edited by E. Patrick Johnson and Mae G. Henderson, 69–89. Durham, NC: Duke University Press, 2005.

McCole, John. *Walter Benjamin and the Antinomies of Tradition*. Ithaca, NY: Cornell University Press, 1993.

McDonald, Boyd. *Cruising the Movies: A Sexual Guide to Oldies on TV*. London: Semiotext(e), 2015.

McDowell, Deborah E. "New Directions for Black Feminist Criticism." In *The New Feminist Criticism: Essays on Women, Literature, and Theory*, edited by Elaine Showalter, 186–99. New York: Pantheon, 1985.

Mérigeau, Pascal. *Jean Renoir*. Paris: Flammarion, 2012.

Metz, Christian. *Film Language: A Semiotics of the Cinema*. Translated by Michael Taylor. Chicago, University of Chicago Press, 1991.

Michelson, Annette. "*Anémic cinéma*: Reflections on an Emblematic Work." *Artforum* 12, no. 2 (1973): 64–69.

Minnelli, Vincente. "The Show Must Go On." *Stage*, September 1936, 33–35.

Minnelli, Vincente, with Hector Arce. *I Remember It Well*. Garden City, NY: Doubleday, 1974.

Mitchell, Juliet. "Introduction I." In *Feminine Sexuality: Jacques Lacan and the École Freudienne*, edited by Juliet Mitchell and Jacqueline Rose, 1–26. New York: Pantheon Books, 1982.

Mitry, Jean. *The Aesthetics and Psychology of the Cinema*. Translated by Christopher King. Bloomington: Indiana University Press, 1997.

Moraga, Cherríe. *Loving in the War Years: Lo que nunca pasó por sus labios*. 1983. Reprint, Cambridge, MA: South End, 2000.

———. Preface to *This Bridge Called My Back: Writings by Radical Women of Color*, edited by Cherríe Moraga and Gloria Anzaldúa, xiii–xix. Watertown, MA: Persephone, 1981.

Moraga, Cherríe, and Gloria Anzaldúa. Introduction to *This Bridge Called My Back: Writings by Radical Women of Color*, edited by Cherríe Moraga and Gloria Anzaldúa, xxiii–xxvii. Watertown, MA: Persephone, 1981.

Morris, Edmund. *The Rise of Theodore Roosevelt*. New York: Ballantine, 1979.

Morrison, Toni. *Playing in the Dark: Whiteness and the Literary Imagination*. Cambridge, MA: Harvard University Press, 1992.

Moser, Benjamin. *Sontag: Her Life*. New York: HarperCollins, 2019.

Moussinac, Léon. *Sergei Eisenstein: An Investigation into His Films and Philosophy*. Translated by Sandy Petrey. New York: Crown, 1970.

Mulvey, Laura. "Visual Pleasure and Narrative Cinema." In *Movies and Methods: An Anthology*, vol. 2, edited by Bill Nichols, 303–15. Berkeley: University of California Press, 1985.

Muñoz, José Esteban. *Disidentifications: Queers of Color and the Performance of Politics*. Minneapolis: University of Minnesota Press, 1999.

Muschamp, Herbert. "Grand Central as a Hearth in the Heart of New York City." *New York Times*, February 4, 1996, sec. 2, 27.

Nadeau, Maurice. *The History of Surrealism*. Translated by Richard Howard. 1965. Reprint, Cambridge, MA: Belknap Press, Harvard University Press. 1995.

Naifeh, Steven, and Gregory White Smith. *Jackson Pollock: An American Saga*. New York: Clarkson N. Potter, 1989.

Naremore, James. *The Films of Vincente Minnelli*. New York: Cambridge University Press, 1993.

Neale, Steven. "Masculinity as Spectacle: Reflections on Men and Mainstream Cinema." *Screen* 24, no. 6 (1983): 2–17.

Nelson, Emmanuel. "Critical Deviance: Homophobia and the Reception of James Baldwin's Fiction." *Journal of American Culture* 14, no. 3 (1991): 91–96.

Nero, Charles I. "Toward a Black Gay Aesthetic: Signifying in Contemporary Black Gay Culture," In *Brother to Brother: New Writings by Black Gay Men*, edited by Essex Hemphill, 289–323. Washington, DC: Redbone, 1991.

Newton, Huey P. "The Women's and Gay Liberation Movements: August 15, 1970." In *To Die for the People*, edited by Toni Morrison, 153–56. San Francisco: City Lights Books, 2009.

Nochlin, Linda. *Courbet*. London: Thames and Hudson, 2007.

———. "'L'Origine du Monde': The Origin without an Original." *October* 37 (Summer 1986): 76–86.

Novarro, Ramón. "From Screen to Concert Stage: A Popular Motion Picture Player Explains Why He Is Exchanging One Art for Another." *Theatre Magazine*, January 1928, 27, 68.

"Novarro in New Talkie." *New York Times*, June 7, 1930.

Nugent, Richard Bruce. *Gentleman Jigger*. Edited by Thomas Wirth. Philadelphia: Da Capo, 2008.

O'Leary, Liam. *Rex Ingram: Master of the Silent Cinema*. London: BFI, 1993.

Orwell, George. 2015. "What Is Fascism?" *Tribune* (UK), 1944. http://www.orwell.ru/library/articles/As_I_Please/english/efasc.

Peeters, Benoît. *Derrida: A Biography*. Maiden, MA: Polity, 2013.

Pennell, Joseph, and Elizabeth R. Pennell. *The Life of James McNeill Whistler*. 2 vols. Philadelphia: J. B. Lippincott, 1909.

Perry, Nick. "Antipodean Camp." In *Hyperreality and Global Culture*, 4–23. London: Routledge, 1998.

Phillips, Adam. Introduction to *The Renaissance: Studies in Art and Poetry*, by Walter Pater, vii–xviii. Oxford: Oxford University Press, 1986.

Piketty, Thomas. *Capital in the Twenty-First Century*. Translated by Arthur Goldhammer. Cambridge, MA: Harvard University Press, 2013.

Piontelli, Alessandra. "Fetal Sensory Abilities." In *Development of Normal Fetal Movements: The Last 15 Weeks of Gestation*, 111–26. Milan: Springer, 2015.

Polizzotti, Mark. *Revolution of the Mind: The Life of André Breton*. New York: Bloomsbury, 1995.

Proust, Marcel. *Remembrance of Things Past*. Vol. 1, *Swann's Way*. Translated by C. K. Scott Moncrieff. New York: Vintage, 1981.

————. *Remembrance of Things Past.* Vol. 4, *Sodom and Gomorrah.* Translated by
C. K. Scott Moncrieff and Terence Kilmartin, revised by D. J. Enright. New
York: Modern Library, 1999.

"Ramón Novarro Slain on Coast; Starred in Silent Film 'Ben-Hur.'" *New York Times,*
November 1, 1968.

Rank, Otto. *The Trauma of Birth.* 1929. Reprint, New York: Dover, 1993.

Renoir, Jean. *My Life and My Films.* Translated by Norman Denny. New York:
Da Capo, 1974.

Rhodes, Jane. *Framing the Black Panthers: The Spectacular Rise of a Black Power Icon.*
New York: New Press, 2007.

Rich, B. Ruby. "New Queer Cinema." In *New Queer Cinema: A Critical Reader,*
edited by Michele Aaron, 15–22. New Brunswick, NJ: Rutgers University
Press, 2014.

Richardson, Riché. *Black Masculinity and the U.S. South: From Uncle Tom to Gangsta.*
Athens: University of Georgia Press, 2007.

Rimbaud, Arthur. "Wandering." In *Arthur Rimbaud: Complete Works,* translated by
Paul Schmidt, 46–47. New York: Harper Perennial, 2008.

Rodowick, D. N. *Elegy for Theory.* Cambridge, MA: Harvard University Press, 2014.

————. "Unthinkable Sex: Conceptual Personae and the Time-Image." *Invisible
Culture: An Electronic Journal for Visual Studies,* 2000. http://www.rochester
.edu/in_visible_culture/issue3/rodowick.htm.

Rose, Jacqueline. "Introduction II." In *Feminine Sexuality: Jacques Lacan and the
École Freudienne,* edited by Juliet Mitchell and Jacqueline Rose, 27–58. New
York: Pantheon Books, 1982.

Roth, Moira. "Marcel Duchamp: A Self Ready-Made." *Arts Magazine* 9 (May 1977):
92–96.

Roudinesco, Élisabeth. *Jacques Lacan.* Translated by Barbara Bray. New York:
Columbia University Press, 1997.

Russell, Lee [Peter Wollen]. "Howard Hawks." In *Howard Hawks: American Artist,*
edited by Jim Hillier and Peter Wollen, 83–86. London: BFI, 1996.

Said, Edward. *Orientalism.* New York: Vintage, 1979.

San Filippo, Maria. *The B Word: Bisexuality in Contemporary Film and Television.*
Bloomington: Indiana University Press, 2013.

————. *Provocauteurs and Provocations: Screening Sex in 21st-Century Media.*
Bloomington: Indiana University Press, 2021.

Sarris, Andrew. *The American Cinema: Directors and Directions, 1929–1968.* New
York: Dutton, 1968.

————. "Auteurism Is Alive and Well." *Film Quarterly* 28, no. 1 (1974): 60–63.

Sartre, Jean-Paul. *Baudelaire.* Translated by Martin Turnell. New York: New Directions, 1950.

————. *Being and Nothingness: An Essay on Phenomenological Ontology.* Translated and edited by Hazel E. Barnes. 1956. Reprint, New York: Citadel, 2001.

Scott, Darieck. "'Jungle Fever?': Black Gay Identity Politics, White Dick, and the Utopian Bedroom." *GLQ* 1, no. 3 (1994): 299–321.

Sedgwick, Eve Kosofsky. "Queer Performativity: Henry James's *The Art of the Novel.*" *GLQ* 1, no. 1 (1993): 1–16.

————. "Queer Performativity: Warhol's Shyness/Warhol's Whiteness." In *Pop Out: Queer Warhol,* edited by Jennifer Doyle, Jonathan Flatley, and José Esteban Muñoz, 134–43. Durham, NC: Duke University Press, 1996.

————. *Touching Feeling: Affect, Pedagogy, Performativity.* Durham, NC: Duke University Press, 2003.

Sedgwick, Eve Kosofsky, and Andrew Parker, eds. *Performativity and Performance.* New York: Routledge, 1995.

Seton, Marie. *Sergei Eisenstein: A Biography.* New York: Wyn, 1952.

Shambu, Girish. "Time's Up for the Male Canon." *Film Quarterly,* September 21, 2018. https://filmquarterly.org/2018/09/21/times-up-for-the-male-canon/.

Shaviro, Steven. *The Cinematic Body.* Minneapolis: University of Minnesota Press, 1993.

————. "Come, Come, Georges." *Artforum,* May 2005, 53.

Shin, Andrew, and Barbara Judson. "Beneath the Black Aesthetic: James Baldwin's Primer of Black American Masculinity." *African American Review* 32, no. 2 (1998): 247–61.

Shockley, Ann Allen. "The Black Lesbian in American Literature: An Overview." In *Home Girls: A Black Feminist Anthology,* edited by Barbara Smith, 83–93. 1983. Reprint, New Brunswick, NJ: Rutgers University Press, 2000.

Shohat, Ella. Introduction to *Talking Visions: Multicultural Feminism in a Transnational Age,* ed. Shohat, 1–63. Cambridge, MA: MIT Press, 1998.

Siegel, Jerrold. *The Private Worlds of Marcel Duchamp: Desire, Liberation, and the Self in Modern Culture.* Berkeley: University of California Press, 1995.

Silverman, Kaja. *The Acoustic Mirror: The Female Voice in Psychoanalysis and Cinema.* Bloomington: Indiana University Press, 1988.

————. *The Threshold of the Visible World.* New York: Routledge, 1996.

Simmons, Ron. "Some Thoughts on the Challenges Facing Black Gay Intellectuals." In *Brother to Brother: New Writings by Black Gay Men,* edited by Essex Hemphill, 263–88. Washington, DC: Redbone, 1991.

Simmons, Ron, and Marlon Riggs. "Sexuality, Television, and Death: A Black Gay Dialogue on Malcolm X." In *Malcolm X: In Our Own Image*, edited by Joe Wood, 135–54. New York: St. Martin's, 1992.

Sinfield, Alan. *The Wilde Century: Effeminacy, Oscar Wilde and the Queer Moment.* New York: Columbia University Press, 1994.

Sitney, P. Adams. *Visionary Film: The American Avant-Garde, 1943–1978.* 1974. Reprint, New York: Oxford University Press, 1979.

Slawenski, Kenneth. *J. D. Salinger: A Life.* New York: Random House, 2011.

Slide, Anthony. Foreword to *Beyond Paradise: The Life of Ramón Novarro*, by André Soares, ix–xii. New York: St. Martin's, 2002.

Smalls, James. "Making Trouble for Art History: The Queer Case of Girodet." *Art Journal* 55, no. 4 (1996): 20–27.

Smith, Barbara. "Blacks and Gays: Healing the Great Divide." In *The Columbia Reader on Lesbians and Gay Men in Media, Society, and Politics*, edited by Larry Gross and James D. Woods, 649–52. New York: Columbia University Press, 1993.

———. "Homophobia: Why Bring It Up?" In *The Lesbian and Gay Studies Reader*, edited by Henry Abelove, Michèle Aina Barale, and David M. Halperin, 99–102. New York: Routledge, 1993.

Smith, Paul Julian. *Desire Unlimited: The Cinema of Pedro Almodóvar.* 2nd ed. London: Verso, 2000.

Soares, André. *Beyond Paradise: The Life of Ramón Novarro.* New York: St. Martin's, 2002.

Sobchack, Vivian. Introduction to *Meta-Morphing: Transformation and the Culture of Quick Change*, xi–xxiii. Minneapolis: University of Minnesota, 2000.

Solomon, Deborah. *Utopia Parkway: The Life and Work of Joseph Cornell.* New York: Farrar, Straus and Giroux, 1997.

Solomon, Matthew. "'Twenty-Five Heads under One Hat' in the 1890s." In *Meta-Morphing: Transformation and the Culture of Quick Change*, edited by Vivian Sobchack, 3–20. Minneapolis: University of Minnesota Press, 2000.

Sontag, Susan. "Happenings." In *Against Interpretation*, 263–74. New York: Farrar, Straus and Giroux, 1986.

———. "Notes on Camp." In *Against Interpretation*, 275–92. New York: Farrar, Straus and Giroux, 1986.

Spivak, Gayatri Chakravorty. *A Critique of Postcolonial Reason: Toward a History of the Vanishing Present.* Cambridge, MA: Harvard University Press, 1999.

Steefel, Lawrence D. *The Position of Duchamp's "Glass" in the Development of His Art.* New York, Garland, 1977.

Steinbock, E. A. "Groping Theory: Haptic Cinema and Trans-Curiosity in Hans Scheirl's *Dandy Dust.*" In *The Transgender Studies Reader 2*, edited by Susan Stryker and Aren Z. Aizura, 101–18. New York: Routledge, 2006.

Stewart, Garret. *Cinemachines: An Essay on Media and Method.* Chicago: University of Chicago Press, 2020.

Stoekel, Alan. Introduction to *Georges Bataille: Visions of Excess, Selected Writings, 1927–1939*, ix–xxv. Minneapolis: University of Minnesota Press, 1993.

Stryker, Susan. "(De)Subjugated Knowledges: An Introduction to Transgender Studies." In *The Transgender Studies Reader*, edited by Susan Stryker and Stephen Whittle, 1–17. New York: Routledge, 2006.

Stryker, Susan, and Aren Z. Aizura. "Introduction: Transgender Studies 2.0." In *The Transgender Studies Reader 2*, edited by Susan Stryker and Aren Z. Aizura, 1–12. New York: Routledge, 2013.

Studlar, Gaylyn. "Valentino, 'Optic Intoxication,' and Dance Madness." In *Screening the Male: Exploring Masculinities in Hollywood Cinema*, edited by Steven Cohan and Ina Rae Hark, 23–45. London: Routledge, 1993.

Suárez, Juan. *Bike Boys, Drag Queens, and Superstars: Avant-Garde, Mass Culture, and Gay Identities in the 1960s Underground Cinema.* Bloomington: Indiana University Press, 1996.

Sussman, Elisabeth. "Florine Stettheimer: A 1990s Perspective." In *Florine Stettheimer: Manhattan Fantastica*, edited by Elisabeth Sussman with Barbara Bloemink, 41–68. New York: Whitney Museum of American Art, 1995.

Sussman, Elisabeth, with Barbara Bloemink, eds. *Florine Stettheimer: Manhattan Fantastica.* New York: Whitney Museum of American Art, 1995.

Sutton, Benjamin. "Artist Enacts 'Origin of the World' at Musée d'Orsay—And, Yes, That Means What You Think." *Artnet News*, June 5, 2014. https://news .artnet.com/exhibitions/artist-enacts-origin-of-the-world-at-musee-dorsay -and-yes-that-means-what-you-think-35011.

Terry, Jennifer. "Theorizing Deviant Historiography." *differences: A Journal of Feminist Cultural Studies* 3, no. 2 (1991): 55–74.

Thompson, Kristin. *Breaking the Glass Armor: Neoformalist Film Analysis.* Princeton, NJ: Princeton University Press, 1988.

Thurman, Wallace. *Infants of the Spring.* 1932. Edited by Thomas Wirth. Boston: Northeastern University Press, 1992.

Tinkcom, Matthew. *Queer Theory and "Brokeback Mountain."* New York: Bloomsbury, 2017.

———. *Working like a Homosexual: Camp, Capital, Cinema.* Durham, NC: Duke University Press, 2002.

———. "Working like a Homosexual: Camp Visual Codes and the Labor of Gay Subjects in the MGM Freed Unit." *Cinema Journal* 35, no. 2 (1996): 24–42.

Tomkins, Calvin. *Duchamp.* New York: Owl Book, 1996.

Troy, Hugh. "Never Had a Lesson." *Esquire*, June 1937, 99, 138, 141.

Truffaut, François. *Correspondance avec des écrivains, 1948–1984.* Edited by Bernard Bastide. Paris: Gallimard, 2022.

———. *Truffaut: Correspondences, 1945–1984.* Edited by Gilles Jacob and Claude de Givray. Translated by Gilbert Adair. New York: Cooper Square, 2000.

Tyler, Parker. *Screening the Sexes: Homosexuality in the Movies.* New York: Da Capo, 1993.

Valman, H. B., and J. F. Pearson. "What the Uterus Feels." *British Medical Journal*, January 12, 1980, 233–34.

Vartanian, Hrag. "Performance Artist Does the Impossible, Shows Up Courbet's 'Origin of the World.'" *Hyperallergic*, June 6, 2014. https://hyperallergic .com/131008/performance-artist-does-the-impossible-shows-up-courbets -origin-of-the-world/.

Velocci, Beans. "Standards of Care: Uncertainty and Risk in Harry Benjamin's Transsexual Classifications." *TSQ: Transgender Studies Quarterly* 8, no. 4 (2021): 462–80.

Video Data Bank. "Community Action Center." Accessed July 24, 2022. https://vdb .org/titles/community-action-center.

Walker, David, James Grimwade, and Carl Wood. "Intrauterine Noise: A Component of the Fetal Environment." *American Journal of Obstetrics and Gynecology* 109 (1971): 91–95.

Wall-Romana, Christophe. "'Cinematic Blossoming': Duchamp, Chess, and Infraqueer Mating." *Modernism/Modernity* 27, no. 2 (2020): 323–38.

———. "Epstein's *Photogénie* as Corporeal Vision: Inner Sensation, Queer Embodiment, and Ethics." In *Jean Epstein: Critical Essays and New Translations*, ed. Sarah Keller and Jason N. Paul, 51–71. Amsterdam: Amsterdam University Press, 2012.

———. "L'Homosexualité dans les écrits et les films de Jean Epstein." In *Ganymède, essai sur l'éthique homosexuelle masculine*, by Jean Epstein, 11–21. Paris: Independencia Éditions, 2014.

Warhol, Andy. *The Andy Warhol Diaries.* Edited by Pat Hackett. New York: Warner Books, 1989.

Warner, Michael. *Fear of a Queer Planet*. Minneapolis: University of Minnesota Press, 1993.

Watson, Steven. *Strange Bedfellows: The First American Avant-Garde*. New York: Abbeville, 1991.

Webb, Michael. "Cedric Gibbons and the MGM Style." *Architectural Digest* 47 (April 1990): 100, 104, 108, 112.

Weber, Nicholas Fox. *Balthus: A Biography*. Champaign, IL: Dalkey Archive, 2013.

Weber, Samuel. "After Deconstruction." In *Mass Mediauras: Form, Technics, Media*, 129–51. Stanford, CA: Stanford University Press.

———. *Benjamin's -abilities*. Cambridge, MA: Harvard University Press, 2008.

———. *The Legend of Freud*. Minneapolis: University of Minnesota Press, 1982.

———. "Mass Mediauras; or, Art, Aura and Media in the Work of Walter Benjamin." In *Mass Mediauras: Form, Technics, Media*, 76–107. Stanford, CA: Stanford University Press, 1996.

———. "Television: Set and Screen." In *Mass Mediauras: Form, Technics, Media*, 108–28. Stanford, CA: Stanford University Press, 1996.

———. *Theatricality as Medium*. New York: Fordham University Press, 2004.

———. "Upsetting the Setup: Remarks on Heidegger's 'Questing After Technics.'" In *Mass Mediauras: Form, Technics, Media*, 55–75. Stanford, CA: Stanford University Press, 1996.

Weiss, Allen S. "Poetic Justice: Formations of Subjective and Sexual Identity." *Cinema Journal* 28, no. 1 (1988): 45–64.

Werckmeister, O. K. *The Making of Paul Klee's Career: 1914–1920*. Chicago: University of Chicago Press, 1989.

Wheatcroft, George. "Whose Fascism Is This, Anyway?" *New York Times*, December 15, 2015. https://www.nytimes.com/2015/12/16/opinion/whose -fascism-is-this-anyway.html.

Whistler, James McNeill. "Ten O' Clock." In *Whistler on Art: Selected Letters and Writings of James McNeill Whistler*, edited by Nigel Thorpe, 79–95. Washington, DC: Smithsonian Institution Press, 1994.

White, Edmund. *The Flâneur: A Stroll through the Paradoxes of Paris*. London: Bloomsbury, 2001.

White, Hayden. *Metahistory: The Historical Imagination in Nineteenth-Century Europe*. Baltimore: Johns Hopkins University Press, 1973.

White, Patricia. *Uninvited: Classical Hollywood Cinema and Lesbian Representability*. Bloomington: Indiana University Press, 1999.

Whiting, Cecile. "Decorating with Stettheimer and the Boys." *American Art* 14, no. 1 (2000): 24–49.

Wiegman, Robyn. "What Ails Feminist Criticism? A Second Opinion." *Critical Inquiry* 25, no. 2 (1999): 362–79.

Wikipedia. "Mayhem (crime)." Accessed July 24, 2022. https://en.wikipedia.org/wiki/Mayhem_(crime).

Wilde, Oscar. *The Complete Works of Oscar Wilde: Stories, Plays, Poems, and Essays.* New York: Harper and Row, 1989.

———. "The Critic as Artist." In *The Complete Works of Oscar Wilde*, edited by J. B. Foreman, 970–92. London: Williams Collins Sons, 1966.

———. "The Decay of Lying: An Observation." In *The Complete Works of Oscar Wilde*, edited by J. B. Foreman, 1009–59. London: Williams Collins Sons, 1966.

———. "Phrases and Philosophies for the Use of the Young." In *The Complete Works of Oscar Wilde*, edited by J. B. Foreman, 1205–6. London: Williams Collins Sons, 1966.

———. *The Picture of Dorian Gray.* In *The Complete Works of Oscar Wilde*, edited by J. B. Foreman, 17–167. London: Williams Collins Sons, 1966.

Williams, Alan. *Republic of Images: A History of French Filmmaking.* Cambridge, MA: Harvard University Press, 1992.

Williams, Linda. "Film Body: An Implantation of Perversions." In *Narrative, Apparatus, Ideology*, edited by Philip Rosen, 507–34. New York: Columbia University Press, 1986.

Williams, Tami. *Germaine Dulac: A Cinema of Sensations.* Urbana: University of Illinois Press, 2014.

Wojnarowicz, David. *Close to the Knives.* New York: Vintage Originals, 1991.

———. *Rimbaud in New York, 1978–79.* Edited by Andrew Roth. New York: Roth Horowitz, 2004.

Wollen, Peter. "The Auteur Theory: Michael Curtiz and *Casablanca*." In *Authorship and Film*, edited by David A. Gerstner and Janet Staiger, 62–76. New York: Routledge, 2003.

———. "Godard and Counter-Cinema: *Vent d'Est*." In *Narrative, Apparatus, Ideology*, edited by Philip Rosen, 120–29. New York: Columbia University Press, 1986.

———. "The Last New Wave." In *Fires Were Started: British Cinema and Thatcherism*, edited by Lester Friedman, 35–51. Minneapolis: University of Minnesota Press, 1993.

———. "Out of the Past: Fashion/Orientalism/The Body." In *Raiding the Icebox: Reflections on Twentieth-Century Culture*, 1–34. Bloomington: Indiana University Press, 1993.

———. *Raiding the Icebox: Reflections on Twentieth-Century Culture*. Bloomington: University of Indiana Press, 1993.

———. "Semiotic Counter-Strategies: Retrospect 1982." In *Readings and Writings: Semiotic Counter-Strategies*, 208–15. London: Verso, 1982.

———. "The Situationist International: On the Passage of a Few People through a Rather Brief Period of Time." In *Raiding the Icebox: Reflections on Twentieth-Century Culture*, 120–57. Bloomington: University of Indiana Press, 1993.

———. "Viking Eggeling." In *Paris/Hollywood: Writings on Film*, 39–54. London: Verso, 2002.

Woods, Alan. "Now Let Us Look at the Pictures." *Cambridge Quarterly* 14, no. 3 (1985): 187–204.

Yarbro-Bejarano, Yvonne. "De-constructing the Lesbian Body: Cherríe Moraga's *Loving in the War Years*." In *The Lesbian and Gay Studies Reader*, edited by Henry Abelove, Michèle Aina Barale, and David M. Halperin, 595–603. New York: Routledge, 1993.

———. "Gloria Anzaldúa's *Borderlands/La Frontera*: Cultural Studies, 'Difference,' and the Non-Unitary Subject." *Cultural Critique* 28 (Autumn 1994): 5–28.

Young, Damon. *Making Sex Public and Other Cinematic Fantasies*. Durham: Duke University Press, 2018.

INDEX OF NAMES

CPSIA information can be obtained
at www.ICGtesting.com
Printed in the USA
JSHW022142080123
35908JS00008B/15